CARY GRANT

CARY GRANT

A Class Apart

Graham McCann

Columbia University Press

NEW YORK

Columbia University Press
Publishers Since 1893
New York   Chichester, West Sussex

Copyright © 1996 by Graham McCann

Library of Congress Cataloging-in-Publication Data

McCann, Graham, 1961–
Cary Grant: a class apart/Graham McCann.
p.   cm.
Originally published: London: Fourth Estate, 1996.
Includes bibliographical references and index.
Filmographies,
ISBN 0–231–10884–2
1. Grant, Cary, 1904–   . 2. Motion picture actors and actress—
United Stated—Biography.   I. Title.
PN2287. G675M33   1997
791.43'028'092—dc20
[B]   96—38577
                                                                     CIP

Casebound editions of Columbia University Press
books are printed on permanent and durable acid-free paper.
Printed in the United States of America

C10 9 8 7 6 5 4 3 2 1

For Silvana
and in memory of my dear grandparents,
Frank and Florence Geary

Contents

Contents

INDEPENDENCE

RETIREMENT

List of Photographs

Acknowledgements

I regret – since working on this book proved so much more rewarding an experience than any of my previous efforts – that I cannot begin by thanking the subject himself. In a way, of course, I still can, so I still will: I never had a better time.

I was fortunate enough, before I started, to have an agent – Mic Cheetham – whose loyalty, enthusiasm and expertise gave me the sense of security to plan the project with a renewed feeling of self-confidence. I was fortunate enough, once I started, to have an editor – Christopher Potter – whose intelligence, commitment and good judgement assured me that whatever I might write would be read carefully and thoughtfully. They both have my lasting admiration and respect.

I doubt that I could have completed this book without the support of my friends. Don Cupitt reassured me that gentlemen still exist, even in the academic world; I will not forget his kindness. At King's, I am particularly grateful to Reg Arnold, Alan Belgrove, Bill Burton and Richard Rayner for their invaluable friendship. My students were extraordinarily supportive during this period. I cannot, unfortunately, thank all of them here, but I really must express my deepest gratitude to the following: Matthew Brooks, John Cassy, Lucy Clouting, Suzanne Cohen, Joanne Dearden, Tara Edwards, Nick Forbes, Richard Hall, Cathy Haynes, Liz Moor, Bonnie Muir, Larry Olomoofe, Guy Paisner, Marc Power, Nicola Reindorp, Paul Saw, Sonya Sultan, Esther Szucs, Adrian Thomas, Franni Vincent, Gudrun Young and, especially, Sebastian Doggart, Beccy Keane, David Mikosz and Tim Shakesby. It has not just been a pleasure to teach these people; it has been a privilege to know them, too.

I owe, as always, an inestimable amount to my family. My mother, in particular, continues to teach me – far more effectively than any expensive education – how to live a decent life.

For their special help I would like to thank the following people among many who supplied references, answered specific queries or supplied useful information: Alan Bennett, Terry Major-Ball, Fred Marks and Robert Phillips. The combined efforts of Maurice, Robert and Dorsey Foster, and Justin Semmens, at Videofinders International enabled me to assemble an unexpectedly comprehensive library of Grant's movies. To Ann Toseland at the University Library at Cambridge, and to the staffs of the Margaret Herrick Library and Academy Film Archives in Los Angeles (the beneficiary of Cary Grant's papers), the British Film Institute Library in London, the *Bristol Evening Post* and the British Library's splendid Newspaper Library, I extend my sincere gratitude for their uncommon courtesy and kind assitance.

I am indebted to everyone at Fourth Estate, but I am particularly grateful to Emma Rhind-Tutt for her tireless efforts on the book's behalf. Monica Schmoller's precise, patient and tasteful copy-editing not only gave the text a welcome final polish but also taught me a great deal in the process. Silvana Dean typed the book many times, swiftly, accurately and stylishly. She also helped me locate certain articles, check facts and clarify particular ideas; I was extraordinarily fortunate to work with her.

Everybody wants to be Cary Grant.
Even I want to be Cary Grant.
CARY GRANT

Interviewer:	*Do you know the important people in the world today?*
Two hour old baby:	*Well, some. I don't know, I'm not sure.*
Interviewer:	*You don't know what you know?*
Two hour old baby:	*No.*
Interviewer:	*Do you know, for instance, Mickey Mantle?*
Two hour old baby:	*No.*
Interviewer:	*Queen Elizabeth?*
Two hour old baby:	*No.*
Interviewer:	*Winston Churchill?*
Two hour old baby:	*Ah, no.*
Interviewer:	*Fidel Castro?*
Two hour old baby:	*No.*
Interviewer:	*Pandit Nehru?*
Twohour old baby:	*No.*
Interviewer:	*Have you heard of Cary Grant?*
Two hour old baby:	*Oh, sure! Everybody knows Cary Grant!*

Carl Reiner and Mel Brooks, 'The Two Hour Old Baby'

PROLOGUE

A mask tells us more than a face.
OSCAR WILDE

Some might say they don't believe in heaven
Go and tell it to the man who lives in hell.
NOEL GALLAGHER

Cary Grant was an excellent idea. He did not exist, so someone had to invent him. Someone called Archie Leach invented him. Archie Leach did not know who he was, but he knew what he liked. What he liked was what he came to think of as 'Cary Grant'. He discovered that it was an extraordinarily popular conception. Everyone really liked the idea of Cary Grant. Archie Leach liked it so much that he devoted the rest of his life to its refinement.

It is easy to see why. Cary Grant was the man that most men dreamed of being, an exceptional man, the 'man from dream city'.[1] He was that most unexpected but attractive of contradictions: a democratic symbol of gentlemanly grace. No other man seemed so classless and self-assured, as happy with the world of music-hall as with the *haute monde*, as adept at polite restraint as at acrobatic pratfalls. No other man was equally at ease with the romantic and with the comic. No other man seemed sufficiently secure in himself and his abilities to toy with his own dignity without ever losing it. No other man aged so well and with such fine style. No other man, in short, played the part so well: Cary Grant made men seem like a good idea. As one of the women in his movies said to him: 'Do you know what's wrong with you? *Nothing!*'[2]

There was nothing wrong with Cary Grant. His colleagues admired him. 'Cary's the only actor I ever loved in my whole life,' said Alfred Hitchcock.[3] 'If there were a question in a test paper that required me to fill in the name of an actor who showed the same grace and perfect timing in his acting that Fred Astaire showed in his dancing,' said James Mason, 'I should put Cary Grant.'[4] To Eva Marie Saint, Grant was 'the most handsome, witty and stylish leading man both on and off the screen.'[5] James Stewart described him as a 'consummate actor',[6] and Frank Sinatra remarked that 'Cary has so much skill he makes it all look so easy'.[7] Stanley Donen, the director, regarded him as 'absolutely the best in the world at his job':[8] 'If you asked almost any man in those days who would he like to be, you'd often get the answer "Cary Grant" – much more often than you would get the answer "the President of the United States".'[9]

There was nothing wrong with Cary Grant. Movie audiences loved to watch him. In the era when movies were made with and around stars, the initial attraction being the name above the title, no fewer than twenty-eight Cary Grant movies – more than a third of all those he made – played at New York's Radio City Music Hall (the largest, most important and prestigious movie theatre at that time in the United States) for a total of 113 weeks – a long-standing record.[10] Again and again he was acknowledged as that theatre's leading box-office attraction. One of his movies was the very first to earn $100,000 in a single week; another was the first to earn $100,000 in a single week at a single theatre. In the pre-eminent popular cultural medium of the twentieth century, Cary Grant was one of its most successful stars. His pulling-power stayed with him until the end of a movie career which lasted for over three decades; even in the year of his retirement, the Motion Picture Association of America voted him the leading box-office attraction.[11] There was no decline, no fall from fashion. He was an exceptionally and enduringly popular star.[12]

There was nothing wrong with Cary Grant. Critics warmed to him. 'We smile when we see him,' wrote Pauline Kael, 'we laugh before he does anything; it makes us happy just to look at him.'[13] Richard Schickel suggested that 'the only permissible response to him is bedazzlement'.[14] In 1995, *Premiere* magazine lauded him as, 'quite simply, the funniest actor the cinema has ever produced'.[15] David Thomson judged him to be nothing less than 'the best and most important actor in the history of the cinema', in part because of his singular disposition, his 'rare willingness to commit himself to the camera without fraud, disguise, or exaggeration, to take part in a fantasy without being deceived by it',[16] and in part because of the extraordinary richness of the results of this commitment, an art mature and elaborate enough to embrace the ambiguities of a self shown in close-up.

There was nothing wrong with Cary Grant. There was much, however, that was extraordinary about him. That accent: neither West Country nor West Coast, neither English nor American, neither common nor cultured, strangely familiar yet intriguingly exotic (as someone in *Some Like It Hot* exclaims: '*Nobody* talks like that!'). That expression: capable of blending light and dark inside a single look, hinting at much more than it holds up for show. That walk: confident, athletic and slightly rubber-legged, fit for slapstick as well as for sophistication. He was, in an unshowy way, unusually versatile: he could play submissive, naïve, child-like characters (such as in *Bringing Up Baby*) or worldly-wise charmers (as in *Suspicion*) or world-weary cynics (as in *Notorious*). John F. Kennedy thought that Grant would be his ideal screen *alter ego*, but then so did Lucky Luciano;[17] Grant's exceptionally broad appeal was in part to do with his bright roundedness, the promise of completion, showing the coarse how to have class and the over-refined how to have the common touch, teaching the unruly how to behave and the repressed how to have fun. What was so remarkable was how Cary Grant himself seemed to be so conspicuously complete. No one else was quite like him. There was something odd, something peculiar even, about his perfection.

'Everybody wants to be Cary Grant,' said Cary Grant. 'Even *I* want to be Cary Grant.'[18] It was not meant as a boast, but rather as an admission of vulnerability. Cary Grant appreciated – more so than anyone else – how difficult it was to be 'Cary Grant', because he knew that *he* was far from perfect. 'How can anyone', asked David Thomson, '*be* "Cary Grant"? But how can anyone, ever after, not consider the attempt?'[19] It is really not so strange that even Cary Grant could not always succeed in being 'Cary Grant'. It is not as if Archie Leach had always found it easy to be Archie Leach. The difference is that everyone knows who 'Cary Grant' is supposed to be, everyone knows the *rules*, while not even Archie Leach was ever very sure of who Archie Leach was supposed to be.

Everybody knows Cary Grant. What everybody knows about Cary

Grant, however, is largely what he wanted us to know. Leslie Caron, one of his last co-stars, recalled: 'He would say, "Let the public and the press know nothing but your public self. A star is best left mysterious. Just show your work on film and let the publicity people do the rest."'[20] He lived much of his life on the screen, in the movies, making us believe in Cary Grant, showing his image at each stage in its slow and subtle evolution. When he retired, he withdrew from view. There were no opportunities for disenchantment: no kiss-and-tell memoirs, no television specials, no embarrassing scenes, no political pronouncements, no diet books or diaries, no talk-show appearances, no authorised biographies, no comebacks, no second thoughts. He never told us how he had managed to be Cary Grant so well for so long. He cared too much, or too little, to let on; he liked to keep us guessing. To accept definition was to invite disqualification. He was content, it seemed, just to live with – or behind – the mystery. The mystery had, after all, served him very well. Why let in daylight upon magic?[21] 'Besides,' he said, with a playful insouciance, 'I don't think anybody else really gives a damn.'[22]

Cary Grant was an excellent idea. The last person who wanted to deconstruct that idea was Cary Grant:

> Who tells the truth about themselves anyway? A memoir implies selectiveness, writing about just what you want to write about, and nothing else. To write an autobiography, you've got to expose other people. I hope to get out of this world as gracefully as possible without embarrassing anyone.[23]

It was typically Cary Grant: polite, urbane, decent and discreet – and very much in control. He looked on with wry amusement as the old tales were retold and the new myths manufactured: he ignored all the parodies and pretenders, all the old quotations and well-worn misconceptions, all the 'Judy, Judy, Judys' and the 'How old Cary Grants'. He did not rise to the bait. He refused to involve himself in the investigations. He kept his self for himself. 'Go ahead, I give you permission to misquote me,' he told his uninvited chroniclers. 'I improve in misquotation.'[24]

Cary Grant, in more than one sense, was a class apart. Socially, he was a glorious enigma, eluding every pat classification. Artistically, he was, in his own particular field, without peers. In a leading article in the *Washington Post* shortly after his death, it was said that the name 'Cary Grant', 'in the absence of anyone remotely like him on the screen, continued to be a synonym for a set of qualities his friends and admirers inevitably summed up as "class"'.[25] Cary Grant did indeed have class. He was a master of the 'high definition performance', a term defined by Kenneth Tynan as 'the hypnotic saving grace of high and low art alike', characterised by 'supreme professional polish, hard-edged technical skill, the effortless precision without which no artistic enterprise – however strongly we may sympathise with its aims or ideas – can inscribe itself on our memory'.[26]

Everybody wanted to be Cary Grant. Everyone else, before and since, failed. It took someone special to succeed. It took Archie Leach.

BEGINNINGS

It is not dreams of liberated grandchildren which stir men and women to revolt, but memories of enslaved ancestors.
WALTER BENJAMIN

Peace. That's what I'm looking for. I want peace. With happy hearts and straight bones without dirt and distress. Surprises you, don't it? Peace — that's what us millions want, without having to snatch it from the smaller dogs. Peace — to be not a hound and not a hare. But peace — with pride to have a decent human life, with all the trimmings.
NONE BUT THE LONELY HEART

CHAPTER I

Archie Leach

Don't I sound a bounder!
CARY GRANT

Take it from me: it don't do to step out of your class.
JIMMY MONKLEY

Cary Grant was a working-class invention. His romantic elegance, as Pauline Kael remarked, was 'wrapped around the resilient, tough core of a mutt'.[1] It is one of the greatest and most mischievous cultural ironies of the twentieth century that the man who taught the privileged élite how a modern gentleman should look and behave was himself of working-class origin. It took Archie Leach – poor Archie Leach – to show the great and the good how to live with style. It was Archie Leach, born into such inauspicious circumstances, who became the man others liked to be seen with, a role model for the socially ambitious, the well bred and even the royal. 'When you look at him', said Kael, 'you take for granted expensive tailors, international travel, and the best that life has to offer.'[2] Cary Grant exuded urbane good taste and inoffensive prosperity: 'There were no Cary Grants in the sticks'; Grant represented the most distinguished example of 'the man of the big city, triumphantly suntanned'.[3]

The transformation of Archie Leach into Cary Grant was contemporaneous with, but different from, that of James Gatz into Jay Gatsby. The mysterious and glamorous figure in F. Scott Fitzgerald's *The Great Gatsby* 'sprang from his Platonic conception of himself',[4] suddenly, out of sight, without explanation. Cary Grant, on the other hand, took time to take over Archie Leach. Both Leach and Gatz came from poor backgrounds, their parents 'shiftless and unsuccessful';[5] both longed to grow, to change, to escape (Leach from Bristol,

Gatz from West Egg, Long Island) and reinvent themselves as the kind of attractive, successful, stylish young man of wealth and taste 'that a seventeen-year-old boy would be likely to invent';[6] and both possessed an extraordinary 'gift for hope',[7] a quality commented on by another character in the novel:

> If personality is an unbroken series of successful gestures, then there was something gorgeous about him, some heightened sensitivity to the promises of life, as if he were related to one of those intricate machines that register earthquakes ten thousand miles away.[8]

The two men differed, however, in their relationship with their old identities; Gatsby was a tense denial of Gatz whereas Grant was a warm affirmation of Leach. With Gatsby, all the careful gestures – the pink suits, the silver shirts, the gold ties, the Rolls-Royce swollen with chrome, the pretensions to an Oxford education, the clipped speech, the 'old sports', the formal intensity of manner – helped to conceal the unwelcome persistence of the insecure 'roughneck', James Gatz. With Grant, however, the accent, the mannerisms, the values, the sense of humour, continued to underline the strangeness of his cultivation. To Gatsby, any memory of Gatz, any recognition of the prosaic facts of his existence, represented a threat to his new identity. To Grant, on the contrary, Archie Leach remained with him, an intrinsic part of his life and character, an affectionate point of reference in his movies and his interviews: Archie Leach was no threat to his – or others' – sense of himself. Archie Leach was the measure of his success and, in a profound sense, a reason for it.

Cary Grant's life was lived in the midst of a vibrant American modernity, but Archie Leach's English childhood was solidly Edwardian. Queen Victoria had died just three years before he was born, and he grew up in a world of gas-lit streets, horse-drawn carriages, trams and four-masted schooners. The culture of the time discouraged – and sometimes mocked – thoughts of upward social mobility. E. M. Forster's *Howards End* (1910), for example, depicted the *petit bourgeois* Leonard Bast as limited fundamentally by his undistinguished background: he was 'not as courteous as the average rich man, nor as intelligent, nor as healthy, nor as lovable';[9] he has a 'cramped little mind',[10] plays the piano 'badly and vulgarly'[11] and is married to a woman who is 'bestially stupid';[12] his hopeless pursuit of culture is curtailed when he dies of a heart attack after having a bookcase fall on top of him. This was the England of Archie Leach. In this England the story of Cary Grant would have seemed incomprehensible.

Archibald Alexander Leach[13] was born on Sunday, 18 January 1904, at 15 Hughenden Road, Horfield, in Bristol. Elias James Leach, his father, was a tailor's presser by trade, working at Todd's Clothing Factory near Portland Square. He was a tall, good-looking man with a 'fancy' moustache, soft-voiced but convivial by nature and at his happiest at the centre of light-hearted social occasions. Elsie Maria Kingdon Leach,[14] his mother, was a short, slight woman with olive skin, sharp brown eyes and a slightly cleft chin; she came from a large family of brewery labourers, laundresses and ships' carpenters. She had married Elias in the local parish church on 30 May 1898. Some of Elsie's friends felt that Elias was rather irresponsible and, worse still, 'common', more obviously resigned than she to their humble position; but it seems that she was, at least for the first few years of their relationship, genuinely in love with him. The family lived at first in a rented two-storey terraced house situated on one of the side streets off the main Gloucester Road leading out of Bristol. Built of stone and heated solely by relatively ineffectual coal fires in small fireplaces, the house was bitterly cold in winter and chillingly damp the rest of the time.

Archie Leach was born in the early hours of one of the coldest mornings of the year. Like most babies at that time, he was delivered at home in his parents' bedroom. The uncomplicated birth, and the baby's subsequent good health, were greeted with particular relief by the couple. Their first child, John, had died four years earlier – just two days short of his first birthday – in the violent convulsions of tubercular meningitis.[15] Elsie had sat beside his cot night and day until she was exhausted; the doctor had ordered her to sleep for a few hours, and, as she slept, the baby died.[16] The loss had left Elsie – who was only twenty-two at the time – seriously depressed and withdrawn, and Elias, living in the city that was the centre of the wine trade, had taken to drink. The marriage was put under considerable strain. Eventually, the family doctor advised the couple to try for another child to compensate for their loss. They did so. Archie was to be, in effect, their only child.

It is at this very early stage that one encounters the first of several points of contention in Grant's biography. Archie Leach was circumcised,[17] which was a fact that later encouraged some biographers to identify him as Jewish.[18] It is not, however, as simple as that. Pauline Kael, among others, has suggested that Elias Leach 'came, probably, from a Jewish background',[19] and it has been said by some that Cary Grant himself believed that the reason for the circumcision must have been due to his father being partly Jewish, but, curiously, there is no record of any Jewish ancestors in Elias's family tree, nor is there any solid evidence to suggest that he thought of himself as Jewish. We do know that Elias and Elsie attended the local Episcopalian Church every Sunday. Circumcision was not, however, it has to be said, a common practice outside the Jewish community in England at that time;[20] it is possible, of course, that the Leaches were advised that it was – in Archie's case – an action that was necessary or prudent for particular medical reasons (and, after the death of their first child, they would surely have taken any such advice extremely seriously), but, again, there is nothing recorded which could clarify the matter.

It is not even clear whether or not Cary Grant lived his life *believing* himself to be Jewish. His closest friends – indeed even his wives – have offered conflicting information and opinions on the matter. In the early 1960s, for example, Walter Matthau, who had heard the rumours that Grant was Jewish, was surprised when Grant denied it. 'So, I asked him why everyone thought he was. He said, "Well, I did a Madison Square Garden event for the State of Israel and I wore a yarmulke." He pronounced the *r* in "Yarmulke". An Englishman wouldn't pronounce the *r*, so I still think he might be Jewish. Besides, he was so intelligent. Intelligent people *must* be Jewish.'[21] There is no reason to think that Grant would have tried deliberately to hide his Jewishness: he was a uniquely powerful and consistently popular star, less easily intimidated than most by anti-Semitic producers and gossip columnists, and he was a frequent contributor to, and supporter of, Jewish charities.[22]

If all (or even most) of the testimonies by his friends are sincere, one has to acknowledge that Grant gave some people the impression that he was Jewish and others that he was not. The extraordinary farrago of conjecture, confusion and wild theorising that this apparent inconsistency has engendered is at times almost comic in its incoherence. An outstandingly bizarre example is the contribution made by

Grant's first wife, Virginia Cherrill, who was convinced (on the rather scant evidence of his deep tan and the fact that he could perform a *temsulka*, which is a word of Arabic derivation for a special double forward somersault) that he was of Arabic origin.[23] In 1983, Grant – then aged seventy-nine, long retired from acting and surely at a stage in his life when it made no sense to continue to be dishonest or evasive about such a matter – replied to a fan's question about his late 'Jewish mother' by stating that she was *not* Jewish.[24]

The theory which has been most controversial, however, was put forward shortly after Grant's death by two of his most assiduous biographers, Charles Higham and Roy Moseley.[25] They claimed, with a suitably bold theatrical flourish, that Grant had been 'the illegitimate child of a Jewish woman, who either died in childbirth or disappeared'.[26] Although this thesis helps to make sense of the circumcision and of the possible reasons for Grant's own inconsistent references to his background (Jews define Jewishness through the maternal line), it is not based on any documentary proof. Indeed, the authors strain one's credulity with their scattershot references to such 'circumstantial evidence' as the fact that Grant's relationship with his mother in later years appeared 'artificial and strained'[27] to some observers, and that 'she consistently refused to visit Los Angeles'[28] once Grant was established as a star. They do, however, make use of two further facts which are rather more intriguing: one is that, until 1962, Grant, in his entry in *Who's Who in America*, listed his mother's name as 'Lillian', not Elsie, Leach; the other is that in 1948 he donated a considerable sum of money to the new State of Israel in the name, according to the authors, of 'My Dead Jewish Mother'.[29]

It is quite true that, until 1962, it is 'Lillian Leach' who is listed in *Who's Who in America* as being Grant's mother;[30] it is also true – although Higham and Moseley do not refer to it – that the 1941 article on Grant in *Current Biography* refers to his mother as 'Lillian', whereas the 1965 edition reverts, without any explanation, to 'Elsie'.[31] This discrepancy, while certainly noteworthy, is not, in itself, 'proof' of the existence of Grant's 'real' mother: the entries in both publications contain numerous inaccuracies, such as the spelling of Elsie/Lillian Leach's maiden name as 'Kingdom' rather than 'Kingdon' (one would have expected greater care if these entries had been intended to set the record straight), the description of Fairfield

mar School as the more American-sounding 'Fairfield Acad-
...y and the inverted order of Grant's forenames as 'Alexander
Archibald'.[32] Higham and Moseley do not make it clear why Grant
took the seemingly perverse step of 'disowning' Elsie while she was
still alive and in a fragile condition and then reclaiming her more
than two decades later: such inconstancy, surely, merits some kind
of explanation. Another puzzling detail, if one is to take seriously
the interpretation of these entries as some kind of rare act of candour
on Grant's part, is why, after acknowledging his secret Jewish mother,
he then proceeded to describe himself as a 'member of the Church
of England'.[33]

It is a bewilderingly odd little mystery. Higham and Moseley,
having convinced themselves that the 'real' mother of Archie Leach
was a mysterious and hitherto unknown Jewish woman called
'Lillian', struggle to weave her into the facts of his life in spite of
having no documentary (or even anecdotal) evidence that she, or
anyone like her, ever existed. They also fail to explain why Grant,
once Elsie Leach had died in 1973, did not make any attempt to
acknowledge the identity of his 'real' mother at any point during
the remaining thirteen years of his life. Other accounts shed no light
on the question of Grant's alleged Jewishness or the reason for the
absence of any records which could corroborate it. We are left, in
short, with one of those intriguing puzzles which together with
others make up a peculiar constellation of ambiguities in the life of
Cary Grant.

The first few years in the life of Archie Leach were marked by
both material and emotional impoverishment. The Leach family
moved house several times during Archie's childhood, and each
change of address marked a further decline in the Leaches' finances.[34]
'We could afford only a bare but presentable existence,' he later
recalled.[35] It did not take long for Archie to become conscious of
the fact that his mother and father were increasingly unhappy in each
other's company. There were 'regular sessions of reproach' as Elsie
castigated Elias for his failure to provide the family with a better
standard of living, 'against which my father resignedly learned the
futility of trying to defend himself'.[36] Elias started drinking more
heavily and frequently – often, it seems, in the company of women
who were more convivial than his wife. 'He had a sad acceptance
of the life he had chosen,' said Grant.[37] Elsie – partly out of necessity,

partly by inclination – became the disciplinarian of the family, working hard to keep her young son under control.

Looking back, Grant observed that his old photographs of Elsie Leach failed to do justice to the complexity of her adamantine character, showing her as an attractive woman, 'frail and feminine',[38] but obscuring the full extent of her strength and her will to control. When Archie was born, she became – rather understandably given the circumstances – single-minded in her concern for his well-being (she had, superstitiously, waited six weeks before allowing Elias to register the birth) and during his childhood she remained, if anything, a little over-protective of him; she 'tried to smother me with care', he said, she 'was so scared something would happen to me'.[39] She kept him in baby dresses for several years, and then in short trousers and long curls. In an attempt to provide him with an opportunity to have a better and more rewarding life than his father's, and in the belief that her son was a bright and talented boy, Elsie arranged for Archie to start attending the Bishop Road Junior School in Bishopston; he was only four-and-a-half years old, whereas five was the usual age for admission. She also managed, on an irregular basis, to save enough money to send Archie for piano lessons. Such forceful ambition was not, one should note, so unusual within a working-class family at the time; Charlie Chaplin also recalled how his mother would correct his grammar and generally work hard to make him and his brother 'feel that we were distinguished'.[40]

Archie did not escape from his mother's influence when he started attending school. Although few of his new schoolfriends came from poorer families than his own, Archie was eye-catchingly smart; Elsie made sure that he wore Eton collars made of stiff celluloid, and she had taught him always to raise his cap and speak politely to any adult he met. His pocket-money was sixpence a week, but he seldom received all of it; Elsie would fine him twopence for each mark he made on the stiff white linen tablecloth during Sunday lunch. Elias was uncomfortable with the idea of such exacting, sometimes overly fastidious, strictures governing Archie's upbringing, but he rarely interfered in matters concerning their son.

When Archie was eight years old, his father left the family for a higher-paying job (and, it seems likely, a clandestine love-affair) eighty miles away in Southampton. War had broken out between Italy and Turkey, and, while Britain was not involved directly, arma-

ment activities were accelerated. Elias was employed making uniforms for the armies. 'Odd,' said Grant, 'but I don't remember my
father's departure from Bristol . . . Perhaps I felt guilty at being
secretly pleased. Or was I pleased? Now I had my mother to myself.'[41]
The job only lasted six months, in part because of the considerable
financial strain on Elias of maintaining two households. He was,
however, fortunate that, with so many workers entering into war-
related industries at that time, his old presser's job in Bristol was still
vacant on his return.

Elias and Elsie were living together again, but their marriage had
disintegrated further. Absence had hardened their hearts; neither
person cared enough to communicate with the other. Elias was rarely
to be found at home, preferring instead to spend most of his free
time in pubs, and, when he returned in the evenings, he would retire
immediately after finishing his meal in order to avoid any further
confrontations with Elsie. Although Archie was often overlooked
during this increasingly tense period, his parents would sometimes,
separately, make an effort to entertain him.

Both Elsie and Elias enjoyed visiting the local cinemas, but, typically, they each did their movie viewing in their own distinctive
way. Archie's mother would, on the odd occasion, take him to see
a movie at one of the more 'tasteful' cinemas in town; he soon
became addicted to the experience, and started going on his own
or with schoolfriends to the Saturday matinees.[42] 'The unrestrained
wriggling and lung exercise of those [occasions], free from parental
supervision, was the high point of my week.'[43] Elias also found time
to accompany him but, whereas Elsie usually favoured the rather
refined atmosphere of the Claire Street Picture House (where tea
and refreshments were served on the balcony during the intermissions
and the movies tended to be romance and melodramas), Elias, who
'respected the value of money',[44] preferred to take Archie to the
bigger, brasher and cheaper Metropole (a barn-like building with
hard seats and bare floors, where men were permitted to smoke,
fewer women were present and the movies were usually popular
thrillers – such as the Pearl White serials[45] – comedies and westerns).

Archie was grateful for all such excursions, but he particularly
enjoyed his visits to the Metropole. It was a loud, exciting place,
with a piano accompaniment which, he recalled, tended to aim more
for plangency than for any discernible tune. It showed the kind of

movies and performers he liked most (such as slapstick comedies and stars like Charlie Chaplin, Chester Conklin, Fatty Arbuckle, Ford Sterling, Mack Swain and 'Bronco Billy' Anderson), and these occasions were probably the only times when he had the opportunity to establish any real rapport with his father, who sometimes treated him to an apple or a bar of chocolate.

Elias also took his son to the theatre. At Christmas it was pantomimes at such grand places as the Prince's and Empire theatres. At other times of the year it was music-hall acts, such as magicians, dancers, comedians and acrobats. Elias, 'in a tight-throated untrained high baritone',[46] taught his son how to mimic some of the singers of the time (in such songs as 'I Dreamt I Dwelt in Marble Halls' and 'The Man Who Broke the Bank at Monte Carlo'), as well as encouraging him to learn some of the magic tricks he had seen. Archie was enchanted. He started to visit the theatre whenever he had the opportunity. He was often alone and unsettled at home, an only child who was 'loved but seldom ever praised',[47] but now he had found an attractive distraction. 'I thought what a *marvellous* place.'[48]

CHAPTER II

A Mysterious Disappearance

Death merely acts in the same way as absence.
MARCEL PROUST

[I made] the mistake of thinking that each of my wives was my mother,
that there would never be a replacement once she left.
CARY GRANT

Archie Leach was just nine years of age when it happened.[1] He had just arrived home, shortly after five o'clock, after an ordinary, quiet, uneventful day at school. He was shocked to discover that his mother had disappeared. She had said nothing to him on the previous day to prepare him for her absence. No one, in fact, had said anything to suggest to him that his mother might not be waiting for him, as usual, at this particular time on this particular afternoon. It was, quite simply, a mystery.

His mother had, it was true, grown stranger, more unpredictable in temperament and behaviour, over the past few months, and he had been aware, to some extent, of the change. She had become increasingly – perhaps even obsessively – fastidious: Archie had noticed that she would sometimes wash her hands again and again, scrubbing them with a hard bristle brush; she would also lock every door in the house, regardless of the time of day, and she had taken to hoarding food; there had even been odd occasions when, inexplicably, she would ask no one in particular, 'Where are my dancing shoes?';[2] and on some evenings she would sit motionless in front of the fire, saying nothing, gazing at the coals, the small room draped in darkness. Archie had also grown accustomed – but by no means immune – to the noisy quarrelling between his parents, as well as to the equally common periods of icy silence which usually followed these arguments.[3] Nothing, however, prepared him for such a sudden and dramatic disappearance as this.

Two of his cousins were lodging in part of the house at the time, and, when he realised that his mother had gone, he sought them out to see if they knew of her whereabouts. According to one source, they told Archie that his mother 'had died suddenly of a heart attack and had had to be buried immediately'.[4] The more common version, however, first put forward by Grant himself, has Archie being told that his mother had gone to the local seaside town of Weston-super-Mare for a short holiday.[5] 'It seemed rather unusual,' he recalled much later, with a bizarre attempt at English understatement which perhaps had come to serve, in public, as a relatively painless way of obscuring a painfully disturbing memory, 'but I accepted it as one of those peculiarly unaccountable things that grown-ups are apt to do.'[6]

If his father attempted to reassure him that his mother would soon come home – and it seems that he did so – then it was not long before Archie realised that she was never going to return:

> There was a void in my life, a sadness of spirit that affected each daily activity with which I occupied myself in order to overcome it. But there was no further explanation of Mother's absence, and I gradually got accustomed to the fact that she was not home each time I came home – nor, it transpired, was she expected to come home.[7]

Towards the end of his life he admitted that, once some of the shock had worn off, 'I thought my parents had split.'[8]

What had really happened to Elsie Leach was that her husband had committed her to the local lunatic asylum, the Country Home for Mental Defectives in Fishponds, a rustic district at the end of one of Bristol's main tramlines.[9] Elias had arranged for the hospital's staff to collect her from their home earlier in the day, and then, after settling her in, he went back to work. He never told his son the truth about the matter.

The asylum at Fishponds was, by quite some way, the worst of the two institutions for the mentally ill in Bristol at that time. Conditions were filthy, and supervision negligible. It cost Elias just one pound per year to keep Elsie inside as a patient. She stayed there for more than twenty years, until, in fact, her husband's death in the mid–1930s. Was he her gaoler? British law prohibits the unsealing of psychiatric case records until a hundred years after the patient's death, and, as Elsie lived on until 1973, the actual reasons for her incarceration may remain ambiguous until well into the next century. Dr Francis Page, a Bristol physician, has said that it was 'always presumed she was a chronic paranoid schizophrenic', but he also acknowledged that he 'never did know the official psychiatric diagnosis' that had been used to keep her institutionalised.[10] She was, it is clear, prone to periods of acute depression, and it is conceivable that she could have suffered a nervous breakdown at this time. It is not so obvious, however, why this in itself should have convinced Elias that the only possible solution would be to abandon her inside the most wretched institution he could find. Ernest Kingdon, a cousin, visited Elsie regularly in Fishponds, and he has insisted that he found her to be resilient and intelligent: 'She used to write beautiful letters asking why she could not be released.'[11]

Although the precise state of Elsie Leach's mental health remains a matter for speculation, it is much easier to establish the reasons why Elias Leach was prepared – or perhaps determined – to have her committed and out of his life. It was a fact – a fact that Cary Grant never acknowledged or commented on in public – that Elias Leach had a mistress, Mabel Alice Johnson. It might have been the shock of her husband's indiscretion which precipitated Elsie's breakdown, although, by that time, their marriage was probably not much more than a sham, and Elsie was unlikely to have been entirely unaware of her husband's numerous earlier affairs. Divorce was both socially unacceptable and financially impracticable. Once Elsie was shut away, however, Elias was at liberty to establish a common–law marriage with his lover and, eventually, have a child with her.[12]

Archie Leach was kept ignorant of his father's other family. He and his father moved in with Elias's elderly mother, Elizabeth, in Picton Street, Montpelier, nearer to the centre of Bristol. Elias and Archie occupied the front downstairs living-room and a back upstairs bedroom, while Archie's grandmother (whom he later remembered as 'a cold, cold woman'[13]) kept to herself in a larger upstairs bedroom at the front of the house. This arrangement provided, at least in theory, someone to look after Archie while his father was spending time with his new family, and it saved Elias the expense of renting two separate houses for his double life.

Archie Leach never knew the full extent of the extraordinary deception perpetrated by his father.[14] Cary Grant discovered the truth (or at least a part of it) two decades later, in Hollywood, after the death on 1 December 1935[15] of his father from the effects of alcoholism – or, as the official account put it, 'extreme toxicity'[16] – when a lawyer wrote to him from England to inform him that his mother was in fact still alive.[17] Through the London solicitors Davies, Kirby & Karath, Grant arranged for the provision of an allowance and moved her to a house in Bristol. Elsie Leach was fifty-seven years old, her son thirty-two. She barely recognised the tall, well-dressed sun-tanned star who arrived back in England to be reunited with her. 'She seemed perfectly normal,' maybe extra shy. But she wasn't a raving lunatic.'[18] As Ernest Kingdon put it, 'Cary Grant knew very little of his mother. She was a stranger. Late in life, they had to come together and learn to know each other. It was a tragedy, really – a great tragedy.'[19]

Suddenly to re-acquire a mother in one's early thirties must have been, to say the least, a strange experience, just as the sudden reappearance of an adult son one last saw leaving for school at the age of nine must have been profoundly unsettling. 'I was known to most people of the world by sight and by name, yet not to my mother,'[20] Grant would say. He, in turn, would never know how ill she had been. Their subsequent relationship, unsurprisingly, might best be described as 'difficult'.

Opinions differ as to *how* difficult the relationship actually was. Any references to mothers in his movies – no matter how slight or frivolously comic – have been pounced upon by some writers for their supposedly deeper 'significance': in one, for example, his charac-ter – a paediatrician – has written a book entitled *What's Wrong With Mothers*.[21] According to his biographers Charles Higham and Roy Moseley, there was never any real warmth or affection shared by mother and son; Elsie, it is claimed, was a 'hard, unyielding woman' who never showed much gratitude for her famous son's regular flights to Bristol, nor did she allow him 'to make her rich', and she 'remained stubbornly independent and uninterested in his film career till the end'.[22] She was not, according to some accounts, a physically demon-strative person, and she could sometimes appear aloof and brusque in the presence of strangers.[23] Dyan Cannon, Grant's fourth wife, after spending some time with her new mother-in-law, described her as an 'incredible' woman with a 'psyche that has the strength of a twenty-mule team'.[24] Grant himself, after her death in 1973, two weeks short of her ninety-sixth birthday, admitted that he had often been exasperated and sometimes hurt by Elsie's stubborn and misplaced sense of independence:

> Even in her later years, she refused to acknowledge that I was supporting her . . . One time – it was before it became ecologically improper to do so – I took her some fur coats. I remember she said, 'What do you want from me now?' and I said, 'It's just because I love you,' and she said something like, 'Oh, you . . .' She wouldn't accept it.[25]

According to Maureen Donaldson, who lived with Grant for a brief period in the mid-seventies, he said that his mother 'did not know how to give affection and she did not know how to receive it either'.[26] He is said to have told one interviewer that his mother – in part because of her prolonged absence – had been, until quite late on, 'a serious negative influence' on his life.[27] Bea Shaw, a friend of Grant's, recalls him as being 'devoted to his mother, but she made him nervous. He said, "When I go to see her, the minute I get to Bristol, I start clearing my throat." '[28]

It seems, however, that the relationship was not as grim as some have suggested. Speaking in the early 1960s, when his mother was in her eighties, Grant described her as 'very active, wiry and witty, and extremely good company'.[29] According to some interviewers, Grant remembered visits to his mother when the two would talk and laugh together 'until tears came into our eyes'.[30] In a letter to the *Bristol Evening Post*, Leonard V. Blake recalled first seeing Elsie – 'a rather plainly dressed woman' – in a department store in the city, telling someone, 'I have heard from Archie.' Blake went on to observe that she 'would visibly glow as his name was mentioned . . . I believe she would wander around Bristol just waiting to talk about Archie. He was the Sun to her.'[31] Clarice Earl, who was a matron at Chesterfield Nursing Home in Bristol, where Elsie lived during her last few years, describes how when Elsie knew that her son was due to visit she would dress herself up and become excited: 'She would sit by my office and look along the corridor toward the front door. When she saw him, she'd give a little skip and throw up her arms to greet him.'[32] Years earlier, when the strangeness of her son's celebrity was far fresher in her mind, she still showed much more interest in him and his career than has usually been suggested. Writing to him at the end of 1938, for example, she confessed: 'I felt ever so confused after so many years you have grown such a man. I am more than delighted you have done so well. I trust in God you will keep well and strong.'[33] After the end of the Second World War, when Elsie was almost seventy years old, she was interviewed by a Bristol newspaper about her son: 'It's been a long time since I have seen him,' she said, 'but he writes regularly and I see all his films. But I wish he would settle down and raise a family. That would be a great relief for me.'[34]

Elsie Leach, it is true, did not accept her son's offer – which was put to her on more than one occasion – to move to California, but her refusal was prompted by reasons other than any alleged ill-feelings towards her son. At the end of his life, Grant explained:

> She wouldn't join me in America. She told me: 'Never lived anywhere but Bristol. Don't want to [leave], only place I know.' At her own request she lived in a nursing home but we kept her house although we knew she would never return there. I didn't want to get rid of it. It would have seemed like I was packing her off.[35]

Elsie was, it seems, as concerned about her son as he was about her. In 1942, when war prevented him from flying over to see her, she wrote to him: 'Darling, if you don't come over as soon as the war ends, I shall come over to you . . . We are so many thousands of miles from each other.'[36] A friend of Elsie's recalled seeing two large chests of food which had been gifts from Grant. When she was asked why they remained unopened, Elsie is said to have replied, 'I want to have them until they're really needed . . . You never know . . . Cary might be hard up one day.'[37] When Grant tried, unsuccessfully, to persuade her to let him hire someone to do her housework for her, he was amused and impressed rather than upset by her negative response: 'she avers that she can do it better herself, dear, that she doesn't want anyone around telling her what to do or getting in her way, dear, and that the very fact of the occupation keeps her going, you see, dear'.[38]

The earliest letter from Elsie in Cary Grant's papers is dated 30 September 1937, sent from Bristol to Hollywood, and it gives one the impression of a much warmer, caring and humorous person than many biographers have described:

MY DEAR SON,

Just a line enclosing a few snaps taken with my own camera. Do you think they are anything like me Archie? I am still a young old mother. My dear son, I have not fixed up home waiting to see you. No man shall take the place of your father. You quite understand. I am desperately longing waiting anxiously every day to hear from you. Do try and come over soon . . .

Fondest love, your affectionate MOTHER.[39]

In her letters and postcards – and Grant saved hundreds in his personal archive – she was usually rather garrulous and good-natured, addressing her son as 'Archie' or 'My Darling Son' and closing with 'Kisses', 'Fondest Love' or 'Your Affectionate Mother'.[40] Grant, in turn, cabled or wrote to her regularly,[41] usually addressing her as 'Darling', ending with 'Love Always' and 'God Bless', and signing his name as 'Archie'. In one letter, sent in 1966 shortly before the birth of his (and Dyan Cannon's) daughter, Grant wrote:

Watching, and being with, my wife as she bears her pregnancy and goes towards the miraculous experience of giving birth to our first child, I'm moved to tell you how much I appreciate, and now better understand, all you must have endured to have me. All the fears you probably knew and the joy and, although I didn't ask you to go through all that, I'm so pleased you did; because in so doing, you gave me life. Thank you, dear mother, I may have written similar words before but, recently, because of Dyan, the thoughts became more poignant and clear. I send you love and gratitude.[42]

Phyllis Brooks, who was once engaged to Grant in the late 1930s and who remained a close friend, remembered him being reunited with Elsie: 'Cary called his mother a dear little woman. But he didn't talk much about her. I didn't probe. It was such a traumatic thing to have happen to anybody.'[43] If the reunion had been an act, prompted by fears of adverse publicity, he seems to have invested an unnecessary amount of time, energy and emotion in maintaining the union during the next thirty-five years. It seems likely that Grant and his mother *did*, slowly, develop a relationship that was, in the circumstances, relatively stable and mature.

It is probably true that he had found it much easier to feel affection for his father.[44] He had, after all, enjoyed an uninterrupted relationship with him, and, after his mother's disappearance, he may have come to regard his father, like himself, as a victim of that traumatic episode.[45] His mother, it seemed at the time, had, without any explanation, deserted him, whereas his father had stayed and raised him. When Elias died, his son expressed the belief that his death had been 'the inevitable result of a slow-breaking heart, brought about by an inability to alter the circumstances of his life'.[46] It would be wrong, however, to accept uncritically the common perception today of Elias as the deferential working-class man and Elsie as the somewhat snobbish woman with grand ambitions, just as it would be wrong to believe that Grant sided consistently and completely with one or the other of his parents. He once said that, when he looked back on the family arguments that dominated his childhood, he felt unable to 'say who was wrong and right'.[47] Both Elsie and Elias Leach possessed a strong sense of working-class pride: in Elsie, this showed itself in her determination to avoid giving anyone an opportunity to regard her family as 'common', as well as in her dreams of financial security and her hopes for her son's social advancement; in Elias, this pride evidenced itself in more prosaic and pragmatic ways, such as in his advice to his son to buy 'one good superior suit rather than a number of inferior ones', so that 'even when it is threadbare people will know at once it was good'.[48] Elsie craved prosperity whilst Elias would have settled for the appearance of prosperity; Archie respected his mother's boundless determination, as well as sharing some of her aspirations, and he also sympathised with his father's gentle stoicism.

Eventually, Cary Grant came to look back on his childhood, and both of his parents, with a generous spirit: 'I learned that my dear parents, products of *their* parents, could know no better than they knew, and began to remember them only for the most useful, the best, the nicest of their teachings.'[49] According to one of his friends

– Henry Gris – it was only relatively late in his life that Grant 'realised the depth of his guilt complex about his mother's disappearance. He believed *he* was the subject of his parents' many bitter quarrels.'[50] Archie Leach, however, during those traumatic months following the mysterious disappearance of his mother, was unable to come to terms with what had really happened to his family; he could only attempt to adjust to what he *thought* had happened, and he thought that his mother had deserted him. 'I thought the moral was – if you depend on love and if you give love you're stupid, because love will turn around and kick you in the heart.'[51]

CHAPTER III

A Place to Be

Regardless of a professed rationalisation that I became an actor in order to travel, I probably chose my profession because I was seeking approval, adulation, admiration and affection: each a degree of love. Perhaps no child ever feels the recipient of enough love to satisfy him or her. Oh, how we secretly yearn for it, yet openly defend against it.
CARY GRANT

Our dreams are our real life.
FEDERICO FELLINI

Archie Leach's adolescence was marked by absence: the absence of his mother, the absence of a stable home life, the absence of money, the absence, it seemed, of a promising future. Not long after his mother's disappearance, his world was disrupted again: Britain was at war, and material conditions grew even worse for working-class families. His father, it seems, simply withdrew himself from his son's life. There was no open breach; there was just a vague and gentle separation. They left the house at different times – Elias for work, Archie for school – and they returned at different times. They seldom saw each other. Archie became, in effect, a latch-key child.

In September 1915, at the age of eleven, he won a scholarship to the local Fairfield Grammar School[1] – a gabled, red-brick establishment about ten minutes' walk from Picton Street. The Liberal government of the time offered 'free places' to a limited number of children whose parents could not afford to contribute financially to their education.[2] Archie still had to pay for his books, school uniform and other necessities, however, and, in the absence of his mother, he soon came to suspect that he would probably not be able to get through Fairfield on the little money that his father gave him. As a result, his 'aspirations for a college education slowly faded'.[3]

Elsie Leach's smart young son was now, according to one of his former classmates, 'a scruffy little boy'[4] who was a promising scholar and a good athlete, but who also had a mischievous streak and was often a disruptive influence. 'It depressed me to be good, according to what I judged was an adult's conception of good', Grant recalled, 'and matters around me were not going well.'[5] When Cary Grant made his triumphant return to Bristol on a visit in 1933, Archie Leach's old teachers told reporters of their memories of 'the naughty little boy who was always making a noise in the back row and would never do his homework'.[6] The irascible piano teacher whom Archie was obliged to visit had taken to rapping the knuckles of his left hand with a ruler (he was naturally left-handed,[7] which caused him to struggle sometimes to play as she instructed). 'My head seemed stubbornly set against the penetration of academic knowledge,'[8] although he admitted, grudgingly, that he quite enjoyed studying geography, history, art and chemistry. What he *did* become was an avid reader of comics, such as *The Magnet* and *The Gem*, as well as a popular and eye-catching footballer (playing in goal and experiencing the 'deep satisfaction' of being cheered when making a good save – 'one of those fancy ballet-like flying jobs'[9]). It was, in fact, as a result of his increasingly uninhibited sporting exploits that he suffered an accident that would alter his appearance in a subtle way: he snapped off part of a front tooth when he fell over in the school playground; the gap closed up in time, but he was left with only one front-centre tooth.[10] Similar – if less dramatic – mishaps followed. His teachers began to give up on him: 'I was not turning out to be a model boy.'[11]

He found an additional outlet for his energies in the 1st Bristol Scout troop. At the end of his first year at Fairfield he volunteered for summer work wherever his Boy Scout training could be used for the war effort: 'I was so often alone and unhappy at home that I welcomed any occupation that promised activity.'[12] He was assigned to working as a messenger and guide on the military docks at Southampton. For two months he watched thousands of boys not much older than himself sail off towards France; some had already lost an arm or a leg in combat but were being sent back for a second time. It was a poignant experience for him, but it was also, in an odd way, an exhilarating period in his life. When he returned to Bristol, he began to spend time at the docks, where schooners and steamships sailed right up the Avon into the centre of the city. 'You always had a sense that Bristol was a port, a gateway to somewhere else,' he said, and, seeing the ships 'that could take you all over the world', he came to see the city as 'a place you could leave, if you wanted to, and, at that age, I did.'[13] He was restless and lonely, and it appears that he contemplated signing on as a cabin-boy until he discovered that he was too young.[14] Although, years later, he described Bristol as 'one of my favorite places in the world',[15] he admitted that, at the time, 'I didn't like it where I was, and I wanted to travel'.[16]

Back at the dark, quiet, cramped house in Picton Street, he was aware that his father, on those irregular occasions when he saw him, was growing increasingly withdrawn and melancholic. 'He was a dear sweet man, and I learned a lot from him,'[17] but as a father he no longer exerted much influence on Archie's life. The shadow of Elsie hung over them both. Years later, Cary Grant wrote of a long-held desire to 'cleanse' himself 'perhaps of an imagined guilt that I was in some way responsible for my parents' separation'.[18]

An opportunity to escape from the emptiness of his home life opened up unexpectedly when he encountered an electrician who was helping out in the school laboratory as a part-time assistant. Grant remembered him as a 'jovial, friendly man'[19] whose attitude towards his own family was considerably more responsible and positive than that of Elias Leach. This unnamed benefactor took a kindly interest in the bright but rather pathetic young boy who was clearly eager for companionship. He was also working at that time at the Hippodrome, Bristol's newest variety theatre, which had opened in 1912; a fully electrified theatre was still something of a novelty in those days, and he offered Archie the chance to explore the house that he had helped to wire. Archie, without any hesitation, accepted:

The Saturday matinee was in full swing when I arrived backstage; and there I suddenly found my inarticulate self in a dazzling land of smiling, jostling people wearing and not wearing all sorts of costumes and doing all sorts of clever things. And that's when I *knew*! What other life could there *be* but that of an actor? They happily travelled and toured. They were classless, cheerful and carefree.[20]

From that moment on, Archie Leach spent as much time as he possibly could at the theatre. The electrician introduced him to the manager of the Empire, another Bristol theatre, where he was invited to assist the men who worked the limelights. There he began to learn the ways of showbusiness people, absorbing the lore of the theatre. This unofficial job came to an abrupt and embarrassing end when, working the follow spot from the booth in the front of the house, he accidentally misdirected its beam, revealing that one of an illusionist's tricks was achieved with the aid of mirrors. Archie reappeared, his enthusiasm undimmed, at the Hippodrome, where he became a familiar sight, running errands and delivering messages backstage. His father and grandmother were, it seems, quite content to allow him to pursue his new activity without any interference. 'I had a place to be . . . and people let me *be* there.'[21]

During 1918, Archie recorded his daily activities in his Boy Scout's notebook and diary, a four-by-three-inch leather-bound volume which was preserved by Cary Grant in his personal archive. A few typical entries from January of that year give one a good sense of how his free time had come to be dominated by the theatre:

14 Monday. After school I went and bought a new belt. And a new tie. Empire in evening. Daro-Lyric Kingston's Rosebuds.
17 Thursday. Stayed home from school all day. Went to Empire in evening. Snowing.
18 Friday. My birthday. Stayed home from school. In afternoon went in town. In evening, Empire.
21 Monday. School. Wrote letter to Mary M. Empire in evening. Not a bad show. Captain De Villier's wireless airship at the top of the bill.
22 Tuesday. School all day. In evening, Empire. All went well, first house. But second house, wireless balloon got out of control and went on people in circle. Good comedy cyclist called Lotto.[22]

He was nearing the age when he could leave school, and he was convinced that he wanted to work full-time in the theatre as soon as he possibly could. He was watching – and often meeting backstage – a broad range of music-hall acts, and he was eager to begin performing himself. At some unrecorded point during that period, probably late in 1917,[23] he made contact with Bob Pender, who was the manager of a fairly well-known troupe of acrobatic dancers and stilt-walkers known as Bob Pender's Knockabout Comedians.[24] He had never achieved the kind of success enjoyed by Fred Karno, but he was an established and respected figure on the music-hall circuit.[25] Leach had heard that the troupe was being depleted regularly as the younger performers reached military age: 'When I found out that there were actually touring companies who would let you perform, and take you around the world, I was amazed, and it became my ambition to join one of these travelling shows.'[26] In a letter on which he signed his father's name, he wrote to Pender – who was on tour at the time – offering his services (but neglecting to note that he was not yet fourteen).[27] Pender replied favourably, inviting Archie to report to Norwich as an apprentice.[28]

According to Cary Grant's version of what happened, he intercepted Pender's letter, ran away from home, caught the train to Norwich (paying the rail fare with money sent by Pender) and was placed in training with the troupe, practising cartwheels, handsprings, nip-ups and spot rolls.[29] It took Elias more than a week to find him, eventually catching up with him in Ipswich, but whatever anger he had felt was swiftly assuaged by Pender, who was, Elias discovered, a fellow Mason.[30] The two men agreed, over a drink, that Archie could return to the troupe as soon as he was allowed to leave school – an event that Grant later claimed he tried to hasten by getting himself expelled: doing his 'unlevel best to flunk at everything' and by cutting class after class.[31]

On 13 March 1918, for some undocumented reason, Archie Leach was suddenly expelled from Fairfield. In front of the school assembly, it was announced that he had been 'inattentive . . . irresponsible and incorrigible . . . a discredit to the school', and that he would be leaving immediately.[32] There are at least four distinct versions of what had happened to precipitate such a radical measure. His own account, repeated and embellished in numerous interviews, was that he and another boy had been caught as they investigated the interior of the girls' lavatories.[33] A second, rather less racy, version, put forward by a classmate, claims that he was found in the girls' playground: 'His expulsion was so unfair. Several of us girls were in tears over it, because we didn't like to lose him.'[34] Another contemporary insists that the reason why he was expelled was that he had been 'involved in an act of theft with two other boys in the same class in a town named Almondsbury, near Bristol'.[35] Years later, G. H. Calvert, a headmaster of Fairfield, could not clarify the matter: 'I have heard various accounts of the reason for his leaving the school, but have no reason to suppose that any one of them is truer than another. Probably only Mr Grant and the headmaster of the day knew the facts of the matter, and memories play tricks . . .'[36] A fourth, and perhaps most plausible, theory is that the decision to expel Archie Leach was not inspired by some singularly dramatic misdemeanour but rather was the act of a broadly utilitarian headmaster (Mr Augustus 'Gussie' Smith) who had – along with the practically minded Elias Leach – reached the conclusion, after a string of petty incidents, that it would be best for all concerned if Archie Leach and Fairfield School parted company sooner rather than later.[37]

Three days later, Archie rejoined Bob Pender's troupe. His father, on this occasion, made no attempt to restrain him, and 'quietly accepted the inevitability of the news'.[38] There was no legal hindrance to his re-employment. The contract between Bob Pender and Elias Leach, written in longhand, is preserved in Grant's personal archive:

MEMORANDUM OF AGREEMENT

Made this day 9th Aug. 1918 between Robert Pender of 247 Brixton Road, London, on the one part, *Elias Leach* of 12 Campbell Street, Bristol, on the other part.

The said Robert Pender agrees to employ the *son* of the said *Elias Leach* Archie Leach in his troupe at a weekly salary of 10/- a week with *board* and *lodging* and everything found for the stage, and *when not* working full board and lodgings.

This salary to be increased as the said *Archie* Leach *improves* in his *profession* and he agrees to *remain* in the employment of *Robert Pender* till he is 18 years of age or a six months notice on either side.

Robert Pender undertaking to teach him dancing & other accomplishments needful for his work.

Archie Leach agrees to work to the best of his abilities.

Signed, BOB PENDER[39]

He began taking lessons in ground tumbling and stilt-walking and acrobatic dances. He practised using stage make-up. He studied the best ways to make full use of a wide range of stage props. He was also coached in the ways of 'working' an audience, of conveying a mood or a meaning without having recourse to words, establishing silent contact with an audience – a skill that he later acknowledged as having helped prepare him for the special challenge of screen acting.

Archie Leach had found a teacher he trusted. Bob Pender, a stocky, robust man in his early forties, was one of the most experienced and versatile physical comedians in England at that time. His real name was Lomas, the son and grandson of travelling players from Lancashire. His wife and co-director, Margaret, was former ballet mistress at the Folies Bergère in Paris. Archie, once he joined the troupe, lived with the Penders and the other young performers, either in their house in Brixton (the area long established, because of its close proximity to the forty-one London music-halls, as the home base of many professional entertainers[40]) or in boarding-houses on the tour circuit. It was an intense, practical and rapid education. Three months after he had left Bristol, Archie returned with the troupe to appear at the Empire. After the final curtain, Elias Leach, who had been in the audience, walked with his son back to his home. 'We hardly spoke, but I felt so proud of his pleasure and so much pleasure in his pride, and I remember we held hands for part of that walk.'[41] It was the closest that he had ever felt to his father.

The Pender troupe toured the English provinces and played the Gulliver chain of music-halls in London. The theatre became Archie Leach's world, the source of his new identity; when he was not on stage, he was usually studying the other acts. 'At each theatre I carefully watched the celebrated headline artists from the wings, and grew to respect the diligence it took to acquire such expert timing and unaffected confidence, the amount of effort that resulted in such effortlessness.'[42] He became determined to learn how to achieve the illusion of effortless performance: 'Perhaps by relaxing outwardly I thought I could eventually relax inwardly; sometimes I even began to enjoy myself on stage.'[43]

While on tour, the troupe was informed that it had been engaged for an appearance in New York. It was an extraordinary opportunity for all the young performers. There were twelve boys in the company, but provision for only eight in the contract that Pender had signed with Charles Dillingham, a New York theatrical impresario. Archie Leach – much to his relief – was one of the first of the troupe to be selected. On 21 July 1920, he joined the others on the RMS *Olympic* – sistership to the *Titanic* – and set sail for the United States of America.

CULTIVATION

Hughson: You're a man of obvious good taste in, well, everything. How did you, I mean, why did you . . .

Robie: You mean, why did I take up stealing? Oh, to live better. To own things I couldn't afford. To acquire this good taste which you now enjoy.

Hughson: You know, I thought you'd have some defense, some tale of hardship. Your mother ran off when you were young, your father beat you, or something.

Robie: No, no. I was a member of an American trapeze act in the circus that travelled in Europe. It folded, and I was stranded, so I put my agility to a more rewarding purpose . . .

To Catch a Thief

David: What do you want?
Aunt: Well, who are you?
David: Who are *you*?
Aunt: Who are *you*?
David: What do you want?
Aunt: Well, who *are* you?
David: I don't know. I'm not quite myself today!

Bringing Up Baby

CHAPTER IV

New York

It was an age of miracles, it was an age of art, it was an age of excess, and it was an age of satire. A stuffed shirt, squirming to blackmail in a lifelike way, sat upon the throne of the United States; a stylish young man hurried over to represent to us the throne of England.
F. Scott Fitzgerald

Good manners and a pleasant personality, even without a college education, will take you far.
Cary Grant

Archie Leach wanted to become a self-made man. The *idea* of being a self-made man appealed to him. It made sense. He had a fair idea of what he wanted to make of himself. As Pauline Kael observed, he 'became a performer in an era in which learning to entertain the public was a trade; he worked at his trade, progressed, and rose to the top'.[1] Archie Leach craved realism, not magic: *he* did not want to be dazzled, he wanted to *learn*: 'Commerce is a bind for actors now in a way it never was for Archie Leach; art for him was always a trade.'[2] Not for Archie Leach the debilitating struggles with one's conscience about the artistic merit of what one was doing; what he was doing was, it seemed to him, eminently preferable to what he would otherwise have been forced to do back home in Bristol. His initial struggles were, primarily, materialistic rather than intellectual; the practical experience he acquired furnished him with a certain toughness of spirit that subsequent generations of performers, from more privileged, middle-class backgrounds, lacked. In Bristol, he had seen the future, and it was work – work of the soul-destroying, demeaning kind which his father had come to accept as the bald and bleak sum of his life and identity. It was not a fate that Archie Leach was prepared to face: 'I cannot remember consciously daring to hope I would be successful at anything, yet, at the same time, I knew I would be.'[3]

Archie Leach was there, at the ship's rail, as the RMS *Olympic* steamed into New York harbour in the early morning sunshine of 28 July, and he thought he knew precisely where he was going; he had seen the famous sights of New York many times before, back in Bristol, on the movie screen. He had spent much of his free time, as a child, gazing at visions of American life in the dark. Archie Leach had imagined America long before he set foot on Manhattan Island.

The Pender troupe was met by a Dillingham representative, who took them directly to the Globe Theater. It was explained, as soon as they arrived, that the plans had been changed; instead of appearing in the comic Fred Stone's show, the Pender troupe would now open in a new revue, *Good Times*, at the Hippodrome. Although there was little time for them to rehearse, the troupe was not disappointed about the unexpected change. The Hippodrome, then on 6th Avenue between 43rd and 44th streets, was the world's largest theatre:[4] it could accommodate several hundred performers at once on a huge revolving stage; it had a ballet corps of eighty, a chorus of one hundred, and it required around eight hundred backstage employees to mount a show that included over ninety of the most celebrated and spectacular acts from around the world; the auditorium seated 5,697 people.

Archie Leach and his companions had arrived at a fortuitous time. New York, in 1920, was the centre of the world's blossoming entertainment business. Not only was it a period in which vaudeville theatres were attracting huge audiences, but it was also a period in which a new popular cultural medium – the movies – was in the process of transforming, and expanding, the realm of commercial entertainment in America.[5] At the turn of the century, vaudeville exploited movies as a new attraction; a pattern of movie presentations as single acts in commercial vaudeville had soon been established, and, indeed, vaudeville provided the forum in which many urban Americans were introduced to the movies. By the 1920s, however, the relationship had changed, and one of the ways in which the heightened sense of competition between the two showed itself was the determined pursuit by vaudeville producers of increasingly grand

and elaborate stage shows and a greater range of unusual and eye-catching acts.[6] The Hippodrome housed many of the most spectacular of these.

When they arrived the Pender troupe, with its modest if expert knockabout routines, must have felt rather intimidated (or possibly even, as Cary Grant put it, 'petrified'[7]). The other acts were certainly diverse: Joe Jackson, the tramp cyclist; Marceline the clown; the Long Tack Sam Company of Illusionists; 'Poodles' Hanneford and the Riding Hanneford Family; and, perhaps most memorable of all, Powers Elephants, described by Cary Grant as 'an amazing water spectacle in which expert girl swimmers and high divers appeared in an understage tank containing 960,000 gallons of water'.[8] Looking back, he reflected: 'Today you cannot imagine the size of it . . . It really was *show* business.'[9] The Hippodrome was not a place for the disorganised or the undisciplined: all performers were obliged to check in for work at a time clock – a necessary measure, as far as the management was concerned, in order to keep track of the extraordinary number of acts.

Archie Leach, along with the other boys in the troupe, lived under the authoritarian eyes of Bob and Margaret Pender in a cramped apartment just off Eighth Avenue. The Penders were severe task-masters. After each evening's performance at the theatre, the troupe would return to the apartment and line up at the kitchen sink to wash their socks, handkerchiefs, towels and shirts, and then on to the ironing-board – a ritual that usually lasted until well into the night. Leach was also given his own special duties, such as keeping accounts and cooking many of the meals. He grew up quickly.

Good Times was a considerable success, and the Pender troupe, although appearing in just one sequence in the show, attracted praise from several critics. Archie Leach found himself part of a 'remarkable international family', an 'astonishing assemblage'[10] of talented performers from diverse backgrounds, and he made the most of the opportunities open to him to learn everything that he could from all of the acts – including special acrobatic tricks, drunken walks, dance steps and illusions. It was an extraordinary time for him.

'The first thing I loved about America', he said, 'was how *fast* it all seemed.'[11] He found New York itself endlessly fascinating. It was a place that breathed possibility. With the Hippodrome dark on Sundays, he was free to explore the city: 'I spent hours on the open-air tops of

Fifth Avenue buses . . . I contentedly rode from Washington Square, up the Avenue and across 72nd Street, to the beauty of Riverside Drive, with its quiet mansions and impeccably kept apartment buildings.'[12] He wanted to feel at home in New York, and, in time, he *would* do so, but, to begin with, he found it simply exhilarating: the size, the sights, the sounds, the scope, the pace, the opportunities (real and imagined) – the initial exoticism of it all was thrilling.

Good Times ran for nine months, giving 455 performances before closing at the end of April 1921. Exploiting the success of the show, Bob Pender was able to book the troupe on a tour of the B. F. Keith vaudeville circuit (the major vaudeville power at that time in the eastern United States), visiting most of the major cities east of the Mississippi River. In mid-1922, the tour closed with an appearance at the prestigious New York Palace, and then, without definite prospects, Pender – ever the pragmatic professional entertainer – decided to return to England. Not all of his troupe, however, agreed with the decision; some of the members, including Archie Leach, were keen to stay on in New York.

Although Pender clearly had a great deal of respect and affection for Leach, as, indeed, it was evident that Leach had for him, it seems that their relationship had, by the end of the tour, grown tense. Pender by now was tired, middle aged and increasingly cautious; Archie Leach was eighteen years of age, good looking, tall (6' 2"), fit, energetic, with an increasingly forceful personality, and relishing life away from home. The manner in which they parted reflected the change in the relationship, with Leach, along with some of his fellow members of the troupe, deceiving Pender about their plans for the immediate future. Pender's letter to Elias Leach not only marks – with regret and exasperation – the end of his association with Archie, but it also suggests that he had been knowingly misinformed as to Archie's real intentions:

> 244 West Thayer Street,
> Philadelphia, PA
> May 21, 1922

DEAR MR. LEACH:

I am writing this to inform you that Archie is coming home. He leaves New York by the Cunard Liner Berengaria on May

29th and should arrive Southampton June 2 or 3. He has made up his mind to come home. I offered him 35 dollars a week which is about G8 [eight guineas] in English money, and he will not accept it, as he says he cannot do on it so I offered him £3/10 a week clear and all his expenses paid but he says he wishes to come home. The wage I have offered him is the same as my daughter and also another of my boys have been getting so I know he could do very nicely on it but I must tell you he is most extravagant and wants to stay at the best hotels and live altogether beyond his means.

I promised him if he improved in his work and was worth it, I will give him more money, but he is like all young people of his age. He thinks he only has to ask and have. I must tell you he has very big ideas for a boy of his age, and he seems to have made up his mind to come home.

He has been a good boy since he has been with me and I think he is throwing away a good chance but *he* does not think so. Mrs. Pender has talked to him but it is no use. He will not listen. So I should like to hear if he arrives home safely . . . I shall be glad to do anything for him when I return to England.

I remain,

Yours truly, BOB PENDER[13]

Recollecting the event forty years later, Cary Grant commented, 'It must have been very disappointing and difficult for [Pender] to leave so many of his boys behind in America, our land of opportunity: but youth, in its eagerness to drive ahead, seldom recognises the troubles caused or the debts accrued while passing.'[14] He was a young adult who, as he put it ruefully, 'knew that I knew everything'.[15] The only problem, it seemed to him at the time, 'was just that I hadn't *seen* everything'.[16]

Archie Leach, committing his immediate future to the US, spent most of the summer of 1922 searching for ways of making himself employable. Pender had contacts, Leach, thus far, had none; he was a young Englishman in America, with little experience and limited resources in a highly competitive business. 'Before I made my way to some measure of success,' he would recall, 'I had many tough times, but I was always lucky.'[17] He began from the outside in, acquiring 'the corniest habits in my attempts to become quickly Americanised'.[18] The obvious influences, for him, were from the theatre:

> I'd been to the Palace to see the Marx Brothers, billed as the 'Greatest Comedy Act in Show Business; Barring None'. I noticed that Zeppo, the young handsome one, the 'straight' man, the fellow I copied (who else?) wore a miniature, neatly tied bow tie. It was called – hold onto your chair – a jazz bow. Well, if that was the fashion, it was at least inexpensive enough for me to follow.[19]

The over-eager series of restylings did little to help him find regular work. After a few barren weeks, he was forced to start using up the 'emergency money' given to him by Pender for a return passage to England.[20] He had, however, during his search for the right kind of shows, managed at least to meet the right kind of people; Pauline Kael has suggested that he must have been 'an incredible charmer',[21] because he was just eighteen, admittedly tall and good looking, yet found himself invited to a number of exclusive dinner parties in the company of the wealthy and famous. On one such occasion, as the escort of the opera singer Lucrezia Bori,[22] he met George C. Tilyou,[23] whose family owned and operated the Steeplechase Park on Coney Island. The meeting resulted in a job: Tilyou hired him to walk around Coney Island on six-foot-high stilts while wearing a bright-green coat and jockey cap, long tube-like black trousers and a sandwich board advertising the race-track. If, in retrospect, the image of Cary Grant on stilts seems somewhat incongruous, one should also note that the image of, say, Ronald Colman, Rex Harrison or David Niven on stilts seems simply incomprehensible; Archie Leach, with his working-class background and his music-hall training, was, among all of the future Hollywood British, uniquely suited to the potential harshness of life in New York in the twenties. 'If I hadn't been badgered, cajoled, dared, bullied and helped into walking those high stilts when I was a boy in the Pender troupe, I might have starved that summer – or gone back to Bristol.'[24] The pay was forty dollars per week, which provided him with some steady cash while he searched for further vaudeville bookings. Another short-term scheme to earn money involved selling neckties hand-painted by his friend

John Kelly (who later achieved fame as the Hollywood designer, Orry-Kelly).

He was experiencing other anxieties during this period. There seems – judging from the (incomplete) correspondence which has been preserved between Archie Leach and his father, Elias – to have been an ongoing series of increasingly acrimonious exchanges between Archie and Bob Pender. Elias Leach, in a letter to his son, refers to 'the rumour of Mr. B. Pender action towards you'; he advises his son to 'try and get in touch with the national vaudeville artists institute and ask them if they take up such cases as yours [if Pender] tries his game on'.[25] Judging from this letter, it seems that Pender may have attempted to force Archie to return the money he was given for his return fare back to England. It is not inconceivable, however, that Archie Leach, having spent at least part of this sum, was more concerned about the possibility that his father might discover that his account of his dealings with Pender had not been entirely truthful. Elias, rightly or wrongly, accepted his son's version of events, and reassured him that 'if I get any letters from B. Pender or anybody else from New York I will do as you have asked me to do and not take any notice of them'.[26] Elias (who had just become a father again and was struggling to support his new family) also thanked Archie for 'another ten shillings note',[27] which suggests that the pressure on Archie Leach to find more lucrative forms of employment was particularly great at this time.

At the end of the summer, Leach and other former members of the Pender troupe heard that the director of the New York Hippodrome, R. H. Burnside, was planning another extravagant variety show, *Better Times*, which would accommodate an act similar to that of the Penders. They began to practise together, and, in September, they returned to the Hippodrome for the new season, calling themselves 'The Walking Stanleys'.[28] When *Better Times* closed, the troupe prepared a new vaudeville act which toured the Pantages circuit of theatres during 1924, travelling through Canada to the West Coast (giving Leach his first, brief, tantalising glimpse of Southern California) and back across the United States.

Upon returning to New York, the troupe disbanded. A few more went back to England, disenchanted after another exhausting and relatively poorly paid tour.[29] Archie Leach, however, once again, stayed on, living at the National Vaudeville Artists Club on West

46th Street 'where I was again permitted to run up bills while trying to run down jobs'.[30] The Club was a good place for making contact with other – often much better-known – performers, and, sometimes, substitute for them on stage. Leach had to improvise with little or no time for rehearsal or reflection. He worked in juggling and acrobatic acts; he had a short spell as a unicycle rider; in the guise of 'Rubber Legs' (a self-explanatory pseudonym that owed much to his years as a stilt-walker) he played in several comic sketches; he also appeared as 'Professor Knowall Leach' in a mind-reading act; and he was a straight man for a number of comics. The most memorable engagement that he secured at this time, he told people, was a spot as a straight man with Milton Berle in a variety show at Proctor's Newark theatre. Also on the bill was one Detzo Ritter, a man who wrestled with himself on stage, spinning himself through the air, locking himself into an agonising half-nelson before pinning himself, exhausted, to the mat for a spectacular finale.[31] Archie Leach's sense of the absurd – which was already fairly pronounced – could not have remained unaffected by such sights: 'The experiences were of incalculable benefit because it was during these one- and two-day engagements that I began learning the fundamentals of my craft.'[32] It was the kind of work that demanded a considerable degree of self-discipline; there was no room for egotism. Archie Leach was learning how best to husband his own energy; it was, indeed, probably from this period that he started to acquire the lasting reputation as a man who took direction well and did not exert himself to assert himself needlessly at the expense of others.

He learned a great deal from studying the best acts, such as George Burns and Gracie Allen, night after night, when they performed in New York:

> George was a straight man, the one who would make the act work. The straight man says the plant line . . . and the comic answers it . . . The laugh goes up and up in volume and cascades down. As soon as it's getting a little quiet, the straight man talks into it, and the comic answers it. And up goes the laugh again.[33]

Archie Leach had stage experience, but only as a silent performer of physical comedy routines; he had not yet had cause to speak, but he was now, gradually, learning the techniques essential for verbal humour. As a straight man, he learned, in front of an audience, the importance of timing: 'When to talk into an audience's laughter. When not to talk into the laughter. When to wait for the laugh. When not to wait for the laugh. When to move on a laugh, when not to move on a laugh.'[34] As his performances improved, and he became more experienced and self-assured, he received more bookings; he once said that he felt at this time that he had played 'practically every small town in America'.[35] The sheer variety, in terms of venue and composition and mood of audience, gave him further invaluable education in the art of comic technique:

> Doing stand-up comedy is extremely difficult. Your timing has to change from show to show and from town to town. You're always adjusting to the size of the audience and the size of the theater. We used to do matinees, supper shows, and late shows . . . the response would change from night to night and from town to town. The people in Wilkes-Barre and the folks in Wilmington don't necessarily laugh at the same things.[36]

While he was playing some short engagements in and around New York, he met Reginald Hammerstein, a stage director and the younger brother of Oscar Hammerstein II, who suggested, somewhat impetuously, that his true talent might lie in musical comedy. Receptive to the idea, Leach took voice lessons and was engaged on a 'run-of-the-play' basis by Arthur Hammerstein, Reginald's uncle, for *Golden Dawn*, the opening production of the impressive new Hammerstein Theater.[37] Leach had a minor role as an Australian prisoner of war, and doubled as understudy of the juvenile lead. The production opened on 30 November 1927, and ran for 184 performances over a six-month period. Afterwards, Arthur Hammerstein re-engaged him for another musical, *Polly*, in the role that Noël Coward had taken in the London production.

Polly opened to largely negative reviews in Wilmington, Delaware, where one critic remarked that 'Archie Leach has a strong masculine manner, but unfortunately fails to bring out the beauty of the score'.[38] Leach was replaced before the show reached Broadway. He was not, however, out of work for too long. Marilyn Miller, the popular musical comedy star, chose him to replace her current leading man in *Rosalie*. The show's producer, Florenz Ziegfeld, agreed with the choice and asked Arthur Hammerstein – his arch-rival – to release Leach from his contract. Hammerstein was not at all pleased, and, over Leach's 'complaining voice',[39] sold the contract to J. J. Shubert instead.

Shubert, along with his brother Lee, was Broadway's biggest theatrical producer at the time.[40] Ironically, although Leach, impetuously, had tried to resist the move, the change could hardly have done his career more good. Within a few weeks, the Shuberts had cast him in a new musical, *Boom Boom*, with Jeanette MacDonald, and agreed to pay him $350 per week. For a young performer who had been in only two previous productions, one of which he had been fired from, this was a stroke of remarkably good fortune. Leach, to his credit, appreciated this fact, and worked hard to make a success of the role. The show opened in New York at the Casino Theater in January 1929. After a mere seventy-two performances it closed (Charles Brackett, *The New Yorker*'s critic, remarked acidly that *Boom Boom* could 'teach one more about despair than the most expert philosopher'[41]), but both MacDonald and Leach were screen-tested at Paramount's Astoria Studio,[42] though no contracts were offered. Leach's test was not positive; he was, according to the talent scout's report, 'bowlegged and his neck is too thick'.[43] This curt dismissal was not quite as injudicious as the now notorious verdict on Fred Astaire's first screen test: 'Can't act. Slightly bald. Can dance a little.'[44] There was, after all, no shortage of young, tall, good-looking would-be matinee idols seeking employment in Hollywood; the competition was great, and any blemish, any sign of a suspect temperament, could count against one. Archie Leach, at that time, was far from Hollywood's – or, indeed, his own – idea of perfect, and he had not yet learned how to make a virtue out of his distinctive features and mannerisms. The talent scout was not guilty of any gross exaggeration. Leach's collar-size was 17½ inches,[45] and, because he had a gymnast's narrow, sloping shoulders, the thickish neck could sometimes seem even thicker than it actually was. He did indeed have a slightly bow-legged gait, which was not uncommon among those trained in his kind of specialised acrobatic work. The depressing verdict, therefore, was probably not entirely unexpected.

It was some consolation to Archie Leach that he was kept, in his words, 'happily, gainfully and steadily employed' by the Shuberts for almost three years.[46] He was, in fact, doing about as well in the theatre at that time as he would have done with comparable work in Hollywood. The Shuberts were paying him $450 per week, which allowed him to purchase his first car, a Packard sport phaeton, then considered one of the finest of American-made automobiles. He was a young man who was sharply aware of the value of appearances. 'That was my trouble,' he recalled, 'always trying to impress someone.'[47]

His next stage role was as Max Gunewald, a vain, superficial young man, in *A Wonderful Night*, Fannt Mitchell's rather loose re-working of Johann Strauss's *Die Fledermaus*. It opened at the Majestic Theater on 31 October 1929, two days after the blackest day of the Wall Street Crash, and closed, promptly, in February 1930. It had received mixed reviews, as had Archie Leach. One critic wrote, somewhat gnomically, that 'Mr Archie Leach, as the soprano's straying baritone, brings a breath of elfin Broadway to his role', but another disagreed, claiming that Leach, 'who feels that acting in something by Johann Strauss calls for distinction, is somewhat at a loss as to how to achieve it. The result is a mixture of John Barrymore and cockney.'[48]

After a few weeks back working in vaudeville, Leach received a new assignment from the Shuberts, but at a somewhat reduced salary. On the verge of bankruptcy, the Shuberts were packaging streamlined versions of some of their earlier successes to offer to the public at 'pre-war prices' from three dollars down to fifty cents. Leach went on tour in the musical *The Street Singer*;[49] for the next nine months, he toured through the provincial towns where unemployment was starting to put many people out on the streets. The show had to gross two thousand dollars a night just to break even. It failed, and was one of the contributing factors that caused the Shubert Corporation to file for receivership in 1931.

That year was the most dismal one for legitimate theatre in the US for two decades. Almost half of all Broadway theatres were closed. The only work that Archie Leach could find was at the open-air Municipal Opera in St Louis, Missouri, where J. J. Shubert produced a summer-long series of musical revivals. Although Cary Grant later recalled the 8,000-seat amphitheatre in Forest Park as being 'delight-ful',[50] and the summer season as 'glorious',[51] it was gruelling work, with a new role to be learned every two weeks. The plots were often extravagant, the productions lavish and the lighting effects, in particular, were spectacular. Audiences were rather less discriminating than on Broadway, but they appreciated professional performances. Leach, usually playing the romantic lead, stood out as a darkly hand-some young man. Local reviews were generally positive. He was noticed. When the season ended, and Leach returned to New York, he was invited to appear in a one-reeler movie entitled *Singapore Sue*. He was engaged on 8 May 1931,[52] for six days, by the Paramount Public Corporation; the movie was shot at Paramount's Astoria Studio, and he was paid $150 for his performance.

In the 1930s, short subjects served not only to flesh out an exhibi-tor's bill, but also allowed the studios (particularly Paramount and Warners, who both had major production centres in New York which enabled them to lure stars from Broadway and vaudeville) to test new talent inexpensively. *Singapore Sue* was not destined for any special promotion, but it was, none the less, the first serious opportu-nity that Archie Leach had to attract the attention of Hollywood producers. He played one of four American sailors visiting the Chinese character actor Anna Chang's café in Singapore. Dressed in a white tropical uniform, handsome in a rather over-ripe way and wearing make-up that made him appear eye-catchingly pale, he smiled falsely and mumbled, through clenched teeth, his few lines of dialogue without any conviction. It was, quite clearly, a dis-comforting experience, and one which remained a sufficiently painful memory to cause Cary Grant in 1970 to seek to persuade the organ-isers of the Academy Awards tribute to him to omit the planned excerpt from *Singapore Sue*.[53] His friend Gregory Peck, who was president of the Academy at the time, sympathised:

> In that early shot Cary hadn't acquired the poise and confidence, the kind of looseness before the camera that he later had. He still looked like English music-hall. I know how I would feel if someone showed a lot of footage of me before I had smoothed out my craft.[54]

Nothing came of the work.[55] In August 1931, Leach asked to be released from his Shubert theatre contracts. The Shuberts obliged. At the end of that month he was engaged to play a character named Cary Lockwood opposite Fay Wray in her husband John Monk Saunders's play *Nikki*. It opened at the Longacre Theater in New York on 29 September 1931. Leach was paid $375 for each of the first three weeks, and $500 per week for the remainder of the run. The show, however, did not endear itself to audiences for whom the theatre was now an expensive luxury, and, although it was moved to the George M. Cohan Theater in a desperate bid to save it, *Nikki* closed after only thirty-nine performances.

In November 1931, shortly after *Nikki* closed, Archie Leach sublet his small apartment and decided, along with his friend Phil Charig (who had written the music for the show), to visit California. Having worked steadily for more than three years, he felt he could now afford to take a vacation. Fay Wray, to whom he had become very close during the run of the show, had been offered a part in the movie that RKO Radio was planning from Edgar Wallace's story *King Kong*. She had invited Leach to follow her.[56] Other people had, at various times during the previous two years, encouraged him to move on and attempt to establish a movie career in Hollywood, and now, after yet another show had ended – in his view – prematurely, the time, at last, seemed right.

CHAPTER V

Inventing Cary Grant

Yes, despite his appearance, he was really a very complicated young man with a whole set of personalities, one inside the other like a nest of Chinese boxes.
NATHANAEL WEST

I guess to a certain extent I did eventually become the characters I was playing. I played at being someone I wanted to be until I became that person. Or he became me.
CARY GRANT

If Archie Leach, as he left New York for Hollywood, had come to think of himself as a self-made man, then Cary Grant, as he stepped out into the Southern Californian sunlight, would come to think of himself as a man-made self. Archie Leach had learned a great deal in a short period about how to perform, but, so far, he had learned little about how best he might use this technical knowledge to lend a certain distinctiveness to his own performances. Cary Grant would bring an unusual, attractive, imaginative personality to complement the existing solid technique. The change of name, in itself, was banal; it was common practice in Hollywood, where words were put to the service of pictures and one's name functioned as a sub-title for one's image. The change of identity, however, was profound; the new name heralded a new self.

Archie Leach did not arrive in Los Angeles with any great expectation of such a rapid and dramatic transformation. He was hopeful of employment in Hollywood, but he was not desperate; he knew that the Shuberts were eager to use him again, should he wish, or need, to return to Broadway. He could afford, therefore, to approach this new challenge with enthusiasm rather than trepidation.

There are, perhaps predictably, several versions of how Archie Leach managed to secure for himself a studio contract. One account, which was popularised by Mae West, has it that she 'discovered' him when he was a humble extra on the Paramount lot.[1] This is quite untrue; indeed, it was a canard that continued to infuriate Cary Grant whenever he saw it in print.[2] He was never an extra, and he had made seven movies before he first appeared with Mae West. Another version – more plausible but still with no documented evidence to support it – was put forward by Phil Charig: according to his account, he took Archie Leach with him when he was summoned for an interview at Paramount's music department, and, although he was not offered a job, the interviewer was sufficiently impressed by Leach's good looks to recommend him for a screen test.[3] There is, however, another version which, since it originated with Grant himself and there is no obvious reason to doubt him on this matter, may be regarded as authoritative: according to Grant, a New York agent – Billy 'Square Deal' Grady of the William Morris agency – gave him the office address in Hollywood of his friend Walter Herzbrun, and Herzbrun, in turn, introduced him to one of his most important clients, the director Marion Gering.[4]

Archie Leach did not just have handsome features – plenty of other young, out-of-work actors in Los Angeles at that time were that good looking – he also had genuine charm. It is clear that Archie Leach found it remarkably easy to find people who were able and willing to support his embryonic career. As had happened in New York, Leach became a popular new guest at Hollywood social occasions, and it was not long before he had the opportunity to impress a number of producers and directors. His new, unofficial patron Marion Gering was planning to screen-test his wife, and he thought that Leach could play opposite her. Gering took Leach to a small dinner party at the home of B. P. Schulberg, the head of production at Paramount's West Coast studio. Schulberg was, it seems, happy to accede to Gering's request, and a screen test and the offer of a long-term contract (worth $450 per week) were the results.

Archie Leach had achieved, with what seems like remarkable ease, the basis for a movie career. Before he could begin acting in any movies, however, he first needed to work on his identity. As with many young contract players, the studio questioned the marquee value of his name. 'They said: "Archie just doesn't sound right in America."' 'It doesn't sound particularly right in Britain either,' was his rather embarrassed reply.[5] He was told, without any intimation that the matter might be open to negotiation, that 'Archie Leach' was unacceptable, and was instructed to come up with a new name 'as soon as possible'.[6] That evening, over dinner with Fay Wray and John Monk Saunders (the author of *Nikki*), it was suggested that Leach might adopt the name of the character he had played in their show: Cary Lockwood. Leach liked 'Cary' as his first name, but he was told by someone at the studio that there was already a Harold Lockwood in Hollywood,[7] and so the search for a new surname continued.[8] The studio advised him to choose a short name: it was the era of Gable, Cooper, Cagney and Bogart. A secretary gave Leach the standard list of suggestions which had been compiled for such a purpose. 'Grant', according to his own recollection of the deliberations, was the surname which 'jumped out at me'.[9]

Paramount, it seems, was equally satisfied with the combination. 'Cary' sounded pleasingly ambiguous, a supple name which, when pronounced to rhyme with 'wary', could suit a sophisticated image, and, when pronounced to rhyme with 'Gary', could fit with a more plebian persona. The name's new owner never seemed particularly interested in proposing a definitive pronunciation: some of his friends, such as Alfred Hitchcock, favoured the former, while others, such as David Niven, favoured the latter (he himself managed, typically, to find a subtle *via media*, and he only ever protested when anyone attempted to call him '*Car*'). 'Grant', on the other hand, sounded reassuringly American; it had more simple and solid connotations, a nod perhaps to the Hero of Appomattox, General Ulysses S. Grant, eighteenth president of the United States. Someone noticed that Cary Grant's initials were the same as Clark Gable's and the reverse of Gary Cooper's; it seemed a good omen – Gable and Cooper were the most popular matinee idols of the day.

Cary Grant was born, in effect, on 7 December 1931,[10] the day that he signed his Paramount contract and consigned 'Archie Leach' to relative – but by no means complete – obscurity at the age of twenty-seven years and eleven months. Cary Grant was not a new man, but rather a young one with the rare opportunity to restyle himself in a manner which would suit his aspirations. The name change itself was a fairly routine, pragmatic decision by the studio;

it was not intended as an invitation to Archie Leach to embark on any profound voyage of self-discovery. Paramount had already decided who Cary Grant should be: a cut-price, younger, dark-haired substitute for Gary Cooper.[11] Cooper had joined Paramount in 1927; by 1931, he was complaining that he was being worked too hard. While he was filming *City Streets* that year, he suffered a near collapse from the combined effects of jaundice and exhaustion. When the movie had been completed, he left for Europe, and began to spend more time with the Countess Dorothy di Frasso than his studio felt was desirable. Archie Leach, smoothed out into the more refulgent form of 'Cary Grant', was to be used to remind Cooper – gently at first – that he was not quite as distinctive nor as valuable as he might have thought he was. The two men did have a number of things in common: both had English backgrounds (Cooper's parents were both English, and he had been educated in Bedfordshire[12]); both were physically powerful men who could also show their vulnerability; and both were versatile enough to play comic as well as romantic roles.

Cary Grant, it was reasoned, could be groomed for stardom by taking the 'Gary Cooper roles' that Gary Cooper turned down, and, by playing on the perceived similarity between the two men, Paramount hoped that Cooper's ego could be held in check by the constant presence of a possible replacement at the studio. A fan magazine of the time – possibly with some covert encouragement from Paramount's publicists – noted that 'Cary looks enough like Gary to be his brother. Both are tall, they weigh about the same, and they fit the same sort of roles.'[13] Cooper had been warned. It was a common tactic employed by all studios at the time to prevent their most popular stars from becoming too 'difficult': Metro-Goldwyn-Mayer, for example, had brought in James Craig as a threat to Clark Gable, and Robert Young as a threat to Robert Montgomery. It was good insurance. If Gary became too demanding, Cary could take over (only a modest dash would need to be erased on the dressing-room door); it was considered unlikely, and, as often happened in similar cases elsewhere, it was probably thought more likely that Cary Grant would become a useful romantic lead in a string of relatively modest movies.

Cary Grant, however, had a quite different outlook on the possibilities opened up by his sudden change of identity. He did not wish to live indefinitely within quotation marks; he wanted to create a 'Cary Grant' that he could grow into. Whoever this 'Cary Grant' was to be, he would have to be someone who seemed real to Archie Leach as well as to others. 'If I couldn't clearly see out, how could anyone see in?'[14] All that he started with, he admitted, was a façade, and 'the protection of that façade proved both an advantage and a disadvantage'.[15] It offered him both the chance to change and an excuse *not* to change. Archie Leach *wanted* to change. The playwright Moss Hart remembers him back in his New York days, mixing with a group of 'have nots' at Rudley's Restaurant on 41st Street and Broadway. According to Hart, Archie Leach had appeared to be 'a disconsolate young actor' whose 'gloom was forever dissipated when he changed his name to Cary Grant'.[16]

Archie Leach saw his reincarnation as 'Cary Grant' not as the end of his self-reinvention but rather as the start of it. The writer Sidney Sheldon, who came to know and work with Grant in the forties, used him as the prototype for Rhys Williams, a character in the novel *Bloodline*; Williams is described as 'an uneducated, ignorant boy with no background, no breeding, no past, no future', but with 'imagination, intelligence and a fiery ambition', he transforms himself from 'the clumsy, grubby little boy with a funny accent' into a 'polished and suave and successful' man.[17] Archie Leach was eager to learn, to absorb as much as he could from the places and people he encountered. His lack of formal education remained one of his lifelong regrets.[18] Since his arrival in the US, he had made a point of making the acquaintance of people who were gifted and highly educated. Rather like the character in *Bloodline*, he 'was like a sponge, erasing the past, soaking up the future'.[19] He was not ashamed of his working-class background, but he did want to take every opportunity to pursue the project of self-improvement; he was, in part, eager to educate himself, but also he was reacting, with bitterness, to the memory of the routine humiliations suffered by himself, his family and his friends back in England. He studied other people's dress sense, table manners, gestures and accents. He was not going to be 'caught out'. The composer Quincy Jones, who formed a friendship with him in later years, remarked that when he was growing up, 'the upper-class English viewed the lower classes like black people. Cary and I both had an identification with the underdog. My perception is that we could be really open with each other because there was a serious parallel in our experience.'[20] John Forsythe, who acted alongside him in the forties, made a similar point: Archie Leach had been 'a poor kid. He did scrape his way to the top. That meticulous quality he had – knowing how to best use himself – was one of the key things to his nature.'[21]

The *idea* of America – its promise of liberty and equality – inspired Archie Leach, as it had inspired many other English people from similar backgrounds. Betsy Drake, who became Cary Grant's third wife, recalled that 'in Cary's day you got nowhere – *no*where – with a lower-class accent. The fact that he survived all that speaks very well for him.'[22] Though America had its own casual snobberies, it was, none the less, considerably more democratic in outlook and disposition than the England that Archie Leach had grown up in. Categories in England were particularly rigid then, and social distinctions emphatically made and scrupulously preserved. In America, on the other hand, Archie Leach could, to some extent, avoid such potential disadvantages. Only an expert in contemporary English class distinctions could have contemplated slotting him firmly into a particular niche; to most people he was just a good-looking and personable young man.

Archie Leach had some sense of what kind of person he wanted Cary Grant to be. Glamorous, for instance. Archie Leach wanted Cary Grant to be the epitome of masculine glamour. To this end his first chosen role-model was Douglas Fairbanks. He had met Fairbanks before he even set foot in America. Fairbanks and his wife, Mary Pickford, had been passengers on the RMS *Olympic* on the same voyage to the US as Archie Leach and the rest of the Pender troupe. The couple were returning to America after their much-publicised six-week honeymoon in Europe. Fairbanks fascinated Archie Leach. Tall, dark and handsome, an international screen idol, a 'self-made man' (with just a little help from Harvard), a fine athlete and, as his young admirer noted, 'a gentleman in the true sense of the word. A gentle man. Only a strong man can be gentle.'[23] Archie Leach was thoroughly impressed by Fairbanks, off screen as well as on; Fairbanks symbolised the kind of man – and star – that the then still somewhat gauche teenage Archie Leach wanted one day to become. What is more, Archie knew enough of Fairbanks's biography, gleaned from movie magazines and newsreels, to see that they had much in common: disrupted and largely unhappy childhoods, alcoholic fathers, acrobatic training, apparently limitless high spirits and a capacity to enjoy their own good luck. Fairbanks had triumphed; he had achieved fame, wealth and power, as well as marrying 'America's sweetheart'.[24] 'For a man coming out of darkness into light,' commented the critic Richard Schickel, 'there was, possibly, a promise in Fairbanks.'[25]

At one point, late on during the crossing, Archie Leach found himself (probably less fortuitously than he later liked to suggest) being photographed alongside his hero during a game of shuffleboard: 'As I stood beside him, I tried with shy, inadequate words to tell him of my adulation. He was a splendidly trained athlete and acrobat, affable and warmed by success and well-being.'[26] Archie's glimpses of Fairbanks on that first Atlantic crossing provided him with his initial, and possibly most enduring, image of modern elegance and style. Cary Grant always attributed his almost obsessive maintenance of a perpetual sun-tan to that first sighting of Fairbanks's deeply bronzed complexion,[27] and he was also equally impressed by the relatively thoughtful and understated elegance of Fairbanks's dress sense (he was not the only one: many of the studio bosses had started out in the clothing trade, and there were few sights more likely to have them purring with delight than that of a well-tailored suit[28]). An Anglophile, Fairbanks had his suits made in Savile Row by Anderson & Sheppard, his evening clothes by Hawes & Curtis, his shirts by Beale & Inman and his monogrammed velvet slippers by Peel. Grant never forgot the subtle precision of that celebrated sartorial flair. Ralph Lauren has said that, years later, Grant described, in minute detail, how Fairbanks looked, and he urged Lauren to make a double-breasted tuxedo 'like the one worn by Fairbanks, same lapel and all'.[29]

Archie Leach was aware, however, that he could not, and should not, simply replicate the Fairbanks look. Cary Grant could not be another Fairbanks. Fairbanks was, at least on the screen, an all-American hero and Cary Grant, whatever, whoever, he might become, was never going to pass for an all-American hero. Gary Cooper would be able to grow into the role of the westerner, his voluptuous, gentle-looking face changing gradually – as though it had long been left thoughtlessly outside at the mercy of the elements – into a harder, rougher complexion, but Cary Grant could not go far in that particular direction. If Cary Grant's future was American, his lineage was English. He could change the way he looked rather more effectively, and speedily, than he could change the way he sounded. His accent, when he arrived in Hollywood, was the oddest thing about him. Nobody talked like that, not even Archie Leach in earlier years.

There is no reason to believe that Archie Leach, during his child-hood and early adolescence, sounded in any way different from other working-class Bristolians. There are, indeed, some who claim to be able to discern the distinctive 'burr' of his old Bristol accent beneath the assumed American tones.[30] It seems likely that Archie Leach's accent first began to change during the period he spent in London with the Pender troupe. It was not just that he was, at the impression-able age of fourteen, exposed to the distinctive dialects associated with South London, but also, more specifically, that he was drawn into the London music-hall community, which had developed its own semi-private patois, something described by one performer as 'a mixture of Cockney, Romany and Hindustani'.[31] Archie Leach, in time, would speak in his own odd hybrid of West Country and mock-cockney, with an increasingly distinctive staccato enunciation. Ernest Kingdon, his cousin, believed that this peculiar accent was to some extent the result of the fact that he was 'trying to maintain English speech, and he had trouble with his diction . . . It's not cultured English talk [but] very precise . . . as if he'd been taught elocution.'[32] This very individualistic way of speaking was probably made even more noticeable during the years Leach spent touring the music-halls in Britain and America with the Penders. Peter Honri, a member of one of Britain's most famous music-hall families, has noted that the so-called 'music-hall voice' relied not so much on volume as on 'pitch and resonance' – it was 'a voice with a cutting edge'.[33]

Archie Leach, as he struggled to survive in New York, realised that being – or, more pointedly, *sounding* – English limited the number of stage roles he could, with any seriousness, audition for.[34] 'I still spoke English English, and I knew that to get jobs here, I'd have to learn American English.'[35] He was not trying consciously to erase the sounds that associated him with a certain geographic and class back-ground; he was simply trying to make himself more employable in his new environment. As Richard Schickel has argued, he was probably aiming not for affectation but rather for 'something unplaceable, even perhaps untraceable', a malleable accent that could lend a 'democratic touch of common humanity' to an aristocratic role and a 'touch of good breeding' to the more raffish parts.[36]

He did his best, and, of course, his accent had already begun to change during those first formative years he had spent in the United States,[37] but the transformation process was both slow and incomplete. Some New Yorkers during this time mistook him for an Australian,[38] and a number of his colleagues, for a brief period, took to calling him 'Boomerang', 'Digger' or 'Kangaroo' Leach (years later, in *Mr Lucky*, he referred back to this strange misconception, having his character explain his use of cockney rhyming slang by saying, 'Oh, it's a language I picked up in Australia'). Although his accent, once he had settled in Hollywood, grew gradually into its now-familiar transatlantic timbre, it continued to strike some American admirers as beguilingly exotic. The critic Richard Corliss, for example, writing on the occasion of Cary Grant's death, recalled the 'cutting tenor voice that refused to shake its Liverpool origins'[39] (which is rather like suggesting that James Stewart never quite managed to lose his Texan twang). Grant himself remained appealingly unpretentious and self-effacing when referring to his accent: when Jack Warner offered him Rex Harrison's role in the movie version of *My Fair Lady*, he exclaimed, 'I cannot play a dialectician – a perfect English teacher. It wouldn't be believable . . . I sound the way 'Liza does at the *beginning* of the film.'[40]

If the accent was, and would continue to be, unique, it was distinctive in the 'right' kind of way as far as Hollywood producers were concerned. There was a demand at the time for British (or at least British-sounding) actors, because the diction of so many American performers was, it was thought, ill-suited to the technical limitations of the early 'talkies'. Although Archie Leach had arrived in Hollywood with his accent a volatile mixture of West Country, South London and New York, Cary Grant was able to attract attention by the way he sounded as well as by the way he looked. That accent, as a critic, Alexander Walker, has pointed out, gave the new personality an 'edge'; it impressed on the voice 'the sharpness that comedy needs if it's to be slightly menacing'.[41] It would, in time, become the kind of accent that could underline the humour in well-written dialogue and disguise the absence of it in the most mediocre of lines. Writers, as a consequence, were among Cary

Grant's most genuine admirers. Listen to the way, in *The Awful Truth* (1937), that Grant, serving a rival with a glass of egg-nog, manages to make the innocent question, 'A little *nutmeg?*' sound like a threat, or how, in *The Grass is Greener* (1960), he places such an artfully sardonic emphasis on the question, 'Do you like *Dundee* cake?', that it succeeds in mocking both the place-name and the antiquated mannerisms of his upper-class character. Cary Grant would become the kind of person who, as David Thomson put it, 'could handle quick, complex, witty dialogue in the way of someone who enjoyed language as much as Cole Porter or Dorothy Parker', with a memorably serviceable accent, caught between English and American, working-class and upper-class, that produced a tone that could be made to sound 'uncertain whether to stay cool or let nerviness show'.[42]

If Cary Grant was going to be someone who *sounded* unorthodox, he was also, in rather less obvious but equally significant ways, going to be someone who *looked* unorthodox. Whereas most other actors in Hollywood at that time were known either for their *physical* or *verbal* skills, Archie Leach, unusually, possessed both. Silent screen comedy had demanded performers who could be as funny as possible physically, noted the critic James Agee, 'without the help or hindrance of words'. The screen comedian, before sound took hold of Hollywood, 'combined several of the more difficult accomplishments of the acrobat, the dancer, the clown and the mime'.[43] The advent of the 'talkies' marked a change in direction. Archie Leach, with his vocal mannerisms and his acrobatic training, had the rare opportunity to make Cary Grant an appealing hybrid: a talented physical performer with a rare gift for speaking dialogue, someone who could, whilst remaining in character, utter a string of sophisticated witticisms before slipping suddenly on a solitary stuffed olive and landing ignominiously on his backside. One movie historian commented on what it was like to grow up in the 1920s with but one wish: to be 'as lithe as Fairbanks and as suavely persuasive as Ronald Colman'.[44] Cary Grant had the rare chance to realise such a wish.

Archie Leach did not take long to see that the opportunity existed, and Cary Grant exploited it. He brought athleticism to elegance, physical humour to the drawing-room. It was the kind of unexpected versatility which undermined the rigid screen stereotypes, and it would help Cary Grant to become 'an idol for all social classes'.[45] As

Kael explains, other leading men, such as Melvyn Douglas, Henry Fonda and Robert Young, could produce proficient performances in screwball comedies and farcical situations, 'but the roles didn't release anything in their own natures – didn't liberate and complete them, the way farce completed Grant'.[46] It was as though the grace of Fred Astaire had combined with the earthiness of Gene Kelly. David Thomson observed: 'Only Fred Astaire ever moved as well as Cary Grant, but Grant moved with more dramatic eloquence while Astaire cherished the purity of movement. Grant could look as elegant as Astaire, but he could manage to look clumsy without actually sacrificing balance or style.'[47]

Cary Grant's potential could not be realised, however, until Archie Leach found the confidence to start acting like Cary Grant, and to start he needed first to develop a reasonably sharp sense of who Cary Grant should act like. Cary Grant, Archie Leach decided, should act like those stars who, up until then, had most impressed him. By his own admission, Cary Grant was in part, at the beginning, patterned on a combination of elegant contemporary Englishmen:

> In the late 1920s I'd wavered between imitating two older English actors, of the natural, relaxed school, Sir Gerald DuMaurier and A. E. Matthews, and was seriously considering being Jack Buchanan and Ronald Squire as well; but Noël Coward's performance in *Private Lives* narrowed the field, and many a musical-comedy road company was afflicted with my breezy new gestures and puzzling accent.[48]

Coward's unapologetically reinvented self – and accent – was of particular relevance. Alexander Walker comments how Coward's example – above all others – probably encouraged Archie Leach 'to abandon the stigmata of English class'.[49] Archie Leach had admired another British playwright, Freddie Lonsdale, because he 'always had an engaging answer for everything',[50] but Coward's supremely confident manner and sparkling wit, as well as his success on both sides of the Atlantic (*The Vortex* had broken box-office records on Broadway), were particularly influential. Leach's imitation, fixed as it was on the surface aspects of self, was graceless at first, but he learned from its limitations. 'I cultivated raising one eyebrow, and tried to imitate those who put their hands in their pockets with a certain amount of ease and nonchalance. But at times, when I put my hand in my trouser pocket with what I imagined was great elegance, I couldn't get the blinking thing out again because it dripped from nervous perspiration!'[51]

In addition to the English role-models, Archie Leach also looked to those examples he had noted of American charm and elegance. Fairbanks was, of course, an important influence, but so too were Fred Astaire and the man described by Philip Larkin as 'all that ever went with evening dress',[52] Cole Porter (whom Cary Grant later portrayed – much to his discomfort and Porter's delight – in the 1946 musical *Night and Day*). Another significant figure for Archie Leach was the actor Warner Baxter, described by one journalist at the time as 'a Valentino without a horse',[53] the 'beau ideal' who had been the first screen incarnation of Fitzgerald's *The Great Gatsby* (1926) as well as the leading man in the first version of *The Awful Truth* (1925) – the re-make of which confirmed Cary Grant as a star.

A Hollywood star persona was cultivated, typically, through a combination of performance – carefully-chosen screen roles – and publicity – studio press releases and magazine stories.[54] Cary Grant emerged at a time when audiences had started reading rather more than before about the performers they saw on the screen; the fan magazine detailed every aspect of the stars' lives, real and imaginary, and they sold by the million:

> The success of the fan magazine phenomenon of the 1930s was a co-operative venture between the myth makers and an army of readers willing to be mythified. The magazines rewarded their true believers with a Parnassus of celluloid deities who climbed out of an instant seashell like Botticelli's Aphrodite.[55]

Motion picture magazines soon began referring to Paramount's 'suave, distinguished' Cary Grant, a new star-in-the-making for whom, it was said, 'the word "polished" fits . . . as closely as one of his own well-fitting gloves'.[56] He was, readers were told, a 'handsome' and 'virile' young man who 'blushed "fiery red"' when embarrassed', and, it was added, he had the 'same dreamy, flashy eyes as Valentino'.[57] While his studio worked hard to find the right kind of publicity to promote its own version of 'Cary Grant', he was advised, in the short term, to say little of any consequence himself. However, the studio soon realised that Grant was actually being rather *too* reticent for his own good. A Paramount publicist at the time came to regard the task of securing coverage for the relatively unknown Cary Grant as probably the most difficult and frustrating experience of her whole career as a press agent.[58] Having grown up with very few close personal ties, he had developed the habit of keeping his thoughts and beliefs to himself, and, having recently transformed his public self, he was over-cautious when subjected to journalistic requests for all the 'facts' about Cary Grant rather than Archie Leach. As one reporter noted after a very early encounter with him, 'Anything he says about himself is so offhand and perfunctory that from his own testimony you get only the sketchiest impression of him.'[59] A writer on *Motion Picture* magazine was similarly frustrated: 'Seldom have I seen a man so little inclined to pour out his soul, and you have to scratch around and dig in order to discover even the bare facts of his life from him.'[60]

Paramount could package Cary Grant but it could not control entirely how he impressed himself on a movie audience. If Cary Grant was in danger of resembling a *tabula rasa* in the journalistic profile, on the movie screen he would soon seem, as Katharine Hepburn put it, 'a personality functioning'.[61] On the screen Cary Grant could *be* himself rather than explain himself (and that alone, in a sense, provided one with an adequate explanation). The actor Louis Jourdan has spoken of the impact that Cary Grant's early movie performances had on him: 'I was in awe of this persona, the look, the walk . . . The Cary Grant I fell in love with on the screen hadn't yet discovered he was Cary Grant.'[62] This new, unfamiliar, intriguing character called 'Cary Grant' was, as Jourdan appreciated, someone who did not fit neatly into the stereotypical roles but who was, on the contrary, a character in conflict with himself:

> Behind the construction of his character is his working-class background. That's what makes him interesting. That's what makes him liked by the public. He's close to them. He's not an aristocrat. He's not a bourgeois. He's a man of his people. He is a man of the street pretending to be Cary Grant![63]

It was one of the most admirable achievements of Cary Grant: that he never had, or wished, to renounce his past in order to embrace his future. Unlike those stars who seemed ashamed of, or embarrassed by, their humble origins, Cary Grant seemed content to stand upon his singularity; it would, for example, have taken a reckless person to risk calling Rex Harrison 'Reg' to his face, but Cary Grant delighted in slipping references to his former name into his movie dialogue – such as the ad-libbed line in *His Girl Friday* (1940): 'Listen, the last man who said that to me was Archie Leach just a week before he cut his throat.'[64] It was a knowing wink to the audience, *his* audience, a secret shared with strangers; it was the kind of gesture that would have endeared someone like Cary Grant to someone like Archie Leach.

Archie Leach did not cease to exist when Cary Grant was created. 'Cary Grant' was just a name, a cluster of idealised qualities. Cary Grant became something other than the sum of his influences, and he preserved more than it might have appeared from his own personal history in that charismatic conformation. Cary Grant was not conceived of as the contradiction of Archie Leach, but rather as the constitution of his desires. If Cary Grant succeeded, Archie Leach, more than anyone else, more than any other influence or ingredient, would be responsible. Cary Grant would always appreciate that fact. Fifty years after he changed his name, when he was the subject of a special tribute,[65] he requested that the cover of the programme for the occasion should feature a photograph of himself at the age of five – signed by 'Archie Leach'.

CHAPTER VI

Hollywood

Since I was tall, had black hair and white teeth, which I polished daily, I had all the semblance of what in those days was considered a leading man. I played in the kind of film where one was always polite and perfectly attired.
CARY GRANT

You must not forget who you are . . .
FEDORA

It was an anxious Cary Grant who reported to work for the first time at Paramount. Archie Leach had a new name, but he had yet to make a new reputation. Here he was at the studio of Marlene Dietrich, Gary Cooper, Maurice Chevalier, Fredric March, the Marx Brothers, W. C. Fields, Claudette Colbert, Tallulah Bankhead, Miriam Hopkins, Sylvia Sidney, Carole Lombard and Harold Lloyd – big stars, experienced performers. The only person with whom Archie Leach was acquainted was Jeanette MacDonald, but her option had not been renewed and she was leaving the studio. Cary Grant was on his own.

If Cary Grant was intimidated by his new surroundings, he was not disheartened. Jean Dalrymple, who had given Archie Leach his first paid speaking role in vaudeville, recalled:

> I had lunch with him at the Algonquin just before he went to California. He was so excited. He felt it was his great opportunity. I remember telling him not to get stuck in California but to come back to the theater from time to time.
>
> I didn't know he was going to be a sensational hit. He didn't always have that marvelous, debonair personality. He was often

very quiet and reserved. But when he got in front of a camera, his eyes sparkled and he was full of life. The camera loved him.[1]

Cary Grant's Hollywood was the Hollywood of the thirties. The effects of the Wall Street Crash were still being felt, and yet memories of the event, which had hit movie-makers in the West as well as more conventional businessmen in the East, were already – for some – receding. Audiences were still visiting America's vast rococo and Moorish picture palaces, those strangely aristocratic arenas of the new democratic art where visitors were greeted with an anxious show of opulence – fountains and waterfalls, painted peacocks and doves, huge mirrors and grand arcades, thick carpeting and air-conditioning, all designed to project, for a few hours, an illusion of prosperity. If it seemed to the weary, depression-ridden citizen that the American dream could not be lived, then Hollywood studios worked hard to remind people that it could still be imagined. 'There's a Paramount Picture probably around the corner', the studio told *Saturday Evening Post* readers. 'See it and you'll be out of yourself, living someone else's life . . . You'll find a new viewpoint. And tomorrow you'll work . . . not merely worry.'[2] It was a relatively successful strategy. In the midst of the Great Depression, audiences were still exhibiting what in the circumstances appeared a remarkable appetite for the products of Hollywood. In the first half of the decade, however, Paramount, ruled by Adolph Zukor, lacked the rock-like business stability of, for example, Metro-Goldwyn-Mayer, and the profit or loss incurred by one movie tended to affect unduly the studio's financial climate.[3] In the year that Cary Grant joined the studio, Paramount had made a sixteen-million-dollar loss, with possible bankruptcy ensuing.

Paramount – not surprisingly – had no intention of starting Cary Grant in important leading roles, but he would have more than enough opportunities to attract the attention of movie audiences. The company (after a policy of wild and rashly over-optimistic expansion during the second half of the 1920s) owned the largest circuit of theatres in the world, which it kept supplied by producing around sixty feature films per year. Operating on increasingly strict factory lines, it completed and shipped at least one new movie every week, so there was always a place for a new contractee somewhere along the assembly line. As a newcomer, Cary Grant was expected to work extremely hard for his $450 a week. He was there, without doubt, to do what he was told. It was a six-day schedule, Monday to Saturday, with no extra pay for overtime (which was common). The bare statistics of his first year with the studio reflect the production-line smoothness of the times: he made seven movies in 1932, working a full fifty-two weeks.

During Grant's first few hectic weeks at the studio he found a supporter in Jack Haley, the comedian, who later achieved his greatest Hollywood success in the role of the Tin Man in *The Wizard of Oz* (1939). As his son, Jack Haley, Jnr., remembers, Grant was grateful to know someone else who had made the transition from vaudeville to movies:

> When Cary was first at Paramount, he made a bee-line for my father, who had already done six or seven pictures there . . . Cary wanted to know what making movies was all about. My father told him, 'The first thing you learn is not to use your stage makeup. So find a good makeup person. And don't talk to the leading actress. She'll steer you wrong. She's your competition. Talk to the character people. They'll teach you the ins and outs.'
>
> Cary loved Charlie Ruggles, Arthur Treacher, and all those character people who came from Broadway or vaudeville. He felt secure with them. Years later Cary told me, 'Your father was the only one who gave me advice for my first picture'.[4]

Grant first appeared, billed fifth, in Frank Tuttle's farce *This is the Night*. Playing the supporting role of an Olympic javelin thrower whose wife is having an affair with a millionaire playboy, Grant was described in the advertisements for the movie as 'the new he-man sensation of Cinemerica!'[5] Tuttle left Grant largely to his own devices, which were still those of a stage-trained actor, and, as a consequence, his performance showed no appreciation of the importance of under-playing. At eighth in the cast list, he was less noticeable as a rich roué in Alexander Hall's *Sinners in the Sun*, his first of two dis-appointing movies with Carole Lombard, although he did have his first chance to show audiences how good he looked in evening clothes. Equally facetious, and even more devoid of opportunities for Grant to impress, was Dorothy Arzner's *Merrily we go to Hell*, in which his contribution, billed ninth, was always going to be negligible. A slightly more promising role was then given to him by Marion Gering in *The Devil and the Deep*, the stars of which were Tallulah Bankhead, Charles Laughton and Gary Cooper.[6]

Of the three other movies in which Grant appeared in 1932 – *Blonde Venus*, *Hot Saturday* and *Madame Butterfly* – by far the most significant was Josef von Sternberg's *Blonde Venus* starring Marlene Dietrich. It was the first good, substantial, role he had been given, one that would provide him with a serious opportunity to show that he could convince audiences as a romantic consort. He was playing opposite the nearest thing that Paramount had at that time to a screen 'goddess', and she was treated accordingly; her custom-built four-room dressing-suite had cost the studio $300,000 (about sixty times the cost of an average US family dwelling in 1932), she had the right to veto her publicity and, with von Sternberg as her director and mentor, an unusually influential say in the selection, and production, of her starring vehicles.

It was while making this, his fifth, movie, and the first that Gary Cooper had rejected, that Grant's image underwent a minor but significant cosmetic transformation. The director, von Sternberg, ever the meticulous *auteur*, changed Grant's hair parting from the left to the right. According to Alexander Walker, the main reason why von Sternberg decided to change the parting was to annoy and unsettle Grant.[7] 'Joe loved to throw you,' Grant told Walker. 'Could you do anything worse to an actor than alter his hair parting just a minute before he starts shooting a scene? I kept it that way ever since, as you may have noticed. To annoy *him*.'[8] It also, as he (and von Sternberg) probably knew, improved his appearance; his 'best side', for the camera, was his right (he disliked the mole on his left side), and the new ramrod-straight parting (which became the single most simple and straightforward thing about him) complemented his other features.

The inexperienced and under-confident Grant did not enjoy working for von Sternberg. There were periods when he was left to look on bemused as the director and the star argued with each other in German, and there were other times when the director seemed intent on turning his fury onto him: 'I could never get a scene under way before Joe would bawl out "Cut" – at me, personally, across the set. This went on and on and on. I felt like someone doing drill who kept dropping his rifle, but wasn't going to be allowed to drop out of ranks.'[9] Grant was miscast as Nick Townsend, a politician ('he runs this end of town') who makes Dietrich his mistress, enabling her to pay for her ailing husband, played by Herbert Marshall, to travel to Germany in search of a cure for his illness. Marshall – who as Richard Schickel has rather cruelly remarked, 'always played civility as if it were a form of victimisation'[10] – should have provided Grant with a useful contrast for his own characterisation; von Sternberg, however, allowed Grant to throw away even his passionate speeches, and for too much of the movie he appears so self-effacing as to be almost invisible. He was, however, beautifully lit and photographed – as were all the leading actors – and he looked good in his fine clothes and glamorous environment. It was, in short, a helpful movie for an ambitious young actor, even if von Sternberg left him feeling, if anything, even less confident than before.

Amidst the unfamiliarity of his new surroundings, Cary Grant, like countless other new arrivals with British backgrounds, sought and found, at least for a short while, a relatively reassuring sense of security and stability in that tightly-knit community of émigré English actors and writers sometimes referred to as the 'Hollywood Raj' or the 'British movie colony'.[11] A few English performers, such as Charlie Chaplin and Stan Laurel, had arrived as early as 1910 as refugees from Victorian music-hall, but the coming of sound had been the signal for a further wave of stage-trained English actors. Though the British mixed fairly freely with the rest of Hollywood society, they seemed, in spite of it, to retain a certain separateness. In the mid-thirties, the *Christian Science Monitor*, reporting on foreigners in Hollywood, was particularly struck by the obduracy of the British in their preservation of their culture:

> Several English cake shops now exist, catering almost exclusively to the English, who maintain a stricter aloofness than do most other resident aliens; steak and kidney pies have miraculously made their appearance all over town and are sometimes even eaten by the natives; Devonshire cream is also manufactured, but in very small quantities . . . Once a year, on New Year's Eve, the principal members of the British colony gather in a Hollywood café to hear the bells of Big Ben ring out over the radio . . . Billiards are now played regularly at the homes of

most British stars, and officers of the British warships visiting in California harbors entertain and are entertained by a group founded by Victor McLagen and known as the British United Services Club, comprised in large part of actors who have served in one of the branches of the British military; while on many a film set old members of the same London club [usually the Garrick], meet and fraternise.[12]

Many of these English actors had found work in Hollywood *because* of their 'exotic' qualities – their looks, their mannerisms and their accents. Their relative insularity, therefore, was not merely the result of homesickness or cultural taste but also, in many cases, professional necessity; to mix too freely and too frequently with one's American colleagues was to risk becoming fully assimilated by, and acculturated in, American society. The commercial appeal of many English actors was their Englishness; English actors who looked and sounded American, unless they were remarkably talented, faced much fiercer competition for roles. Many of the most successful English actors of the time were well aware of the danger. Ronald Colman, Artur Rubinstein recalled, possessed a 'beautiful' English accent which actually 'became better and more marked with time instead of becoming American-ised',[13] while C. Aubrey Smith, specialising in playing a limited range of crusty English colonel types, developed and preserved a lucrative cluster of *echt*-English mannerisms for the enchantment of American audiences. There were some for whom the need, or desire, to maintain their cultural distinctiveness caused them, gradually but usually inexorably, to settle into a comfortable form of self-parody. Aubrey Smith – who once summed up his experience of working with Garbo in *Queen Christina* in the remark, 'She's a ripping gel',[14] and who lived in a house on Mulholland Drive that boasted a weather vane made out of three cricket stumps, a bat and a ball – was a comically anachronistic figure even for most of his compatriots, while Gladys Cooper, taking tea one warm afternoon at the Pacific Palisades home of Robert Coote, reacted with typical mock-horror to the arrival of George Cukor by exclaiming disapprovingly: 'Darling . . . there seems to be an *American* on your lawn.'[15]

Although as time went on Cary Grant continued to enjoy the company of many of the Hollywood British, he was not eager to become *too* closely identified with them. The least appealing aspect of the British colony was that it was a kind of microcosm of British society, with the same hierarchical structure and snobbery. There were other working-class Englishmen in Hollywood, but few of them seem to have embraced – or been embraced by – the colony. Chaplin was sufficiently powerful and secure to have no need of such a self-consciously exclusive community, whereas others from similar backgrounds, such as Stan Laurel, Alfred Hitchcock and Charles Laughton, found the prospect of enduring the old class tensions for a second time, this time on foreign soil, too unpleasant to contemplate for very long.[16]

At a time when Archie Leach was just beginning to get used to being Cary Grant, the stalwart members of the British colony – after the initial pleasantries were over with – were the most likely people to remind Cary Grant that he was 'really' just Archie Leach. Established members of the colony did nothing to disguise their privileged backgrounds: Aubrey Smith (Charterhouse and Cambridge), Basil Rathbone (Repton), Boris Karloff (Uppingham), John Loder (Eton) and Clive Brook (Dulwich) were among those who were known to attend the annual public-school dinner organised by the Hollywood British. David Niven (Stowe and Sandhurst), who arrived in 1934, found it relatively easy to ingratiate himself with this exclusive group,[17] whereas Grant, who struck some of the expatriates as 'socially insecure',[18] simply had no choice but to 'go native'.

He became friends with another Paramount contract player, Randolph Scott, when the two co-starred in *Hot Saturday*, and they decided to pool their resources and share a house. Handsome, amiable and increasingly successful, the two men began to attract precious publicity as two of Hollywood's most eligible young bachelors.[19] Scott introduced Grant to Howard Hughes, who, in turn, provided Grant with an entrée into Hollywood's most glamorous social circles, introducing him to a period of grand and incessant parties, sophisticated and affluent new friends, and all the paraphernalia of California high society. In a sense, Grant found that he could have the best of both worlds: the established British stars were, at least early on, useful contacts, while the rest of the Hollywood community appreciated his unusual sociability. Cary Grant became known as an Englishman who genuinely enjoyed – and felt comfortable in – the company of Americans, and that, in the early thirties, was a rarity which he exploited to the full.

On the movie screen, Cary Grant was still struggling to improve as an actor. Josef von Sternberg had made an ill-conceived attempt to shout him into producing a more assured performance, but the stiffness remained: 'Joe bemoaned, berated and beseeched me to relax, but it was years before I could move with ease before a camera. Years before I could stop my right eyebrow from lifting, a sure sign of inner defenses and tensions.'[20] The majority of the roles he was being given by Paramount simply capitalised on his good looks, putting him into smart uniforms or elegant evening clothes at every opportunity. His success, such as it was, struck him as shallow. Jack Haley Jnr. sympathised: 'It must have been miserable for Cary. As a foreigner . . . he was at the bottom of the barrel in terms of parts. The first choice went to Gary Cooper. The second went to George Raft. Even Fred MacMurray was getting better parts than Cary.'[21] A publicist put it more bluntly: 'Gary Cooper or Freddie March, they were *actors*. Cary Grant? He was kind of a *stick* . . . He was there to look tall, dark and handsome.'[22] When he was forced to play Lieutenant Pinkerton in the movie version of Puccini's *Madame Butterfly*, and sing 'My Flower of Japan' to Sylvia Sidney's Cio-Cio-San, it seemed that his career, if it was progressing at all, was doing so painfully slowly.

Cary Grant's fortunes changed suddenly and unexpectedly. Before he had finished shooting *Madame Butterfly*, he found himself cast in *She Done Him Wrong*, opposite Mae West. In his autobiography, *Fun in a Chinese Laundry*, von Sternberg boasted that he had 'rescued' Grant from a possible career of being 'one of Mae West's foils' in order to launch him 'on his stellar career'.[23] The memories of Hollywood celebrities are notoriously unreliable: as the call to work with West came some months *after* Grant had finished *Blonde Venus*, von Sternberg's role in the advancement of Grant's 'stellar career' was somewhat overstated. West claimed in *her* (equally unreliable) autobiography, *Goodness Had Nothing To Do With It*, that she noticed 'a sensational looking young man' – Grant – on the Paramount lot, and cast him on the spot: 'If this one can talk,' she claims she said at the time, 'I'll take him.'[24] According to West, she saw immediately that Grant 'had poise, a great walk, everything women would like'.[25] In truth, Grant was probably first spotted by West on the screen in one of his earlier movie appearances ('I liked his voice first, but I saw right away that the rest of him measured up'[26]). As far as his casting for *She Done Him Wrong* was concerned, it seems likely that B. P. Schulberg had favoured pairing his new leading man with the aggressive West,[27] and it is also known that Lowell Sherman, the director West had chosen for the movie, had liked Grant's performance in *Blonde Venus*.[28]

The movie was an adaptation of West's stage success of 1928, *Diamond Lil*. She played Lady Lou, 'one of the finest women who ever walked the streets', who runs a Bowery saloon; Grant played Captain Cummings, from the nearby church mission, who is really 'the Hawk', a government agent. It was the first opportunity since Grant had been in Hollywood for him to make use of his vaudeville training as a straight man. 'Haven't you ever met a man who can make you happy?' he asks her. 'Sure,' she replies, 'lots of times.' West had usually played opposite men who appeared as tough and as coarse as her own character, and Grant's more vulnerable performance provided an interesting contrast to her brash sexuality. 'Why don't you come up sometime, see me?' she says to him, staring into his eyes. 'Come up. I'll tell your fortune.'

Shooting began on 21 November 1932, and was completed in a mere eighteen days. For an outlay of $200,000, it earned $2 million within three months in the US alone. This movie, in effect, saved Paramount from bankruptcy. Cary Grant emerged from the triumph as someone who had the potential to be much more than a mere straight man to Mae West. As Pauline Kael observes, West brought out Grant's passivity, giving him an aloof charm, 'a quality of refinement in him which made her physical aggression seem a playful gambit'.[29] Kael also noted that the success of the performance was achieved in spite of Grant's relative lack of confidence in his own abilities as a movie actor: he did not 'yet know how the camera should see him', and he appeared, when he had little to do in a scene, 'vaguely ill at ease', standing 'lunged forward as if hoping to catch a ball'[30] (this might be a little unfair: Grant's character was meant to seem uneasy in his duplicity, and his physical awkwardness provided West with the opportunity for yet more *double entendres*: 'That's right. Loosen up. Unbend. You'll feel better'). He was, none the less, the 'classiest' leading man whom West had appeared with, and the critics appreciated that fact. 'Hi, tall, dark and handsome,' she said to him; it was a nice welcome for Cary Grant. His good looks, under-playing and good comic timing combined to suggest a very promising future. After roles in three more formulaic movies – *The Woman Accused*, *The Eagle and the Hawk* and *Gambling Ship* (all 1933) – Paramount seized on the opportunity to cast Grant alongside West for their second movie together: *I'm No Angel*. The weak story-line never threatened to distract one's attention from the comic dialogue:

Grant: Do you mind if I get personal?

West: I don't mind if you get familiar.

Although it was a poor movie in comparison with *She Done Him Wrong*, it was another great success at the box-office. Paramount raised his salary to $750 per week. Fan mail began to arrive in increasing amounts, and the fan magazines started to compete for his interviews.[31]

He was grateful for the exposure afforded him by his association with West – who was among the top ten box-office attractions in the country at that time – but he became increasingly resentful of the shameless way in which she sought to take all of the credit for his stardom: 'She always got a great deal of publicity for herself . . . I could never understand the woman. I thought she was brilliant with that one character she portrayed, but she was an absolute fake as a person. You would shudder from it.'[32] At the time, however, Grant – who *thought* more than most about the technique behind a performance – was well aware of what an excellent teacher in the art of screen comedy West was: 'She knows so much . . . Her instinct is so true, her timing so perfect, her grasp of the situation so right. It's the tempo of the acting that counts rather than the sincerity of the characterisation. Her personality is so dominant that everyone with her becomes just a feeder.'[33] One of the most impressive qualities of the young Cary Grant was this capacity for quiet observation; he never missed an opportunity to learn from performers more experienced, and more skilled, than himself, and he learned much of immense value from his working experience with Mae West.

Grant was now in the process of becoming something of a Hollywood celebrity. He inherited the dressing-room formerly occupied by George Bancroft, a star of silent movies who had recently been demoted to the ranks of supporting players. Paramount's most illustrious top dozen stars were quartered side by side in implied order of importance. Mae West had taken possession of dressing-room number 1, followed by the other leading women: Claudette Colbert, Marlene Dietrich, Sylvia Sidney, Miriam Hopkins and Carole Lombard. Then came the leading male stars: Gary Cooper, Fredric March, Bing Crosby, George Raft, Cary Grant and Charles Laughton. Grant's personal life was also beginning to change: he became engaged in 1933 to Virginia Cherrill, who had played the blind girl in Chaplin's *City Lights*, and in November he took her back to England,[34] where they were married on 9 February the following year. He was thirty years old. The marriage, however, was soon in trouble; in the spring of 1935 they separated, and Grant began a series of brief relationships with other women.[35] The couple were granted a divorce that March.

Professionally, the years 1934 and 1935 did not see Grant offered many movie roles by Paramount which provided him with much opportunity to exploit his new-found popularity. *Thirty Day Princess*, *Born to Be Bad*, *Kiss and Make Up*, *Ladies Should Listen* (all 1934) were largely forgettable affairs. After making *Wings in the Dark* (1935), Grant was given six months off; Paramount had a backlog of Grant movies which had yet to be released.[36] It seemed as though the studio was undecided as to how best it should utilise his talents, and his dissatisfaction with Paramount deepened: 'They had a lot of leading men at Paramount with dark hair and a set of teeth like mine, and they couldn't be buying stories for all of us.'[37] In November 1935 he returned to England to make *The Amazing Quest of Ernest Bliss*[38] for the independent company, Garrett Klement Pictures; if he had hoped to find temporary relief away from Hollywoood, he was disappointed – during the filming, his father died.

When Grant returned to Hollywood early in 1936 he was anxious to sort out his future. He feared that he was in danger of being eclipsed by some of his contemporaries, such as James Cagney (who had just reached number ten in the list of top box-office draws) and Errol Flynn (who had starred recently in the very successful *Captain Blood*). It had become obvious to insiders that Grant was unhappy at Paramount. When *Sylvia Scarlett*, which he had made on loan at RKO the previous year, was released, the generally positive reviews of his contribution encouraged him to persevere in his struggle for more control over his career.

Grant later acknowledged *Sylvia Scarlett* as 'my breakthrough',[39] but it was, in many ways, a spectacular failure. Based on Compton Mackenzie's picaresque novel, it starred Katharine Hepburn and was directed by George Cukor. Grant played Jimmy Monkley ('gentleman adventurer'), a cockney con-man who teams up with Sylvia Scarlett (Hepburn) and her father (Edmund Gwenn) in various embezzlement schemes. The most unusual aspect of the movie was that the plot called for Hepburn to masquerade as a boy through most of the story.[40] Coded motifs and hidden implications abound in the script: Monkley wants to cuddle up to Sylvester 'like a hot-water bottle'; a housemaid wants to daub a moustache on Sylvester and kiss 'him'; and a bohemian artist is given a 'queer feeling' by his fascination with the boy. For a woman to appear on the screen in drag, in spite of the moralistic Production Code of the time, was a daring departure for a Hollywood movie, but the conceit was only allowed after Cukor had been ordered to add what he later described as 'a silly, frivolous prologue, to explain *why* this girl was dressed like a boy, and being so good at it. We weren't allowed to give the impression that she liked it, or that she'd done it before, or that it came naturally.'[41]

The movie proved to be both a personal watershed and a professional catastrophe for several of the people who made it. Its dismal reception set in motion Katharine Hepburn's boycotting by the nation's movie exhibitors as 'box-office poison'. Hepburn's accent flits from French to cod-cockney to Bryn Mawr, and, in her stylised boy's clothes and principal-boy's gestures, she appears − far from seeming unnervingly androgynous − merely epicene (an American cousin, perhaps, of the English camp comic actor Kenneth Williams). The dialogue − 'why, then I *won't* be a girl! I *won't* be weak and I *won't* be silly! I'll be a boy and be rough and hard' − did nothing to discourage her irritatingly mannered performance. At one point during the shooting of the movie, Hepburn confided in her diary: 'This picture makes no sense at all.'[42] It was a perceptive remark. RKO executives were furious long before *Sylvia Scarlett* was confirmed as the studio's worst box-office failure of the year. The movie's shell-shocked producer, Pandro Berman, told Hepburn and Cukor (but not Grant) that he never wanted to work with either of them ever again.[43]

What was extraordinary was how Grant managed to emerge from

this débâcle not merely unscathed but with an enhanced reputation. 'That was really the beginning for Cary,' Katharine Hepburn remembered. 'He was the only reason to see *Sylvia Scarlett*. It was a terrible picture, but he was wonderful in it.'[44] One reason why Grant *was* so effective in it was the fact that he was playing an Englishman, and several scenes were set in a travelling fair (performing songs like 'The Winkle on the Boarding 'ouse Floor'). There is, indeed, more than a trace of Archie Leach in Grant's performance. Jimmy Monkley was formed by the same society that had shaped Grant: first glimpsed in a black hat and coat on a boat crossing the English Channel, he later refers to himself sarcastically as 'a little friend of all the world, nobody's enemy but me own', and more soberly as 'a rolling stone' who is neither a 'sparrow' nor an ''awk'. 'Take it from me,' he tells Scarlett, 'it don't do to step out of your class.' In contrast to Archie Leach, however, Jimmy Monkley sees no way of escaping, merely surviving. 'You have the mind of a pig,' Scarlett tells him. 'It's a pig's world,' he replies. As Richard Schickel has suggested, the role of Jimmy Monkley offered Grant the opportunity 'to get in touch with what was usable in his past, lay it out in public, and discover that his bright new, light new world would not collapse inward upon him, that, indeed, it was capable of vast expansion'.[45] George Cukor agreed: until then, he said, Grant had been 'a successful young leading man who was nice-looking but had no particular identity'.[46] This movie, he added, changed that: '*Sylvia Scarlett* was the first time Cary felt the ground under his feet as an actor. He suddenly seemed liberated. It was very exhilarating to see.'[47] The critics were also impressed: writing in *Variety*, one declared that Grant 'steals the picture', while the *Motion Picture Herald* reviewer praised Grant's performance as 'the most convincing' and in stark contrast to the 'overstrained' attempts at characterisation by his more experienced co-stars.[48]

Sylvia Scarlett, or rather Grant's role within it, was his ticket to leave Paramount. His contract was about to run out, and the success of his portrayal of Jimmy Monkley, combined with the increasingly cavalier treatment he felt he was receiving from Paramount (vetoing his request to go on loan to MGM for *Mutiny on the Bounty*, putting him in a mystery called *Big Brown Eyes*, loaning him out again to MGM for a second lead in *Suzy* and then putting him in the insipid screwball comedy *Wedding Present*), made up his mind for him. He would refuse to renew his contract. Not only would he break away from Paramount, he would, he resolved, from that point on, after twenty-one movies, refuse to commit himself exclusively to any one studio.

It is difficult today to appreciate just how astonishing and courageous (or reckless) Grant's decision seemed in the mid-thirties. No one of his stature had contemplated acting as a freelance performer since the days before the studio system took hold of Hollywood. He had, however, come a long way on his own, further than most, and, although his own vision of himself was still somewhat out of focus, it was considerably sharper than the vision of Cary Grant found among the producers at Paramount. It seems possible that even the executives at Paramount were beginning, grudgingly, to realise that this was the case. Adolph Zukor, who was anxious to keep him at the studio, offered Grant thirty-five hundred dollars per week to stay. Grant, however, was adamant that his future lay in independence and the freedom to choose not only his roles but also, eventually, his co-workers and his scripts. Jack Haley Jnr., has stressed the peculiarity of Grant's independent spirit:

He was constantly a maverick, rebelling against what everybody expected him to do. He had the confidence to say good-bye to Pender and look for work in the theater. Later he'd walk out on the Shuberts. Then he walked out on Paramount, which offered him a great deal of money to stay. And that was right toward the end of the Depression. It took *cojones* to do that.[49]

Many other promising young actors were stunned by such an urgent and uncompromising attitude. 'If I had stayed at Paramount,' he said, 'I would have continued to take pictures that Gary Cooper, William Powell, or Clive Brook turned down.'[50] The rivalry between Grant and Cooper, in particular, had been growing increasingly intense during the previous couple of years. Cooper had once dismissed the challenge of Grant by claiming that he was 'a crack comedian, no competition for me',[51] but things had since become rather more unnerving, and *Photoplay* magazine said of the two men: 'They know that they're pitted against each other, and when the final gong sounds, one of them will be on the floor.'[52]

In the autumn of 1936, Grant bought out what little remained of his contract and announced that he was open to offers from other studios. The first movie he accepted was Columbia's *When You're in Love*. While working on it, he was also offered a prominent role in *The Toast of New York* by RKO. He worked on the Columbia movie by day and the RKO project by night. Neither movie did particularly well at the box-office, but both studios were impressed with his performances and offered to sign him to contracts. His financial demands nearly deterred them: he asked for a flat fee of $75,000 per movie. Both studios felt the sum was exorbitant. The only way to break the stalemate was for Grant to prove to Columbia and RKO that he could find a similar offer elsewhere. Hal Roach approached him to co-star in the fantasy comedy *Topper*, offering to pay him $50,000 if the movie was successful. It was. For very little work (he was actually on the screen for far less of the movie than it seemed), Grant experienced his first undisputed commercial success as a star. He played an elegant ghost in a high society world of nightclubs, champagne, pink ladies and fast cars, a magical figure who exuded what would come to be thought of as the essence of Grant's image – playful and unflappable sophistication. After its release there was a further huge increase in his fan mail, over two hundred letters each week. It showed producers that he could carry a movie, and it also marked the beginning of his reputation as one of Hollywood's most gifted light actors. Through his agent, Frank Vincent, Grant worked out a unique deal whereby he would work for both Columbia *and* RKO, alternating between the two.[53]

Cary Grant won the freedom to shape the future course of his career. He now had the power to take control over the creating of his screen (and off-screen) persona. It was not, of course, complete control: he would still have to rely on screenwriters and cameramen and directors, as well as on the compatibility of his co-stars, but, none the less, it was a far greater liberty than other actors of the time had experienced before. Cary Grant was now free to really become Cary Grant.

STARDOM

Sullivan: Good morning, Burroughs. How do you like it?
Dressed in rags
Burroughs: I don't like it at all, sir. Fancy dress, I take it?
Sullivan: What's the matter with it?
Burroughs: I have never been sympathetic to the caricaturing of the poor and needy, sir.
Sullivan: Who's caricaturing? I'm going out on the road to find out what it's like to be poor and needy and then I'm going to make a picture about it.
Burroughs: If you'll permit me to say so, sir, the subject is not an interesting one. The poor know all about poverty, and only the morbid rich would find the topic glamorous.
SULLIVAN'S TRAVELS

I'll let someone else photograph the ugliness of the world. It's larceny to remind people of how lousy things are and call it entertainment.
CARY GRANT

CHAPTER VII

Never a Better Time

I have seen an individual, whose manners, though wholly within the
conventions of elegant society, were never learned from there, but were
original and commanding, and held out protection and prosperity; one who
did not need the aid of a court-suit, but carried the holiday in his eye; one
who exhilarated the fancy by flinging wide the doors of new modes of
existence; who shook off the captivity of etiquette, with happy, spirited
bearing, good-natured and free as Robin Hood; yet with the port of an
emperor, – if need be, calm, serious, and fit to stand the gaze of millions.
RALPH WALDO EMERSON

Happy thoughts!
CARY GRANT

It is a delightful moment: in a nightclub, on the dance floor, a large,
cumbrous man is engaged in a frenzied jitterbug with his slight,
refined, embarrassed-looking partner; a handsome young man in
evening dress has just bribed the orchestra leader to repeat the music,
thus sentencing the embarrassed-looking woman – who is actually
his ex-wife – to further public agitation opposite her dancing partner
– who is actually her over-eager new suitor; the handsome young
man in evening dress, having accomplished his scheming, pulls up
his chair to the edge of the dance floor, sits down, crosses his legs,
folds his arms, breathes a self-satisfied sigh, and smiles a broad, contented, joyous smile as he faces the dancers, and, implicitly, the
camera, and us, his audience. This man – elegant, blithe, mischievous,
delightful – carries the holiday in his eye;[1] he is a man, quite simply,
having the time of his life. This man is a star. This man is Cary
Grant.

The movie in which this scene takes place is *The Awful Truth*
(1937). It was the first of a remarkable run of five movies – the

others were *Bringing Up Baby* (1938), *Holiday* (1938), *Gunga Din* (1939) and *Only Angels Have Wings* (1939) – which not only justified Grant's gamble on a freelance career but also established him, beyond any doubt, as one of Hollywood's most distinctive and popular movie stars. Each of these movies would come to be thought of as a classic of its kind, each one was quite different from the others, and each one added something extra to Grant's range as an actor. Two years, five movies and, at the end of it, one hugely successful performer, secure in his on-screen identity and confident of his ability to attract and entertain his audience. There would never be a better time for Cary Grant; there would, of course, be more good movies, more memorable performances, more box-office records, more critical plaudits, but never again would all of the crucial components – the roles, the story, the dialogue, the directors, the cast, the mood – combine so felicitously and consistently to provide Cary Grant with quite so memorable, so rewarding, so rich a succession of starring vehicles. This, more so than any other, was Cary Grant's moment.

This extraordinary period in Grant's career began, oddly enough, darkly, with Grant coming close to dropping out of *The Awful Truth*, demoralised, convinced that he had made a disastrous error of judgement. The critic Richard Schickel has described this movie as 'a kind of tuning fork; by its reverberations one can test the comic pitch of almost any movie on a similar theme – and find them, to varying degrees, just off the note'[2], yet it was made in spite of the fact that all of the co-stars (Grant, Irene Dunne and Ralph Bellamy) spent the first few days of shooting in varying states of nervous tension. The director, Leo McCarey, had made his name at Hal Roach's studios, first as a gag writer and then as the director of movies by Charlie Chase, W. C. Fields, Mae West, the Marx Brothers and Laurel and Hardy. His methods, however, bemused and alarmed the cast of *The Awful Truth*. Ralph Bellamy remembers the unnerving sense of chaos early on in the production: 'McCarey came in every morning with a small piece of brown wrapping paper on which he'd written his ideas. He'd say, "Cary, you come in that door on the right, and Ralph, you come in over there on the left. I'll run the dog through, and Irene, you come through . . ."'[3] Hal Roach, who had worked with Grant on *Topper*, knew that he would be surprised and unsettled by McCarey's 'odd' methods: McCarey, said Roach, 'kept improving on things. He'd give Cary something in the morning and then tell him,

With first wife Virginia Cherrill in 1934. 'My possessiveness', Grant said, 'brought about the very condition it feared: the loss of her.'

With second wife Barbara Hutton in 1942. 'Our backgrounds – family, educational and cultural – were completely unalike.'

With third wife Betsy Drake in 1952. 'It was terribly frustrating to be married to him', she recalled, 'because he's a very self-sufficient man.'

With fourth wife Dyan Cannon in 1965. 'I loved the man', she said, 'but I couldn't live with him.'

With fifth wife Barbara Harris in 1980. 'My best piece of magic', he said, 'was marrying Barbara.'

Grant with his daughter, Jennifer: 'From the time she was born, she's been the joy of my life.'

North by Northwest (1959): Planes, trains and fine tailoring – the last romantic hero.

Suspicion (1941): Grant as the man who lied too much, blending light and dark inside a single look.

"I'm not going to do that." Cary decided that Leo didn't know what the hell he was doing and tried to get out of the picture.'[4]

'At the end of the first day,' Bellamy recalled, 'Irene was crying – she didn't know *what* kind of a part she was playing. Cary said, "Let me out of this and I'll do another picture for nothing".'[5] At the end of the first week of filming, Grant sent an eight-page memorandum entitled 'What's Wrong With This Picture' to the head of Columbia, Harry Cohn. He also offered to pay five thousand dollars in return for being released from his contract. Cohn ignored it.[6]

It was not long, however, before Grant started to change his mind. One of the things that helped reassure him was McCarey's eagerness to exploit certain aspects of his actors' own personalities in order to make the characters more believable: for example, when Bellamy told McCarey that he did not even know what his character should wear, McCarey told him, 'The jacket and trousers you have on are just what I want!'; when McCarey discovered that Bellamy could not 'get from one note to another', he tricked him into accompanying a strained-looking Irene Dunne in a rendition of 'Home on the Range' ('you blast it out with your Oklahoma accent').[7] Grant began to see that McCarey was well aware of his strengths and more than willing to help him put them to good use. Once he trusted McCarey, Grant felt liberated by the absence of a settled script and seized the opportunity to improvise.[8] 'Cary caught on quickly,' said Bellamy. 'It was right in his groove, his kind of comedy, of humor . . . He could laugh with you as you were watching him. He knew you were laughing and he was encouraging it.'[9]

Grant played Jerry Warriner, a man who deceives his wife by pretending to go on vacation to Florida whilst really staying in New York City playing cards with 'the boys'. When he returns, complete with false tan and a basket of oranges, he is surprised to find his wife Lucy (Irene Dunne) arriving with a handsome foreign voice coach, Armand (Alexander D'Arcy). Each comes to suspect the other of being unfaithful (he probably has been, she might well have been).[10] They argue, and they divorce, with Lucy (through trickery) gaining custody of their beloved dog, Mr Smith. Lucy takes up – rather hesitantly – with Daniel Leeson (Ralph Bellamy), a slow-witted but wealthy oil heir from Oklahoma who is staying just down the hall from her with his doughty mother. Mr Smith provides Jerry with the opportunity to come and go at Lucy's apartment, and these triangular encounters cause comic tensions. Lucy eventually realises that Jerry still loves her, and she loves him, and she therefore has to scheme to get him back – and shake off the increasingly irritating and lovesick Leeson.

'The trouble with most marriages', complains Jerry, 'is that people are always imagining things.' It turns out that it is not the fact that people use their imagination that is the trouble, but rather that some people do not use it enough, or in the right ways. When Jerry and Lucy – both arch fantasists, both excited more by the idea of infidelity than by the fact of it – separate, they find new partners whose lack of imagination serves only to remind them of what they miss most of their old married life. Jerry moves on from a dim exhibitionist to a dour débutante, looking increasingly unsure of himself as he is surrounded by the literal-minded. Lucy is courted by a parvenu of stunning obtuseness, and she, like her ex-partner, appears lost in this prosaic environment. The awful truth is that Jerry and Lucy need each other, love each other, even if they are too proud, and too devious, and too stubborn, to admit it. When they meet up again just before they think they are about to begin their lives again with their more reliable new partners, Lucy recites a poem written in an earlier time for her by Jerry: 'Lend an ear, I implore you;/This comes from my heart, I'll always adore you.' It was meant to make them look back in amusement, but it only reminds them of what they are on the verge of losing. They try to toast each other's new beginning with champagne, but the life has gone out of it, flat, like their future, unless they return to each other.

Grant's performance is beautifully judged. He moves from the smooth, suave, self-assured character of the early scenes to the almost timid, boyish character of the final scene without ever appearing unnatural or forced. Early on, for example, in the (partly impro-vised) restaurant scene, Grant (assisted by his two superb co-stars) is delightfully knowing as Jerry teases Lucy and mocks the naïve Daniel:

Jerry: So you're going to live in Oklahoma? Oh, *Lucy*, how I *envy* you. Ever since I was a small boy that name has been filled with magic for me. [*He closes his eyes ecstatically*] *Oklahoma*!

Daniel:	[*Proudly*] We're going to live right in Oklahoma City!
Jerry:	Not Oklahoma City itself? Lucy, you *lucky* girl! No more running around the nightspots, no more prowling around in New York shops. I shall think of you every time a new show opens and say to myself, 'She's well out of it!'
Daniel:	New York is alright for a visit, but –
Daniel & Jerry:	[*In unison*] I wouldn't want to live here.
Lucy:	[*Struggling to hide her discomfort*] I know I'll enjoy living in Oklahoma City.
Jerry:	[*Triumphantly*] But of course! And if it *should* get dull, you can always go over to *Tulsa* for the week-end!

Later on in the movie, Grant shows Jerry's insecurity as he barges into his ex-wife's recital and ends up falling off his chair with an undignified crash. In the final scene, when Lucy and Jerry are about to go to their separate (but adjoining) bedrooms as the last hour of their married life ebbs inexorably away, it is Jerry who now seems awkward and vulnerable as Lucy seizes the opportunity to make him even more confused:

Jerry: In half an hour we'll no longer be Mr and Mrs – Funny, isn't it?

Lucy: Yes, it's funny that everything's the way it is on account of the way you feel.

Jerry: Huh?

Lucy: Well, I mean, if you didn't feel the way you feel, things wouldn't be the way they are, would they?

Jerry: But things are the way you made them.

Lucy: Oh no. They're the way you *think* I made them. I didn't make them that way at all. Things are just the same as they always were, only you're just the same, too, so I guess things will never be the same again. Ah-h, good night.

Jerry, downcast, dressed in an absurdly large and loose nightshirt that makes him look like a lost little boy, reappears later on, unsure of what he might say to make Lucy take him back into her bed:

Lucy: You're all confused, aren't you?

Jerry: Uh-huh. Aren't you?

Lucy: No.

Jerry: Well . . . you *should* be, because you're wrong about things being different because they're not the same. Things *are* different, except in a different way. You're still the same, only I've been a fool. Well, I'm not now. So, as long as I'm different, don't you think things could be the same again? Only a little different?

Grant's improvisations contributed to the success of the scenes, as well as demonstrating his own talent for comic invention. An example is an early scene in which Jerry returns to the apartment after their separation. Irene Dunne was told to open the door, discover Grant standing there and say with surprise, 'Well, if it isn't my ex.' Grant was not told to reply, but he ad-libbed one of the movie's best-remembered lines: 'The judge says this is my day to see the dog.' It was not just the fact that he did, and would, ad-lib lines like this, but also that he did so with such speed and composure; Dunne and Bellamy were the first of many of his co-stars to 'corpse' after his more unexpected comic improvisations.

When *The Awful Truth* was released, in the autumn of 1937, it made the studio (whose net profit for the whole year was $1.3 million) more than half a million dollars, and reviewers praised it as 'the season's funniest and smartest drawing-room comedy'.[11] It received six Academy Award nominations (for Best Picture, Best Actress – Dunne, Best Supporting Actor – Bellamy, Screenplay, Film Editing and Director), with McCarey winning the Oscar for Best Director. Inexplicably, Grant was the only one of the leading actors who was overlooked by the Academy, although the critics had all praised his performance. It is unlikely, however, that he was too disappointed by the snub; he believed that it was his best work to date, and he knew that it had enhanced his stature both within the Hollywood community and among the movie-going public. As

Phyllis Brooks, one of his closest friends of the time, recalled, 'The *Awful Truth* came out, and Cary suddenly became very important. He was so happy. Everybody who knew him was thrilled.'[12]

The Awful Truth showed that Grant was a leading man who could also make people laugh. George Cukor noted the significance of the unusual and unexpected combination of what he called 'this dash, this dapper thing'[13] with what was considered to be comic relief:

> You see, he didn't depend on his looks. He wasn't a narcissist; he acted as though he were just an ordinary young man. And that made it all the more appealing, that a handsome young man was funny; that was especially unexpected and good because we think, 'Well, if he's a Beau Brummell, he can't be either funny or intelligent', but he proved otherwise.[14]

Cary Grant became a star who often played wealthy, privileged characters who never seemed to have any need to work in order to maintain their glamorous and hedonistic lifestyle. He became a star whose characters were good looking, quick witted, funny and athletic, a star whose characters seemed to win the hearts of women without even trying. Audiences in Depression America should, one might think, have envied him, perhaps even hated him, but in fact they seemed to adore him. They did so, in part, because he represented a certain kind of gentleman, a Hollywood gentleman, who had the common touch.

The Hollywood movies of the time tended to reflect certain ideas about elegance and luxury. The Hollywood gentleman was pictured as a breed apart: he played among the privileged without himself symbolising privilege; he lived with them but he remained one of us. The ordinariness of the extraordinary was important. As the sociologist Leo Lowenthal remarked:

> It is some comfort for the little man who has become expelled from the Horatio Alger dream [of distinguished endings from humble beginnings], who despairs of penetrating the thicket of grand strategy in politics and business, to see his heroes as a lot of guys who like or dislike highballs, cigarettes, tomato juice, golf, and social gatherings – just like himself.[15]

In *Top Hat* (1935), for example, Fred Astaire, who seemed to wear spats even for those quiet days at home, showed audiences his *real* loyalties by waking up the old fogies in London's crusty Thackeray Club with a noisy and thoroughly 'improper' tap dance. Wealth, one was reassured, had not, in this case, won out over virtue; our hero was just an innocent swell – still one of us, even if he now had the good fortune to be more materially secure than us. The Hollywood gentleman, blessed with the modern democratic spirit, needed to be shown to be a common man at heart, unspoilt in spite of it all. Emerson said that

> A man should not go where he cannot carry his whole sphere or society with him, – not bodily, the whole circle of his friends, but atmospherically. He should preserve in a new company the same attitude of mind and reality of relation, which his daily associates draw him to, else he is shorn of his best beams, and will be an orphan in the merriest club.[16]

Grant's gentleman was elegant yet down-to-earth, refined without seeming effete, comfortable with the style of the patrician shorn of the rough edges of pride, complacency and aggression. Grant's gentleman just wants a better life, a happier life; he does not wish to escape from his past so much as to embrace his promising future. On those rare occasions when his new social environment threatens to weaken his resolve and dazzle him with its air of superiority, an old friend intervenes to break the spell and rescue his best self from corruption. In *The Awful Truth*, for example, such a moment of weakness occurs when Jerry, newly-engaged to débutante and heiress Barbara Vance, tries to impress his snobbish and stuffy future in-laws with a story about his father's days at Princeton; in mid-anecdote he is startled by the sudden appearance of his ex-wife masquerading as 'Lola', his tipsy showgirl 'sister'. As soon as she sees how deferential Jerry has become, she saves him by destroying his credibility in the eyes of his upper-class audience:

Jerry: I was just telling one of father's stories. Er, you've heard it. You see, there was a minute to go, Dad had the ball and was running –

Lola: 'The ball?' *What* ball?

Jerry:	The football.
Lola:	Oh, what in the world would Dad be doing with a football?
Jerry:	[*Becoming irritated*] Look, I was, er, just telling a story about when father was at Princeton. You remember when –
Lola:	Yes, of *course* I remember. Pop loved Princeton. He was there nearly twenty years. If ever a man loved a place, he did. He just adored it – and he certainly kept it looking beautiful. You've seen the grounds, of course?
Mrs Vance:	Of course.
Jerry:	[*Visibly embarrassed*] I'm afraid that my sister has a somewhat *distorted* sense of humor. What she really meant to say was that father presented the College with some of its finest landscapings . . .

After 'Lola' interrupts again to perform an impromptu and unsolicited song and dance routine, Jerry has no option but to flee with her in disgrace, although the anger he felt at first for her interference has by now given way to a kind of grudging admiration of the witty manner by which she punctured his pretensions. Although he will not admit it – at least not immediately – he is greatly relieved to be free from such a suffocatingly snobbish and humourless family.

'Without the rich heart', wrote Emerson, 'wealth is an ugly beggar.'[17] Cary Grant's characters were good-natured populists, not mean-spirited patricians; audiences could imagine Grant enjoying the company of servants and showgirls just as much as – and probably rather more than – he enjoyed the company of socialites. In contrast, for example, to the bovine demeanour and graceless materialism of Ralph Bellamy's rich American in *The Awful Truth* ('I got cattle and horses and chickens and alfalfa . . .'), who idealises Lucy Warriner as his ticket to social respectability, Grant's wealthy man-about-town, when he is deprived of Lucy's company, is happy enough to spend the evening with a woman called 'Toots' – he has his faults, it is implied, but he is not a snob. His gentleman was also appealingly mid-Atlantic in both deportment and disposition. The traditional image of the English gentleman, with his bespoke suits and his general air of social superiority, was, for American audiences, too foreign, too obviously a symbol of Old World inequality, to be thought of sympathetically, let alone to identify with. There was also, for some, something androgynous about the English gentleman, as though he had failed to live up to Emerson's insistence on 'manhood first, then gentleness'.[18] The common images of the new American gentleman, on the other hand, were less precise and not much easier to admire. There was Henry James's melancholic portrayal of the old-fashioned New York gentleman, rigid in evening dress, distinguished by 'gleaming silk lappet and white linen . . . pearl button and gold watch-guard and polished shoe', haunted by a terrifying *alter ego*, an 'evil, odious, blatant, vulgar' yet psychologically unavoidable modern market-place type.[19] Edith Wharton's East Coast gentlemen were changing in similar ways, their Old World decency in the process of being crushed by scheming, their refined tastes conquered by fashion and their traditional principles dissolved by 'the new spirit of limitless concession',[20] and F. Scott Fitzgerald's gentlemen were forced to see that there are people of worth who are not tasteful members of the upper middle class.[21] American culture was, in short, suspicious of the idea of the gentleman, afraid of being bewitched by form at the expense of content, afraid, in Emerson's words, of the 'false gentleman' who 'almost bows the true out of the world',[22] but it was, none the less, unable or unwilling to abandon the idea entirely.

What the Hollywood gentleman projected was meant to be neither fustily nostalgic (English, effeminate, aristocratic) nor harshly modernist (American, brutish, materialistic), but rather something that synthesised the more appealing qualities from both traditions and styles. The Hollywood gentleman, therefore, looked like an Englishman and thought like an American; he had the deportment of the Old World and the disposition of the New; he had 'class', but he was classless; he combined strength with sensitivity, elegance with exuberance, was able to 'out-pray saints in chapel, out-general veterans in the field, and outshine all courtesy in the hall', a man who was 'good company for pirates and good with academicians'.[23]

Cary Grant – an Englishman who had embraced American values, a sophisticated-looking man who was capable of high-spirited acrobatics, a prosperous man from a working-class background – offered Hollywood the rare dialectical combination it had been searching for. Cary Grant was – for audiences, for writers, for critics, for producers – a fascinating hybrid. C. L. R. James, the Trinidadian political activist and theorist, arrived in the United States just as Grant's first series of successful star vehicles was bringing him to a genuinely mass audience, and he was struck by the novelty of the image:

> Cary Grant is a new and very important symbol. He is an Englishman but far removed from Ronald Colman and Leslie Howard, representative of a new type of Englishman on whom the influence of American civilisation has been very strong. He has the freedom, natural grace, simplicity and directness which characterise such different American types as Jimmy Stewart and Ronald Reagan. But behind it all there is the British reserve. He anticipates, so to speak, the emergence of a new social type, the inevitable result of increasingly close relations between Britain and America.[24]

The Awful Truth had shown how Grant could take a very confident, physical, 'man's man' type of character and make him seem vulnerable and sensitive. His next movie, *Bringing Up Baby*, saw him take a naïve, timid, unworldly character and find in him a strange kind of quiet dignity and moral strength. He played a palaeontologist, Dr David Huxley (modelled, in terms of appearance, on Harold Lloyd), whose plans to marry Alice Swallow, an intimidatingly 'proper' woman, and to obtain funding for his museum and complete the reconstruction of his brontosaurus skeleton, are always being derailed by an eccentric young woman called Susan Vance (Katharine Hepburn). To begin with, Huxley's life seems destined to unfold in a ruthlessly logical and disciplined manner. When his fiancée hears him talking excitedly about their honeymoon, she is quick to disenchant him:

Alice: Going away? Why, what are you thinking of, David?

David: Oh, well, we planned it.

Alice: Why, as soon as we're married, we're coming directly back here and you're going on with your work.

David: Oh, *Alice*, gee whiz . . .

Alice: Now once and for all, David, *nothing* must interfere with your work.

David: Oh . . .

Alice: Our marriage must entail no domestic entanglements of any kind.

David: You mean, you mean . . .

Alice: I mean of *any* kind, David.

David: Oh, well, Alice, I was sort of hoping . . . well, you mean, you mean children and all that sort of thing . . . ?

Alice: Exactly. This [*making a sweeping gesture in the direction of the brontosaurus*] will be our child.

David: Huh?

The life of David Huxley, like his work, is too safe, too enclosed, too airless, too tidy, all bone and no blood. As the movie develops, however, he discovers – unwillingly at first – that he knows very little about life, and the series of extraordinary events that follow serve as his new university. Outside of his orderly museum, David finds only chaos ('Susan, you look at everything upside down!'). He is obliged to ingratiate himself with a certain Mr Peabody (George Irving), who has the means to unlock a million-dollar gift for the museum, but their golf match is interrupted by Susan Vance, who takes his golf-ball by mistake, then gets into his car by mistake, and then drives off with the helplessly confused David ('I'll be with you in a minute, Mr Peabody!') trapped on the running-board.

When, that evening, he makes a fresh attempt to win over Mr Peabody in a fancy restaurant, Susan again intrudes into his life. First he slips on an olive she has just dropped on the floor ('*You* drop an olive and then *I* sit on my hat. It all fits perfectly'); then she asks him to hold someone else's purse by mistake ('it never *will* be clear as long as *she's* explaining it'); and then she rips the back seam of his tailcoat by accident ('Oh, you tore your coat'). It is only when Huxley loses his temper and tries to escape from this absurdity once and for all ('Let's play a game. I'll put my hand over my eyes and then you go away. And I'll count to ten. And when I take my hand down, you will be *gone*!') that he ties himself even closer to her and her peculiar view of the world. As she starts to leave, he forgets to step off the train of her gown, pulling it off without her realising it and exposing her vented backside to the eyes of the world. His desperate series of sudden improvisations (covering the gap with his hat, pressing close to her with his entire body) attempts to protect her modesty and spare her embarrassment, but it also marks the very first time that he has acted spontaneously, and, indeed, intimately, and thus begins the education that will help transform him into a more appealing kind of American male.[25]

The following morning, David's priceless intercostal clavicle, the last bone to complete his brontosaurus exhibit, finally arrives. Susan, meanwhile, has taken delivery of a tame leopard called Baby, sent by a brother in South America, and telephones David, pretending to be attacked. He races in alarm to her apartment (even though he had, just a few hours before, wished her out of his life – he is not thinking clearly now at all), absent-mindedly clutching his bone. She then tricks him into driving to her Connecticut farm, heedless of the fact that he is due to be married in the afternoon, and sends his clothes, dishevelled after an incident involving a poultry truck, out to be dry-cleaned while he is showering. Wearing a fluffy negligée, he is surprised by the arrival of Susan's dowager Aunt Elizabeth (May Robson) and, in exasperation, explains to her that 'I just went *gay* all of a sudden!'.[26]

Susan's dog, George (played by Asta,[27] the same remarkable fox terrier that had appeared in *The Awful Truth*), steals the bone and buries it. The leopard escapes; another leopard, of a savage disposition, escapes from a nearby circus. A small big-game hunter (a superb Charlie Ruggles), who arrives for dinner, is astonished to hear that leopards roam the Connecticut woods. Somehow almost everyone ends up in gaol, but Susan escapes by pretending to be a gangster's moll who will spill the beans. Both leopards reappear, and David, much to his surprise, saves Susan from being attacked.

David – his spell in the country over – retreats back into the museum. His fiancée has left him after hearing of his adventures with another woman. When Susan reappears, having found the precious intercostal clavicle, David – perched on the scaffolding around the top of the skeleton – panics ('Thank you very much, Susan. Put it down there on the table and go away'). As she begins to confess that many of the 'accidents' had been devised by her in order to keep him near her, David's response takes her (and perhaps him) by surprise:

David: But . . . I ought to *thank* you!

Susan: *Thank* me?

David: Yes . . . You see, well, I've just discovered that was the *best* day I ever had in my whole life.

Susan: David, you don't mean that?

David: I never had a better time!

Susan: But, but *I* was there.

David: Well, that's what made it so good!

Bringing Up Baby, although only a moderate critical and box-office success at the time,[28] is now seen as the most sublime example of the Hollywood screwball comedy. Pauline Kael described it as American cinema's 'closest equivalent to Restoration Comedy'.[29] At its heart are the immaculately timed comic performances of Grant and Hepburn; whereas their previous collaboration – the infamous *Sylvia Scarlett* – had left Hepburn with an unwelcome notoriety as 'box-office poison', this movie enhanced the reputations of *both* stars.[30]

Howard Hawks, the director, observed that Grant's performance was exactly what he had wanted: 'It's pretty hard to think of anybody but Cary Grant in that type of stuff. He was so far the best that there isn't anybody to be compared to him.'[31] As Kael remarked of Grant at this point in his career:

He became Cary Grant when he learned to project his feelings of absurdity through his characters and to make a style out of their feeling silly. Once he realised that each movement could be stylised for humor, the eyepopping, the cocked head, the forward lunge, and the slightly ungainly stride became as certain as the pen strokes of a master cartoonist. The new element of romantic slapstick in the mid-thirties comedies – the teasing role reversals and shifts of mood – loosened him up and brought him to life. At last, he could do what he had been trained to do, and a rambunctious, springy side of his nature came out.[32]

As had happened on the set of *The Awful Truth*, the director and cast of *Bringing Up Baby* improvised several of the most memorable lines and scenes. Hawks recalled that Grant, after the experience of *The Awful Truth*, was the most keen, and the most able, of the improvisers: 'He was so marvelous. We finally got so that I'd say "Cary, this is a good chance to do Number Seven." Number Seven was trying to talk to a woman who was doing a lot of talking. We'd just do Number Seven. And he'd have to find variations on that.'[33] Hawks was acutely aware of the fact that he was working with Grant at a particularly important and exciting stage in his career:

> I've seen it happen time and again. A performer goes along for years and is never better than satisfactory. Then, suddenly, he becomes brilliant. It's a matter of confidence. Cary Grant became a star when he became confident of himself. He's doing things now, little gestures, facial expressions, that he wouldn't have dared to do when he first came to Hollywood because he lacked confidence. Now he's got it. Confidence brings poise and polish and what I call 'style' to a player. Once a performer has it, his reading of lines and his reactions take on sparkle. Right now, Cary is hot.[34]

One reason why Grant was considered 'hot' was that he was benefiting greatly from the advice and expertise of directors such as Hawks and Leo McCarey. Referring to Grant's breakthrough performance in *The Awful Truth*, the writer Garson Kanin argues that 'McCarey furnished him with more than a part – he gave him a character, a personality, an image', one that he would continue to use, with subtle refinements, for the rest of his career.[35] It was an overstatement – Grant had been working on this 'character' for some time, and there was no *radical* change in his look or deportment between *Topper* and *The Awful Truth* – but it is clear that McCarey helped Grant to think more carefully about what precisely it was that he was trying to *do* in front of a camera. Whereas von Sternberg had discouraged Grant from contributing his own ideas on how a scene should work, McCarey welcomed any thoughts that Grant had to offer. Howard Hawks, in this sense, was a similar kind of director. An example of the new spirit of collaboration was observed by the critic and director Peter Bogdanovich:

There's a scene where Cary's supposed to get angry, and Howard said, 'That's pretty dull. You get angry like Joe Doakes down the block. I know a guy, when he gets angry, he kind of whinnies like a horse. Why don't you do that?' So Cary went like this . . . [*makes whinnying sound*]. And then *that* became part of his persona. Now, you could say that Hawks could have given that direction to anybody. But it wouldn't necessarily have worked. It wouldn't have worked with Bogart or Cooper or Gable. It worked with Cary Grant. Perhaps Hawks was inspired by the qualities Cary brought to the scene and knew Cary could make it work.[36]

Grant's contribution went beyond his own particular role in *Bringing Up Baby*.[37] He also played a significant advisory role in the cutting of the movie, and he helped his co-star, Katharine Hepburn, deal with much of the comic business that was unfamiliar to her. Hepburn had been perceived by audiences of the time as being cold, lofty and contemptuous, but, alongside Grant, they saw in her a different, warmer, funnier kind of person. Hawks had not been impressed by her initial attempts at comedy, so he encouraged Grant (and another crafty old vaudevillian, Walter Catlett, who played the sheriff) to coach her on set. One problem was that she was trying to *act* comically; Grant showed her 'that the more depressed I looked when I went into a pratfall, the more the audience would laugh'.[38] Grant's expertise was used to most dramatic effect at the very end, when Hepburn was supposed to climb up a ladder to face Grant at the top of the brontosaurus skeleton, and then grab at his hand when the skeleton collapses. Grant recalled, 'I told her when and how to let go. I told her to aim for my wrists, an old circus trick. You can't let go of that kind of grip, whereas if you go for the hands, you'll slip. She went right for my wrists, and I pulled her up. Kate was marvelously trusting, if she thought you knew what you were doing.'[39]

It was a strange, intriguing screen partnership, with Hepburn's noisy verbal pyrotechnics made increasingly funny by Grant's silent reaction shots. Their relationship evolves but never really settles down: they never kiss, they never laugh, they never really fight, they rarely, in fact, understand what the one is trying to say to the other, and yet, somehow, they grow closer, close enough to make their last-minute confessions of faith comprehensible. Every scene they share has a sense of excitement about it, a kind of comic danger: she refuses to let him have his golf-ball back, she drives off in his car, he tears her dress, she tears his coat, he stamps on her foot, she invents a new name and profession for him, he avoids her and then he defends her. As the writer Patrick McGilligan has said, it was a different kind of partnership – more volatile, more quirky – to the one Hepburn enjoyed with Spencer Tracy: 'Tracy and Hepburn tended to get comfortable with each other. Any truce between Cary Grant and Hepburn could be safely assumed as temporary.'[40]

Grant worked with Hepburn again for his next movie, *Holiday*.[41] The two actors enjoyed each other's company as well as respecting each other's talents. 'Cary was a lovely, very generous actor. A good comedian. And so *funny*. He had a wonderful laugh. When you looked at that face of his, it was full of a wonderful kind of laughter at the back of the eyes.'[42] Grant, in turn, admired her professionalism. 'Kate's a joy,' he said, praising her willingness to work on scenes until every detail seemed perfect.[43] George Cukor was the director, and the three survivors from the traumatic *Sylvia Scarlett*, now reunited, worked well together.[44]

In *Holiday* Grant and Hepburn played quite different characters from those in *Bringing Up Baby*. Grant played Johnny Case, an unspoilt and industrious young man (a Harvard man, too) who stumbles into a world of débutantes and bankers – the Fifth Avenue home of his fiancée Julia Seton, her wealthy father, her tormented brother Ned, and her frustrated sister Linda (played by Hepburn). Johnny dreams of taking a year or two off to get a bearing on what he really wants to do and be, an idea that makes as little sense to Julia as it does to her father. The movie works out the conflicts of an easygoing gentleman as he tries to detach the upper-class idea of play from the upper-class facts of accumulation. The audience watches as Johnny and Linda attempt to put the patricians in touch with a kind of fun that is innocent and free of the cold hand of Wall Street. Johnny's flip-flop in the imposingly grand drawing-room, for example, is the equivalent of Astaire's outburst in *Top Hat*, a playful gesture amid the museum-quality furniture. Johnny may be rising up the class hierarchy, and he may be about to marry into a rich and powerful family, but he is still 'one of us': he arrives at the house on Fifth Avenue via the servants' entrance, and, after being taken up to the first floor by elevator, he looks down at the stairs and says to himself, 'I could've *walked* that.' Linda likes him for the very qualities that disturb his fiancée and future father-in-law: he has not yet been 'bitten by the reverence for riches'.

Most of the characters in the movie have chosen wealth over virtue; they have money but no happiness, leading lives of quiet but comfortable desperation. 'Oh, now come on, darling,' Johnny says at one point to his humourless fiancée. 'Let's not let the *fun* get out of it!' It is clear, however, that there is no fun to be found in the company of these people; they are too preoccupied with thoughts of social standing, of power and reputation, to entertain thoughts of idle pleasure. The redeemable characters, in contrast, take an easy ride through the tangled landscape of obligations, money and privilege. One of them, Nick Potter (Edward Everett Horton), a Columbia professor, is patronised when he arrives with his equally unspoilt wife at the formal party to celebrate the engagement; he simply rises above the snobbery with an ironic look and a quiet determination to have a good time even in a house packed full of upper-class killjoys. Potter is the right kind of gentleman, with Emerson's 'rich-heart' and a natural willingness to treat others as equals. It is Potter who helps Johnny resist the empty glamour of high society, mocking his anxiety to please his sternly materialistic fiancée with the remark, '*That's* not Johnny Case. *That's* a very important person!' Johnny's reaction – a look of contrition, a boyish ruffle of the hair and an invitation to Potter to kick his backside – shows that he has not lost the common touch. 'I'm a plain man of the people,' he avers. 'I began life with these two bare hands.' As the most sympathetic of the rich people, who stores her dreams 'upstairs' in a room full of fond memories and secret hopes carefully cordoned off from the rest of the house, Linda's unexpected feelings of love for Johnny save her from the stifling life of the Setons. She and Johnny are soul mates, both genuinely uninterested in social convention or class obligations.

The role of Johnny was probably a relatively easy one for Grant to identify with. A young man of natural intelligence and style, working his way up to a position where he can appear – if not feel – at ease in the grandest surroundings: Johnny Case must have seemed very familiar to him (he later played a tragic version of the same kind of role, as Ernie Mott in *None But the Lonely Heart*,[45] but here, in *Holiday*, the bitterness that lurks behind the achievement is never glimpsed).

If Johnny Case was a character close to the man that Cary Grant had become, his next role, as the cockney Sergeant Archibald Cutter in *Gunga Din*, was more reminiscent of the man he used to be. The movie itself was quite a departure for Grant: it was a major action picture by RKO (allocated two million dollars – the studio's biggest budget up to that time) and was shot on location in the Alabama Range, near Lone Pine, with a company of twelve hundred actors and workers. With Kipling's heroic water-bearer doing little more than lending his name to *Gunga Din*, Ben Hecht and Charles Mac-Arthur wrote an original screenplay that combined elements from their own *The Front Page* with *The Three Musketeers* and *Lives of a Bengal Lancer*. Cutter (Grant), MacChesney (Victor McLaglen) and Ballantine (Douglas Fairbanks, Jnr.) are three British soldiers of the Royal Engineers in nineteenth-century India, the first two trying their hardest to prevent the third (a kind of military-version of Hildy Johnson) from leaving the service to get married and run a tea plantation.

After an outstation is attacked, the three sergeants are sent on a mission to discover what happened. They find a temple hidden in the mountains where the Thuggee cult listen to their leader and make plans to destroy the British troops in the area. The three sergeants, along with their loyal water-carrier, Gunga Din (Sam Jaffe), are taken prisoner and tortured. They then escape and capture the cult-leader, enabling them to hold off his men until the British troops arrive. Gunga Din (in a curiously camp scene that would be parodied so memorably by Peter Sellers at the beginning of *The Party*), although badly wounded, climbs the dome of the temple to blow a bugle-call, warning the troops of an ambush and saving the army from massacre.

Everyone seems to have enjoyed the experience of making *Gunga Din* (and Grant later referred to it as one of his favourite movies). Described by a reviewer as 'one of the most enjoyable nonsense-adventure movies of all time',[46] it is a playful piece of work, full of in-jokes and clowning as well as lively action scenes and grand dramatic gestures. Grant looks at the peak of his youthful self-confidence; from the very first scene, he has a manner that suggests that he would be willing to attempt *anything*. George Stevens, who took over the direction early on from Howard Hawks, allowed Grant to improvise in scene after scene. Grant's round-eyed, bright-eyed flamboyance makes Cutter appear simultaneously heroic and comical: 'You're all under arrest . . . and you know why!' he says at one point in his knowingly broad cockney accent. 'Her Majesty's very *touchy* about having her subjects strangled. Wrap up your gear. You're coming with me!' As one critic said of Grant, 'he's never been more of a burlesque comic than when he arrives at the gold temple of the religious cult of thugs and whinnies with greedy delight at the very moment he's being shot at'.[47]

'Archie Cutter' (he chose his first name himself) refers us back, of course, to Archie Leach. Cutter is a working-class Englishman, unspoilt, principled and defiantly optimistic. He is a creature of the great outdoors, not the smoke-filled drawing-room; he provided Grant with the chance, at long last, to emulate his old idol, Douglas Fairbanks, Snr., leaping through the air, performing somersaults, punching out his opponents and brandishing a sword against the hostile hordes. *Gunga Din* was the second-highest grossing movie of 1939 and RKO's most profitable movie in years.[48] Grant had once again significantly expanded his range as a performer, and enjoyed another major box-office success.

He followed *Gunga Din* with a more serious adventure movie, *Only Angels Have Wings*. On this occasion he combined his abilities as romantic lead with a strong masculine story so typical of the movie's director, Howard Hawks. Grant played Jeff Carter, the tough-talking head of an air-freight service flying mail out of the banana port of Barranca. His co-star was Jean Arthur, who played the role of Bonnie Lee, a stranded showgirl who competes for his affections with his former wife, Judy (Rita Hayworth).[49] Jeff Carter is a much darker, harder, more serious character than Grant had played before, all clipped abruptness and dark-eyed stares; he caught the mood, and gave one of his most memorable performances. The men in Hawks's world were unsentimental professionals who played down the dangers in their lives. Women who intruded into this unapologetically masculine world were treated with suspicion; only after a woman had shown total acquiescence to its rules could she be considered for admission.

For most of the movie, Bonnie is brushed aside whenever she tries to express her feelings for Carter:

Carter: You're not making sense.

Bonnie: You're telling me. If I'd taken that boat I'd have gone out of here remembering a swell guy, someone who lived up to a screwy ideal that I –

Carter: Look, I didn't ask you to stay, I wouldn't ask any –

Bonnie: I know, you'd never ask any woman to do anything.

Carter: That's right. What's more, there's something else I wouldn't do.

Bonnie: What?

Carter: Get burned twice in the same place. There's another boat leaving next week.

Bonnie: I'll be on it.

Carter: Good.

Bonnie shows her grief when Joe, one of their number, dies when he crashes in bad weather. 'What's the use of feeling bad about something that couldn't be helped?' asks Carter. Later, chastened, she tells Carter, 'I hadda behave like a sap.' 'Grown up?' asks Carter. 'Hope so,' she replies. 'Good girl,' he says, before testing her toughness by inquiring, 'Who's Joe?' 'Never heard of him,' she answers, confirming that she has learned at last how to behave in a man's world.

Carter – however – stands out from the common crowd of men. His dandified appearance is certainly striking: oversized panama hat, dark leather jacket draped over the shoulders and gaucho trousers. His behaviour, although designed to seem brusque, is governed by the gentlemanly code: he does what he thinks is right to keep the community alive, even if that means sometimes putting his own safety at risk. When his closest colleague dies, it is Bonnie who discovers, in private, that he remains vulnerable beneath the surface sang-froid: 'Oh Jeff, you're crying.' He looks lost. He needs her more, not less, than the others.[50]

Only Angels Have Wings was another great success for Grant. The man who just two years before had been seen by many producers as merely an ersatz Gary Cooper was now an international star in his own right, recognised and admired by millions of movie-goers throughout the world. He was deluged with fan mail, and Cary Grant fan clubs were being formed all over America. He was earning around a quarter of a million dollars a year at a time when the average weekly wage was less than $100, and his professional independence gave him the power to choose his studios, directors and co-stars. Most important of all, he had found himself, and acquired the self-assurance to really *enjoy* being Cary Grant.

Hollywood had found its ideal gentleman, a gentleman for a democratic culture. He was an amalgam of tradition and modernity, wealth and virtue, élite and mass, high and low, great and good. It *should* not have worked, but somehow it did. As he sits and faces the camera during that early scene in *The Awful Truth*, he looks at us with an expression that suggests that he knows as well as we do that the audacious trick has, against all the odds, actually come off. He smiles at us, sharing with us his extraordinary good fortune. He smiles a smile like Gatsby's smile:

> It was one of those rare smiles with a quality of eternal reassurance on it, that you may come across four or five times in life. It faced – or seemed to face – the whole eternal world for an instant, and then concentrated on *you* with an irresistible prejudice in your favour. It understood you just so far as you wanted to be understood, believed in you as you would like to believe in yourself, and assured you that it had precisely the impression of you that, at your best, you hoped to convey.[51]

It was, from that moment on, the smile one associated with Cary Grant.

CHAPTER VIII

The Intimate Stranger

What is it that attracts one's curiosity toward a public face? Do we want to see if their eyes are the same color we thought they were? If they have freckles, warts or blemishes? If their appearance holds some secret that we can fathom? If they're still as tall or short or older or younger than we expect them to be? Do we want to make sure that they are human and therefore not unlike ourselves? And why would we want to do that anyway? I've never been certain what people expect to find. I just hope they aren't too disappointed when it concerns me.

CARY GRANT

It is not true that the more you love, the better you understand; all that the action of love obtains from me is merely this wisdom: that the other is not to be known; his capacity is not the screen around a secret, but, instead, a kind of evidence in which the game of reality and appearance is done away with. I am then seized with that exaltation of loving someone unknown, someone who will remain so forever: a mystic impulse: I know that I do not know.

ROLAND BARTHES

Cary Grant, by the end of the thirties, had become one of the major international Hollywood stars. It was, as it turned out, a particularly propitious time to become a major star. In 1939, the studio system was at its peak.[1] The Depression was lessening; admission to local movie theatres cost twenty-five cents, and more people than before had twenty-five cents to spend, and, at the movies, they got more for their money than ever before or since.[2] The movie-goer could expect to see an A picture (a big-budget feature with big stars), a B-picture (a low-budget feature with a shorter running time), a newsreel, a comedy short and a cartoon. The movie-goer, at the end of the thirties, would also see many of the most popular movies ever made in Hollywood – such as *Gone with the Wind*, *The Wizard of Oz*, *Stagecoach*, *Mr Smith Goes to Washington*, *Ninotchka* and *Gunga Din* – and many of its greatest stars – such as Bette Davis, Clark Gable, James Cagney, Gary Cooper, Jimmy Stewart and Cary Grant. Hollywood had come of age, and so had Cary Grant.

Grant's appeal was unusually broad. He was not the kind of star who tended to attract only one or the other of the sexes. Grant, as Pauline Kael puts it, was 'the male love object. Men want to be as lucky and enviable as he is – they want to be like him. And women imagine landing him.'[3] On the screen, as Archie Cutter, Grant had shown men that he could look good doing physical 'manly' things, like punching other men through windows and standing firm as the bullets brushed past his ears; as Jeff Carter, he showed them he could be a 'man's man', cool, calm, strong willed and unsentimental; as Jerry Warriner, he showed them he could look good, and have fun, and make them laugh. It was, for many men, a rare and rich and fascinating sight. As Burt Reynolds, one of Grant's admirers, recalled: 'Cary was magical. He was touched by the gods in the sense that he was different from everyone else. When he walked into a room, you *had* to look at him. Men liked him as well as women, and that is incredibly rare. Men found him non-threatening. If a woman said, "I'm in love with Cary Grant", most men couldn't blame her.'[4] Other men agreed: 'Men don't find many men appealing, but Cary was attractive to everybody. Men wanted to look, dress, and be like him.'[5] 'When Cary walked into a room, not only did the women primp, the men straightened their ties.'[6] Kael, again, puts it well when she says that although on one level men might have wanted to be Clark Gable, 'supremely confident and earthy and irresistible', on another level, 'a few steps up the dreamy social ladder', there was the 'more subtle fantasy of worldly grace – of being so gallant and gentlemanly and charming that every woman longs to be your date. And at that deluxe level, men want to be Cary Grant.'[7]

Grant had shown women, as Jerry Warriner, that he could be amusing as well as good looking; as David Huxley, he showed them that he could be gentle, vulnerable and pliable; as Jeff Carter that he could be a real challenge. In all of his roles, he revealed different shades of a protean personality; he portrayed a man that was interesting, and, just as importantly, and unusually, that he was interested in *them* – not only, or even primarily, sexually, but also intellectually, as people, as friends. Women *talked* to him, more so than was usual with most other leading men, and he *listened*, which was even rarer. For Pauline Kael, many women, 'if the roof leaks, or the car stalls, or you don't know how to get the super to keep his paws off you', might have wished for a Clark Gable to appear and assist them, 'but when you think of going out, Cary Grant is your dream date – not sexless but sex with civilised grace, sex with mystery'.[8] With a man like Gable, she argues, 'sex is inevitable', as well as being prosaic, because he is the kind of man who 'thinks women are good for only one thing', whereas with a man like Grant, 'there are infinite possibilities for mutual entertainment. They might dance the night away or stroll or go to a carnival – and nothing sexual would happen unless she wanted it to.'[9] Cary Grant was 'the sky that women aspire to. When he and a woman are together, they can laugh at each other and at themselves.'[10]

Grant had become a major star, but also a very distinctive one, a star who appealed to both men and women, a star who symbolised the ideal of the democratic gentleman: not only was his an image that was enjoyed by both sexes but also by all classes.[11] 'He was comfortable in all aspects of show business,' said Gregory Peck, 'acrobatics, singing, music, comedy, drama, the circus. Underneath that suave manner and sophisticated style, he was dyed-in-the-wool, grass-roots, down-to-earth show business. A performer.'[12] He was, for audiences, an 'intimate stranger',[13] the same as them but different, familiar yet intriguingly exotic, easy to warm to but hard to work out.

Richard Schickel has written of the unworldliness of Grant's screen persona, a persona as real as a character in a recurring dream, 'effortlessly entering people's messed up lives in his heavenly tailoring, an ironic eye cocked on these mortals, his every gesture and expression implying a knowingness that would have been awesome if he did not so casually throw it away'.[14] He was like a member of the family whom everyone had only just noticed, the loved one the lover had never met, homely yet uncanny.[15] 'Mr Grant,' said a young interviewer, meeting Cary Grant for the first time, 'I keep telling myself that you're just a person. Right? But you're not just a person. You're just not. I'm supposed to sit here and talk to you like you're an old friend and you're not my friend. I don't even know you.'

'Sure you know me,' said Grant, and he reached across the table and, very lightly, touched her hand, and smiled: 'We're friends.'[16] That was his gift: he had only to smile at us to see our anxiety turn to trust, our reserve to warmth, and still we would not really know who he was. 'It was always part of his essential screen character that he rarely had any visible means of support or any discernible roots,' said Schickel. 'He was always as much the man from nowhere as the hero of any western, always as much the man from no discernible place as the man from dream city.'[17] It seemed apt when he played an alluringly handsome angel in *The Bishop's Wife*, charming all the women, inspiring all the men, before disappearing – not just from sight, but also from memory – without leaving a trace: 'They seldom send us to the same place twice,' he tells one woman. 'We might form attachments.'

This intensely private man, who had driven a succession of studio publicists to distraction with his studied reticence in the presence of journalists, had become someone whom many movie-goers identified with, or felt great affection for, or modelled themselves on. The lightness of his public persona, the imaginative grace of his performances, had not come easily to him: 'I've often been accused by the critics of being myself on the screen . . . But being oneself is more difficult than you'd suppose.'[18] Grant remembered the reluctance he had felt, early on in his movie career, to come to terms with the way the camera highlighted his features – 'The way I sound. The way I move. The way I look' – and the struggle he had had before he could accept 'the magnification of all my imperfections'.[19] He learned that it was far from easy to 'be natural' on screen, for the scrutiny of millions: 'None of this comes naturally. It comes from experience. It takes practice. Just as a writer says he improves from year to year – and looks back upon his old stuff and says, "My God!" well, so does an actor.'[20] Stanley Donen, who later worked with Grant, stressed the fact that his intimate play of elegance owed much to his skill as a movie actor:

> Cary was unique. You see it and feel it in the reactions and the characterisation. There's not a false moment. And it seems like it's just happening, that he's experiencing it at that moment. He projected ease and comfort, and he was always concentrated. You never saw any fear in him when he was acting. His scripts were full of little notes to himself. The minute detail of it all:

that's really what all art is about. The tiniest details: that's what he was great at. He always seemed real. It wasn't a gift from God. It was the magic that came from enormous amounts of work.[21]

Other actors appreciated the achievement. Tony Curtis remarked that one could 'learn more by watching Cary drink a cup of coffee than by spending six months with a Method actor'.[22] Marlon Brando was similarly impressed: 'Tracy, Muni, Cary Grant. They know what they're doing. You can learn something from them.'[23]

Grant's peculiar appeal for audiences had something to do with the odd way in which – especially in his comedies – he seemed to be aware of their presence. Richard Schickel touches on this when he speaks of Grant's sly gift of being able to 'pull back into a funny distractedness, a way of talking to other people as if he were talking to himself'.[24] By this Schickel did not mean that Grant resorted to a kind of cynical ploy, 'akin to the slight holding back from full commitment . . . that other actors and actresses – especially the handsome ones – sometimes employ to indicate to their fans that they are not really as undignified or stupid as the role seems to indicate they are'.[25] What he means is that Grant had a sharp alertness, 'a way of being bemused by the lunacies with which he is involved that does not set him apart from them but in the end allows him to plead innocent on the ground of temporary insanity. "Look at me," he seems to say, "I'm too intelligent to be doing this. Oh, well. Here goes." We can identify with that. It's what we are compelled to say to ourselves all the time when events get out of hand.'[26]

Kael remarks on the 'absence of narcissism' in his acting, 'the outgoingness to the audience'.[27] Audiences could see that he was a generous and serious performer, working hard at making the scenes play, never making himself look good at the expense of his fellow performers, and so they appreciated the occasional sly reference – 'readable but not underlined'[28] – he shared with them in the spirit that it was intended, not as the cynical wink of the fake but rather as the playful nod of someone having the time of his life. Sometimes it involved a passing reference to Archie Leach,[29] sometimes a fleeting glance at the camera, but on certain occasions the in-jokes were rather more subtle.[30] In *The Awful Truth*, for example, audiences saw Irene Dunne embarrass Grant's character in front of his future in-laws by claiming that he has a drink problem: 'We call him "Jerry the Nipper". He likes to sneak 'em when nobody's looking. Awful cute about it, too. I've seen him go along a whole evening and apparently not have a thing to drink and all of a sudden fall flat on his puss!' In his next movie, *Bringing Up Baby*, audiences saw Katharine Hepburn embarrass Grant's character in front of a police constable by 'confessing' the news that his 'real name' was Jerry: 'You mean to say you don't remember "Jerry the Nipper"?' Grant's character responds by exclaiming, 'Constable, she's making all this up out of motion pictures she's seen!'[31]

The Awful Truth featured a memorably awkward three-way conversation between the mischievous character played by Grant, his irritated ex-wife played by Irene Dunne and her new dim-witted fiancé played by Ralph Bellamy. Grant's character teased his ex-wife about leaving the bright lights of the city for a quiet life in Oklahoma with her new husband and his mother.[32] Two years later, in *His Girl Friday* (1940), there was a remarkably similar awkward three-way conversation between a mischievous Walter Burns (Grant), his irritated ex-wife Hildy Johnson (Rosalind Russell) and her new dim-witted fiancé Bruce Baldwin (Ralph Bellamy):

Walter: Where are you going to live?

Bruce: Albany.

Walter: Albany huh? Got a family up there?

Bruce: Nah, just my mother.

Walter: Just your mother, eh? Oh, you're going to live with your mother?

Bruce: Well, just for the first year.

Walter: Oh, well that *will* be nice. Yes, yes, a home with mother. In *Albany* too!

Later on in the same movie, when asked by someone to describe what Bellamy's character looks like, Grant ad-libs the response: 'He looks like, er, that fellow in the movies . . . you know, Ralph Bellamy.' A special kind of playful complicity had been established between Grant and his audience.

A movie star like Grant, said one critic, carried his movie past with him. He became 'the sum of his most successful roles, and he has only to appear for our good-will to be extended to him'.[33] Although the character that he had evolved to project into the world had grown out of his real self, it was not exactly like that real self; it was a part of him, and, as time went by, it would become the greater part of him, but it was not all of him. Stars had secrets; those stars like Grant, who proved most fascinating, were those who could reveal themselves in public and yet control the process of self-disclosure, choosing how far to strip and how much to tease. As the critic Richard Corliss remarked: 'The true subtleties of acting and character, of revelation and concealment, took place in the arc of admiration that bound Grant to his audience, and set him apart . . . To see him was to love him. To love him was never to know him.'[34]

It was Pauline Kael who first described Cary Grant as 'the most publicly seduced male the world has known'.[35] She had a point. Of all the leading men in Hollywood, none was led as often as Cary Grant. 'You can be had,' Mae West had said to him, looking him up and down, in *She Done Him Wrong*. In the presence of such a sexually aggressive woman, Grant's character seemed elusive and defensive, more prey than predator. West was merely the first, however, of a series of female co-stars who were forward in ways that Grant's characters were backward. 'Women went for him as if they had heard the starter's gun,' wrote Alexander Walker, adding that Grant, of course, 'had heard it, too, and began running even earlier'.[36] In *Bringing Up Baby*, for example, Susan has to resort to a desperate assortment of ruses (such as tricking him into thinking that she is being attacked by a leopard, hiding his clothes and telling people he has suffered a nervous breakdown) in order to keep the hapless David near her; she confesses to him, at the very end of the movie, that 'all that happened happened because I was trying to keep you near me, and I just did anything that came into my head', but the extraordinary thing is that she *needed* to. Rather like Marilyn Monroe's character in *The Seven Year Itch* (1955), who fails to notice that the man sitting next to her at the piano as they play 'chopsticks' is about to attempt to seduce her ('Why did you stop?' 'You know why.' 'Why?' 'Because now I'm going to take you in my arms and kiss you, very quickly and very hard.' '*Hey, wait a minute!*'), some of the men whom Grant played seemed unaware of their sexual allure, needing to be ambushed into intimacy with women. In a later movie,

I Was a Male War Bride (1949), for example, the first kiss that Grant's character shares with his female colleague (played by Ann Sheridan) comes about through her cool manipulation of his emotions:

Catharine: Henry, what's all this 'darling' business you were mumbling about a moment ago?

Henry: '*Darling?*' Did I say that?

Catharine: I heard you.

Henry: Er, it was probably fright. It's only natural –

Catharine: Did you mean me, Henry?

Henry: Er, I think I was *stunned* momentarily.

Catharine: Well, maybe you were, but you looked like you were going to kiss me when you saw me.

Henry: I *what*?

Catharine: I wish you had. I've never been kissed by a Frenchman.

Henry: Well, there's nothing – well, what's so strange about *that*?

Catharine: Well, you know what people say . . .

Henry: [*Embarrassed*] Oh, that's nonsense . . . We're no different than anybody else.

Catharine: Well, I don't *know*, Henry. I've just heard talk.

Henry: Well, that's *silly*!

Catharine: Why don't you try it just once and let me see?

Henry: Oh, *Catharine*!

Catharine: Well, that's the only way to find out, isn't it?

Henry: But I tell you, it's so *silly*!

Catharine: Well, there's no harm in trying, is there?

Henry: [*Confused*] N-No, I suppose not.

Catharine: Alright, go ahead.

She is calm, he is agitated; she is cunning, he is clueless; her voice is deep, his gets higher. The woman is in complete control; he does precisely what she wants him to do, the way she wants him to do it, when she wants him to do it, without him ever quite comprehending what it really is that he is doing:

Catharine: Oh, *that* was no good! that wasn't the *least* bit different!

Henry: [*Defensively*] Ah, I *told* you it wasn't going to be any different!

Catharine: But I thought it'd be better than *that*.

Henry: But after all, you didn't give me much of a chance!

Catharine: That wasn't fair, was it? I really should give you another chance.

Henry: Yes, you ought!

Catharine: Oh, alright, try again.

Henry: Come here [*kisses her again*].

Catharine: [*Smiling*] Well, that was a little better!

It would have been easy for a leading man to have played this kind of scene in such a way as to make his character seem ludicrous. Grant's achievement was to emerge from such comically awkward situations seeming *more* attractive and complicated than before.[37] As Kael observes, he never looked like becoming a public joke, not even when Billy Wilder had Tony Curtis parody him in *Some Like It Hot*, encouraging Marilyn Monroe to ravish his recumbent body ('I've got a funny sensation in my *toes*'). Grant's ability to look shy and reserved made him 'pure box-office gold', and the fact that many of his characters were pursued and seduced by women, far from making him appear 'weak or passively soft', actually made him seem 'glamorous – and, since he is not as available as other men, far more desirable'.[38]

Cary Grant's characters could indeed be had, but not without guile and persistence and a considerable amount of patience. Indeed, in some of his more serious roles, that enticing innocence of his could look more like indifference, suggesting to the viewer that, although he might *like* the women who pursued him, 'he nevertheless didn't actually *need* them'.[39] In such roles, intimacy was still a possibility, but it was only a possibility, and it carried with it a certain danger.

David Thomson has written of Grant's ability to reveal the dark, as well as the light, side in his more serious characters, showing 'malice, misogyny, selfishness, and solitariness beneath good manners and gaiety', as well as 'a sense of grace-in-humor buoying up a near-sadistic playing upon lesser people's nerves and good nature'.[40] There is also something of Baudelaire's modern dandy about him, 'an air of coldness which comes from an unshakeable determination not to be loved; you might call it a latent fire which hints at itself, and which could, but chooses not to, burst into flame'.[41]

Jeff Carter, the sombrero-wearing flyer in *Only Angels Have Wings*, is just such a character. He works in a world in which 'real men' can always do without women; real men are 'hard men', their hearts shielded from the tender thoughts of others. His best friend describes him as 'a good guy for gals to stay away from'. Bonnie (Jean Arthur) 'half falls apart waiting for him to make a move'.[42] The more Carter shows Bonnie his stoical masculinity, the more Grant shows *us* his vulnerability. Carter needs her too much, not too little, to allow his real feelings to show:

Bonnie: Say, someone must have given you an awful beating once!

Carter: Hey, you're a queer duck.

Bonnie: So are you!

Carter: I can't make you out.

Bonnie: Same here. What was she like, anyway?

Carter: Who?

Bonnie: That girl that made you act the way you do?

Carter: A whole lot like you. Just as nice, almost as smart.

Bonnie: Chorus girl?

Carter: Only by temperament.

Bonnie: Well, at least you're true to the type.

Carter: Sit down, make yourself comfortable.

Bonnie: Still carrying the torch for her, aren't you?

Carter: Got a match?

Bonnie: Say, don't you ever have any?

Carter: No, don't believe in laying into supply of anything.

Bonnie: Matches, marbles, money or women.

Carter: That's right.

Bonnie: No looking ahead. No tomorrows, just today.

Carter: That's right.

Bonnie: Is that why she gave you the air?

Carter: Who?

It would be wrong, however, to turn Kael's observations on that particular quality evident in many of Grant's performances – 'shyness and reserve' – into an account of the sum of his screen self.[43] He was not *always* passive or introspective or naïve. As Nick Townsend in *Blonde Venus*, he pursues the woman: 'C'om, Helen, give me a little kiss, will you?' As the brash Joe Adams in *Mr Lucky* (1943), he is positively flirtatious. As Walter Burns, in his third collaboration with Howard Hawks – *His Girl Friday* – he is always active, abrasive, scheming and sardonic; Hildy is fleeing from him, not he from her, and, although he does not go so far as to articulate his feelings fully and unambiguously, he makes it clear enough to her – and us – that he wants her back. Introduce a rival for the affections of a woman and Grant's characters seldom fail to rise to the challenge: note, for example, the way that Jerry in *The Awful Truth*, or Walter in *His Girl Friday*, does all that he possibly can to mock and humiliate his rival and win back his partner. These characters are not often intimate on screen with the women in their lives, but, when necessary, they are prepared to threaten to draw attention in public to the private intimacy of their relationship in order to warn off any competitor: think of Jerry in *The Awful Truth*, in the presence of his ex-wife and her new suitor, making his deliberately indiscreet references to their honeymoon night ('Remember when they sent the bell-boy? Gosh, we didn't want ice-water!') or of Walter in *His Girl Friday*, starting and then stopping himself from recalling, in the presence of his ex-wife and her shocked fiancé, an extraordinary anecdote concerning their over-night stay in Albany. C. K. Dexter Haven, in *The Philadelphia Story*, wants Tracy Lord so badly that he sorts out his drink problem, compromises himself with the magazine he despises and returns to reclaim her love. Even the unusually unworldly David Huxley, in *Bringing Up Baby*, lets his heart rule his head, his body his brain, by allowing himself to be sidetracked by Susan, because he knows, deep down, that what he really wants is warm flesh, not dry bone – 'children and all that sort of thing'.

There was, more often than not, something more subtle, more complex going on than there seemed, at first glance, on the surface whenever women pursued Grant's more elusive characters. The woman who chases him understands, deep down, that he wants to be caught by her (and probably *only* by her). As Kael admits, the game, more often than not, 'is an artful dodge';[44] he does not need to act like a conqueror in order to end up a winner. 'He gets the blithe, funny girl by manoeuvering her into going after him.'[45] Even on those occasions when his characters seemed less sure about themselves, Cary Grant knew exactly what *he* was doing: 'Always allow the woman to come to you in a love scene . . . Don't make the move to her. It puts you in a very commanding position.'[46]

It also made him very helpful to his female co-stars. His vulnerability gave them strength, his silences allowed them to talk. Women had more to do when they acted alongside Grant, and many of them gave better, more interesting, more confident performances when they appeared in movies with him. Katharine Hepburn and Irene Dunne, for example, appreciated the generosity of his acting; in the comedies they shared with him, they had many – if not the majority – of the wittier lines.[47] Grant, said Kael, was 'the greatest sexual stooge the screen has ever known: his side steps and delighted stares turn his co-stars into comic goddesses. Nobody else has ever been able to do that.'[48]

Cary Grant knew the value of his intimate strangeness. He was a chivalrous leading man, not slow in coming forward because he really came forward by holding back. Billy Wilder – who tried on many occasions to work with Grant, but, in spite of his friendship with him, never quite managed to[49] – spoke often about an idea he had for a movie about the Crusades.[50] It would, he said, open on knights in shining armour as they prepared to ride off to war. There would follow a montage of the crusaders as they kissed their wives farewell and locked them securely into their chastity belts. We would see the knights mount their horses and ride off for the Holy Land. Then,

Wilder said, he would cut to a modest little shop on a cobble-stoned lane. A wooden sign would wave gently in the twilight: 'PIERRE COUR DE LION, LOCKSMITH.' We would then move in for our first sight of the village locksmith. It would be Cary Grant.

CHAPTER IX

Suspicions

There's so much junk written. I never understand why people write these wicked and malicious things. They keep stacks of 'information' on you – much of it misinformation – and then shove it into a book.
CARY GRANT

He would, wouldn't he?
MANDY RICE-DAVIES

Cary Grant appeared in three movies in 1941 – the tenth anniversary of his arrival in Hollywood. All three were among the highest-grossing movies of the year, underlining his status as a major star. Each one featured Grant playing a character wary of public scrutiny. As C. K. Dexter Haven in *The Philadelphia Story*, he finds himself blackmailed into co-operating with the very 'society snoops' he most despises; as Roger Adams in *Penny Serenade*, he struggles to hide his family's precarious financial situation from the head of an adoption society; and as Johnnie Aysgarth in *Suspicion*, he charms a woman, marries her and gives her good cause to suspect him of plotting to murder her. These were all characters who were careful to keep their private affairs hidden from view. They had secrets; they were deceitful; they were the subjects of gossip, rumour and innuendo. They were all under suspicion.

The most mysterious of these was Johnnie Aysgarth. 'There was something strange about Johnnie Aysgarth . . . Even his reassurances seemed almost sinister.'[1] He is adored by women, but they know that they cannot rely on him. He can make most men warm to him, but few of them trust him. He convinces one woman that he loves her, and then he betrays her. He can sometimes seem unusually sensitive, and sometimes chillingly uncaring. He promises happiness one day and threatens misery the next. He is a dangerous enigma, attractive yet repellent, easy to like but hard to know. He is not the kind of character that audiences of the time expected Cary Grant to play.

Alfred Hitchcock, the director of *Suspicion*, had wanted Grant for the role precisely because of such audience expectations. He knew that audiences on seeing Johnnie Aysgarth would know that he was Cary Grant, so that however bleak the situation might become, they would not believe that a character played by Grant could really turn out to be a murderer. Hitchcock, therefore, planned to execute an audacious double-bluff, revealing Grant's character to *be* as bad, as cold, as evil as he had seemed to be, thereby administering a shock far beyond anything that the plot itself could have been expected to deliver. The ending that Hitchcock intended featured Johnnie Aysgarth bringing his wife a glass of poisoned milk; just before she drinks it, she hands him a letter in a sealed envelope for him to mail. The letter names him as her murderer. Then, still in love with the man that she knows is her killer, she drinks the poison. 'I thought the original was marvelous,' Grant remarked. 'It was a perfect Hitchcock ending. But the studio insisted that they didn't want to have Cary Grant play a murderer.'[2]

The revised ending, in which Aysgarth is revealed merely as the victim of his wife's distrustful nature, although thoroughly unsatisfactory, still managed, perversely, to make Cary Grant's performance appear unnervingly ambiguous. It now seemed as though the darkness of the character, the glimpses of violence and misogyny from behind the cheerful and charming façade, were not the mere outward signs of his inner designs, but, even more disturbingly, they were constant, irremediable elements in the disposition of a flawed but innocent man. The bewildering swings of mood, of countenance, of behaviour, were the qualities of an ordinary man rather than an extraordinary murderer. The charm was real, but it was revealed to be a dangerous charm, with the power to enthral. The viewer was left feeling peculiarly uneasy. How much of this was Johnnie Aysgarth, and how much was Cary Grant?

Hitchcock had seen in Cary Grant that saturnine quality that had only been hinted at in earlier roles. Jeff Carter, in *Only Angels Have Wings*, kept his distance from the woman who loved him not because he felt nothing for her but rather, on the contrary, because he feared he felt too much; we see his coldness towards women as artificial rather than natural, a contrivance more to do with conscience than contempt. Hitchcock, however, had seen something else in that face than merely the look of a conventional, handsome leading man; he also saw a potential to be menacing, to be equivocal, to be mysterious.

Hitchcock, each time he worked with Grant, pushed a little further, a little deeper, played a little more knowingly on that seductive ambivalence. As John Robie in *To Catch a Thief* (1955), for example, his secrecy fascinates the woman who pursues him:

Frances: You're just not convincing, John. You're like an American character in an English movie. You just don't talk the way an American tourist ought to talk.

John: But don't you know that all the guidebooks say *don't* act like a tourist?

Frances: You're just not American enough to carry it off.

As Roger Thornhill in *North by Northwest* (1959), his reticence and the mystery that surrounds his identity are unnerving, suggesting a peculiarly dangerous sensuality:

Eve: This is ridiculous. You know that, don't you?

Roger: Yes.

Eve: I mean, we've hardly met.

Roger: That's right.

Eve: How do I know you aren't a murderer?

Roger: You don't.

Eve: Maybe you're planning to murder me right here, tonight.

Roger: Shall I?

Eve: Please do.

It was not that Hitchcock had been the first to glimpse the hidden depths in Grant's screen persona. Such depths, such complex under-tones, had been part of his appeal for some time; he held something back, he under-played, he invited further speculation. What was intriguing about Hitchcock's use of Grant was the *extent* of this emphasis upon his intimate strangeness. The secret shielded from view by most of Grant's earlier characters was the fact that he really wanted the women who were trying so hard to seduce him. The secret, or secrets, shielded by Johnnie Aysgarth in *Suspicion*, on the other hand, seemed more difficult to fathom; perhaps he really wanted the woman he had charmed, or perhaps he really despised her, or perhaps he really did not know what his true feelings were. His was a personality that aroused suspicions without ever entirely assuaging them.

Cary Grant, as a celebrated new star, came under ever greater public scrutiny. Some observers began to grow suspicious of him, too. How much of his characters' diffidence in the company of women was due to how the role was written, and how much was due to how it was played? Was Grant's appealing screen personality an exaggeration or a fabrication of his off-screen self? Was the elegant self-restraint he showed when women sought him out for seduction a sign of the respect he had for them or of the indifference he felt? Was he, by Hollywood's standards, a new kind of man, or not a 'man' at all? How 'gentle' could – should – a gentleman be? At what point does elegance become emasculation?[3] As Cary Grant won admirers, willing to accept the magic without seeking to explain it, he also attracted his share of critics, eager to work out how the trick was done. 'Cary Grant's man', wrote one such critic, 'gives me the feeling that he offers a woman satisfaction of her senses and affections in return for his peace ... [and] one does not feel that love will interest Grant permanently, only that he will give it a good try, and if that fails, he'll do his best not to let on.'[4]

Such speculation, perhaps, was the price Grant had to pay for the distinctiveness of his public image. People who met him in private were often surprised to find that although in certain ways he was just as he had seemed on screen (when Clint Eastwood was first introduced to him, for example, he turned to the others in the room and said: 'Oh, my God. He talks just like he does in the movies'[5]), in other ways he behaved quite differently. His cultured reserve, for instance, was more to do with acting than with any 'natural' inhibition. Peter Bogdanovich, seeing him on the set one day, recalls 'thinking, "He's just like Cary Grant". The only difference I noticed was that I'd never seen him laugh on the screen as he did in life –

because in person he really *laughs*, his eyes tear, and he looks joyous.'[6] Bogdanovich often remarked on the unexpectedness of this aspect of Grant's off-screen personality: 'It was something really open and giving. The most memorable thing about Cary for me was his sense of joy.'[7] It was considerably easier, of course, to discover the truth about some aspects of Grant's private self than it was to clarify other ambiguities. Perhaps he laughed more readily off screen than on, but, wondered his critics, did he love more readily, too? His intense heterosexual glamour glittered a little too brightly for those spectators who were used to more rugged, down-to-earth leading men. It was not, of course, impossible for observers at the time to suspect that the aggressive, pumped-up, swaggering masculinity displayed by the more 'conventional' men of the period, the 'tough guys' (such as Cagney, when he smacked Mae Clarke in the face with a cut grapefruit in *The Public Enemy*[8]), hid a deep-felt insecurity about their sexuality. It was not impossible, but it was not very common. Grant's more relaxed, more understated masculinity, on the other hand, was easier for contemporary critics to question.

Some of them took encouragement for their suspicions from the fact that Grant, as his stardom increased, became even more protective of his privacy. What, they wondered, did he have to be protective about? What did he, could he, have to hide?[9] As far as most reporters of the time were concerned, although his reticence frustrated them, they were prepared not to pry too often, nor too deeply, into his private life. They appreciated the fact that he was far from being the only uncooperative star in Hollywood, and, rather like the reporters who pursued C. K. Dexter Haven in *The Philadelphia Story*, they admired the stylish ways in which he sought to shut them out:

Liz: I was the only photographer whose camera you didn't smash. You were terribly nice about it – you threw it in the ocean.

Macauley: Oh. One of *those*, huh?

Dexter: Yes. I had a strange idea our honeymoon was *our* business.

Liz: Incidentally: he paid for all the cameras. I got a nice little letter of apology, too.

Macauley: Always the gentleman, huh?

Dexter: Except on occasion.

Most journalists were content to reach some kind of understanding with Grant. In the mid-thirties, for example, in Bristol – after an unfortunate altercation at the funeral of his father, during which a photographer's camera was smashed – Grant offered the Bristol press a deal: in return for promising to leave him and his family in peace, he would notify local reporters of forthcoming visits and make himself available for a brief picture session and interview.[10] Certain journalists in Hollywood, such as Jim Bacon, Roderick Mann, Sheilah Graham and Joe Hyams, had similar informal arrangements that proved to be mutually beneficial. Others, however, came to resent the long silences, the refusal to confide in them, the reluctance to criticise or gossip about other stars. 'Why should a publicised person cause special excitement?' Grant complained. 'Why is it not sufficient to see and enjoy the performance of a great entertainer or athlete and then leave him or her alone?'[11] Abigail Van Buren, author of the syndicated 'Dear Abby' column, confirms that, to her knowledge, Grant 'never gossiped. You would never hear him say, "Don't tell anyone, but . . ."'[12] A publicist also noted that Grant 'seemed a little put out when people asked him even seemingly innocent questions that sounded as though they could be gossipy'.[13] Some reporters, and, in particular, Hedda Hopper and Louella Parsons – the two most prominent and powerful gossip columnists in Hollywood during the 1940s – saw Grant's stubborn refusal to co-operate as an act of provocation, a challenge that, as a matter of principle, they could not fail to take up.

Most of Grant's contemporaries, as his friend David Niven recalled, 'played a humiliating game of subterfuge and flattery having long since decided that it was far less troublesome to have them with us than against us'.[14] If there had to be gossip, most stars concluded, then it was important for them to do whatever they could to ensure that only the gossip that reflected favourably on their reputations would make it into print. Slurs about someone's 'deviant' sexuality could be countered by the gossip columnist agreeing to 'reveal' the news of a reassuring (and sometimes entirely non-existent) romantic entanglement, and extra-marital affairs could be explained away by tales of on-set arguments or 'innocent clowning' in fashionable night-spots. 'They could help careers and they could hinder careers,' wrote Niven, 'and they could make private lives hell, but if there was talent they could not stop enough people getting to the top and . . . if there was no talent, they could not manufacture it.'[15]

Grant, however, would not play along:

> As a younger man it puzzled me that so many people of prominence seemed so carelessly eager to reveal intimate, and what I considered to be private, matters about themselves, in public print. Why did they do it? Was it vanity? Did they crave publicity at any cost? Were they desperate to correct or revise past impressions by telling what *they* thought to be the truth about themselves? Did they write about themselves rather than suffer a further succession of inaccuracies written by someone else? Or did they hope that by personally telling their own personal experience they might help their fellow men?[16]

If others were too obtuse, or insecure, or cynical, to appreciate the difference between a principled discretion and a morbid secrecy, that, argued Grant, was their problem.

He was a freelance. Even when he was under contract to Paramount in the early thirties, he had made little effort to court the gossip columnists, or, indeed, to respond to their occasional criticisms and insinuations about him. He became more, rather than less, dismissive of their self-important posturings after his actions – beginning very early in his career – appeared to many onlookers to have been either shockingly imprudent or ill-advisedly mischievous. The first – and most notorious – act of defiance, or ingenuousness, was Grant's decision in the early thirties to share an apartment with his fellow actor, Randolph Scott.

Both men were contract players at Paramount. Scott, a year older than Grant, came from a much more prosperous background and was considerably more extrovert and less prone to worry than his friend. They appeared together in two movies: *Hot Saturday* (1932) and, more memorably, *My Favorite Wife* (1940). They decided, shortly before making the first of these movies early in 1932, to pool their resources and share an apartment at 1129½ North Sweetzer Avenue in West Hollywood, and then, a few months later, moved to a more substantial residence at 2177 West Live Oak Drive in the Los Feliz district. Early in 1934, after Grant had married his first wife, Virginia Cherrill, he moved with her into an apartment on Havenhurst. In the late summer of 1935, after Grant's traumatic divorce from Cherrill, he and Scott rented a beach house at 1018 Ocean Front Road in Santa Monica.[17] They continued to co-rent it until 1942, when Grant married Barbara Hutton (although they had made a deal that whichever one of them re-married first would keep possession of the house, Grant decided to move out and he sold his share to Scott). It was a relationship and a living arrangement which, as time went on, struck many people in Hollywood as odd, and the gossip columnists whom Grant had treated with such contempt seized on the story with relish.

Ben Maddox, a 'tame' journalist as far as Grant was concerned, had been a guest at one of the first dinner parties hosted by the two men. His published remarks were just the kind of thing that Paramount had wanted to hear: 'Need I add', he concluded, 'that all the eligible (and a number of the *in*eligible) ladies-about-Hollywood are dying to be dated by these handsome lads? Cary tears around in a new Packard roadster and Randy flashes by in a new Cadillac. Oh-oh-oh, how the girls want to take a ride!'[18] It was not long, however, before the studio-prompted press coverage began to appear counterproductive. Photographs of Grant and Scott relaxing by their swimming pool, having breakfast together and sharing the washing-up, moved one columnist to suggest tartly that Paramount's two young stars were 'carrying the buddy business a bit too far'.[19]

The apparent 'cosiness' of the living arrangements was not quite as it seemed. The house was fairly spacious, with seven bedrooms, and it was rare for Scott and Grant not to have any guests staying with them. David Niven and Robert Coote (and, on occasion, Errol Flynn) were their near-neighbours, also sharing a beach house (which became such a notorious centre for alcoholic over-indulgence and marathon partying that Grant referred to it affectionately as 'Cirrhosis by the Sea').[20] On various occasions during that time such friends of Grant and Scott as Ginger Rogers, Howard Hughes, Dorothy Lamour, Niven, Coote, Flynn, Carole Lombard, Noël Coward and Phyllis Brooks spent time there as guests, most Sundays would feature star-studded parties and William Randolph Hearst, Jnr., remembered the house as 'a bachelor's paradise', with 'girls running in and out of there like a subway station'.[21] Decoys, said the doubters. 'I let people think or say whatever they want to,' Grant told those few reporters he was prepared to confide in. 'I can't control anyone's thoughts. I have enough trouble controlling my own.'[22]

It made no difference. As far as certain gossip columnists were concerned, it was 'unnatural' for the two men to live under the same roof for so long, and Grant, as the bigger star and more aloof of the two, became a target of Hollywood's most homophobic reporters. Edith Gwynn, for example, a *Hollywood Reporter* columnist, was one of the first to start the whispering campaign. After her first few oblique references to the 'situation' had not had the desired effect of forcing Grant – or Scott – to treat her with greater respect, she grew ever more provocative and knowing in her remarks. In one column, for example, she shared with her readers her ideas for a party game, in which each star would represent a famous movie title: Greta Garbo, she suggested, might be *The Son-Daughter*, Marlene Dietrich could arrive as *Male and Female*, while Cary Grant, she thought, would be just right as *One Way Passage*.[23] When Grant was seen at a string of social events with Betty Furness,[24] Gwynn refused to believe that the relationship was genuine: 'Betty is still wearing a high hat . . . Be sure to ask Cary what is the height of indifference.'[25] Perhaps Grant knew that there was little he could say or do to change the minds of gossips such as Gwynn, but he certainly does not appear to have wavered in his determination to refuse to play the game according to their rules. He was, after all, the man who had the temerity to tell the redoubtable Hedda Hopper that 'my personal affairs are none of your Goddamned business'.[26]

As a consequence, the rumours of Grant's bisexuality circulated around Hollywood for the rest of his life. After his death, somewhat predictably, such rumours were made more well known with the publication of a number of sensationalistic articles and biographies,[27] the most brazen of which was Charles Higham and Roy Moseley's *Cary Grant: The Lonely Heart*, published in 1989.[28] It is clear that Grant had expected such a development: writing to Nancy Sinatra, he had said, 'The victimised dead cannot defend themselves. Though the fabrications are refuted by others close to them, the damage has been done. I've always conditioned my wife and daughter to expect the biographical worst . . .'[29] *Cary Grant: The Lonely Heart* was, in some ways, a serious and thorough study of the man, but, unfortunately, it proved to be a thoroughly prejudiced survey of the gossip. This self-consciously revisionist biography began by announcing solemnly that 'the honest biographer cannot shirk the painful truth, even at the risk of being called deliberately sensationalist'.[30] The 'facts', the authors insisted, were 'unavoidable': Cary Grant was a bisexual who was forced for all of his life to hide behind the fiction of his heterosexual image.[31]

If there was some shard of previously obscure and undocumented 'fact' about Grant's sexuality embedded in this biography, it was a virtually impossible task to extract it from the mire of rumours, falsehoods, red herrings, internal contradictions and groundless rhetoric. First, it was alleged that Grant's 'cruel and despotic' mother caused him to 'wreak vengeance' upon the women who loved him throughout his adult life.[32] Then there was the first of innumerable attempts at cod–Freudian analysis: Grant had once said that his earliest memory was of being 'publicly bathed in a portable enamel bathtub . . . protesting against being dunked and washed all over in front of my grandmother'; Grant, looking back on this moment, wondered to himself why he, as a 'mere baby', had experienced 'such overwhelming modesty'.[33] Higham and Moseley had no doubts as to what the experience revealed: namely, that he had been 'ashamed even at that four-year-old stage of exhibiting his genitals to a woman'.[34] They wink and nudge knowingly at the reader a little further on, when they recount his early stage performances, when, dressed in certain costumes, 'he even looked positively effeminate, as though he were aching to appear in drag'[35] (as, one presumes the implication is, all bisexuals do). Much of the remainder of the biography does its best to suggest that the kind of company he kept was proof enough of his 'true' nature: in New York, John Orry-Kelly ('a handsome, effeminate youth'[36]), Moss Hart ('quietly genteel'[37]) and Phil Charig; in Hollywood, Randolph Scott (of course), Howard Hughes, Noël Coward, Cole Porter and Clifford Odets. The authors show themselves to be capable of trusting anyone as long as he or she suits their purpose: they are satisfied, for example, that Grant had an affair with Howard Hughes (although they admit 'it can only have been brief and superficial') because it was 'testified to by three of Hughes's lieutenants and his publicist'[38] (one presumes that all four of them must have been hiding in the bedroom closet at the time), whereas when Greta Thyssen, a former Miss Denmark, is quoted on the subject of the passionate affair she had with Grant (she recalled him telling her that she had 'the sexiest-looking body I have ever seen'), the authors feel that it is, in *this* instance, advisable to point out that 'whether this relationship was as romantic as Miss Thyssen claimed is uncertain'.[39] At times the authors are simply inconsistent: referring to the serious love-affair that Grant is thought by most people to have had with Sophia Loren, they point out, somewhat disingenuously, that 'there is no evidence that the relationship . . . was consummated'[40] (Howard Hughes's voyeuristic 'lieutenants' and publicist, presumably, being otherwise engaged at the time), but, four pages on, the *louche* spirit of the discussion moves them to describe Loren as Grant's 'former lover'. Later in the book, when it is mentioned that Grant hired a personal assistant who, the authors glumly admit, 'was not homosexual', they explain this anomaly by pointing out that this 'provided good cover for Cary (a gay assistant would have instantly drawn untoward gossip)'[41] (which is why, one imagines, Grant had shared a house for so long with Randolph Scott!).

One 'truth' that does emerge, inadvertently, from such sensationalist accounts is that it is quite possible to find someone somewhere in Hollywood who is prepared to 'confirm' almost any rumour about almost any star.[42] A producer once complained that if 'you're not everything to everybody, you're nobody in Hollywood'.[43] Patrick McGilligan remarked on the subject of rumours about certain stars' homosexuality: 'Interestingly, that's the first bit of juicy gossip you hear about *everyone* in Hollywood.'[44] It is, indeed, harder to find Hollywood stars from the thirties and forties who were *not*, at any time, the subjects of such gossip, than it is to find those who *were*. The excitable and unpleasantly homophobic Edith Gwynn, for example, writing in the mid-thirties, alluded to the possibility of Hollywood becoming a 'long-haired town for males', mentioning by name Gary Cooper, James Cagney, Grant and Scott.[45] In 1951, *Motion Picture* magazine made the entirely unfounded allegation that 'Jimmy Stewart didn't get married for so long because he was the type of male with no great interest in the opposite sex', adding that 'Cary Grant heard this one about himself, too, although no one who knows Cary can exactly figure out why'.[46]

Englishmen in Hollywood were regarded with especial suspicion.[47] David Niven recalled a conversation he had with Hedda Hopper in which she told him that she had once warned Elizabeth Taylor against marrying Michael Wilding because he had 'long indulged in homosexual relations with Stewart Granger'.[48] He did his best to assure her that she had been mistaken. 'Isn't it true', she replied, 'that Michael Wilding was kicked out of the British Navy during the war because he was a homosexual?' Nonsense, said Niven, who described Wilding's 'gallant record and explained the true meaning of being "invalided" out of the service'.[49] 'Well, I know that he and Granger once had a yacht together in the South of France and I know what went on aboard that yacht.' 'So do I,' answered Niven, 'and it's a miracle that the population of France didn't double.'[50]

It is notable that Sal Mineo, who spoke openly about his own bisexuality late on in his life, was not prepared to accept uncritically many of the allegations about other stars: 'Everyone's got those rumors following him around, whether it's true or not . . . *Everyone*'s supposed to be bi, starting way back with Gary Cooper and on through Brando and Clift and Dean and Newman and . . . you want me to stop?'[51] He also noted how some of the gossip began: 'there's always the roomie thing in Hollywood – Brando and Wally Cox, Brando and Tony Curtis, Cary Grant and Randolph Scott – and there are always rumors about them, even if they aren't true . . . I think Hollywood secretly *wants* to think it's true.'[52] Others agreed: 'Facts don't interest people. Everyone likes to be in on the inside story. Whether it's true or not is a secondary consideration. If it's spicy, then it's interesting.'[53] Katharine Hepburn dismissed the rumours out of hand: 'Everyone is called a homosexual in Hollywood.'[54]

As far as the rumours concerning Grant are concerned, his friends and colleagues have always refuted them. One said that 'I was *amazed* at what I heard. They never could have known him.'[55] Virginia Cherrill, speaking in 1989, complained: 'I read a few pages in a recent book about Cary and knew right away it was a complete fabrication . . . I don't know why people have to destroy someone's name after he's dead.'[56] Joe Hyams, who was not usually particularly unwilling to be indiscreet about Grant, has told interviewers that he 'never found an inkling of Cary Grant's bisexuality'.[57]

It is certainly undeniable that Grant did have close relationships with women throughout his adult life. According to Fay Wray, his co-star in *Nikki*, they were both tempted to have an affair in 1931, during the run of the play: 'His eyes would flash when he looked at me . . . They said, "I love what you have to say. I like you." But I was married. The timing was not right for romance.'[58] She also claimed that three years later, after Grant had begun his movie career, 'Randolph Scott told me, "Cary is in love with you". Many years later, in 1945, after I had married Bob Riskin, I overheard Cary at a party say to Bob, "Be good to her. I was so in *love* with her! But I wouldn't have been a good husband. I pay too much attention to the position of a sofa!"'[59] The screenwriter Robert Lord remembers spending many days in the company of the young Archie Leach at San Simeon, the palatial Santa Monica beach house William Randolph Hearst had purchased for his mistress, Marion Davies; Leach, recalled Lord, 'was laying Marion Davies, or trying to'.[60] Hal Roach said of the Cary Grant of the mid-thirties in Hollywood, 'I never knew any man that was in love with so many gals as Cary was.'[61] Betty Furness, an actor and close friend, several decades after her relationship with Grant had ended, confessed to still feeling angry about the gossip columnists' cynicism: 'I would simply like to state that my relationship with Cary was a romance on both parts. It was not set up by anyone . . . he was beyond any question the most attractive, charming, funny, sweet, marvelous man I've ever known . . . and I haven't met his rival yet.'[62]

In 1935, it seems, Grant considered marrying Mary Brian, his co-star in *The Amazing Quest of Ernest Bliss*, which he was making in England. 'He was the most fun and the most romantic man I've ever known.'[63] According to Brian's account, 'We had fallen in love and talked about marriage and children.'[64] Grant, it seems, had second thoughts, and, back in Hollywood, started dating Phyllis Brooks, whom fan magazines referred to as 'the next Mrs Grant' for the following two years or so.[65] 'I'm going to marry Brooksie', he told his friends, 'and have all the children we can. That's what life's all about.'[66] Although the marriage was being planned, Grant and Brooks's mother loathed each other with increasing intensity: 'My mother never liked anybody I went out with, but Cary presented the biggest threat.'[67] Eventually, under the strain of family arguments, the relationship ended, but Brooks, fifty years later, still referred to Grant as 'the love of my life':[68]

He was imperfect as are all we mortals, but he was my love. He was careful, gentle, kind, tender and fatherly to me. So far as I knew, he was a loving and passionate heterosexual. He had a very strict moral code as to loyalty, fidelity and like virtues, and lived by them when I knew him.[69]

Had Grant been anxious to disguise his real sexual proclivities, one might suppose he would have encouraged stories which cast him in a reassuringly heterosexual light, but that does not appear to have been the case. When Sophia Loren – whom some of Grant's friends regarded as the great love of his life, and to whom Grant proposed marriage in the late fifties – announced her plans for a television movie based on her autobiography, it became clear that her affair with Grant would feature prominently. Far from welcoming this opportunity to have his masculine image reaffirmed through association with the lusciously feminine Loren, Grant threatened a lawsuit to prevent the production from reaching the screen. 'I cannot believe that anyone would exploit an old friendship like this,' he was reported as saying at the time.[70]

'Cary wasn't a womaniser,' Jean Dalrymple has remarked, 'but he loved women. He was always looking for one to make him happy. I don't know why his wives didn't in the beginning.'[71] Bill Weaver, who became Grant's assistant in the late sixties, wrote that 'there was never any doubting' Grant's affection for women: 'He needed their company, took pleasure in their presence, and seemed absurdly hopeful, as his first four marriages showed, of one day finding the ideal companion.'[72] Grant was married five times. 'He went head-first into the affrays,' wrote David Niven, 'throwing caution to the winds and quite convinced, in his boundless enthusiasm, that each romance was the one for which he had been put into the world.'[73] His first marriage, to Virginia Cherrill, was the shortest, lasting barely seven months: 'My possessiveness and fear of losing her brought about the very condition it feared: the loss of her.'[74] Seven years later, in 1942, he married the Woolworth heiress Barbara Hutton. It lasted three tempestuous years: 'Our marriage had little foundation for a promising future. Our backgrounds – family, educational and cultural – were completely unalike.'[75] It had not helped when a waspish society columnist wrote about Hutton's new husband as a 'former Coney Island hot dog salesman'.[76] The couple were dubbed 'Cash and Cary', which made things even worse (it was only made public years later that Grant had insisted on signing a pre-nuptial agreement relinquishing any claim to Hutton's fortune in the event of a divorce). Grant disliked Hutton's high society friends: 'If one more phony noble had turned up, I would have suffocated.'[77] All the old class tensions returned. When Hutton hosted her elaborate dinner parties, Grant would usually stay upstairs reading scripts, or, on those rare occasions when he did make an appearance, he would 'entertain' her friends with a series of deliberately vulgar mock-cockney routines: 'I was ostracised by all the people I hoped to be ostracised by, and I couldn't have been happier.'[78] Years after their divorce, Hutton commented that 'Cary Grant had no title, and of my four husbands, he is the one I loved most . . . He was so sweet, so gentle, it didn't work out, but I loved him.'[79] His marriage to Betsy Drake, his third wife, lasted considerably longer – from Christmas 1949 until 1962 – but it was put under a great deal of strain for much of that period.[80] There were two more marriages – first to Dyan Cannon in 1965 (ending in divorce in 1968), and finally to Barbara Harris in 1981.[81]

In *North by Northwest* (1959), a woman asks Grant's character, 'What happened to the first two marriages?' 'My wives divorced me,' he replies. 'Why?' 'They said I led too dull a life.' Cary Grant, when interviewers asked him what happened to the first four marriages, gave them a similar reply:

> They all left me. I didn't leave any of them. They all walked out on me. Maybe my marriages were heavily influenced by something in my subconscious that's related to my early years and the way I envisioned my mother. That's a pat answer, I know, but it's very possible. However, I'm not really sure why they left me. Maybe they just got bored.[82]

On another occasion he said: 'My wives and I were never one. We were competing.'[83] Reflecting on past failures, he remarked that 'when I am married, I want to be single, and when I am single, I want to be married'.[84] 'If his disillusionments were many,' wrote David Niven, 'his defeats were few and he always, with great gallantry, took the blame when things went wrong, saying that he had been too egocentric to give the union a proper chance'.[85] Most women, Grant said, 'are instinctively wiser and emotionally more mature than men. They know our insecurities. A man rushes about trying to prove himself. It takes him much longer to feel comfortable about getting married.'[86] He admitted that he was not proud of his marriage record: 'It was not the fault of Hollywood, but my own inadequacies. Of my own inconstancy. My mistrust of constancy.'[87] By the time he met Barbara Harris, he believed, he had finally 'learned that love demands nothing and understands all without reproach';[88] for much of his life, he confessed, 'I really didn't understand love. I wanted to be, you know, macho.'[89]

As to the long-standing gossip about his sexuality, which seemed to grow ever more widespread after each of the first four marriages ended in divorce, Grant did, after his movie career had ended, break his silence. A few months before he died, he told one movie critic that he had read some of the publications about himself: 'They all repeat the rumors that I'm a tightwad and that I'm a homosexual. Now I don't feel that either of those is an insult, but it's all nonsense.'[90] A few years earlier, in 1977, he said:

> When I was a young and popular star, I'd meet a girl with a man and maybe she'd say something nice about me and then the guy would say, 'Yeah, but I hear he's really a fag.' It's ridiculous, but they say it about all of us. Now in fact, that guy is doing me a favor. Number one, he's expressed an insecurity about the girl. Number two, he has provoked curiosity about me in her. Number three, that girl zeroes in on my bed to see for herself, and the result is that the guy has created the exact situation he wanted to avoid.[91]

'Look at it this way', he suggested to another persistent interviewer who asked him about the rumours:

> I've always tried to dress well. I've had some success in life. I've enjoyed my success and I include in that success some relationships with very special women. If someone wants to say I'm gay, what can I do? I think it's probably said about every man who's been known to do well with women. I don't let that sort of thing bother me. What matters to me is that I know who I am.[92]

The gossip columnists' stream of innuendoes about Grant's sexuality were not the only rumours that dogged him during the forties.

When war broke out in Europe, Grant, along with other British actors in Hollywood, was vilified in some quarters for his apparent reluctance to return and sign up. One 1942 article in *Picturegoer*, for example, declared that all Englishmen still working in Hollywood should be filmed exclusively in black and white, 'since Technicolor would undoubtedly show up the yellow of their skin'.[93] The British press was quick to depict the Hollywood British as having 'gone with the wind up' in their country's hour of need. Some, such as David Niven, had promptly disengaged themselves from whatever commitments they had in Hollywood and left to join up.[94]

Although Grant had been planning for some time to apply for US citizenship, he still thought of himself as British, and, during the 'phoney war' of 1939–40, he had been keen to do (and be seen to do) his duty. The problem was that nobody – least of all the British government – seemed ready and able to define precisely what that duty was. 'You feel so damn helpless here,' Grant told an American war correspondent. 'I want to go back. I could be an ARP warden. I could be a fire-fighter. I could do something.'[95] Although it was not widely known at the time, it appears that he volunteered for service in the Royal Navy, but the Foreign Office advised the Admiralty that he, along with several other applicants, would be of more use in Hollywood, promoting positive images of the British to the American public.[96]

In the summer of 1940, Grant and Cedric Hardwicke, as representatives of the British colony, flew to Washington for a meeting with Lord Lothian, the British ambassador, to solicit his advice about how best to serve the war effort. Lothian instructed those British actors, writers and directors who were regarded, as far as the military was concerned, as 'mature' (and Grant, at thirty-six, would have been classed among them), to 'stay put and carry on doing what you do best'.[97] If this directive had been as well-publicised in Britain as it was in the US, a great deal of the subsequent scurrilous gossip and negative press coverage might have been avoided; unfortunately, it was not, and Grant, along with the other Englishmen abroad, was subjected to frequent movie-magazine demands to 'come home like David Niven'.[98]

In fact, according to some sources, it seems possible that Grant was – and had been since the late thirties – working as a special agent for the British Intelligence Services.[99] This has yet to be proven,[100] but, on 18 April 1947, King George VI awarded Grant the King's Medal for Service in the Cause of Freedom, citing his 'Outstanding service to the British War Relief Society'.[101] The award was not made public at the time. He had become an American citizen on 26 June 1942,[102] but he remained, it was said, 'very pro-British' and continued to be 'terribly British-minded'.[103]

The FBI was, apparently, concerned about just how 'American-minded' Grant was. He was known to have friends and colleagues who held strong left-wing views, and, during the forties, he appeared in several movies with themes or dialogue which seem to have alarmed those on the alert for signs of 'un-American' ideology.[104] In 1944, the Los Angeles office of the FBI issued a memorandum entitled 'Communist Infiltration of the Motion Picture Industry', listing the personnel of *Citizen Tom Paine*, *The Master Race*, and Grant's collaboration with Clifford Odets, *None But the Lonely Heart*. The FBI also noted that Lucille Ball, Ira Gershwin, John Garfield, Walter Huston and Cary Grant were among those people in Holly-wood who had 'Communist connections'.[105] On the list of movies produced or released between 1 January and 20 November 1944 that were said to be 'loaded' with Communists were three that starred Grant: *Mr Lucky*, *None but the Lonely Heart* and *Destination Tokyo*. In 1947, Lela Rogers (the mother of Ginger Rogers and RKO's 'expert' on Communist infiltration in the movie industry) told the House on Un-American Activities Committee that *None but the Lonely Heart* – which featured Grant speaking such lines as 'You're not going to get me to work 'ere and squeeze pennies out of little people poorer than I am' – was blatantly anti-capitalist in its sentiments.

The movie role which seemed almost to have been fashioned from the multiple suspicions and rumours about Cary Grant was that of Devlin, the FBI agent in Alfred Hitchcock's romantic thriller *Notorious* (1946).[106] Devlin is a spy; he is a professional dissembler, secretive, deceitful, emotionally impotent and, beneath the cool exterior, acutely vulnerable. The plot concerns Alicia Huberman (Ingrid Bergman), whose father has been apprehended as a Nazi agent. She is approached by Devlin with the chance to work as a counter-spy in Brazil, uncovering enemy secrets connected with a man named Alexander Sebastian (Claude Rains). Devlin and Alicia fall in love, but he is unable to override her orders, which tie her to Sebastian, who proposes marriage. Devlin, demoralised, has to continue to see her, even though he believes that she had not loved him enough to defy the orders. When Sebastian realises that she is an American agent, he contrives to murder her by slow poisoning, and Devlin, suspicious of her declining health, tries to rescue her.

All of the central characters in *Notorious* are purveyors or victims of sexual intrigue. Devlin, for example, is unable to articulate his true, most intimate feelings for Alicia:

Alicia: This is a very strange love-affair.

Devlin: Why?

Alicia: Maybe the fact that you don't love me.

Devlin: When I don't love you, I'll let you know.

Alicia: You haven't said anything.

Devlin: Actions speak louder than words.

'I've always been afraid of women,' he says early on, 'but I'll get over it.' Soon, however, he has to let her be sent into sexual enslavement to Sebastian. Sebastian, too, is a sexual blackmailer: jealous of Alicia's friendship with Devlin, which had been designed to appear to him as merely tourist-innocent, he challenges her to put an end to his suspicions: 'Would you care to *prove* to me that he doesn't matter to you?'

Hitchcock – assisted by Ted Tetzlaff's extraordinary key lighting – again plays on the darker side of Grant's screen persona. Devlin's first appearance is suitably curious; we see only the back of his head as he sits, silent and in silhouette, observing the bright and animated people who face him. In almost every scene, Devlin wears a tightly-knotted tie, a buttoned-down collar and coat, and an expression of guarded unease. His voice is buttoned-down, too: deep, clipped and deadly serious, each word withdrawn before it can be weighed up by the listener. On those rare occasions when he smiles, it is usually purely for the deception of onlookers, such as when he discusses in public with Alicia the secrets she has uncovered. In the earlier memorable kissing scene that begins on the balcony, Devlin and Alicia talk of their plans for supper as they nibble each other's lips and ears, and the camera follows them as they move, slowly, whispering, embracing, through shadow and light, through the living-room, to the telephone in the hall, and finally to the door of the apartment, tracking quietly, closely, the kiss that opens and closes, the casual carnality of their exchange. What impresses itself on the viewer, apart from the technical virtuosity of the scene, is Devlin's coolness, his eerie stillness, as Alicia kisses him, lets her cheek brush against his, her hand stroke along his shoulder, her eyes open into his gaze. She lives in the light, he lurks in the shadows; she is open, he is closed; she wears a bold striped blouse with a bared midriff, he covers it up before they go outside. Later, when obliged by his own sharp sense of self-imposed duty to ensure that she continues with her orders, this reserve allows him to wear the mask of indifference without evident discomfort:

Alicia: Oh, I see: now's the time for you to tell me you have a wife and two adoring children and this madness between us must stop immediately.

Devlin: I'll bet you've heard that line often enough.

Alicia: Right below the belt every time, Dev.

The next time that they will kiss will be to fool her new husband, to distract him from the evidence of their espionage. Devlin, now that he is only acting, kisses her more passionately, more dramatically, than before. Only when there is no genuine risk to his own feelings can he behave affectionately to another. He fears love, he avoids pain, he refuses to trust; he seems prepared to subject himself, and the woman he cares for, to the harshest political expediency rather than save himself from the aridity of lovelessness. 'Why won't you believe in me, Devlin – just a *little* bit?' she begs him. One watches the slow, methodical death of a woman and the inexorable descent into quiet desperation of a man, step by step, scene by scene, until Devlin begins, at last, to break down his own emotional constriction. 'I couldn't stand it any longer,' he whispers to her, 'I had to tell you that I love you.' She is astonished, and relieved, and thrilled by his sudden wakefulness: 'Oh, you love me!' The camera moves in tight to his face, his dark eyes: 'I couldn't tell you before,' he confesses, 'I was a fatheaded guy . . . full of pain.'

It is a mark of Grant's understanding of the nature of the role that the character's emotional infantilism is revealed not in what he does, but rather in what he does not do. His love is apparent but not acted upon – because of the chronic risk of self-disclosure. By this character's association with a well-known element in Grant's screen persona, audiences were encouraged to confront one of the most seductive and troubling aspects of the man who is in love but so 'full of pain' that guilt comes close to winning out over the admission of need.

Was Devlin Grant? Some of the gossip-mongers of the time – and long after – wanted to think so. Higham and Moseley, for example, did not hesitate to make the connection: Devlin's 'possessiveness, sexual ambiguity and deep-seated guilt and fear are from beginning to end Cary Grant's own.'[107] It is true that Grant himself had spoken of his struggle to become less possessive after the failure of his first marriage. As, however, for the rumours concerning his sexual ambiguity, and the guilt and fear that were supposed to have followed from it, they were, and they remain, just rumours.

What *is* clear is that, in at least one very significant way, Cary Grant was very unlike Devlin. Devlin is, for most of the movie, a moral marionette, responsive to the demands of his superiors and professional politics. Grant, admirably, was not. He refused to conform to the conventional expectations about how a Hollywood celebrity should behave. He kept his own counsel. He treated the self-important gossip columnists of the time with the contempt that many of his colleagues thought that they deserved, but were too fearful to say out loud. 'I guess,' he said, 'that anyone that's publicised is not allowed to be a fairly decent individual.'[108] At its worst, his behaviour seemed secretive and stubborn just for the sake of it, and it may, perhaps, have encouraged precisely the kind of suspicious attitudes towards him which he, and those close to him, found so galling. At its best, however, there was a certain rare gallantry about it which was capable of shaming the cowardice of so many of his Hollywood contemporaries.

One instance of this occurred at the end of the forties, when his co-star in *Notorious*, Ingrid Bergman, left her husband and first child for the Italian director Roberto Rossellini, with whom she soon became pregnant. Hollywood blacklisted her; religious groups in the US denounced her, and senators attacked her as 'a powerful influence for evil'.[109] Most of her old colleagues and friends in Hollywood – even some who had been her lovers – did not dare to defend her and incur the wrath of the moralising columnists and pressure groups. Cary Grant, however, spoke out, on several occasions, in support of her:

> Ingrid Bergman is a fascinating, full-blooded yet temperate woman who has the courage to live in accord with her needs, and strength enough to accept and benefit by the consequences of her beliefs in an inhibited, critical and frightened society. Ingrid needs no uninvited busybody to proclaim her debts; she knows and pays them herself. I commend her highly to you.[110]

When she won an Oscar in 1957 for her performance in *Anastasia*, she asked Grant to accept it on her behalf. 'For years [Cary] was the only one in Hollywood who ever contacted me,' she said. 'I had done no wrong in his eyes.'[111] Grant, who knew that among those people who had denounced her conduct were many who had done much worse, and much more often, said simply, 'I can't stand hypocrisy.'[112] That was not how Johnnie Aysgarth, or Devlin, or even C. K. Dexter Haven would have behaved, but it was typical of the kind of man that Cary Grant really was.

INDEPENDENCE

Eve: I ought to know more about you.

Roger: Well, what more could you know?

Eve: You're an advertising man, that's all I know.

Roger: That's right. Oh. Train's a little unsteady.

Eve: Who isn't?

Roger: What else do you know?

Eve: You've got taste in clothes, taste in food . . .

Roger: . . . and taste in women. I like your flavor.

Eve: You're very clever with words. You can probably make them do anything for you. Sell people things they don't need, make women who don't know you fall in love with you . . .

Roger: I'm beginning to think I'm underpaid.

NORTH BY NORTHWEST

CHAPTER X

The Actor as Producer

I'm no longer just the nice young man who knew how to put his hands in his pockets and smile broadly. I know the entertainment industry requires hard work, studies, determination and the drive for perfection, which one never achieves.

CARY GRANT

I invent inventions . . . I happen to be working on my greatest invention at the present time: a human animal which don't look for a master. Ain't easy!

ERNIE MOTT

'I was never interested in acting in films, I was interested in the economics of the business.'[1] It was a knowingly misleading remark – not only was Grant an enthusiastic performer, he was also fascinated by the craft of acting in front of a camera – but it was right in one respect: Cary Grant, more so than most other movie stars of the period, had a pronounced interest in, and talent for, the economy of stardom. The director Stanley Kramer said of Grant: 'When he exhibited himself, he was "Cary Grant" – the handsome leading man, star-incarnate. Grant never gave the appearance of being "commercial", and he was probably as commercial an actor that ever lived.'[2] The forties witnessed not only the consolidation of Grant's success as a performer, but also the confirmation of his expertise as a businessman. The actor became a producer.

Grant had always craved both artistic and financial independence; he achieved both through a combination of courage, good fortune, intelligence and prudence. David Niven once said of Grant that 'long before computers went into general release, Cary had one in his own brain: a brilliant business man himself, he was fascinated by the rich and the ultra-successful'.[3] Howard Hughes was a particularly great influence on Grant. As a very young millionaire, Hughes had formed the Caddo Corporation and begun making movies, such as *Hell's Angels* (1930); later on, after a break from the industry, he returned in 1947 to buy himself into RKO. Since he first met Hughes early on in his movie career, Grant had come to rely on him for advice: 'He was a brilliant man. Way ahead of his time. I would listen to him for hours, not always understanding at the time exactly what he meant. But as time went by, his thoughts would be proven correct.'[4] Grant appears, in fact, to have learned from his business colleagues just as quickly and effectively as he learned from his fellow performers. By the late thirties, he had begun to devote much of his spare time to his multiple commercial activities. Douglas Fairbanks, Jnr., remembers that

> Cary used to do a lot of arbitrage. He would buy Japanese yen and sell English pounds and buy Italian lire or German marks. He did that every morning before work on *Gunga Din*. He'd look over the paper and buy and sell things and send messages to buy so many pounds and then sell so many yen, and so forth. I was fascinated.[5]

By the early forties, Grant's long-term success as a freelance actor was assured.[6] He had been the first major Hollywood star to escape the exclusive long-term studio contract, and also the first to negotiate a ten per cent cut of the gross deal for his movies. He had power. He had control. He had ambition and vision. He had his own business. Frank Vincent, whom Grant had first met, as Archie Leach, back in New York in 1922, had become his business partner in 1936; although, formally, Vincent was, from that point on, Grant's representative, Grant would, in reality, be his own agent.[7] Having invested a considerable amount of his own money into what became known as the Frank Vincent Agency, Grant had come, by the end of the thirties, to play an increasingly active role in the firm's other business dealings: in 1940, for example, he helped re-negotiate a deal at MGM for another Vincent client, Greta Garbo, and a new contract for Rita Hayworth at Twentieth Century-Fox.[8] His behind-the-scenes negotiating skills were alluded to in 1944 by a columnist when Myron Selznick, the most important agent in Hollywood at that time, died: 'Now that Myron is gone, Cary Grant is the best agent in Hollywood.'[9] Grant also refurbished the agency's offices on Sunset Boulevard, making them the most luxurious in Hollywood. When Vincent died in 1946, Lew Wasserman at MCA took over the formal responsibility for negotiating Grant's movie contracts, but Grant did not sign on as a client; in an exceptional arrangement, Grant became MCA's sole non-exclusive client. Both Wasserman and Grant's lawyer-manager, Stanley Fox, represented him on each negotiation and split the customary ten per cent commission.

Stanley Fox became Grant's closest business colleague. He had persuaded Fox to give up private practice and represent him exclusively. Together they would, eventually, form a series of companies in order to produce his movies.[10] Fox explained the strategy:

> Ninety percent of Cary's income was being taxed, but we never took advantage of any dodges. We thought the dangers involved in those deals could, in the end, cost more money than the high taxes. So we formed different corporations for different situations. When Cary did a film, he was employed by the company for a salary that was less than he could get if he were working for a studio. But we owned the picture. The company would get seventy-five percent of the profits, and the studios would get the other twenty-five percent for putting up all the money and giving us whatever backing we needed. We got offices and an expense account.[11]

In the early 1940s, the memory of Paramount's cavalier (but by no means untypical) treatment of him was still fresh in Grant's mind. He did not much *like*, let alone *trust*, the studio bosses of the time, agreeing with Chaplin's description of them as 'inconsiderate, unsympathetic and short-sighted'.[12] The studios, in turn, were not keen to see Grant's bid for independence become a trend, and, as a result, there was a certain amount of negative publicity surrounding his business activities, alluding to his supposed 'money mad' attitude. 'I *like* money,' Grant declared, to no one's great surprise. 'Anybody know anyone who doesn't?'[13] Some writers, such as Sheilah Graham, sought to explain Grant's ambitions by claiming that he had 'an almost pathological fear of poverty'[14] – the persistence of which surprises only those fortunate enough never to have been poor themselves – while others, such as Alexander Walker, have chosen to focus on Grant's belief in the virtue of self-reliance: 'he didn't like things being done for him: he preferred to look after himself.'[15] His success may well have been envied by some of his fellow actors, but many others admired his nerve and his high ideals. His contract evolved over the years: each time something happened on a movie that he regarded as unacceptable, he remembered to cover that issue in the next agreement he made. He conducted his career boldly and enthusiastically, with relatively little thought given to the conventional wisdom, and the choices that he made demonstrated the courage to go anywhere he wanted – needed – for a challenge, a surprise, something memorable.

Grant was independent, but he was still fallible. In spite of his eye for the box-office and his extremely careful – sometimes torturous – deliberations before committing himself to new projects, he was still capable of making some injudicious choices.[16] *The Howards of Virginia* (1940), for example, was probably (alongside *Sylvia Scarlett*) the worst movie he ever made, and featured what was almost certainly his worst performance. It is, indeed, difficult to imagine just what he thought he was doing when he agreed to appear in this story set in eighteenth-century America during the period of the Revolutionary War. He played Matt Howard, a backwoodsman from Virginia – a friend of Thomas Jefferson, to boot – who marries the daughter of an aristocratic family. Looking absurdly awkward in buckskin, pony-tailed hairpiece and tricornered hat, and sounding equally awkward in a bewildering range of accents (Somerset, Scottish, Irish), he could surely not have seemed more obviously miscast. 'I don't belong in costumes,' he admitted years later. 'I was so bad in *The Howards of Virginia*.'[17] He was better in *Night and Day* (1946), a thoroughly fanciful 'biopic' about the life and music of Cole Porter, and it was hugely successful at the box-office, but it was still a mediocre piece of work (the most risible moment probably being the scene in which Porter is inspired by the sound of raindrops to compose the title tune). 'If I'm ever stupid enough to be caught working with you again,' Grant is said to have told the director in a rare outburst, once the movie had been shot, 'you'll know I'm either broke or I've lost my mind.'[18] Another strange choice was the role of a famous brain surgeon in *Crisis* (1950), which proved to be so unpopular with audiences expecting a more conventional 'Cary

Grant movie' that an executive in the studio's sales department remarked that 'we could've made more money with that picture if we'd cut the film up and sold it for mandolin picks'.[19]

Grant not only had cause, on occasion, to regret his decision to appear in certain movies; he also had good cause to regret his decision to decline certain movie offers.[20] In 1953, for example, he was offered the starring role of Norman Maine, the drunken, fading actor who adopts a young and struggling singer, in George Cukor's re-make of *A Star is Born* (1954). James Mason, who accepted the role, heard that Grant had 'reached the point of participating in at least one story conference . . . before it dawned on him that he was wasting their time'.[21] Some have sought to explain Grant's decision by pointing to the fact that, for a time in the early forties, he had gone through a phase of – for him – heavy drinking, and, as a consequence (and remembering his father's alcoholism), the prospect of the part of the moody drunk may have struck him as too reliant on painful personal memories.[22] Whatever the reasons for Grant's refusal to take the part, the fact remains that he missed out on a prestigious movie, and a challenging role for which James Mason received an Oscar nomination. Being a free agent did not make the maintenance of Grant's successful career any easier than it would have been under the paternalistic aegis of a long-term studio contract; if anything, it made it even harder. Grant, unlike other stars, had the licence to be unpredictable, to surprise his audience, to stretch himself and revise his image. He also had, as a result, the freedom to stall or ruin his career through making the wrong choices and alienating his admirers. The pressure on him was unusually great. Throughout the forties, therefore, Grant, as a freelance actor, went through periods of grand artistic ambition and cautious commercial calculation, his business sense sometimes in harmony with his artistic sense and sometimes at odds with it.[23]

Arsenic and Old Lace (1944) was perhaps *the* movie of Grant's from the forties that best captured the way in which his commercial and creative concerns sometimes contradicted each other. If Grant had really been, as he once joked, only interested in the business and not in the performance, he should have been reasonably pleased with *Arsenic and Old Lace*. This black comic farce, about drama critic Mortimer Brewster and his two sweet little aunts who happen to serve their guests elderberry wine laced with arsenic, had already proved itself to be an extremely popular stage play on Broadway, and the screen version, directed by Frank Capra, was well received by the critics and enormously popular with audiences.[24] Capra had persuaded Grant to play the role of Mortimer Brewster by offering him a salary of $160,000, which was $35,000 more than Capra's own salary.[25] Grant's popularity, and bank account, were enhanced by his taking part in the project. He should have been pleased with it, but he was not.

Grant's attitude to *Arsenic and Old Lace* was more that of the serious performer than of the cynical businessman. He donated all of his salary to wartime charities, and he took on the project knowing that it would not reach the public for a considerable time (the deal for the movie rights had stipulated that it could be released only after the play had closed on Broadway).[26] He had wanted to work with Frank Capra, and needed to try his hand at a more expressive, dramatic kind of comedy than the kind he was associated with. It did not, however, work out to his satisfaction. Although he found Capra to be 'a dear, dear man',[27] he did not feel that the director quite understood the nature of his comic style. As Gregory Peck remarked, 'Capra was a very strong, determined, hands-on director, and he had Cary doing a lot of squirrely things . . . I think Capra pushed him too far in the direction of old farce – the kind of farcical playing that was a bit strained'.[28] Grant himself regarded it as his 'worst performance',[29] which was wildly unfair, but it was undoubtedly one of his most uncomfortable pieces of work. For the first twenty minutes, he looks assured – indeed, he had rarely before seemed quite so charmingly confident – and then, suddenly, when he discovers the first of the dead bodies his aunts have hidden in the window-seat, he switches to a different kind of performance altogether: uncomfortable, edgy, uneven, with a near-constant look of pop-eyed mock-horror. He still has some good lines which he delivers beautifully ('Insanity runs in my family. It practically *gallops!*'), and he shares an enjoyable scene with Peter Lorre (as Einstein, the timid and tipsy sidekick of a psychopath) which works because Lorre's familiar repertory of facial tics, nervous gestures and anxious whispers allows Grant to slip back momentarily into his more restrained comic style:

Einstein: Get out of this house now, will you, please?

Brewster: Eh? What you say? Speak up, sonny! I can't hear you.

Einstein: Johnny, he-he's in a bad mood! You-you get out of here!

Brewster: Will you stop under-playing? I can't hear you!

The little, gently sardonic, ad-lib was probably one way of coping with the frustration. He later said of the experience of making the movie:

> I was embarrassed doing it. I overplayed the character. It was a dreadful job for me, and yet the film was a very big success and a big money-maker, perhaps because of the reputation it had as a play. The fellow who played the role on stage, Allyn Joslyn, was much better than I was. Jimmy Stewart would have been much better in the film.[30]

Grant disliked commercial failures, but he probably disliked artistic failures even more. He was a perfectionist, and he had struggled to achieve full control over his career in order to ensure, more than anything else, that his contribution to his movies would be as full and as effective as possible: 'I'm not a writer or a director, I'm an improver.'[31] Garson Kanin, who directed him in *My Favorite Wife*, appreciated the value of his contributions:

> He worked very hard. I remember that indelibly. Almost more than any other quality was his seriousness about his work. He was always prepared; he always knew his part, his lines, and the scene. And he related very well to the other players. He took not only his own part seriously, he took the whole picture seriously. He'd come and look at the rushes every evening. No matter how carefree and easygoing he seemed in the performance, in reality he was a serious man, an exceptionally concentrated man. And extremely intelligent too.[32]

Grant sought out those directors with whom he expected to be able to work in a suitably collaborative spirit. He singled out five in particular for special praise: Howard Hawks (who directed Grant in *Bringing Up Baby, Only Angels Have Wings, His Girl Friday, I Was a Male War Bride* and *Monkey Business*); George Stevens (*Gunga Din, Penny Serenade* and *The Talk of the Town*); Leo McCarey (*The Awful*

Truth, Once Upon a Honeymoon and *An Affair to Remember*); George Cukor (*Sylvia Scarlett, Holiday* and *The Philadelphia Story*); and Alfred Hitchcock (*Suspicion, Notorious, To Catch a Thief, North by Northwest*). These directors were, it seems, particularly open to Grant's own creative ideas:

> Each of those directors permitted me the release of improvisa-
> tion during the rehearsing of each scene – rather in the manner
> that Dave Brubeck's musical group improvises on the central
> theme, never losing sight of the original mood, key or rhythm,
> no matter how far out they go. [These directors] permitted me
> to discover how far out *I* could go with confidence, while
> guided by their quiet, sensitive directorial approval.[33]

Stanley Donen, who directed Grant on four occasions from the late fifties onwards, commented that Grant's commercial viability as one of Hollywood's major stars gave him considerable authority: 'Let's tell it like it is. If you were trying to make a movie and needed twenty million, you'd have a hell of a time getting it. But if you could say, "I've got Cary Grant", there was no more money trouble. Cary was entitled to have an opinion. He was more than the star. He was the reason the picture got made!'[34] Gradually, as his career developed, Grant would assume more and more responsibility for the movies he was involved in. Although the studios formally had the final cut of his movies, Stanley Fox helped Grant negotiate a handshake deal which, in effect, transferred that right to him: 'He would sit day after day with the film editor. He wanted a film to move and did not want it to run more than a hundred and twenty minutes. His sense of good timing extended to the pace of the film itself.'[35]

The first thing that Grant took full control of was his own appearance, showing a meticulous attention to detail. He would insist on only being photographed in close-up from the right side of his face (the left side, he believed, looked 'dead', although most cameramen could see nothing odd about it).[36] Few men looked so good in a suit, but Grant grew increasingly obsessive about his clothes. All of his shirts were made specially for him; if any of them were deemed short of perfect they would be sent back with such instructions as 'extend the collar tips by ⅛ inch'.[37] One of his long-suffering tailors said that he would measure the lapels of his jackets with a ruler, insisting on corrections if there was even a fraction of an inch between the angle of the cut and the lapel.[38] Some of his colleagues were bemused by such fussiness, but none of them doubted his expertise in this area. Edith Head, Hollywood's best-known and most successful costume designer, said that Cary Grant's taste was 'impeccable':

> I consider him not only the most beautiful but the most beautifully dressed man in the world. His is a discerning eye, a meticulous sense of detail. He has the greatest fashion sense of any actor I've ever worked with. He knows as much about women's clothes as he does about men's.[39]

Grant insisted that 'it takes 500 small details to add up to one favorable impression'.[40]

His attention to detail, however, went far beyond his own appearance. A reporter visiting Grant as he began shooting a new movie observed, 'On the set, he was the only star I have ever known who personally examined each extra before a scene to make sure they were dressed right.'[41] His perfectionism was not always appreciated by his colleagues. The production manager of *Night and Day* wrote in his daily memorandum, 'I don't think there is a set in this picture that hasn't been changed by Cary, and it has cost this studio a terrific amount of money.'[42] There are countless stories of Grant's insistence on minor and major changes to the dialogue, the costume design and the décor: rooms that looked, he is supposed to have said, too small or too large, paintings that needed to be replaced, doorknobs painted different colours, windows changed, camera angles altered, lenses switched – it all became too much for a few people, such as the highly experienced but no-nonsense English cinematographer Christopher Challis, who complained that Grant, although a 'consummate artist' and not 'in any way unpleasant', was also 'the biggest "old woman" I have ever worked with'.[43] Normally, however, he had an unusually clear sense of what it was that he wanted, and, just as importantly, why he wanted it. The actor Thelma Orloff noted when she worked with Grant that he 'had grasped every aspect of the business ... He never did anything that wasn't right on the button'.[44] When Peter Bogdanovich asked several of Grant's directors about certain 'particularly delightful moments in their Grant films', he often received the same reply: 'That was Cary's.'[45] Alfred Hitch-cock, who did not often welcome the advice of his cast on technical (or any other) matters, always showed considerable respect for Grant's opinions. On the set of *North by Northwest*, for example, Grant assisted Hitchcock on the choreographing of several complicated scenes, such as the commotion in the auction-room.[46]

Some might have been exasperated by Grant's meticulousness, but others were fascinated by it. When James Mason worked with him on *North by Northwest*, he began by studying Grant's playing in an early scene in which his character is kidnapped: 'I had been most eager to watch this Grant at work and figure out the secret of his perfect comedy playing. He was earnest, conscientious, clutching his script until the last moment. Then onto his feet and it would just happen.'[47] Many of his fellow actors welcomed and benefited from his contributions. Douglas Fairbanks, Jnr., who co-starred with Grant in *Gunga Din*, recalled the generosity of Grant's approach to the movie:

> He was wonderful, and the most generous player I've ever worked with. He wasn't just taking his salary. He was concerned that the picture be a good picture. He thought that what was good for the picture was good for him, and he was right. He was a master technician, which many people don't realise, meticulous and conscious of every move. It might have looked impetuous or impulsive, but it wasn't. It was all carefully planned. Cary was a very sharp and intelligent actor who worked out everything ahead.[48]

Martha Scott, who appeared alongside Grant in only her second movie – the ill-fated *The Howards of Virginia* – remembers how he helped her grow more confident and relaxed:

> He never made me feel he knew I was nervous. Once in a while, in a close shot over his shoulder, in a full-head close-up of me, he would put his foot next to mine so I wouldn't move my body out of the frame. Sometimes he'd reach over and touch my elbow – to remind me not to move out of the light. I was so used to the theater that I was apt to do my scenes and not care about anything. But Cary wanted it to be right for me.

He was conscious of body movement, like a dancer. It was wonderful to watch. Working with him was such a loving and happy experience. The most outstanding thing was his commitment to perfectionism, his help in surreptitious ways. During a shot, if somebody mumbled, he'd mumble, too, forcing another take.[49]

He was equally helpful to Sophia Loren when they co-starred for the first time together in Stanley Kramer's *The Pride and the Passion* (1957). Kramer remembers how Grant 'was extremely co-operative and did not play the big star at all. He was very human and thoughtful':

Cary had a thing about Sophia's presentation to a worldwide audience and to an American audience particularly . . . He didn't want her to have the image of an Italian sex symbol. He didn't want her to fall into that pit. He thought she was beyond that . . . It was her first English-speaking film, and Cary was thoughtful and very helpful to her. He never hesitated to say, 'why don't we do another take? I don't think her line was clear there.' Or, 'I think she can do a little bit better, don't you think so, Sophia?' He encouraged and bolstered her. As he did everybody.[50]

Grant's willingness to put the interests of the movie as a whole before the interests of his own personal contribution was perhaps one reason why he was so often overlooked when it came to Academy Award nominations. He received just two Best Actor nominations during his career, both for roles which did not make use of his prodigious comic talents: the first for the mawkish *Penny Serenade* (1941), in which he cries in one scene (and which was described by Richard Schickel as 'an act of retribution – against him for having so much fun for the past few years, against us for joining in on it'[51]), the second, four years later, for *None But the Lonely Heart*, in which again he cries. Grant said, with only a slight tinge of bitterness, that the best light comic acting, perversely, worked against its critical recognition: the easier it was made to look the less it looked like 'acting'. He added that he would 'have to blacken my teeth first' before the Academy would take his work seriously.[52] There can, however, be few other performers who appeared in so many movies for which their co-workers received Academy Awards: Leo McCarey, for example, won an Oscar for Best Director for *The Awful Truth*; Sidney Sheldon won Best Screenplay for *The Bachelor and the Bobbysoxer*; Gordon Sawyer, Best Sound Engineer for *The Bishop's Wife*; Ethel Barrymore, Best Supporting Actress for *None But the Lonely Heart*; Joan Fontaine, Best Actress for *Suspicion*; and James Stewart, Best Actor for *The Philadelphia Story*. Peter Stone, when he accepted his Best Screenplay Oscar for another of Grant's movies, *Father Goose*, recognised this point when he expressed his gratitude to Grant, 'who keeps winning these things for other people'.[53]

If the Academy Awards voters tended to overlook Grant's own contributions, his fellow actors, in contrast, respected his attitude. James Stewart, for example, who was himself one of the most intelligent screen actors in Hollywood, was somewhat embarrassed when he received an Oscar for his role in *The Philadelphia Story* while Grant was, once again, left empty-handed. Both actors had enormous admiration for each other's abilities and professionalism, and both had worked particularly well together in the movie. 'He came to work fully prepared,' Stewart said of Grant. 'He didn't like rehearsals, and neither did I.'[54] They acted for, rather than against, each other, confident enough in each other's company to persuade the director, George Cukor, to let them improvise some exchanges – such as in the scene where Stewart's character – drunk – visits C. K. Dexter Haven for a late-night conversation:

It was time to do the scene, and Cary said, 'George, why don't we just go ahead? If you don't like it, we'll do it again.' So, without a rehearsal or anything, we started the scene. As I was talking, it hit me that I'd had *too* much to drink. So, as I explained things to Cary, I hiccupped. In answer to the hiccup, Cary said – out of the clear blue sky – 'Excuse me.' Well, I sort of said 'Umm?' It was very difficult for me to keep a straight face, because his ad-libbed response had been so beautifully done . . . Cary had an almost perfect humor.[55]

Stewart had given (in *Mr Smith Goes to Washington* and *The Shop Around the Corner*), and would give (in *It's a Wonderful Life* and *Vertigo*), better performances and yet receive no award from the Academy, but Grant's subtle, under-played acting in *The Philadelphia*

Story was, Stewart noted, exceptional. Joseph L. Mankiewicz, the movie's producer, acknowledged this in a letter he wrote to Grant after it was released:

> Whatever success the picture is having . . . is due, in my opinion, to you in far greater proportions than anyone has seen fit to shout about. As what is laughingly called 'the producer' of the film, but still, perhaps, closer to it than anyone – believe me, your presence as Dexter, and particularly your sensitive and brilliant playing of the role, contribute what I consider the backbone and basis of practically every emotional value in the piece. I can think of no one who could have done as well or given as much.[56]

As the forties progressed, however, it proved increasingly difficult for actors like Grant to find other similarly popular and well-written comedies. Preston Sturges reflected on the change in his satirical movie, *Sullivan's Travels* (1941), which told the story of a commercially successful writer-director of such audience-pleasing movies as 'Ants in Your Pants of 1941' and 'Hey! Hey! In the Hayloft' who decides that the time has come for a serious movie like his proposed 'Oh Brother, Where Art Thou?' Ernst Lubitsch was nearing the end of his run of gloriously sophisticated and witty comedies, Leo Mc-Carey was in the process of leaving behind his anarchic, screwball fantasies in favour of more sentimental comic dramas, and Howard Hawks and Frank Capra had turned their attention to the war in Europe. Cary Grant, like a number of his contemporaries in Hollywood, found himself in danger of seeming a mere light comedian stranded in dark times. 'After 1940', wrote Pauline Kael, 'he didn't seem to have any place to go – there were no longer Cary Grant pictures.'[57] That Grant survived where several other similar comic performers faded away was due in part to the fact that he had shown himself in the past to be an unusually versatile leading man, and in part to the fact that, as a free agent, he could anticipate the change in mood and adapt more promptly and effectively than most who were constrained by their studios.

Grant began to exploit this opportunity to take on more challenging roles in movies which reflected some of the anxieties and concerns of the time. He sought assistance for this move from among that sub–community in Hollywood that he probably had most faith in: the writers. He found them more than willing to help. As one screenwriter said: 'A writer in Hollywood, even when he's doing well, is looked down upon by everyone else. In radio, television and motion pictures, all writers were called the boys . . . Cary called us authors. You can't realise what a compliment that was.'[58] Another noted the unusual respect that screenwriters showed to Grant: 'At every studio there used to be a writers' table in the commissary. Nobody could sit there unless they were a writer. One time at Paramount Adolphe Menjou sat at the writers' table, and all the writers got up and left. But they invited Cary to join them.'[59] They regarded him as being on their side. Yet another recalls Grant giving him some advice when he began working at MGM: 'He said, "watch the wastebaskets. Metro has a new efficiency expert. He checks the writers' wastebaskets at the end of the day. Be sure your wastebasket has a lot of half-written papers in it".'[60] Grant, more often than not, had, in the past, helped a number of writers look rather better than they were by the clever way that he delivered their lines. Now he sought out the kind of talented writers who could help him develop new roles.

Three movies in particular – *The Talk of the Town* (1942), *Mr Lucky* (1943) and *None But the Lonely Heart* (1944) – bear the hallmarks of Grant's independence. Each of them represented something of a departure for him. Each took him out of the brightly elegant sur-roundings of his recent movies and placed him in darker, grimmer circumstances. Each of them was a gamble – artistically: could he make these, for him, unorthodox characters convincing?; commer-cially: would audiences accept Cary Grant in movies other than 'Cary Grant movies'?; and politically: would his use of predominantly left-wing screenwriters, some of them, indeed, card-carrying members of the Communist Party, have any serious long-term rami-fications for his career?

The Talk of the Town is one of Grant's most underrated movies. Although it dealt with an ambitious range of themes and issues, drawn from America's democratic tradition – the small town as the incubator of virtue versus the small town as the breeding ground of bigotry; formal education versus practical experience; self-reliance versus civic duty; the letter of the law versus the spirit of the law – it manages, thanks to a fine screenplay (co-written by Irwin Shaw and the populist Sidney Buchman[61]) and an excellent cast headed by three outstanding performers (Grant, Ronald Colman and Jean Arthur), to be entertaining, accessible and intelligent where the more 'serious' *The Howards of Virginia* (also written by Buchman) is merely insultingly trite and asinine. Grant played Leopold Dilg, a mill-hand with a reputation for plain-speaking ('Some people write novels. Some people write music. I make speeches on streetcorners'). Dilg, after being arrested on trumped-up charges of arson and murder ('he's the only honest man I've come across in this town for twenty years – naturally, they want to hang him'), escapes and hides in the house of Nora Shelley (Arthur). Before she has time to decide what to do with Dilg, her new tenant arrives – the eminent legal scholar from Harvard, Michael Lightcap (Colman). When Lightcap catches sight of Dilg, Nora is forced to pretend that he is their unusually argumentative gardener, Joseph. With a mixture of relief and anxiety, she watches as the two men, one a fugitive from justice, the other a scholar of justice, take a liking to each other and engage in increasingly combative debates about the interpretation of the law:

Lightcap: If feelings had any influence on the law, half of the country would be in gaol. *Facts*, Miss Shelley, *facts*!

Dilg: My dear professor, people wind facts around each other like pretzels. Facts alone? That's a nut without a kernel. Where's the soul, where's the instinct, where's the warm human side?

Lightcap: All right, Joseph, you conduct the law *your* way on random sentimentality and you will have violence and disorder.

Dilg: Uh-huh, and *your* way you'll have a Greek statue – beautiful but *dead*!

Lightcap: All right: two schools of thought – I see your point of view, theoretically, in fact I respect it . . .

Dilg: I wish I could respect *yours*, professor!

Nora: Ah, Joseph puts it a little strongly, professor. He *does* respect you, of course, but, as you can see, he's for the practical side, the everyday, garden variety type of human experience.

Lightcap: Yes, and makes the law up as he goes along.

Dilg: Out of common sense, yes. In fact, professor, the way I see it, you don't *live* in this country, you just take a *room* in it! . . . All you know about the American scene is what you read in newspapers and magazines – somebody else's impressions hashed up for lazy people. If you don't feel it yourself you've learned nothing, just like having somebody tell you about his operation.

Lightcap is, says Dilg, 'an intelligent man, but cold – no *blood* in his thinking'. He spends his time perusing the paper description of American democracy while Dilg spends his experiencing its living reality. Lightcap – beautifully played by Colman – believes in those principles 'which are above small emotions, greed and the loose thinking of everyday life'; Dilg fears that the law, in reality, is merely 'a gun pointed at somebody's head – it all depends which end of the gun you stand whether the law's "just" or not'. He challenges Lightcap to 'spend half the day with your books and the other half finding out what people *do*'. For the remainder of the movie, we see the two men edge closer to each other, Dilg coming to have more respect for Lightcap's idealism, Lightcap coming to appreciate the importance of practice as well as theory, actions as well as words ('You laugh at my kind of law and wink at the other,' teases Dilg, 'which one do *you* practice?'). By the end, both men have learned from the other, both have reached that point at which they can face the mob together and argue as one:

Lightcap: This is *your* law and your finest possession: it makes you free men in a free country. Why have you come here to destroy it? If you know what's good for you, take those weapons home and burn them – and then, *think*. Think of this country, and of the law that makes it what it is. Think of a world *crying* for this very law, then maybe you'll understand why you ought to guard it, and why the law has got to be the personal concern of every citizen – to uphold it for your neighbour as well as yourself. Violence against it is one mistake; another mistake is for any man to look upon the law as just a set of principles, just so much language printed on fine, heavy paper [*exchanges glances with Dilg*], something he recites and then leans back and takes it for granted that justice is automatically being done. *Both* kinds of men are equally wrong! The law must be engraved on your hearts and practiced every minute – to the letter and spirit. You can't even exist unless we're willing to go down into the dust and blood and fight of battle every day of our lives to preserve it – for our neighbor as well as ourselves!

The resolution of the movie's romantic entanglements – should Nora Shelley go with Lightcap, stay with Dilg, or be with neither? – was solved, in somewhat cowardly fashion, by the director George Stevens shooting three different endings and then gauging the reactions of preview audiences. Dilg's reward in the most popular version reflected, perhaps, Grant's reward as his stardom eclipsed that of Colman's. The movie, in general, proved a triumph for Grant, as well as for the rest of the cast and crew; it was a critical as well as a commercial success, earning seven Academy Award nominations. The gamble had paid off.

Mr Lucky was, if anything, a slightly bolder venture yet. The original story was by Milton Holmes, a tennis pro at a club where Grant sometimes played. He had approached Grant with the idea, Grant had liked it enough to ask RKO to commission a script, co-written by Holmes and the more experienced Adrian Scott (who later achieved notoriety – along with Sidney Buchman – as one of the Hollywood Ten). Grant played Joe Adams, a draft-dodging gambler who falls in love with the high-born Dorothy Bryant (Laraine Day). It was particularly ironic that Barbara Hutton, whom Grant had recently married, had attempted, ultimately unsuccessfully, to persuade a highly placed RKO executive to cast her opposite her new husband.[62] Grant resisted the idea, and, as Hutton had never acted in front of a camera before, it is hardly surprising that he did so, but, bearing in mind the class-conscious dialogue, it could have made for some remarkably poignant scenes.

'Nobody ever knew what he was – except tough,' says his friend, narrating the story after it appears that Joe Adams has died an heroic war-time death. Adams is, like Jimmy Monkley from *Sylvia Scarlett*, a working-class man who has had to fight to survive a precarious early life on the edge of poverty, and who has come to the conclusion, as a consequence, that he can rely on no one but himself. 'How long has it been since anyone had any control over you?' asks Dorothy.

'Nobody ever had,' he replies, 'and nobody ever will.' Adams treats his call-up papers with contempt: 'Listen, this isn't *my* war! I *had* my war: crawling out of the gutter – the hard way. I won *that* war!' In one particularly memorable scene, when Adams suspects Dorothy of dismissing him because of his humble origins, Grant delivers his lines with unusual passion, each word underscored with bitterness, as though, for a moment, it is not Joe Adams speaking, nor Cary Grant, but Archie Leach:

> To people like you, folks like me are animals! We're so *bad*, and you're so very *good*. What do you expect – *credit* for it? How could you be anything else with what you had to start out with? You ought to be horsewhipped if you *didn't* turn out right! And what are *you* so high and mighty about? What did *you* ever do? *He's* the guy who made all the dough for you [*pointing at a portrait of her ancestor*], and he was born in a log cabin! You know where I grew up? In a one-room shack with a dirt floor. You talk about 'this side' of your family and 'that side' of your family. As far as I know we only had one side and it was awful poor! Lots of times there was what-for to eat. That's why I ran away when I was nine; I got tired of being hungry and seeing my old lady go hungry until she died!

Adams finishes by looking at Dorothy and saying, 'I just know that your kind can look through me like I was a pane of dirty glass.' At the time that Grant was making *Mr Lucky*, he was growing increasingly angry about having to share a house with all of Barbara Hutton's aristocratic guests. 'Now, hi' comes from Lime 'ouse', he is said to have snapped at them on one occasion, 'I'm just a bloody cockney. Where's me fish an' chips?'[63] It could not, at that time, have been difficult for Grant to have summoned up many of his old painful memories when he played the part of Joe Adams.

Both *The Talk of the Town* and *Mr Lucky* did well at the box-office (the latter, in fact, became RKO's biggest profit-maker of 1943). *None But the Lonely Heart*, on the other hand, did not, which depressed Grant profoundly, because this was probably the most personal project that he would ever be involved in. Made expressly at his instigation, the story – based on the novel by Richard Llewellyn – became a gesture toward his own roots. He played Ernie Mott, a restless cockney drifter, a self-styled 'tramp of the universe', trying to make a better life for himself and his aged, ailing mother, who runs a second-hand store in London's East End slums. Ernie Mott's plight might have been that of Archie Leach had he never left home, and Grant, without doubt, was drawn to the story for that reason: 'I was usually cast as a well-dressed, sophisticated chap . . . This time I was an embittered cockney. In many ways the part seemed to fit my nature better than the light-hearted fellows I was used to playing.'[64]

Although Grant's working-class background was not unknown, its full significance was rarely understood, the residue of pain usually obscured by the perception of the 'proletarian charm' that had helped endear his elegant image to the masses. One writer, for example, remarked simplistically on those so-called 'characteristic' British working-class qualities that Cary Grant was supposed to have pre-served, such as 'cockiness, obstreperousness, love of vulgar humour, fondness for fish and chips, sausages and mash and tripe and onions, and [an] affection for old music-hall songs [such as] "Yes, We Have No Bananas".'[65] Grant himself, however, had not the slightest desire to indulge in such a patronising, Disney-style romanticism. He craved realism, or at least as much realism as a Hollywood movie starring Cary Grant could accommodate. He gave careful instructions to the set designers, ensuring that the dimensions and décor matched those of the sitting-rooms and bedrooms he had once inhabited in Bristol. He wanted low dark ceilings to emphasise the claustrophobic atmos-phere of life in the old East End, with narrow cobblestone streets and cramped semi-detached houses. He had first-hand knowledge of what it was like to be poor, to want to break free, to find a better life, and he wanted that knowledge to be utilised.

His choice of screenwriter had signalled his intentions: Clifford Odets, the left-wing playwright, founder member of the Group Theater, author of *Waiting for Lefty* (1935) and *Golden Boy* (1939), supporter of the Communist Party of the USA. Grant was so impressed with the screenplay Odets produced that he also insisted that Odets should direct it. 'If he believes in you,' said Odets of Grant, 'he'll gamble his entire career with you.'[66] Odets brought in another unconventional figure, Hanns Eisler, an associate of Brecht's, to compose the score.[67] It seems unlikely that the executives at RKO looked on these well-known activists without a sense of foreboding, but the fact that they were hired – and stayed hired – was a sign of Grant's authority. 'Cary sat for hours with Odets and talked about Bristol,' Jack Haley, Jnr., recalled. 'He had a wonderful love of writers. That's why he helped several of them become directors. It was extraordinary the way he put his career on the line to give all those guys their first shot.'[68]

The finished movie (a remarkable directorial début by Odets) was dark and richly melancholic, its strengths those of the cinema (a keen visual sense, some striking combinations of sounds with images), its weaknesses those of the theatre (static dialogue scenes). At its centre are two fine performances – by Grant and, as Ernie Mott's mother, Ethel Barrymore. Grant, Pauline Kael observed, plays Mott with 'an almost stricken look, a memory of suffering'.[69] The opening voice-over describes Mott as a man looking 'for a free, noble and better life in the second quarter of the twentieth century', but unable to realise his full potential because he is always being pushed back into a life of petty crime by poverty. The choice, he notes, seems to be between being a 'victim' or a 'thug', but, he asks, 'suppose you don't want to be neither, like me: not the 'are, and not the 'ound. Then what?' Then, he realises, he must struggle against the odds. 'I'm a lone wolf barking in a corner,' Mott says, 'plain disgusted with a world I never made and don't want none of.' When his relationship with his mother softens, she saves up and buys him a pin-striped suit so that he can go out and show off, 'just like your father did'. 'Did you love my old man?' he asks her. 'Love's not for the poor, son,' she replies. 'No time for it.' The movie ends on an even darker note than the one on which it started: he has been deceived by the mob and left penniless, his mother is in prison, and, as he visits her on her death-bed, they hug each other and sob uncontrollably.

Grant was proud of the movie, and of his performance in it. A quarter of a century later, when he was the recipient of a belated tribute from the organisers of the Academy Awards ceremony, he requested that an excerpt from *None But the Lonely Heart*, featuring the scene in which he cries by his mother's bed, be included in the assemblage of clips: 'I didn't do much of that kind of emotion, but I think that was rather good.'[70] His performance had, at the time, been nominated for an Oscar, only to lose, rather anti-climactically, to Bing Crosby for his performance in *Going My Way*. He told one reporter that he had been reasonably pleased with the critical reception of the movie, but had been very disappointed by its mediocre performance at the box-office; the public, he said, had 'wanted me to make them laugh'.[71] As much as he had appreciated the critical plaudits, Cary Grant remained committed to pleasing a mass audience, and, as a consequence, he came, grudgingly, to the conclusion that *None But the Lonely Heart* had been a gamble that had failed. Except for a ten-minute short promoting the sale of war bonds,[72] he did not make another movie for more than a year – the longest break he had taken in his career. His marriage to Barbara Hutton was coming to an end, and he was in no mood to begin any new projects.

When he did return, he did so with a renewed determination to ensure that whatever artistic ambitions he might entertain would have to be tied more tightly to popular tastes and expectations. It seemed that what most people wanted most to see Cary Grant in were light comedies, elegant romances and well-crafted thrillers. As one critic said of his more 'serious' roles of the mid-forties, they were performed with considerable skill, 'but it was like asking Cole Porter to write a hymn on behalf of the beautification of America: extraordinary natural resources were being left unused'.[73] Grant, ever-practical, took note of this kind of observation. Perhaps he had come to terms with the greater box-office pulling power of comedy, or perhaps he had needed reassurance that what he did best was artistically, as well as commercially, creditable, but, for whatever reason, he re-emerged as an articulate champion of the 'Cary Grant movie':

> People say audiences want 'realism'. They say it has to be garbage cans and lousy two-bit violence. I don't see why it can't be laughs and the Plaza, too. That's part of life. High comedy and polished words, that's the hardest to write and to act it's the best. And it lasts the longest, too. We're the ones who can go on for years.[74]

Cary Grant was back, appearing in Cary Grant movies. He still showed an interest in well-written, unusual, intriguing stories, but his attitude now was more noticeably risk-aversive than before. *The Bishop's Wife* (1947), for example, was a delicate mixture of comedy, drama and fantasy, featuring Grant as Dudley, an angel who descends from heaven to help an overworked bishop (played by David Niven) attempt to raise money for a new church and save his marriage; it was quirky, still something of a minor gamble, but Grant was reassured by a reliable cast, a conscientious director (Henry Koster), and a screenplay that was improved radically by the (unacknowledged) revisions by Billy Wilder and Charles Brackett.[75] It also played on the familiar appeal of Grant's democratic gentleman, with the classless angel doing his best to save the bishop from the 'vulgar rich'. The movie was a critical and commercial success, garnering five Academy Award nominations – including for Best Picture – and Grant's performance was singled out by reviewers for special praise. In the aptly-named *People Will Talk* (1951), an unusually adult and literate movie with a similarly unorthodox combination of comedy, satire and melodrama, writer-director Joseph L. Mankiewicz secularised Dudley, giving Grant the part of a gynaecologist called Noah Praetorius who marries a pregnant young patient (played by Jeanne Crain) in order to prevent her from having an abortion or committing suicide. Again, the risks involved in appearing in such a movie were offset by Grant associating himself with someone who had such a reliable track record as Mankiewicz, the only man to win four Academy Awards in two years. Grant, again, emerged with his popularity secure and his critical reputation, if anything, enhanced (*Newsweek*'s reviewer rated his contribution as 'one of the most intelligent performances of his nineteen-year Hollywood career'[76]).

So for the time being, or at least for most of it, Cary Grant seemed content just to be 'Cary Grant', and appear in the kind of movies Cary Grant had appeared in before, doing the same kinds of things he had done before, and, if some of the critics did not like some of the movies, he could at least console himself with the thought that those movies were making a great deal of money. *Destination Tokyo* (1944), for example, was a very successful but safely formulaic war movie (praised as 'a pippin of a picture' by one easily pleased reviewer[77]); *The Bachelor and the Bobbysoxer* (1947), in which Grant starred alongside Shirley Temple and Myrna Loy, was a contrived but inoffensive comedy which became one of the biggest-grossing movies of 1948; *Mr Blandings Builds His Dream House* (1948) was another amiably light comedy that proved hugely popular with movie-goers; and *I Was a Male War Bride* (1949), directed by Howard Hawks, harked back to the old screwball spirit of the late thirties, and grossed over $4.5 million, making it 20th Century-Fox's biggest box-office hit of the year. 'Grant just kept ambling gracefully, graciously along,' said Richard Schickel, agentless and advisorless, at the top of the popularity polls, no matter what he did or didn't do.'[78]

By 1948, Grant looked, indeed, in most ways, to have reached the very top of his profession. He had made *Fame Magazine*'s list of the ten most popular stars in America:[79] he was receiving a handsome salary and a percentage of the gross from each of his movies: he was the manager of his own career. Soon he would be invited to go through that Hollywood ritual in which his hand and footprints would be immortalised in cement in the forecourt of Grauman's Chinese Theater, joining those of his old role model – Douglas Fairbanks – and his old rival – Gary Cooper. He could, it seemed, go on (and on), into the fifties, and do, more or less, whatever he wanted to do. What he really wanted to do, however, was a question that Grant, on further reflection, found that he could not answer to his own satisfaction.

CHAPTER XI

The Pursuit of Happiness

Tradition is not something a man can learn; not a thread he can pick up when he feels like it; any more than a man can choose his own ancestors. Someone lacking a tradition who would like to have one is like a man unhappily in love.
LUDWIG WITTGENSTEIN

I think it's important to know where you've come from so that you can know where you're going.
CARY GRANT

Cary Grant, by the end of the forties, had grown weary of being 'Cary Grant'. He had been 'Cary Grant' for twenty years. It seemed long enough. He was successful. He was wealthy. He was popular. He was bored: 'To play yourself, your *true* self, is the hardest thing in the world.'[1] It is, he might have added, impossible unless one knows what one's 'true self' is, and, when he reflected on it, he found that he was no longer sure: 'You might say that Archie Leach sat watching a Cary Grant movie one day and said: "Why don't I relax like Cary Grant?"'[2] The answer was not forthcoming: 'You're just a bunch of molecules until you know who you are. You spend all your time getting to be a big Hollywood actor. But then what? You've reached a comfortable plateau and you want to stay on it, you resist change.'[3]

'Celebrity', wrote John Updike, 'is a mask that eats into the face. As soon as one is aware of being "somebody", to be watched and listened to with extra interest, input ceases, and the performer goes blind and deaf in his overanimation.'[4] It was a problem that had come to preoccupy Grant. He feared he was in danger of succumbing to self-parody. He knew the man who writers, producers, critics and

166

fans thought Cary Grant was; now he wanted the opportunity to discover who *he* thought he really was.

Why choose the start of the fifties as the time for such a break? One reason was that Grant feared that audiences were wearying of his kind of movies, perhaps even of his kind of star – perhaps even of him. His 1952 reunion with Howard Hawks for *Monkey Business*, in which he played a character reminiscent of *Bringing Up Baby*'s David Huxley alongside Ginger Rogers and Marilyn Monroe, had not been the major box-office success that everyone involved had anticipated. His next movie, *Dream Wife*, was released by MGM the following year during the slack season, with little support by way of previews and publicity. Hollywood as a whole was undergoing a major transformation, adjusting itself to cater to the tastes of the post-war audience. Major studios were not renewing the expensive long-term contracts of ageing stars such as Clark Gable and Errol Flynn, suspecting that their popularity had run its course. Gradually they were being replaced by younger men, such as Marlon Brando, Montgomery Clift, William Holden and Burt Lancaster, with newer, grittier styles. 'It was the period of the blue jeans, the dope addicts, the Method,' Grant recalled, 'and nobody cared about comedy at all.'[5]

There was another reason for a new start: Grant had married again, and, this time, he was determined to make the marriage work. Betsy Drake was his third wife.[6] He had met her for the first time in August 1947, on board the *Queen Mary*, when he was returning to the US after a short visit to England.[7] They had stayed in touch, and, at the beginning of the following year, he persuaded her to come to Los Angeles to sign a contract he had arranged for her with RKO. Grant then insisted that she appear with him in the romantic comedy *Every Girl Should Be Married* (1948), which, when it was released, received mixed reviews. They married on Christmas Day, 1949, in Phoenix, Arizona, with Howard Hughes in attendance as best man. They appeared together in a movie, for the second and final time, in *Room for One More* (1952), which, once again, was only mildly successful at the box-office.[8] Drake, however, had changed Grant. His friends had noticed it. Grant, one said, 'developed an extra dimension after marrying Betsy'. She had 'opened up a whole new world of ideas' for him.[9] He was more inquisitive, more open-minded, more eager to learn. He was forty-eight years old, had been working since he was fourteen, and was rich enough not to need to work again in his life. He decided that it was time to put his marriage first and his career behind him. He announced his retirement from making movies.

Betsy Drake did not turn Cary Grant from a self-assured and contented celebrity into an inquisitive, restless soul. He had always, off-screen, been prone to bouts of depression, insecurity and introspection. When his first marriage began to fail in the mid-thirties, it was reported in some newspapers that he had attempted suicide.[10] He had been found lying unconscious across his bed, with a bottle of pills nearby, and the police had rushed him to the Hollywood Hospital where his stomach was pumped. At the time, his studio (he had not yet left Paramount) put out a story that suggested that the whole thing had merely been an ill-conceived prank. Later on, however, Grant admitted:

> I had been drinking . . . most of the day before and all that day. I just passed out. The servant found me, became alarmed, and called the cops. You know what whisky does when you drink it all by yourself . . . It makes you very sad. I began calling people. I know I called Virginia [Cherrill]. I don't know what I said to her, but things got hazier and hazier. The next thing I knew they were carting me off to hospital.[11]

David Niven described Grant as a 'will-o'-the-wisp',[12] the 'most truly mysterious friend I have. A spooky Celt really, not an Englishman at all . . . has great depressions and great heights when he seems about to take off for outer space.'[13] When someone once asked Grant what caused his periods of depression and self-doubt, he replied: 'Growing up. Becoming me. My relationship with my parents. Marriage.'[14] The failure of his first two marriages had been particularly painful; 'until thirty-five,' he reflected, 'a man is often a self-centred idiot,'[15] and he regarded his own self-absorption as one of the reasons why his past relationships had broken down.

'Self-importance', wrote Updike, 'is a thickened, occluding form of self-consciousness. The binge, the fling, the trip – all attempt to shake the film and get back under the dining-room table, with a child's beautiful clear eyes.'[16] Grant felt that he needed such a radical strategy in order to rediscover his old zest: 'To be contemporary,' he said, 'one has to mirror the tempo and bent of the time. You watch. You listen. And you reflect what you see and hear. It's fatal to freeze at any point in a career. Standing still means that the parade passes by.'[17] Grant, encouraged by Betsy Drake, decided to take a break from the 'hypocrisies of Hollywood'. They were not seen at any of the fashionable nightspots; more often than not they would stay quietly at home. He had always talked of travelling around the world; now seemed the ideal time to do so. They booked passage on a freighter headed for the Orient. A friend who saw them off recalled: 'Cary figured his career was over. He was wrong, but he thought audiences didn't like his stuff anymore, that the whole business had changed and the style of Marlon Brando and the others had taken over.'[18] Most of Grant's contemporaries were bemused by his departure: 'It was madness,' one of them said. 'Here he was, maybe the most charming actor ever, and it was like pulling teeth. He was absolutely certain that his charm had gone.'[19] In the ensuing weeks, as he travelled with his wife, he attempted to resolve his relationship with the extraordinary figure that Cary Grant had become: 'If I can understand how I became who I am, I can use that to shape my life in the future. I want to live in reality. Dreams aren't for me.'[20]

There had always been something of the auto-didact about Grant, but before he met Drake he had been less focused, more impulsive, in his inquiries. 'Cary had a constant curiosity about everything,' said a friend. 'Life was a process and an adventure. There was always much to learn.'[21] 'Enthusiasm', said David Niven, 'was the most important ingredient in Cary's make-up,'[22] and this enthusiasm showed itself in the invariably brief but intensive fascination he had for new ideas, gadgets and theories. Niven recounts his experiences of several of these short-lived obsessions, including his 'health food period' which led to the installation of a state-of-the-art carrot juice machine in his kitchen: 'Fearful throbbings and crunchings followed us into the garden where we were given a pre-luncheon cocktail of buttermilk, wheat germ and molasses. When the sinister sounds died down, we re-entered the house to find that the machine had gone berserk and had redecorated the kitchen from top to bottom, covering walls, windows, ceiling and linoleum flooring with a fibrous yellow paste.'[23] On another occasion, Grant informed his friends that he had learned how to cure a painful wound on his back – the result of a movie duel – by applying oxygen to the affected area and then commanding his lungs to dissolve the damaged tissue. 'This so impressed us', said Niven, 'that before long we were lying like stranded tuna on his drawing-room carpet waiting for him to bring us round again.'[24]

'I'm not a Peer-Gynt-like searcher,' Grant once said, 'but I think if a man picks up knowledge, if he improves his tolerance, if he reduces his own impatience and irritability, if he can spare a listening ear to the other fellow – well, he can't help but find himself easier to be with.'[25] He had always sought out those people from whom he could learn something: Bob Pender in England; the young intellectuals and artists who socialised at places like the Algonquin and Rudley's in New York; Douglas Fairbanks, Snr., Howard Hughes, Alfred Hitchcock, Cole Porter and Clifford Odets in California. Billy Wilder – who socialised often with Grant – remembers his inquisitiveness: 'We talked about life, food, paintings, collecting, about music – a wide range of things . . . He was a man full of curiosity. He was always drinking everything in.'[26] Spencer Tracy had, in the late forties, introduced Grant to Seymour J. Gray, a professor of medicine at the Harvard Medical School;[27] they became good friends, and their mutual interest in philosophy became the basis of many conversations. At Gray's suggestion, Grant read such texts as Plato's *Philebus* and *Phaedo* dialogues. 'He was a thinking person. I had the feeling [he] wasn't primarily interested in money. His main concern was doing a good job. He was proud of his work. He always pointed out to me in these discussions his humble beginnings. He wanted to impress his mother, I think, to be loved by her. I'm not sure she recognised how much he had accomplished.'[28] Henry Gris noted how Grant worked to make up for what he felt were the inadequacies of his formal education: 'Cary kept notes on everything, including interesting words. Elegant words that meant something different. Words with meaning and sophistication. He wrote them down in a very fine, calligraphic longhand, in alphabetical order.'[29] The words – such as 'avuncular', 'attrition', 'exacerbation' and 'hypertrophies' – were listed at the back of one of Grant's notebooks. Gris recalls asking Grant why he did it, and being told 'it was because he was in love with the English language'.[30] True to George Orwell's characterisation of the English as a 'nation of coupon-snippers',[31] Grant was also careful to cut out and keep anything of interest in the newspapers. Maureen Donaldson, who had a close relationship with him in the seventies, remembers how he 'clipped coupons. He clipped news items. He clipped stories from magazines . . . No matter how trivial the "news" seemed to be, Cary would mark items to be included in his files.'[32] In another notebook he wrote, 'Like everyone else, I shall die before accomplishing even an infinitesimal fraction of what my imagination will – a will of its peculiar own – suggest to me.'[33] His life, he insisted, would continue to be examined; in contrast to F. Scott Fitzgerald's belief that 'the natural state of the sentient adult is a qualified unhappiness',[34] Grant was convinced that knowledge would bring happiness.

When Grant met Betsy Drake, he found someone who was, if anything, even more enthusiastic about the benefits of the process of edification than he was. She was a kind-hearted person, bright but non-academic in approach, a voracious reader, devouring books on metaphysics, ecology, Eastern religions, mythology and psychology. She had countless hobbies, including photography, short-story writing, astronomy, sociology, yoga and gourmet cooking (her not entirely successful culinary experiments were satirised by Alfred Hitchcock – who had been obliged to sample several of them – when he included in 1972's *Frenzy* a running joke about a police inspector's wife and her disastrous 'gourmet' meals[35]). Her self-confidence impressed Grant, and, knowing that she was more knowledgeable than him on a wide range of subjects, and, relishing what seemed to be the novelty and perhaps sometimes the occult quackery of it all, he was prepared, most of the time, to trust her judgements. Early on in their relationship, after reading a book called *Hypnotism Today* by Jean Bordeaux and Leslie M. Le Cron, Drake began hypnotising Grant to cure him of his sixty-a-day smoking habit. It worked, one way or another, transforming him into a staunch anti-smoker for the rest of his life. Soon the couple, inspired by this success, were using hypnosis to relieve tensions and induce sleep; later, when Grant returned to acting, he claimed to use self-hypnosis to learn his lines in his sleep. 'I owe a lot to Betsy,' he said, long after their marriage was over:[36]

Betsy was good for me. Without imposition or demand, she patiently led me toward an appreciation for better books, better literature. Her cautious but steadily penetrative seeking in the labyrinths of the subconscious gradually provoked my interest. Just as she no doubt intended. The seeking is, of course, endless, but, I thankfully acknowledge, of constantly growing benefit.[37]

His 'retirement' did not last long: in the spring of 1953, Grant and Drake returned to California, and, by the middle of the following year, a mere eighteen months since his withdrawal from Hollywood, he was back on a movie set once again. His self-analysis, however, did not end at the same time as his sabbatical; indeed, if anything, it intensified as the decade went on.

Drake was becoming increasingly interested in psychotherapy (eventually she gave up her movie career to train as a psychotherapist[38]), and, after she had separated from Grant (in 1958, but they remained friends), she sought treatment with a Dr Mortimer A. Hartman, a radiologist and internist, who was practising in Los Angeles and experimenting in the field of psychotherapy. Grant had read Freud, and was familiar with the language and techniques of psychoanalysis, but there is no record of him ever undergoing professional psychotherapy himself. He did, however, meet Mortimer Hartman on the advice of his estranged wife, because Hartman, along with a colleague, Dr Arthur Chandler, had started carrying out experiments with the hallucinogenic drug lysergic acid diethylamide (LSD-25).[39] According to Hartman, he saw Grant, as his patient, over a period of three years.[40]

'I took LSD with the hope it would make me feel better about myself,' said Grant. 'I wanted to rid myself of all my hypocrisies. I wanted to work through the events of my childhood, my relationship with my parents and my former wives. I did not want to spend years in analysis.'[41] After three unsuccessful marriages, he reflected, 'either something was wrong with me or, obviously, with the whole sociological and moralistic concepts of our civilisation.'[42] The problem, at root, was, he had come to believe, that the one person who still seemed unconvinced about the identity of Cary Grant was Archie Leach: 'I had lots of problems over the years, but they were Archie Leach's problems, not Cary Grant's.'[43] If he could only shake off the problems from the past, he felt, he could, at last, embrace the promise of the future. LSD, he believed, might be the catalyst that could spark such a revolution. He estimated that he underwent 'about a hundred sessions'[44] (not just with Hartman in the US, but also in England with other doctors[45]) during this period. Lying on a couch, wearing a shield over his eyes and with wax or cotton wool in his ears, he took the drug and tried to relive his past:

At first I found it unbelievably painful. In the beginning I didn't want to go back. The sessions lasted six hours each. I would run the gamut of emotions from deep pain with tears running down my face to light-headed, almost drunken laughter . . . I remember at one point lying on the doctor's couch, squirming around, moving around in small circles, telling myself that I was unscrewing myself. I told myself that I was getting un-screwed-up. When each session ended, I was drained. I'd go home to sleep . . . It took two years, but it was necessary for my evolution.[46]

He would describe himself at the time of this analysis as 'a battle-ground of old and new beliefs':[47]

The first thing that happens is you don't want to look at what you are. Then the light breaks through; to use the cliché, you are enlightened. I discovered that I had created my own pattern, and I had to be responsible for it . . . I went through rebirth. The experience was just like being born for the first time; I imagined all the blood and the urine, and I emerged with the flush of birth.[48]

LSD was, at the time, a government-licensed experiment.[49] The Los Angeles LSD scene was particularly fertile in the mid-fifties; it was here that experiments with the drug had the potential for a healthy financial return if inroads could be made into the chronically analysis-prone movie community. Some people were attracted to the high idea of opening the doors of perception, others to the more prosaic rumour of a 'clever pill', but people, for whatever reason, were fascinated. For a time, Grant was drawn into the inner circle of proselytisers of the new cure-all: others included Aldous Huxley, Timothy Leary, Anaïs Nin and Oscar Janinger. Leary, in fact, claimed that Grant was one of the people who 'converted' him to the positive potential of the drug: 'Cary Grant was always my idol. When I was young I modelled myself on him.'[50] In his view, Grant craved 'a life-changing experience', and LSD provided him with the means to begin it: 'Cary was the focus of a hundred million women lusting after him. You couldn't expect him to be like the guy next-door; he was carrying the weight and freight of the world's fantasies. LSD helped him with his burdens.'[51] Huxley, for one, was suspicious of those therapists who seemed to specialise in lucrative sessions with Hollywood celebrities. He wrote of one social encounter: 'We met two Beverly Hills psychiatrists the other day, who specialise in LSD therapy at $100 a shot – and, really, I have seldom met people of lower sensitivity, more vulgar mind! To think of people made vulnerable by LSD being exposed to such people is profoundly disturbing.'[52] It is not clear who Huxley was referring to, but Hartman's notoriety was spreading, and, by the early sixties, his experiments with the drug had fallen foul of the Californian Board of Medical Examiners: in August 1961 it placed him on ten years' probation, and in October suspended him formally from practising in California.

Grant, however, was convinced that he had benefited from the experience: 'All my life I've been searching for peace of mind. Nothing really seemed to give me what I wanted until this treatment.'[53] He claimed that he had learned 'many things' during therapy: 'I learned to accept the responsibility for my own actions, and to blame myself and no one else for circumstances of my own creating. I learned that no one else was keeping me unhappy but me; that I could whip myself better than any other guy in the joint.'[54] In fact, Grant found his burgeoning enthusiasm for this therapeutic use of LSD increasingly hard to contain, and, eventually, while he was shooting the movie *Operation Petticoat* (1959), he could hold back no longer. Two reporters – Joe Hyams and Lionel Crane – both prepared for the usual amusing but scrupulously bland Grant interview, were stunned to find him unusually relaxed, open and keen to share with them the extraordinary experiences he had undergone.[55]

'I have been born again,' he told the astonished Hyams. 'I have just been through a psychiatric experience that has completely changed me. It was horrendous. I had to face things about myself which I never admitted, which I didn't know were there.'[56] He talked about his desperate desire to change his character so that he could be reunited with Betsy Drake; his need to understand himself more clearly, to escape from the old cycle of depressions that had plagued him for most of his adult life. Hyams, listening open-mouthed, began to realise that he had somehow stumbled into 'the most explosive and controversial' interview of his career. 'Now I know that I hurt every woman I loved,' Grant went on to say. 'I was an utter fake, a self-opinionated bore, a know-all who knew very little.'[57] Hyams – 'tense with excitement' – began to record the revelations as Grant continued:

> First I thought, oh, those wasted years. Second, I said, 'Oh, my God, humanity, please come on in . . .'
>
> For the first time in my life I was ready to meet people realistically . . . Every man is conceited, but I know now that in my earlier days I really despised myself. It's when you admit this that you're beginning to change. Introspection is the beginning of courage.
>
> I was always professing a knowledge I didn't have. If I didn't know about a subject I would disdain it. I was very aggressive, but without the courage to be physically aggressive. I was a bad-tempered man but I hid it.
>
> Now everything's changed. My attitude toward women is completely different. I don't intend to foul up any more lives. I could be a good husband now. I'm aware of my faults, and I'm ready to accept responsibilities and exchange tolerances.[58]

He told Hyams what he would go on to tell Crane: 'Now, for the first time in my life, I am truly, deeply and honestly happy.'[59]

Hyams was not too surprised when, soon after the interview, Grant – and his advisors – began to have second thoughts about publicising his use of LSD. He had not changed completely: the fear that his achievements might be undermined by this sudden, unprecedented spate of self-exposure caused him to pull back. It was too late to kill the story entirely; Crane had published his version already – in London's *Daily Mirror*. Hyams, however, had agreed to use some of the material in a series of articles for the New York *Herald Tribune*, which was, as far as Grant was concerned, too close to home when he had a movie (*North by Northwest*) to promote. Stanley Fox, acting on Grant's behalf, ensured that the story went no further.[60] What public revelations there were at the time did nothing, much to his relief, to detract from his box-office appeal. In the short term, Grant avoided any further confessions, and, in the mid-sixties (after the dangers of LSD had become more apparent and most states had enacted their own bans on its possession and use), he tried to distance himself from the 'counter-cultural' connotations of its changed status: 'I wouldn't dream of taking LSD now . . . I don't *need* it now.'[61] Late on in his life, however, at the prompting of interviewers, some of the original evangelical zeal did re-appear.[62]

Did the experience make him happier? Did it change him? His friends and directors at that time seem to have felt that what little change there might have been was at best superficial and short-lived. Richard Brooks, for example, said that he 'didn't recognise that the changes [in Grant] were from taking LSD, but under LSD he was too placid. He was not his questioning self.'[63] Stanley Donen was, if anything, even more sceptical, claiming that Grant had been convinced – temporarily – by his therapists that 'LSD gave him . . . the real answer to the miracle of how to live. Did I notice any real changes? Not really. He was still exactly Cary Grant after LSD. He had the same attitudes, except he felt more secure perhaps.'[64] To David Niven, it had all seemed 'a most hazardous trip for Cary to have taken to find out what we could have told him anyway: that he had always been self-sufficient, that he had always been loved, and that he would continue to give a damn about himself – and particularly about others'.[65]

In time Grant offered a slightly more circumspect account of the significance of this period of intensive self-scrutiny: 'Sufficient kicks in the rear over the years do make a difference, and I think I learned from experience. At least a little bit.'[66] The old, humane, ironic sense of humour started to return, and, reassuringly, the unforgiving self-excoriation gave way to a more constructive self-mockery. He still craved happiness, and remained committed to its pursuit to the end, but was less convinced of the correct means; he became noticeably less confident about what, precisely, had been 'solved' by the treatment: 'Did I find any answers? I don't know. My life is very important to me. I wanted every moment to be as happy as possible. I've learned not to believe any longer in either high emotions or deep depressions.'[67]

Grant's friend Judy Quine was probably right when she suggested that this period marked not so much a revision as a clarification of self for him: 'I think he realised that he was coming closer and closer to becoming the person he always wanted to be and thought he was . . . Cary said, "I invented the person I wanted to be, and I had to find that person." I think he had done that long ago on the screen, long before he was able to do that in a more spiritual sense inside of himself.'[68] Rather than rid himself, once and for all, of Archie

Leach's problems, Cary Grant, it seemed, came to regard them as his own. 'I suddenly realised', he reflected, 'that I had spent the greater part of my life fluctuating between Archie Leach and Cary Grant, unsure of either, suspecting each. Then I began to unify them into one person. With unity came peace and relaxation.'[69]

CHAPTER XII

The Last Romantic Hero

I played a well-dressed, fairly sophisticated chap who is put into intolerable situations.
CARY GRANT

Life typecasts us. Look at me. Do you think I would have chosen to look like this? I would have preferred to have played a leading man in life. I would have been Cary Grant.
ALFRED HITCHCOCK

'I'm a gentleman,' he said. 'A rough lumberman from the big north-west?' she replied. 'I must remember to yell "timber" occasionally,' he said. Cary Grant was back, playing opposite Grace Kelly in *To Catch a Thief* (1955), two years after he had judged his career to be over, still tall, dark and handsome, still charming, still popular. In the same movie, Jessie Royce Landis played a wealthy widow who was flattered to have Grant flirt with her. Four years later, in *North by Northwest* (1959), she played his mother. She was, in fact, ten months his junior. As other leading men of his generation were showing their age, Cary Grant was defying his. He would dive into the dirt as the crop–duster plane buzzed over his head, run along the rooftops, fight on the edge of Mount Rushmore, dance the odd highland fling, and be pursued by attractive young women on trains and boats and even to the top of the Empire State Building. He seemed, as one writer put it, 'Hollywood's lone example of the Sexy Gentleman',[1] the last romantic hero.

He had not expected to become the last romantic hero. This was, after all, supposed to be the dark decade of, in his own words, 'the blue jeans, the dope addicts, the Method',[2] a grim period in which Hollywood tried to switch from glamour to grit, from romance to

178

realism, to project, as Tom Wolfe put it, 'an awesome montage of swung fists, bent teeth, curled lips, popping neck veins, and gurglings'.[3] Heroes were out, anti-heroes were in. Real men were now supposed to be in the grip of existential angst, not romantic ardour. Wolfe called it 'the era of Rake-a-Cheek Romance on the screen. Man meets woman. She rakes his cheek with her fingernails. He belts her in the chops. They fall in a wallow of passion.'[4] This was not supposed to be an era in which Cary Grant would survive, and yet he did much more than survive: he went from strength to strength, setting new box-office records, attracting increasingly warm reviews and appealing to, if anything, an even broader range of fans than before. He was still there, on his own, 'a peerless creation, a worldly, sophisticated man who has become more attractive with the years.'[5] The new trend for callow rawness and nervy lubricity served only to underline the allure of Grant's exotic elegance. The more fidgety other men became, the more relaxed he looked. 'He knew he'd perfected it,' a critic observed, 'and not only perfected it, but patented it. And you'd never be able to spot the join between reality and illusion, however much you strained your eyes.'[6]

In 1948, at the age of forty-four, Grant had come fourth in the box-office poll of the most popular male stars; by 1958, he had risen to the top of that list, and by the start of the next decade he was named as the number one box-office attraction – male or female – in America.[7] His stardom was secure, and it looked as though he had finally come to terms with that fact. The old zestful playfulness was back, he seemed to be *enjoying* himself again – he seemed, in fact, to enjoy being Cary Grant again. He looked, at last, to be at ease with himself. As Kael has written: 'Grant really had got better looking. The sensual lusciousness was burned off: age purified him.'[8] Grant 'and his slim-line clothes developed such an ideal one-to-one love affair that people could grin appreciatively in the sheer pleasure of observing the union'.[9] Tom Wolfe was one such admirer, marvelling at 'the Cary Grant clothes, all worsted, broadcloths and silks, all rich and underplayed, like a viola ensemble'.[10]

It was Alfred Hitchcock who persuaded Grant to return to the screen. He had driven down to Grant's house in Palm Springs one day early in 1954, armed with a draft version of the script for *To Catch a Thief*. He knew that it was going to be far from easy to coax Grant back to acting. 'Don't count on it, Hitch,'[11] Grant had warned him when he had first raised the subject over the telephone a few weeks before. During lunch beside the pool, Grant explained his reasons for withdrawing from Hollywood and from movies: he was too old to be a leading man, he said; he was tired of the routine politics involved in making big-budget movies; he was out of style, out of fashion; he was anxious about how he would look in the new high-clarity VistaVision process; and he had no good reason to risk an anti-climactic return. 'There isn't a thing wrong with you, old man, that a first-rate screenplay won't cure,' Hitchcock replied, handing him the draft. 'I'd appreciate it if you'd read this as soon as possible.'[12]

Grant admired Hitchcock; he was relaxed in his company. He had just seen *Rear Window*, and had been very impressed. He knew from their two previous collaborations that they worked well together. It did not take long for him to commit himself to the project, enticed by a good, amusing script, a pleasant location in the south of France, a generous contract, and a co-star who was close to the peak of her meteoric career: Grace Kelly. Grant was to play John Robie, a debonair Riviera jewel thief who has paid his debt to society by joining the Resistance and performing heroic feats during the war. Kelly's role was that of a wealthy and wilful young woman, Frances Stevens, on vacation with her lavishly bejewelled mother. The movie opens with a new series of cat burglaries in the area, and Robie suspected of coming out of retirement to commit these crimes. Frances is drawn to Robie, in part because she suspects him of planning to relieve her mother of her jewels, and in part because she is attracted to him and hopes that he will prove her wrong.

Grant was fascinated by Kelly: 'She was the most beautiful woman I'd ever known . . . She had the most incredible ESP about me. She could almost read my thoughts. She was cool and reserved, and then she'd say something about my own mood or attitude and it was like she was completely tuned in.'[13] She could improvise (the result, she told him, of her early days in live television soaps[14]), she was very professional (Grant praised her 'Buddha-like' concentration[15]) and she shared his sense of humour; she seemed to him his ideal female co-star. Hitchcock, in turn, was very close to being Grant's ideal director:

Hitch and I had a rapport and understanding deeper than words. He was a very agreeable human being, and we were very compatible. I always went to work whistling when I worked with him because everything on the set was just as you envisioned it would be. Nothing ever went wrong. He was so incredibly well prepared. I never new anyone as capable. He was a tasteful, intelligent, decent, and patient man who knew the actor's business as well as he knew his own.[16]

Hitchcock's screen heroine was a very distinct type: not 'the big, bosomy blonde', but rather 'the ladylike blonde with the touch of elegance, whose sex must be discovered'.[17] Grant also preferred, according to Leslie Caron one of his co-stars, 'women who had a distinction and a certain education about them.'[18] Grace Kelly appeared perfect both for Hitchcock and for Grant; they both wanted Frances Stevens to be the kind of character of whom, when Robie approaches her, 'the audience should be led to wonder whether she intends to shrink from him or tear off his clothes'.[19] An early scene achieves this effect: at the end of an evening spent formally with her mother, Frances is escorted back to her room by Robie; she opens the door, looks coolly at him, puts an arm around him and kisses him firmly full on the mouth, then moves back, offers the faintest of smiles, and shuts the door in his face. Robie is left looking pleasantly shaken. 'It's as though', said a delighted Hitchcock, 'she'd unzipped Cary's fly.'[20]

Only Grant could have reacted to such an unexpected gesture with such a smart combination of amusement, surprise and embarrassment. The scene was, in a way, a sly reprise of countless moments from earlier Cary Grant movies, with the handsome man, his mind on other things, taken unawares by the beautiful woman, leaving him momentarily disoriented. In *To Catch a Thief*, the woman grows more self-assured, more cunning, more in control as each scene progresses. At the beginning, Robie is relaxed and unruffled, observing Frances dispassionately (describing her to her mother as 'very pretty – *quietly* attractive'). Soon, however, Robie loses much of that sense of calm self-control: caught swimming with another woman, he is unnerved by Frances's knowing sarcasm – 'Are you *sure* you were asking about water skis? From where *I* sat it looked as if you two were conjugating some irregular verbs.' Eventually, the woman is, literally, in the driver's seat: steering her car around the notorious bends and precipices of the Corniches, with Robie grimacing with trepidation each time the edges are grazed.[21] The change in the relationship had been symbolised in similar ways in earlier Grant movies: in *Notorious*, for example, he had 'that grin' wiped off his face when his intoxicated female driver accelerated up to 80 miles per hour, and in *I Was a Male War Bride* he was forced to sulk in a side-car while the woman rode the motorcycle. Grant, however, did not let his character seem diminished by his changed circumstances. He looks – slowly, subtly – as though he is beginning to find the woman interesting, and the woman, in turn, looks as though she is growing more attracted to him. It was an unusual form of foreplay for an unusual kind of man; there was never any doubt, however, what the end-result would be. His appeal was not sexless, but rather, as Kael puts it, 'sex with civilised grace, sex with mystery'.[22]

To Catch a Thief was more a collection of scenes than a movie, but it was entertaining in an undemanding way. Grant enjoyed being, once again, the seduced male, with Kelly's character moving subtly from glacial reticence to sexual efflorescence, spicing the dialogue with the kind of *double entendre* Hitchcock relished:

Frances: [*Offering cold chicken at a picnic lunch*] Do you want a leg or a breast?

Robie: You make the choice.

Frances: Tell me, how long has it been?

Robie: How long has what been?

Frances: Since you were in America last.

Hitchcock later admitted that he rewrote some of the dialogue in order to enhance its suggestiveness, and he left some of these lines in fully expecting the censors to object to them; to his surprise, they allowed them to stay. The dialogue that Grant and Kelly share, as a consequence, positively drips with salty innuendo. In a later scene, set in the hotel suite of Frances Stevens, Robie arrives for a view of the fireworks display in Cannes harbour:

Frances: If you really want to see the fireworks, it's better with the lights off. I have a feeling that tonight you're going to see one of the Riviera's most fascinating sights. [*Robie is caught glancing at her strapless evening gown.*] I was talking about the fireworks . . .

Robie: May I have a brandy? Would you care for one?

Frances: Some nights a person doesn't need to drink . . . Give up, John. Admit who you are. Even in this light I can tell where your eyes are looking. [*Close-up of her necklace and generous décolletage.*] Look. Hold them! *Diamonds* – the only thing in the world you can't resist. [*Fireworks explode in the background as she kisses his fingers one by one, and places his hand beneath the necklace.*] Ever had a better offer in your whole life? One with everything? . . . Just as long as you're satisfied. [*Fireworks explode again.*]

Robie: You know as well as I do this necklace is imitation.

Frances: Well, *I'm* not. [*They kiss. Cut to the climax of the fireworks display.*]

After finishing *To Catch a Thief* in September 1954, Grant did not make another movie for more than a year. He wanted to see how it was received before he decided what his long-term future should be. He agreed to go on a national publicity tour when the movie was released in September 1955. Paramount sent Grant all over the United States, making personal appearances, giving press and radio interviews and meeting theatre owners. In New York, he drew the biggest crowds between opening-day performances of the movie since the heyday of the stage shows when he appeared at the Paramount Theater. He was moved by the applause he received, and *To Catch a Thief* became a major box-office success. Reviewers were not overly impressed with the movie as a comedy-thriller, but Grant's performance was uniformly praised ('everyone,' said one critic, 'was talking about how great he looked'[23]). In the end, his decision was not a difficult one: he was back for good.

Apart from a few ill-conceived projects, such as *Kiss Them for Me* (1957) – a rather awkward comedy-drama – and *The Pride and the Passion* (1957) – a costume drama set in Spain during the Napoleonic Wars, which was regarded as memorable only for the off-screen affair that Grant had with his co-star, Sophia Loren[24] – the rest of Grant's movies during this period celebrate his reputation as the last romantic hero. 'No one else looked so good and so intelligent at the same time,' said David Thomson, '*but* there was always a mocking smile or impatience behind his eyes that knew being beautiful was a little silly.'[25] Critics, directors, even actors, began to speak of him as though he was an endangered species, a man of rare quality, a man who knew not too much but just enough, a man of cultured passion. 'He was impeccably dressed', said Leslie Caron, 'and yet he gave out a feeling of animal strength – almost like a jaguar ready to pounce.'[26] Reality and illusion seemed conjoined, even to those close at hand. 'With his leading ladies,' said Caron, 'he had this wonderful rapport, courtesy and tenderness, but with a great deal of humour – just like on the screen. It was really very pleasant. It was like going out with a gentleman.'[27] Eva Marie Saint, another of his co-stars, stressed what a sympathetic actor she found him to be: 'You just always felt that he was with you every minute – not only for *his* close-ups, but for your close-ups too.'[28] Having outlived or outlasted the competition, Grant's graceful singularity was more precious than ever. As one reviewer observed, Grant's name 'virtually assures box-office success to any picture in which he appears'.[29] Even if one missed the rawness, the edgy excitement, of those earlier performances, one could still appreciate the consummate technique of the mature roles. Richard Schickel noted that Grant now seemed 'to glow, to radiate masculine power perfectly deployed', his stance 'so casual and yet so commanding', causing audiences to share 'an unspoken agreement, democratically arrived at, that the only permissible response to him is bedazzlement'.[30]

It was not an entirely subjective response. Grant really had become a more subtle, a more accomplished, performer: technically, he had grown sophisticated enough to do less but with greater effect. Pauline Kael remarked that age had not just 'purified' his looks, age had also purified his acting:

When he was young, he had been able to do lovely fluff like *Topper* without being too elfin, or getting smirky, like Ray Milland, or becoming a brittle, too bright gentleman, like Franchot Tone. But he'd done more than his share of arch mugging – lowering his eyebrows and pulling his head back as if something funny were going on in front of him when nothing was. Now the excess energy was pared away; his performances were simple and understated and seamlessly smooth . . . His romantic glamor, which had reached a peak in 1939 in *Only Angels Have Wings*, wasn't lost; his glamor was now a matter of his resonances from the past, and he wore it like a mantle.[31]

Kael recalls seeing Anthony Quinn sitting in an airport VIP lounge watching Grant in *To Catch a Thief*, pointing at the screen and announcing loudly to no one in particular, '*That's* the actor I always wanted to be.'[32] She was amused by the remark, because, as she noted, 'Quinn has never learned the first thing from Cary Grant.'[33] One of the reasons why Grant's career settled into such a pleasing equilibrium during the fifties was that he, unlike most of his contemporaries, learned how to avoid self-caricature. As Kael – a particularly shrewd judge of such things – so memorably puts it:

> If you should ask Anthony Quinn 'Do you know how to dance?' he would cry '*Do I know how to dance?*' and he'd answer the question with his whole body – and you'd probably wind up sorry that you'd asked. Cary Grant might twirl a couple of fingers, or perhaps he'd execute an intricate, quick step and make us long for more. Unlike the macho actors who as they got older became strident about their virility, puffing their big, flabby chests in an effort to make themselves look even larger, Grant, with his sexual diffidence, quietly became less physical – and more assured. He doesn't wear out his welcome: when he has a good role, we never get enough of him. Not only is his reserve his greatest romantic resource – it is the resource that enables him to age gracefully.[34]

The screenwriter William Goldman has spoken, more specifically, of how, during this period, Grant mastered the art of editing his own lines, getting 'other people in the scene to do the expository talking'.[35] Grant said at the time that the 'pitfall of most young actors is that they never really listen to a scene. Instead, they worry about how they *look* listening to a scene. The pitfall of most young men is that they rarely listen to a conversation. Instead they worry about what other people think of them listening to a conversation.'[36] It was a significant distinction: Cary Grant used his subtlety as an actor to highlight his subtlety as a man.

Most leading men of the period behaved as though they did not find women interesting as people rather than as mere sex objects or maternal figures ('*Stella!*'); they sometimes seemed ready to have women listen to them, but they seldom seemed prepared to listen to women. They were generally too preoccupied with their own problems to pay much attention to anyone else's. Whether they were strong or weak, young or old, confident or insecure, a rebel or a conformist, the world was their world, it revolved around them, and women, if they were allowed inside at all, were admitted only on certain terms. Cary Grant – strikingly in this sense – was different. He offered women a civilised equality. Although in many ways he was more of an Edwardian than a 'New Man', he seemed, at the time, a refreshingly *courteous* figure. He looked as though he was genuinely interested in the women who appeared opposite him, treating them not merely as attractive women but also as complicated, intelligent, independent, vulnerable, witty human beings. By the fifties, in his more mature roles, he came to treat women with even more respect than before, showing a desire to understand them, to *appreciate* them, rather than merely to bed them. 'Grant is interested in the qualities of a *particular* woman,' wrote Kael, 'her sappy expression, her non sequiturs, the way her voice bobbles. She isn't going to be pushed to the wall as soon as she's with him.'[37]

It was this willingness to listen, to let women think, speak and act in his presence, that made Grant so good at the 'seduced male' roles of this period. Audiences knew so much about him, felt at ease with him, and so, it seemed, did the characters in his movies, encouraging a greater sense of complicity as they examined that extraordinary and well-established screen persona. 'The heroines of the later movies,' said a critic, 'are all aware that he's a legendary presence, that they're trying to seduce a legend.'[38] On occasion, the actors would improvise a line that confirmed this awareness: 'How do you shave in there?' asks a woman in one of these movies,[39] putting her finger to the cleft in his chin. His silent, puzzled, look in response says it all; there is the wariness of the celebrity as well as the coyness of the man in that expression.

An Affair to Remember (1957),[40] is a good example of the way in which the later roles were often written with an arched awareness of the man who assumed them. Grant played Nickie Ferrante, a dilettante artist and man about town, who enters into a shipboard romance with Terry McKay (Deborah Kerr), a refined and independent woman who used to be a nightclub singer. To his role of the faintly *louche bon vivant*, Grant brought irony, not just as a means of light relief in a sentimental story, but also to support the mature conviction that irony is a significant ingredient in any complicated adult experience. In one of the better scenes, featuring some mildly flirtatious comic dialogue between Ferrante and Terry, Grant's own, well-known, history of marital disappointments is woven into the texture of Ferrante's character with an ease and a fine effect that audiences had come to expect of a Cary Grant movie:

Terry: And women . . . ?

Ferrante: Oh, *women* . . .

Terry: You've known quite a few. And I suppose they've all been *madly* in love with you . . .

Ferrante: I doubt it.

Terry: . . . but, er, you haven't had much respect for *them* . . .

Ferrante: On the contrary!

Terry: Still, you've always been very *fair* in your judgements . . .

Ferrante: Yes. I've been *more* than fair. I idealise them. Every woman I meet I put up there [*puts his hand high up*]. Of course, the longer I know her [*starts letting his hand move lower*] and the better I know her [*hand moves lower still*] . . .

Terry: Yes, it's hard to *keep* them up there, isn't it?

Ferrante: Yes, isn't it!

Terry: Pretty soon the pedestal wobbles . . . and then topples . . .

Ferrante: [*smiling*] *C'est la vie!*

Tom Wolfe saw the mature Grant as 'a Romantic Bourgeois Hero',[41] the 'loverboy of the bourgeoisie'.[42] He was wrong. True, most of his characters were comfortable materially, and some were businessmen, but none were brash nor middlebrow, and none of them were so easy to place in terms of background or breeding. There was nothing exclusive about Grant's appeal: he had seemed stateless and classless for some time. There was nothing bland about him, either: Hitchcock acknowledged this, exploiting Grant's witty acceptance of his own foolishness by placing his screen character, time after time, in intolerable, humiliating or unsettling situations; Howard Hawks recognised it, too, seizing on every opportunity to ruffle Grant's smooth elegance (enforced changes into ill-fitting and inappropriate clothes, sudden pratfalls and embarrassing cases of mistaken identity). Unlike, say, Rock Hudson (who was more like a Grant re-drafted by an accountant), there was a hint of disorder lurking below the romantic and orderly surface. A review of *That Touch of Mink* (1962), which co-starred Grant with Doris Day, said that the only significant difference between *Lover Come Back* (1962) and *That Touch of Mink* was that 'in *Lover Come Back* the Cary Grant part was played by Rock Hudson, and in *That Touch of Mink*, the Cary Grant part is played by Cary Grant. When it comes to playing Cary Grant, nobody can beat Cary Grant.'[43]

Although most of Grant's characters from this late period are, ostensibly, middle or upper class, his playfulness distances him from his more conventional colleagues. In *Indiscreet* (1958), for example, he does not hesitate to attempt a high-flung highland fling (indeed, he comes alive during the performance), and in *The Grass is Greener* (1960) he clearly takes great pleasure in mocking his aristocratic character's over-refined tastes and mannerisms. He remained the democratic gentleman, one of us rather than one of them, the fine urbanity still sheltering the old mass allegiances.

Grant's fourth and final movie for Hitchcock, *North by Northwest* (1959), was the most self-conscious in its use of his own image.[44] He played Roger O. Thornhill ('What does the O. stand for?' 'Nothing'), an advertising executive. Thornhill, like Grant, is an intriguingly mysterious, elusive figure, familiar yet with a nimbus of oddity about him:

Thornhill: I know. I look vaguely familiar.

Woman: Yes.

Thornhill: You feel you've seen me somewhere before.

Woman: Mmmm.

Thornhill: Funny how I have that effect on people. It's something about my face.

Woman: It's a nice face.

Thornhill: You think so?

Woman: I wouldn't say it if I didn't.

Thornhill: Oh, you're *that* type!

Thornhill, finding himself accused, inexplicably, of murder, introduces himself, unconvincingly, as 'Jack Phillips, western sales manager for Kingby Electronics', but, even when the woman, Eve Kendall, shows him that she is well aware of his real identity, he gives little away. If he is not assuming a disguise, he finds one imposed on him by others:

Stranger: My secretary is a great admirer of your methods, Mr Kaplan. Elusiveness, however misguided . . .

Thornhill: Wait a minute. Did you call me 'Kaplan'?

Stranger: Oh, I know you're a man of many names, but I'm perfectly willing to accept your current choice.

Another aspect of Grant's screen persona which is played on here is his civilised non-aggressiveness:

Thornhill: Honest women frighten me.

Eve: Why?

Thornhill: I don't know. Somehow they seem to put me at a disadvantage.

Eve: Is it because you're not honest with them?

Thornhill: Exactly . . . What I mean is the moment I meet an attractive woman, I have to start pretending I have no desire to make love to her.

Eve: What makes you think you have to conceal it?

Thornhill: She might find the idea objectionable.

Eve: Then again, she might not.

Thornhill: Think how *lucky* I am to have been seated here!

Eve: Oh, luck had nothing to do with it.

Thornhill: Fate?

Eve: I tipped the steward five dollars to seat you here if you should come in.

Thornhill: Is that a proposition?

Eve: I never discuss love on an empty stomach.

Thornhill: You've already eaten.

Eve:　　But *you* haven't . . .

Hitchcock and his screenwriter, Ernest Lehman, devised a plot that depended on the audience identifying unquestioningly with Grant as a 'normal' man to whom abnormal things happen but who nevertheless still seems – just – to avoid losing control. Hitchcock thus has Grant chased by a mysterious crop-dusting plane, kidnapped, forced to swallow a full bottle of bourbon, humiliated in court, mocked by his mother, made to squeeze into the berth of a train compartment, disguise himself as a redcap, fake his own death and fight on George Washington's Mount Rushmore profile. As he had done before, Hitchcock conceived some additional in-jokes, such as obliging his scrupulously fit ('Say, do I look *heavyish* to you?') and glamorous ('he's a well-tailored one, isn't he?') leading man to ruin several of his own bespoke suits by diving in the dirt before suffering the even greater indignity of being obliged to wear the cheap and ill-fitting suit of an imaginary man who, he complains, 'has dandruff'. The playfulness, further complicating a story that already was more gnomic than even Hitchcock was used to, underlined the confidence the director had in the actor. Grant was perfect for the role, combining the wit, exasperation, inventiveness, disillusionment and wounded passion of the curious Roger Thornhill.

Grant's romantic appeal looked just as strong at the beginning of the sixties. In what was arguably his last truly satisfying movie, *Charade* (1963), he gives a remarkably calm and engaging performance that draws on all those qualities which had contributed so much to his past successes: the fascinating ambiguity of the intimate stranger (he plays Peter Joshua, who may really be Alexander Dyle, or Adam Canfield, or Brian Cruikshank, who is a murderer, or a thief or a government official, and who may be married, divorced or single); the elegant good looks of the leading man ('he's tall – over six feet – rather thin – in good physical shape, I'd say – dark eyes – quite handsome really'); the disposition and tricks of the old music-hall performer (in an improvised scene set in a nightclub, he has to participate in a game that involves, in his case, rolling an orange with his chin over the body of a rather large, matronly woman); the masculine bravado of the action hero (fights on rooftops, chases, shoot-outs); and the timing and skill of the talented light comedian (subtle double-takes, sly one-liners).

He had only agreed to appear in the movie after he succeeded in persuading the screenwriter, Peter Stone, to re-write the central characters in such a way as to bridge the difference between his own age and that of his thirty-three year old co-star, Audrey Hepburn.[45] While he was not, it seemed, self-conscious about his age in his off-screen life (he had started dating Dyan Cannon, who was his junior by some thirty-five years), he had come to feel, at the age of fifty-eight,[46] that there was a danger of him appearing 'a dirty old man'.[47] 'He made me change the dynamic of the characters and make Audrey the aggressor,' Stone recalled. 'She chased him, and he tried to dissuade her. She pursued him and sat in his lap. She found him irresistible, and ultimately he was worn down by her.'[48] This was, therefore, probably the most self-conscious and overt depiction of the 'seduced male':

Reggie: Aren't you allowed to kiss back?

Adam: No. The doctor said it would be bad for my thermostat. [*She kisses him again.*] When you come on, you really come on.

Reggie: Well, come on!

The dialogue recalls the spirited exchanges of Grant's comedies from the late thirties and forties:[49]

Reggie: Won't you come in for a minute?

Peter: No, I won't.

Reggie: I don't *bite*, you know – unless it's called for . . .

Peter: How would you like a spanking?

Reggie: How would you like a punch on the nose? Stop treating me like a child!

The age difference, far from being a problem, becomes the source of a distinctive and fruitful brand of comic repartee:

Reggie: Oh-oh – here it comes. The fatherly talk. You forget I'm already a widow.

Alex: So was Juliet – at fifteen.

Reggie: I'm not fifteen.

Alex: Well, there's your trouble right there - you're too *old* for me.

Reggie: Why can't you be serious?

Alex: There, you just said an 'orrible word.

Reggie: Said what?

Alex: 'Serious.' When a man gets to be my age that's the last word he ever wants to hear. I don't want to be serious — and I especially don't want *you* to be.

Reggie: Okay, I'll tell you what — we'll just sit around all day being frivolous — how about that? [*She starts kissing him*]

Alex: Now, please, Reggie — cut it out.

Reggie: Okay [*Pulling back*].

Alex: What are you doing?

Reggie: Cutting it out.

Alex: Who told you to do that?

Reggie: You did.

Alex: But I'm not through complaining yet!

'Audrey and I had a wonderful time making *Charade*,' said Grant, 'and I think it shows.'[50] It was a great success. According to Tom Wolfe's account, at the movie's première at Radio City Music Hall, 'thousands turned out in lines along 50th Street and Sixth Avenue, many of them in the chill of 6 a.m., in order to get an early seat'.[51] Grant's box-office pulling power had grown even greater. After all the soul-searching, the niggling anxieties and the tiresome routine of a decade or so ago, it had been a triumphant return by Cary Grant.

If, at that relatively late stage in Grant's career, a movie had been designed as a celebration of his special appeal, it would probably have resulted in something very much like *Charade*. It allowed him to combine all of those aspects of his screen persona which had been developed and refined during three decades of working in movies. If the movie was not faultless, the central performance surely was. As Audrey Hepburn's character says to him: 'Do you know what's wrong with you? *Nothing*!'

RETIREMENT

Professor:	You are welcome to stay. I shall sleep in the bathtub.
Actress:	That would be absolutely uncomfortable.
Professor:	A fine American tradition.
Actress:	You can't sleep in the bath.
Professor:	What's good enough for Cary Grant is good enough for me.

INSIGNIFICANCE

Sam:	You call her on the phone and say 'come let's look at Swatches?' She's not gonna see right through that?
Jay:	Well, you don't do it like I do it, you do it in your own suave way. Think: Cary Grant.

SLEEPLESS IN SEATTLE

CHAPTER XIII

The Real World

What do you mean, there's no such person? I've been in his hotel room.
I've tried on his clothes!
ROGER O. THORNHILL

It was time to climb off the celluloid and join the real world.
CARY GRANT

Cary Grant made his last movie in 1966. Although his retirement
was never made official, he knew, after he had completed his final
scene, that his screen career was over. His colleagues, his friends, his
fans were incredulous: there had been no obvious decline in his
performances, nor in his popularity. 'At any age,' said Billy Wilder,
'Cary Grant would still be a heartbreaker. He would still be the most
attractive man on the screen. He did not age one bit. His hair got
gray. That's all.'[1] Stanley Donen agreed: 'I never could understand
why,' he said of Grant's decision, 'but he was determined.'[2]

His two most recent movies had suggested that, far from winding
down his career, he was looking for ways to extend it. *Father Goose*
(1964) had been a significant departure for him. He had played, in
his own words, 'an unshaven old gray-haired sot in sloppy denims'[3]
who is forced to act as a look-out in the Pacific during World War
Two. Leslie Caron played the marooned young teacher of seven girls
whom he rescues and, gradually, is domesticated by. Audiences found
much to admire in a movie that had a good comic script (which
won an Academy Award for its writers, Peter Stone and Frank Tarloff), and, at its centre, a fine, crafty, performance from Grant – as
Walter Eckland – who seemed to relish the opportunity to take so

many liberties with his elegant screen persona. Less distracted by the exceptional looks, viewers took more notice of the exceptional talent. Commercially, the movie was, if anything, even more successful than *Charade*, and the critics were positive (one judging Grant 'as graceful as ever', another describing his performance as 'excellent'[4]). In its first week at Radio City, it took in $210,380, breaking that cinema's previous one-week record (for *Charade*) by more than $30,000.[5] *Time* magazine joked that Grant had now become so rich he could, if he chose, join NATO.[6] *Father Goose* proved that Grant could still attract huge audiences even when he was not playing his usual debonair characters.

His next movie – *Walk, Don't Run* (1966) – was meant to prove that he could also play engaging but more mature, 'fatherly', characters who were not destined to win the love of young leading women. Grant appeared as Sir William Rutland, an English businessman visiting the 1964 Olympic Games in Tokyo and finding accommodation only by persuading a young woman, Christine Easton (Samantha Eggar), to share her apartment with him. The romance, in this case, was between Easton and Steve Davis (Jim Hutton), the American athlete whom Rutland has sneaked into the apartment and acted as matchmaker for. Grant's role was similar to that of the angel in *The Bishop's Wife*, bringing two people together before disappearing as suddenly as he had appeared. Although it compared unfavourably with the highly acclaimed 1943 original (entitled *The More the Merrier*),[7] the reviews were generally favourable (*America* judging Grant 'as deft and winning a light comedian as ever',[8] *Newsweek* remarking that Grant 'could not be unfunny if he tried',[9] and the *New Yorker* adding that Grant had 'never looked handsomer or in finer fettle'[10]) and commercially the movie was by no means unsuccessful.[11] If Grant had been in doubt as to his popularity as the decade entered its second half, he should have been reassured. As the *New Yorker* review concluded, if his appearance, as well as his performance, 'proves anything it is that his attempted abdication as a screen dreamboat is premature and will have to be withdrawn: he is a good ten years away from playing anyone's jolly, knowing uncle, and as for lovable Mr Fixit, he should be ready for that role in about the year 2000'.[12]

Hollywood, however, had changed, and Cary Grant no longer felt at home there. He had, since the early fifties, done his best to avoid Hollywood studio-based productions, preferring to work away, on location, in such places as Spain, France, Italy and London. He complained that he had grown tired of tripping over studio cables,[13] and, as his own producer, he had taken advantage of the economic benefits of shooting movies in Europe, but it was also true that he had come to feel isolated and unhappy in the Hollywood of the sixties. Few of his trusted colleagues were still working regularly – Grace Kelly was now Princess Grace, in 'exile' in Monaco, Katharine Hepburn seemed in virtual retirement, David Niven had moved to Switzerland – and some – Bogart, Flynn, Gable, Cooper – had died. Worse still, for such a private man as Grant, the studios – less stable financially since the fifties – had begun to exploit their own commercial appeal as 'historic cultural centres', starting their own tourist packages. Grant worked – and, on occasion, lived and slept – in one of the bungalows on the Universal lot. Each bungalow had two offices, a kitchen, and secretaries' and writers' rooms; Marlon Brando, James Stewart, Doris Day, Tony Curtis and Elizabeth Taylor were among those celebrities who had their own duplex. Grant had cherished the opportunity this arrangement gave him to mix, in relative privacy, with writers – such as Mel Brooks and Peter Stone – directors – such as Hitchcock – and other performers. He was, therefore, horrified when Universal started organising 'official' $3 tours of the studio for the public: open-topped buses would move slowly past his bungalow throughout each day, announcing, '*That's* Cary Grant's bungalow!', '*That's* Cary Grant's car!' and '*This* is where Cary Grant sunbathes!' He had made *Walk, Don't Run* for Columbia because he had wanted to teach Universal a lesson. 'I'm not an animal in a zoo!' he complained.[14]

He had also become disenchanted with the quality of the scripts he was being sent. Even *Walk, Don't Run* relied on a twenty-three-year-old story. If he was to continue as a leading man, he needed – in spite of such reassuring reviews as *The New Yorker*'s – novel, intelligent, imaginative stories and sensitive writers, and the kind of ironic, knowing, dialogue that had made the 'age issue' in *Charade* seem inoffensive. Most of what he read, however, struck him as either unoriginal or tasteless. As for the somewhat melancholic prospect of switching permanently to scene-stealing 'character' roles, he was gifted enough technically to do so but he was probably vain enough to find the idea too depressing, and he certainly had no need to consider such a move unless he could convince himself that it would interest him more than his other activities. 'I could have gone on acting and playing a grandfather or a bum,' he said, 'but I discovered more important things in life.'[15]

What was more important to Grant, he had discovered, was the prospect of becoming a father for the first time at the age of sixty-two. He had married Dyan Cannon in Las Vegas on 22 July 1965.[16] Seven months later, on 26 February 1966, she gave birth to a baby girl. Grant was, at long last, a father. He had always wanted to have children. As early as 1940, when he was shooting the melodramatic *Penny Serenade* (which concerned a couple's desperate struggle to adopt a child), he told his co-star Irene Dunne of his intention to marry Barbara Hutton: 'I know what my children are going to look like. They're going to be blond with brown eyes.'[17] It was not to be. Although the couple tried for a family, Hutton could not conceive.[18] Grant was bitterly disappointed: 'Barbara was cut to ribbons long before I knew her,' he said.[19] He did, however, become surrogate father to Hutton's son from her earlier marriage to Count Reventlow: Lance, born in 1937, became devoted to Grant, calling himself 'Lance Grant' when he started school (much to his real father's anger).[20] Grant remained very close to Lance after the divorce from Hutton, continuing to refer to the boy, in private, as his 'son',[21] and even after Grant married Betsy Drake he used to have Lance stay with them, helping with his schooling, tutoring him for exams and encouraging him before his first few dates. Grant and Drake – in spite of their mutual desire for a family – remained childless during their marriage.[22] Writing in 1962, recalling his movies of the previous decade, he noted that two of his favourite co-stars, Grace Kelly and Eva Marie Saint, both 'went on to raising happy and beautiful children'; 'I wish', he added, '*I* could say the same.'[23] Four years later his daughter was born.

'She is my best production,'[24] he said of his first (and, as it turned out, only) child. Her parents decided to name her Jennifer. 'She's the most winsome, captivating girl I've ever known,' he told reporters, 'the most beautiful baby in the world.'[25] His friend Peggy Lee remembered the profound effect the birth of his daughter had on him: 'When he had Jennifer, that was the main event. The wonder of having a child never left him. I've seen fathers look at babies but never the way Cary looked at Jennifer.'[26] After her birth – five months before *Walk, Don't Run* was released – Grant was simply too preoccupied with her to commit himself to any new projects. Whenever directors or writers or studio executives would attempt to persuade him to consider a new movie, he just smiled, shook his head and explained that he was no longer interested; when they asked him why, he would reach into his pocket and produce a picture of Jennifer: '*This* is why.'[27]

'I won't say that I'll never make another picture,' Grant told one interviewer at the time, 'because I can't look into the future.'[28] There were, as a result, many attempts to pull him out of his unofficial 'retirement'.[29] It was said that Grant might appear in *The Vicar's Wife*, a new movie with a screenplay by Alan Bennett.[30] Alfred Hitchcock had long harboured hopes of developing an intriguing movie based on *Hamlet* specifically for Grant.[31] MGM wanted him to star in a re-make of the 1932 *Grand Hotel*.[32] At the beginning of the seventies, Joseph Mankiewicz asked him to appear in *Sleuth* (1972)[33] and he was invited to consider a similarly lucrative deal for appearing in *A Touch of Class* (1973).[34] He also had several projects which had, at various times, been commissioned or monitored by him personally, including a script he had, for a brief period, owned, *1,000 Cups of Crazy German Coffee*,[35] another intended for Dyan Cannon and himself, *The Old Man and Me*,[36] a movie based on the life of Buffalo Bill,[37] and a movie version of *Gulliver's Travels* (which had been a long-time ambition, beginning in 1949 when he asked Thornton Wilder to write a screenplay for Howard Hawks and himself to work on).[38] Warren Beatty, as late as 1977, pleaded with Grant (and offered him one million dollars) to appear briefly in *Heaven Can Wait* (1978), in the cameo role that Claude Rains played in the 1941 original, *Here Comes Mr Jordan*; Grant declined, saying it was 'not a good part. Long speeches. Stands around a lot. Everybody else gets the jokes.'[39] A particularly bizarre proposal – dismissed out of hand by Grant – was for him to appear in a re-make of *Harvey*, with Elton John as the invisible rabbit.[40] The most grotesque offer, however, without any doubt, came from Grant's old co-star, Mae West, who wanted him to return with her for *Sextette* (1978);[41] she had tried before to persuade him to reappear with her in a re-make of *She Done Him Wrong*[42] but, on both occasions, he declined politely.

'When Cary retired,' said Billy Wilder, 'I started concocting stories for a man with gray hair in his early seventies, but he told me, "No, I'm not going to do it anymore." He guarded the last few years of his life brilliantly. But to the very end I can assure you there were several pictures for which the studios wanted Cary, but he was just not available.'[43] The producer Robert Evans, who came to know Grant during the sixties, pleaded with him to reconsider: 'When you're an original, you owe it to the world – you can't retire simply because you can't be duplicated.'[44] Evans insisted: 'Everything about Cary was stamped "original" . . . Fashion is temporary. Style lasts forever.'[45] Grant was not unaware of the fact that Hollywood could not replace him: Ryan O'Neal, when he was preparing to appear in the nostalgic screwball comedy *What's Up, Doc?* (1972), asked Grant for advice on how to play 'a Cary Grant-type part'.[46] The director, Peter Bogdanovich, would have preferred to have worked with Grant himself,[47] but he knew that his chance had gone. '[Grant] didn't need the money,' said the agent Irving 'Swifty' Lazar, 'so he wasn't even tempted. I once offered him three million dollars to do a movie, which today [1990] would be twenty million, and he wouldn't do it. He said, "It's not a question of money. I wouldn't do it for any amount."'[48]

'My life changed the day Jennifer was born', he said. 'I've come to think that the reason we're put on this earth is to procreate. To leave something behind. Not films, because you know that I don't think my films will last very long once I'm gone. But another human being. That's what's important.'[49] He seemed content to stay at home and look after his daughter, while Cannon, although she was an attentive young mother, grew increasingly eager to resume her acting career.[50] He visited the baby's room early each morning to gaze at her; he consulted dieticians and supervised the food she was weaned on; he photographed her expressions, tape-recorded her sounds; and fretted over her slightest cough. It was as if nothing else mattered to him any more; all other relationships took second place to that between father and daughter.[51] Years later, he said that he stopped acting because he 'wanted to have the time to spend with her. I wanted to be able to watch her grow up.'[52] At the time, most of his old colleagues expected him to tire of fatherhood, just as he had tired of all other activities and theories which had, for brief periods, obsessed him. In this case, he did not. Although he was careful to avoid any definitive statements about his long-term intentions, he was convinced that it was time to move on to other things – 'the real world',[53] as he later put it. 'I no longer care to see something that isn't actually happening . . . I don't read fiction any more or go to plays or movies,' he said, exaggerating for effect; 'I'm more curious about actuality.'[54] It would become his standard response to any questions about his movie career: 'I'm interested in truth, in reality.'[55]

His relationship with his baby daughter was – at least from his point of view – joyful, but his relationship with his wife was, it seems, deteriorating rapidly.[56] Peter Bogdanovich, who socialised with the couple at the time, was not surprised when the marriage began to disintegrate: 'I somehow felt Cary was more in love with her than she was with him. Certainly he doted on her and seemed to do whatever she asked, and she appeared to enjoy showing him off. "Sing 'em that song, Archie!" she cried out on the way back from a ball game.'[57] Others, however, felt that Cannon, since the birth of Jennifer, had become too submissive. Cannon herself later spoke of her 'Pygmalion relationship'[58] with Grant: he advised her on clothes (elegant, understated), make-up (he disliked it) and career (he would help her find movie roles, but not until their child was older). Grant wanted to stay at home each evening, whereas Cannon preferred to socialise occasionally: 'He dominated me completely, and I was so eager to please.'[59] In the end, she walked out. Grant, horrified that his fourth marriage, in spite of all his self-analysis and LSD therapy, was not working, and desperate to ensure that he did not lose access to his daughter, made several attempts at a reconciliation, but Cannon remained adamant that she wanted her freedom. Towards the end of August 1967, she entered the superior court in Los Angeles and sued for divorce on the grounds that Grant had treated her in 'a cruel and inhuman manner'.[60] A date for the hearing was, eventually, set for 20 March 1968.

Before defendant and plaintiff could appear in court, Grant was involved in a car crash in New York. The accident was fairly serious: his chauffeur was badly hurt and Grant himself was taken to hospital[61] with bruising and grazing to his face and three broken ribs. While Grant was in hospital, the divorce proceedings in Los Angeles began. On the following day, all the newspapers, to Grant's acute embarrassment, reported what Cannon had to say. The New York *Daily News*, America's highest-circulation newspaper of the time, carried a headline on the front page of its 21 March issue: 'Life with Cary Grant a "Nightmare".' Rarely had a celebrity of Grant's stature been so publicly attacked. The court was told that Grant was 'an apostle of LSD' who had attempted to prevail on Cannon 'to use the drug many times';[62] he had been moody, prone to 'yelling and screaming' episodes, and had spanked her; he had become 'violent and out of control' as he watched the Academy Awards ceremony on television, spilling his wine and shouting that 'everyone on the show had their faces lifted'; he had refused to allow Cannon to take along her supply of baby food when they took Jennifer to Bristol to see Elsie Leach, because 'the cows in England are as good as they are in this country'.[63] If some of the assertions were trivial or mildly amusing, the more serious allegations were – or at least appeared at the time to be – extremely damaging to Grant's reputation. His friends were not surprised that he did not respond to the claims – after all, it had long been his custom not to respond to any such reports – but they were concerned that, on this particular occasion, he was seeming to give credence to the allegations through his continued silence. 'I realise I've made mistakes with Dyan,' Grant confided to Sheilah Graham, 'I'll give her all the odds. I won't fight. She can have everything she wants.'[64] His friend Henry Gris recalls that 'all Cary ever said was "After all – she's the mother of my child"'.[65] Eventually, Grant's trial lawyer released a statement: 'If Miss Cannon feels a need to seek public sympathy and approbation through a press agent, that is up to her. As Mr Grant's legal representative we have good reason for our decisions, and each action is carefully considered, and taken, in accordance only to what is best for his child's welfare.'[66]

When Grant left hospital, he flew back to Los Angeles to recuperate. He said that he just wanted to be close to Jennifer. On 21 March, the uncontested decree was granted, but had modified alimony to $50,000 per year in support payments. Cannon lost her plea that Grant's visits to Jennifer should be limited to daylight hours and that he should not visit her overnight or without a nurse being present. It was said that the sum granted was considerably less than Grant's initial offer, and the judge, believing evidence that Grant had not used LSD for more than a year, gave him two months' visiting rights per year without restrictions.[67] As a father, Grant had been exonerated. As a husband, he had been gravely embarrassed. As a star, remarkably, the spectacular disclosures and allegations had, it seemed, left the general public unimpressed; he was still the object of mass affection. The episode had, none the less, been extremely painful for both parties. Grant's closest friends agreed that the months following the end of his marriage were the absolute nadir of his life. Henry Gris recalls that Grant would stay in his house 'all day for word from the nurse as to when he could get to see his little girl for an hour or two. He'd just sit and hope the phone would ring. He wouldn't make plans with *anyone* if he thought there was a chance he could see his child.'[68] Although, eventually, they re-established their friendship,[69] Grant was, for some time after their divorce, very bitter about Cannon's behaviour, and, for a brief period, he seemed to have grown deeply cynical about women in general: 'Once the female has used the male for procreation, she turns on him and literally devours him.'[70]

Coming to fatherhood so late, Grant manifested a near obsession for his daughter's safety and well-being. It had been decreed in court, at his insistence, that her face should never be photographed because of his fear of kidnappers (a fear that, understandably, was made even more acute after it was discovered that Grant's was one of the names on Charles Manson's 'hit list'[71]), and Grant moved around the country to be in close proximity to her whenever her mother was working on location. 'You get desperate to see your child,' he said, 'absolutely desperate.'[72] In time, Grant and Cannon managed to achieve a modicum of give-and-take, agreeing more flexible and amicable arrangements for the access of each to their daughter. 'Cary did some wonderful things for me, and I for him,' Cannon said, towards the end of the decade; 'when he comes to see Jennifer and me now, the circumstances are very much the same as when we were dating. I can talk. We talk a lot about Jennifer . . . She knows she's loved.'[73]

Grant, having distanced himself from the Hollywood community, and finding himself single once again, was not entirely sure what he should do with the rest of his life. Without other obligations, he was, at least in the short term, happy to avail himself of long-standing invitations to visit old friends. In the aftermath of the very public dissolution of his marriage, he was particularly pleased to travel abroad to spend time with Ingrid Bergman in Paris, J. Paul Getty in London, Sophia Loren and Carlo Ponti in Rome, and Grace Kelly and Prince Rainier in Monaco. He still had meetings to attend in Hollywood, and new projects to discuss, but he sensed the aimlessness of his life after decades of making movies. Television was an attractive and lucrative option for some of his contemporaries – Lucille Ball, Bob Hope, Donna Reed and Debbie Reynolds all had their own shows

– but Grant had always been opposed to appearing on the small screen, describing 'television men' as 'a fast trading group and I don't want to get involved with them'.[74] He had not appeared on stage since 1931,[75] and he was certainly not attracted to the idea of a return in his mid-sixties. What *did* appeal to him, however, was the world of business.

Two months after his divorce from Dyan Cannon, the business section of the *New York Times*, on 22 May 1968, announced: 'Rayette-Fabergé Elects Cary Grant to Board.' The news was a considerable surprise: not just because Grant was committing himself to something other than movies, but also because of the irony that Grant – who had refused to wear make-up for his screen appearances, and who had made some fairly disparaging remarks in public about the cosmetics industry in the past – was joining a toiletries firm. Was this, wondered some of Grant's movie associates, the same Cary Grant who had said that he disliked 'an abundance of make-up or perfume', and that he admired a woman 'for her lack of artifice'?[76] They were puzzled, but the business world, and the newspapers, were fascinated. Grant's motives might have been hard to fathom, but Fabergé's seemed transparent: the firm had established a very public connection with a man who epitomised good taste, unforced elegance and style, as appealing to the masses as he was to the privileged minority. His salary, it was announced, was to be $15,000 per year, with $200 extra for each directors' meeting he attended.[77] On the day that he accepted, the company's stock rose two points on the New York Stock Exchange. George Barrie, its founder and president, had, at the very least, pulled off an audacious public-relations coup.

Grant liked Barrie, who had started his career as a jazz musician and shared many of Grant's interests and tastes. He had accepted Barrie's proposal, he said, 'because when it was offered to me they threw in the odd bit of travel and a roof over my head'.[78] The 'odd bit of travel' was made more congenial to Grant by providing him with his own private jet – a luxurious Fabergé Convair plane – equipped with a portable piano and a bar, with two bedrooms and thick carpeting, and the 'roof' over his head may have referred to his office in Fabergé's New York headquarters (the old Rockefeller townhouse) or perhaps to the Fabergé townhouse in London.[79] It was an arrangement that proved mutually satisfying: Grant had a new challenge, and he had the means to fly to wherever his daughter might be whenever there was a sudden opportunity to spend some time with her; Barrie had a new 'creative consultant' who guaranteed media coverage whenever he attended Fabergé functions.

'The toiletries industry is very much like the motion picture industry,' Grant said. 'Distribution and marketing are much the same. Only the percentages are different.'[80] Grant insisted that he enjoyed the work, which took up several days each month and involved turning up unannounced at Fabergé conventions and in department stores all over the world, attending the occasional sales meetings and acting as an advisor on new products, packaging, promotion and marketing matters. 'I wouldn't be doing this if I didn't like it,' he insisted. 'You shouldn't do anything you don't like. You wouldn't be any good at it.'[81] Fabergé, in turn, was, it seems, genuinely impressed with Grant's contribution. 'He has a keen business sense,'[82] said one executive, and an ebullient George Barrie told *Business Week*: 'When we purchased Fabergé five years ago, it was doing $11 million. This year [1968] it will do about $50 million, and I attribute some of that to "Mr G".'[83]

Grant soon started describing himself as a 'travelling businessman'.[84] Rumours of a return to making movies were heard from time to time and, on the evidence of the fan magazines and the public remarks by many producers, directors, writers and other actors, he was – and continued to be – much missed. There was, however, one loose end that was about to be tied up: at the end of the sixties, the Academy of Motion Picture Arts and Sciences finally decided to make amends for the fact that Grant, in spite of his distinguished movie career, had never actually won an Oscar by presenting him with the most prestigious of its prizes: the Special Oscar, awarded only to the most illustrious (and usually the most shamefully neglected) of its stars.

The relationship between Grant and the Academy had been distant for many years. He had never enjoyed attending the annual awards ceremony, even early on in his career, and had eventually withdrawn in protest over what he saw as its progressive degradation. He had also not been afraid of criticising the politics behind the Academy's decisions – a habit which probably cost him some influential friends. The critic David Thomson claimed that it was 'a conclusive failing of the Oscar system that Grant won nothing for a specific performance', and its belated proposal of the special award was, he said, conceived of 'in shame and confusion'.[85] Grant had been considered 'difficult' by some of Hollywood's grandees, but he was also, they realised, extremely popular with both critics and audiences alike. The time, it seemed, was ripe for a pacific gesture: the offer was made, and Grant accepted it. The date for the next Academy Awards ceremony had been set: Thursday, 7 April 1970. The problem was that, in the weeks that followed the announcement of Grant's award, the star himself had not yet made it clear if he was planning to collect the Oscar in person. The organisers, headed by Gregory Peck – president of the Academy at the time and a personal friend of Grant's – were assembling a special montage of excerpts from his most memorable movies, and the pressure was mounting to fix the timing of the speeches and presentations. Grant had been in contact on several occasions to clarify the arrangements, specify any special requirements he had and express his preferences about the clips for the montage, but, more recently, he had proved oddly evasive, and, eventually, Gregory Peck took it upon himself to track Grant down and beg him to make a decision, either way but promptly. Grant did send his secretary of the time, Bill Weaver,[86] to the venue of the ceremony – the Dorothy Chandler Pavilion in Los Angeles – in order to check on the number and location of its exits and entrances, and, following Grant's legendary meticulousness, time precisely how long the proposed walk from dressing-room to stage microphone would take, but he did not, in spite of Peck's pleading, commit himself to the event.

There was a particular reason for the prevarication. Cynthia Bouron, a one-time call-girl and former actor, had recently told Grant that she was going to sue him for the paternity of the child she was about to give birth to, and, it was hinted, she might broadcast her intentions at the Academy Awards ceremony itself. If the baby was a boy she planned to name him 'Cary Grant' (she had already, it transpired, named her English collie dog after him). Grant, who had only met Bouron briefly a few months before, had not taken her threats lightly; she had a reputation in Hollywood as a very volatile individual, with a number of very dubious associations, and Grant's advisors became convinced that she was quite capable of such a gesture. Under California law, alleged fathers are presumed guilty until proven otherwise in the courts, and must bear the costs relating to the pregnancy and birth until the case is heard. Grant, on the advice of his lawyer did not answer his telephone for several weeks and tended to travel from place to place in the months leading up to the Academy Awards ceremony, visiting his mother in Bristol, attending meetings in Manhattan and spending a few days in Jamaica with Noël Coward. He felt trapped, flattered that he was being honoured by his peers but dreading the possible public humiliation of being subpoenaed on prime-time television.

Rumours about the affair had been circulating around Los Angeles for some time, but on 20 March, a mere three weeks before the ceremony, the *Los Angeles Times* reported Bouron's claims and disclosed that she had given birth to a baby girl, whom she had christened Stephanie Andrea Grant.[87] Barely a week before the ceremony, Grant contacted the organisers and asked them to withdraw his name. Eventually, Gregory Peck and Howard Hughes managed to persuade him to go ahead with the ceremony, but he remained anxious about his televised appearance. Grace Kelly was due to fly from Monaco to Hollywood so that she could present him with his award, but Grant, fearing that she might be embarrassed by the possible publicity stunt, told her not to come.

Before the award was made, the montage of clips was shown,[88] tracing the star's career in scenes with Mae West, Jean Harlow, Katharine Hepburn, Jean Arthur, Irene Dunne, Ingrid Bergman, Grace Kelly, Eva Marie Saint and Audrey Hepburn. There were glimpses of Grant as Jerry Warriner, David Huxley, C. K. Dexter Haven, Jeff Carter, Archie Cutter, Ernie Mott, John Robie and Roger Thornhill, shots of him performing somersaults and pratfalls, chasing and being chased, kissing and, most of all, being kissed. The effect was powerful, reminding the audience how talented Grant had been, and how many different periods in Hollywood's history his career had spanned. After it had ended, the Special Oscar was introduced by Frank Sinatra. The inscription below the statuette read:

To CARY GRANT

for his unique mastery

of the art of screen acting

with the respect and affection

of his colleagues

Sinatra, presenting the award, announced, 'It was made for sheer brilliance of acting . . . No one has brought more pleasure to more people for so many years than Cary has, and nobody has done so many things so well.'[89] Grant appeared, looking glamorous and remarkably fit, smiling centre-stage as he received a thunderous standing ovation. He paused, clearly very touched by such a warm reception. When he began his acceptance speech,[90] he thanked the directors he had worked with – Hawks, Hitchcock, McCarey, Cukor, Stevens and Donen – along with the writers – Philip Barry, Dore Schary, Robert Sherwood, Ben Hecht, Clifford Odets, Sidney Sheldon, Stanley Shapiro and Peter Stone. 'I've never been a joiner or a member of any – of a particular – social set,' he went on to say, but he stressed that he felt 'privileged to be a part of Hollywood's most glorious era'. He ended by saying that 'no greater honour can come to a man than the respect of his colleagues'.

He received another standing ovation, and then he was gone. Bouron had not shown up;[91] there had been no disturbances, no embarrassments, and Cary Grant had, much to his relief, given another – and, in a way, his last – 'Cary Grant' performance. It had been, without doubt, one of the most popular, and most emotional, presentations in the history of the Academy Awards ceremonies, and Grant had done himself, and his image, justice. On 2 September, at the request of Daniel Taradash, the Academy president, he reinstated his membership of the Academy, explaining in a letter the reasons for his resignation many years before: 'Because of what may have since become outmoded principles, I deplored commercialising a ceremony, which, in my estimation, should have remained unpublicised and privately shared among the artists and craftsmen of our industry. I'm not at all sure my beliefs have changed; just the times . . .'[92]

The rapprochement was complete: Grant, the discreet rebel, had made his peace with Hollywood's establishment, and Hollywood had, at last, paid its public tribute to one of its most enduring and successful stars. He wrote to Frank Sinatra to thank him for remaining with him on stage during the 'astonishing ovation'; without his support, Grant added, 'I might have burst into tears rather than laughter'.[93] If he had been searching for a suitably neat way to conclude his movie career, he probably felt that he had found it: the reel world could now give way to the real world, the public to the private, the star to the man.

CHAPTER XIV

The Discreet Celebrity

It should not seem paradoxical if the famous seem shy and private. For fame implies that one deeply knows the rules for socially significant behavior, not necessarily that one's temperament is in accord with them. In fact the greater one's talent for fame, the greater may be one's temperamental distaste for society, since it is easier to understand and manipulate social expectations if one is somehow outside to begin with. To be entrepreneurial about one's work or one's public self does not mean that one is an entrepreneur; it means that one knows how to survive in an entrepreneurial world, even to the extent of satirising it by selling what is essentially intangible.
LEO BRAUDY

The older I get the more invitations come my way . . . I think people are just curious to see if I can still walk.
CARY GRANT

Every so often people might catch a fleeting glimpse of him, perhaps leaving a restaurant or entering a theatre or passing swiftly through an airport, the brisk, straight-backed spring-heeled walk still evident, the hair now almost white but still full, the sun-tanned face still unmistakably *him*. Cary Grant led a very active life after he ceased appearing on the movie screen, but it was a life lived largely in private, well away from the harsh and unhappy glare of publicity, a life lived on his own terms, in his own time.

It would be much too simplistic to say that Cary Grant, once he withdrew himself from view, ceased to be 'Cary Grant', that Cary Grant, in retirement, relaxed back into being Archie Leach once again.[1] It would be closer to the truth to say that Archie Leach now took the opportunity to relax and enjoy the fact that he had come

to terms with being Cary Grant. 'At one point in my life', he told
an interviewer, 'I pretended to be a certain kind of man on screen
... and very soon I became that man in life. "I" became him, or
rather "he" became me. Anyhow, at some point ... we met up
with each other. And you know something? This will surprise you
... we're still good friends.'[2] There was, of course, still sufficient
space between the private man and the public persona to allow for
some ironic self-commentary – such as when he would tell his friends
that he would 'just do the Cary Grant thing so no one holds us up',[3]
or the occasion at an Academy Awards show when he replied to
Laurence Olivier's *sotto voce* lament, 'Oh, if only I *were* Laurence
Olivier!', by saying, 'If only *I* were Cary Grant!'[4] – but it never
obscured his basic hard-won self-assurance. Olivier was only half-
joking: his *was*, off-stage, out of character, a phantom presence,
curiously evasive as a person. Grant, in contrast, had matured into a
much more solid, coherent personality, the old 'vague contour' had
finally 'filled out to the substantiality of a man'.[5]

Grant sometimes told journalists that he was, 'in reality', more
like the scruffy, unshaven, misanthrope of *Father Goose* than the
well-tailored charmer of *Charade*, and that he often relaxed at home
in pyjamas or an old pair of blue jeans.[6] The journalists – quite rightly
– were unconvinced. He continued to feature regularly on the list
of the world's Ten Best Dressed Men[7] long after he had made his
last movie, and he was, both in public and in private, as meticulous
as ever about his clothes and his appearance. Bill Weaver, his assistant
in the seventies, recalls that 'there was something about Grant that
made his clothes stay in perfect shape. While on other people clothes
developed stains, creases, and spots, Grant's remained impeccable.'[8]
The elegance did not disappear, like a cheap camera trick, once Grant
had brought his screen career to an end. Weaver was struck by the
fact that, if anything, Grant now seemed 'better looking than he
had been when younger, his appearance astonishingly unmarked by
signs of age'[9] – an impression made all the more remarkable for
the young assistant, who was always worried about his own weight,
when he noticed his employer's habit of resting idly on his bed after
dinner, watching television and 'dipping regularly into a box of
chocolates by his side'.[10] Nature can sometimes appear heartlessly
undemocratic.

It seems that even Grant's elderly mother was a little unnerved by her son's quiet confidence in the longevity of his good looks. Grant recalled:

> We were driving along once and she said, 'Archie, why don't you do something about your hair?' and I asked her why, what was wrong with it? She said I should dye it, that everyone was doing it these days. I said, 'Well, I'm not doing it.' She finally said that my hair made her look old. We about drove off the road. You know, she was already 89.[11]

The 'natural look': it was, one might say, the ultimate Cary Grant conceit. As many other famous men of a similar age began their hair-replacement programmes, their diets and their increasingly frequent trips to the plastic surgeon, straining at least to look tighter if not younger, air-brushing their image to obscure the crueller effects of the passage of time, there was Cary Grant, content, it seemed, to grow old as gracefully as he did most other things, without any fuss or fakery.

It was not easy for any ageing movie star to cope with the creeping sense of disorientation involved in remaining a star after ceasing to appear in movies. One was still well known, but now, suddenly, one was well known for what one *used* to do – well known, in fact, for what one used to *be*. Some, in their desperate search for a second act in their lives, ended up trying to act-out the same life all over again: comebacks, comb-backs, tummy-tucks and face-lifts, stretching out the past to hide from the present ('My God,' exclaimed Grant as he viewed one icon of old Hollywood appear on television, 'there's something *dead* on his head!'[12]). Others, giving up the vain struggle to regain their lost youth, chose instead to give themselves to it, becoming the loyal custodians of their own past, letting history lie on their shoulders like a shawl, their old lines now etched deep in their faces: their future was their past, re-heated for late-night consumption on the talk-show circuit. Neither option appealed to Grant: he claimed to prefer to 'look good for *my* age',[13] rather than for someone else's age, and, as for the business of nostalgia, he said, 'If you've enjoyed your life, why would you want to spend hours going over it again?'[14] He announced that his 'formula for living is quite simple . . . I get up in the morning and I go to bed at night. In between times, I occupy myself as best I can.'[15]

After the trauma of his divorce from Dyan Cannon and the subsequent struggle for custody of Jennifer, Grant began the 1970s intent on leading a quiet and very private life. His plans, however, were delayed when, early in 1970, he was inveigled into making another very public appearance. Alexander Cohen, producer of the Antoine Perry Award Show, asked Grant to present an honorary 'Tony' to Noël Coward. As Grant had always admitted to having been influenced by Coward in the early years of his career – when Archie Leach began to transform himself into Cary Grant – and as the two men had been friends since the late twenties, Grant felt obliged to accept the invitation. Although the presentation itself turned out to be relatively uneventful – in spite of Grant's usual worries – the aftermath was not. Crowds had gathered outside on the street, watching to see the celebrities as they left for their limousines. As each one appeared, the crowd reacted by breaking into applause that ranged from the polite to the boisterous. When Grant appeared, however, the reaction was extraordinary. Bill Weaver witnessed the scene:

> Grant stepped through the door. In a second the police barricade was scattered as fans, young, middle-aged, and old, erupted through the cordon, rushing to try to touch the man they still regarded as their idol, clutching out at him, shoving, pushing, and kicking, tearing at his buttons in order to secure at least one small trophy of the star.[16]

Although he was, in retrospect, heartened by the knowledge that he could still arouse such a strong and positive response some four years after he last appeared in a movie, the experience of being trapped, even temporarily, in the middle of a large crowd caused him to retreat even further from public life. He seldom signed autographs for fear of attracting other admirers, he relied on the use of the Fabergé private jet to avoid any risk of being delayed at airports and, when he was in New York, Bloomingdales consented to open after hours so that he could shop alone.[17]

He was, according to Weaver, 'enormously shy . . . and would work himself into a state of anguish and torment when any event of a challenging nature was suggested'.[18] William McIntosh, one of Grant's business associates, believed that although his dread of crowds was very real, the aloofness that followed from it was not entirely negative. Grant 'sometimes gave the impression of a man rationing his name and his time, with a caution that owed something to natural shyness, but also to a canny awareness of the heightened value that rarity confers'.[19] The risk of over-exposure was considerable. 'There's a banquet every night,' Grant complained. 'Every bloody night out here. There's one for Bob Hope, one for Jack Benny, one for every guy in the world. You can't do them all. I'd rather dine quietly down on the beach.'[20]

He continued to work for Fabergé, travelling on its behalf to Japan and Czechoslovakia, as well as making regular trips to London, Paris and all over the US, attending meetings, making awards and arriving unannounced at countless department stores; he still was, despite his retiring nature, a very effective public relations representative for the company. He did not, however, limit his activities to his association with Fabergé. During the seventies, he also became involved in a land development project in the Irish Republic called Shannonside;[21] he joined the board of Tamboo, a private club on Great Harbor Cay near Nassau in the Bahamas;[22] he invested in, and went on the board of, the Hollywood Park Racetrack;[23] he also joined the boards of the Magic Castle (a private club in Los Angeles for *aficionados* of magic),[24] the Norton Simon Museum in Pasadena,[25] and Western Airlines;[26] and, in 1975, he was made a director of Metro-Goldwyn-Mayer (and, when MGM was broken up into two companies in 1980, Grant sat on the board of both MGM films and MGM Grand Hotels).[27]

What Grant *did* decline to become involved in were all of the new movie projects that were still being sent to him: 'I guess you can say that I'm retired from the movies until some writer comes up with a character who is deaf and dumb and sitting in a wheel-chair.'[28] The one concession that he made was when Fabergé launched its own movie company, Brut Productions, at the beginning of the seventies. It had been George Barrie's idea, not his, but his expertise proved, unsurprisingly, to be invaluable. The company started by releasing *Night Watch* (1973), starring Elizabeth Taylor, and *A Touch of Class* (1973) with Glenda Jackson and George Segal. Grant was particularly supportive of the latter movie, which, although he resisted the temptation to make it into his own starring vehicle,[29] was very much shaped by his distinctive views on romantic comedy; it was an encouraging success, grossing $3.5 million during its first four weeks in the US and receiving four Academy Award nomina-tions.[30] He was not, however, prepared to prolong his involvement: 'As an ex-industry member, I'd become a target [at Fabergé] for people with scripts who want acting jobs, or shareholders who are convinced their daughter is the prettiest in the world and should be in pictures. They all seem to want to get into pictures, I don't know why. Anyway, I must hold all that at arm's length.'[31]

Las Vegas, rather surprisingly, proved more appealing than the new Hollywood to Grant. He had, in fact, been on friendly terms with several of the most important figures involved in the history of the Las Vegas Strip. He first met Bugsy Siegel in the mid-thirties, and the two men were intrigued by each other: Siegel by Grant's glamour, Grant by Siegel's notoriety (it was perhaps not entirely coincidental that Grant made a particular effort to socialise with Siegel at the time when he was preparing to act as the gambling draft-dodger in *Mr Lucky*).[32] Howard Hughes owned property in Las Vegas, as did another old friend, Charles Rich, who kept a Cary Grant suite in his hotel, The Dunes, reserved permanently for him.[33] The person who encouraged Grant to play a more active role in the city, however, was a rival of Hughes: Kirk Kerkorian.[34] Grant was introduced to Kerkorian by Charles Rich in the early 1960s. They quickly established a rapport. Kerkorian styled himself – not entirely accurately[35] – as a self-made man, and a gentleman, like Grant; his fierce ambition, his love of flying, his womanising and his shyness perhaps reminded Grant of a younger Hughes; and, like Grant, he was a very private man who rarely co-operated with the media. Kerkorian made Grant a director of Western Airlines (providing him with the kinds of privileges he appreciated, such as the use of a private L-1011, specially outfitted with an office, a marble bathtub and a gener-ous supply of caviar, *foie gras*, Château Lafite and Cristal champagne), and, when he became the major stockholder in MGM in 1969, he was responsible for inviting Grant to join the board of that company as well (providing invaluable advice to the man who knew so little about Hollywood that he had once asked George Raft to pay a gambling debt[36]). When MGM increased its involvement in Las Vegas,[37] Grant was, once again, a useful advisor and public-relations figure.

Many of Grant's friends could not understand what he could have in common with the brash and tawdry life of Las Vegas; some wondered if it was a symptom of his nostalgia for his early days in vaudeville, others guessed that it was more to do with his fascination with the business side of the entertainment industry, but the fact that he was drawn to some aspects of the place was beyond doubt.[38] His involvement with the city was, indeed, sufficiently well known during the seventies to lead to him being asked to accompany Lord Louis Mountbatten on a social visit to Las Vegas, introducing him to Frank Sinatra and Jack Benny and organising a special photo-session – at Mountbatten's request – with the chorus-girls at The Dunes.[39]

Off-screen, as he had usually been on-screen, Grant remained the democratic gentleman, as attractive a guest for the most exclusive social functions as he was for the more demotic occasions in Vegas. In 1970, he attended a reception at Buckingham Palace and a royal Gala Cabaret overseen by Prince Philip in aid of the World Wildlife Fund. In 1977, he delivered a speech at a Los Angeles Variety Club dinner honouring Prince Charles, and, on the occasion of one of Prince Philip's visits to California, Grant took him to the Magic Castle for the evening. Although he did not crave the respect of royalty, he did not object to it, and there was certainly an air of quiet satisfaction about the manner in which he behaved in the company of the British royal family, discreetly amused, perhaps, by the way in which he now seemed to represent to it the same kind of rare urbanity and style which the young Edward VIII had once symbolised for Archie Leach.

Grant's close friendship with Grace Kelly afforded him the opportunity to combine these normally distinct social spheres on certain memorable occasions. He was a regular visitor to Monaco as a guest of the Rainiers, and, in his capacity as a former tightrope walker and acrobat, he was also delighted to be one of the judges for the annual Monaco circus competition. He enjoyed the variety, and he liked the company. 'Grace loved and admired Cary,' said Prince Rainier. 'She valued his friendship and wanted me to share that with her.'[40] Grant joined yet another board – that of the Princess Grace Foundation – at the request of the Rainiers.

There was a danger, during this period, of Grant's personal life atrophying completely. When he was not attending meetings or travelling, he was often alone, watching television or attending baseball games.[41] He seemed, after the collapse of his fourth marriage and the embarrassment of the Bouron paternity case, to be shying away from the possibility of forming any new close friendships. When he was in New York, he stayed in his penthouse on the twenty-seventh floor at the Warwick Hotel, only rarely going out in the evenings. When he was in Los Angeles, he stayed in his old house on Beverly Grove Drive, which was – and had been for many years – in the process of extensive and complicated renovation, and was not a particularly suitable place to entertain guests.[42] What relationships Grant did have in the early seventies were brief and fairly superficial. He was seen with countless young women – including Raquel Welch (who, it was said, shared with Grant 'a love of special sweet butter and cold meat sandwiches'[43]), Farrah Fawcett-Majors and Victoria Morgan (a 'strictly sexual' relationship, it was said[44]) – but with none of them for very long. On those occasions when he did deign to attend a party, there would always, Bill Weaver recalls, 'be dozens of pressing women competing for his attentions'; wary of being rebuffed, he would sometimes dispatch Weaver to ask a particularly attractive woman 'if she would like to have dinner with an ageing movie star'.[45] Being Cary Grant, Weaver noted, he was not a stranger: 'his face, his voice, his manner, his charm, even his clothes, were immensely familiar. Unless the woman was married, she nearly always accepted.'[46]

By the mid-seventies – perhaps emboldened by the fact that he was able to see more of his reassuringly level-headed daughter – Grant began a serious, four-year relationship with Maureen Donaldson, a young entertainment journalist and photographer from England.[47] Donaldson was twenty-six, Grant nearly seventy, when they first met. They had several things in common: both came from relatively under-privileged backgrounds in England (Donaldson was the daughter of a retired fireman from Muswell Hill), both had left for America at an early age and both had chosen to settle in Los Angeles. They also shared a sense of humour, and a love of British comedy: Grant had often travelled to London to see the best performers – such as Sid Field, Richard Herne,[48] Harry Worth, Arthur Haynes and Eric Morecombe – and he enjoyed listening with Donaldson to tapes of Tony Hancock's old radio shows.[49] After she moved in with him, and Grant saw how popular she seemed to be with his daughter, he began to contemplate the possibility of another marriage. Newspapers took notice, and London's *Daily Mail* carried the headline: 'Cary to Marry Again . . . to Win His Daughter Back!'[50] Donaldson, understandably, was hurt by the suggestion that she was merely a means to an end, and, though she knew that there was no truth in the story, she resisted Grant's subsequent attempts to formalise the relationship. By 1976, she was – like Dyan Cannon before her – growing tired of Grant's perfectionism, his endless lectures on dress sense, hair colour, correct pronunciation and table manners ('I was going to dinner parties with Noël Coward in the twenties,' she recalls him saying in order to conclude one argument, 'so I think you can accept *my* word as final on this matter'[51]). He had encouraged her in her decision to pursue a new career as a free-lance photographer, and had arranged for several of his celebrity friends (in addition to himself) to pose for her, but this, ironically, had given her the independence that enabled her to drift away from him. They parted in 1977, but remained on good terms. Years later, he sent her a poem by Robert Browning, underscoring the line, 'That what began best can't end worst'.[52]

If the end of his relationship with a woman more than forty years his junior caused Grant to feel concerned about his age, another even more profoundly upsetting event had made him grow more sharply aware of his own mortality. His mother had died. Elsie Leach had spent her final few years in a nursing home[53] after several of her relatives in Bristol had become concerned about her living on her own.[54] She had remained active right up to the end of her life, although, in some ways, her behaviour had started to suggest that she was becoming easily confused. A matron recalled that Elsie sometimes discussed her son in terms of the characters he played in the movies she watched on television: '"He's a much better doctor than any of the doctors here", she'd say. Or "He's a very good ship's captain".'[55] Grant had – except in the forties during war-time – visited her in Bristol two or three times each year. He usually arranged to spend his birthday with her each January, when he would collect her in a Rolls-Royce, eat fish and chips in the back of the car and then take her to the Clifton Downs, where they would sit and talk for a couple of hours.[56] The bond between them had grown stronger in the decades since their traumatic reunion in the mid-thirties. She died on the afternoon of 22 January 1973, just a few days short of her ninety-sixth birthday. 'She died in a perfect way,' Grant said. 'She was served a cup of tea, and when they came back to see her, that was it.'[57] He flew to Bristol as soon as he received the news, but, in his customary manner, he kept the details and the funeral arrangements secret until it was too late for the local press to intrude.

Elsie Leach's death, inevitably, loosened Grant's ties with Bristol. His visits became less frequent, and, when his 'favourite cousin', Eric Leach, died in 1982,[58] they became very rare indeed.[59] Although he was always very positive in public about his birthplace, he was not always, in private, happy with the numerous requests he received from various eminent Bristolians for financial support.[60] His own success had helped to raise the city's profile abroad, and he may have felt that he had already made a suitably significant contribution.[61] In 1974, he unveiled a plaque at the United Nations Building recording the opening of a new landscaped area on New York's East Side re-named the Bristol Basin (because it had been built over tons of Second World War blitz-rubble brought over from Bristol in the form of ship ballast), and in 1986 he made a broadcast on the BBC's weekly radio appeal slot on behalf of the University settlement, Barton Hill. Generally, however, he kept his distance, and when the BBC production unit in Bristol proposed to take him back to the city for a television documentary to mark his eightieth birthday, he refused to co-operate.[62]

Now on his own again, he continued to dote on his daughter, building an elaborate fireproof vault in his house to store (for her future use) all the important artefacts from his career. Ironically, the star who hated signing autographs did not hesitate to collect them from other celebrities whom he knew his daughter admired. Woody Allen, for example, recalled being astonished to find Cary Grant waiting to meet him at Michael's Pub in New York, clutching copies of his books for his signature. 'He was stunning to look at and wonderfully charming,' Allen said, still somewhat dazed by the encounter.[63] On her tenth birthday, in 1976, Grant wrote to his daughter:

> Ten years have passed since I first saw your dear face. Ten years. Ten years of loving you. Ten years of regarding you, of thinking of you, and of being with you at every opportunity possible to me ... I am proud to know you. Proud to be seen with you ... You are the dearest daughter a man could have. You have never caused me a moment's anguish or disappointment. Your qualities are of the best, and if you persist in these qualities throughout life, you will enjoy ever-growing happiness, and, by so doing, understand the happiness you bring to others who know you, especially to me.[64]

As the seventies came to a close, Grant remained a busy but elusive figure, moving rapidly from place to place, board meeting to board meeting, rarely pausing anywhere long enough to be noticed by anyone but the most sharp-eyed of onlookers. His scrupulous avoidance of public appearances meant that even in New York – a city whose inhabitants pride themselves on being defiantly unimpressed by the sight of the grandest of celebrities – a rare encounter with Grant was likely to leave people tongue-tied and star-struck. On one such occasion, an unsuspecting waiter brought some tea to Grant's room when he was staying at the Sherry-Netherland Hotel: 'Jesus Christ!' exclaimed the waiter, finding himself face-to-face with the movie star; 'No,' came the reply, in that unmistakable accent, 'Cary Grant.'[65] When he did make contact with people outside of his intimate group of close friends and colleagues, he usually did so by telephone – a practice which, though normal for Grant, often proved frustrating for him or unnerving for the intended recipient of his call. 'He told the receptionist who screened my calls, "Hello, this is Cary Grant",' one of his business acquaintances remembers, 'and she said, "Well, hello! This is Elizabeth Taylor. What can I do for you?".'[66] The journalist Roderick Mann recalls: 'Cary called numerous people to tell them he liked what they wrote. Can you imagine? He called the *Los Angeles Times* film critic. She didn't believe it. He said, "Hello, this is Cary Grant," and she said, "*What?*".'[67]

'I think we tend to live in the past,' Grant remarked, 'to dote on nostalgia and endow certain things with a quality they never had.'[68] At the end of the seventies, he looked back on the past decade with some satisfaction: the vainglorious follies of some of his old colleagues had reassured him that he had been wise not to be tempted by any of the movie offers he had received, and the mirror – as much as anything – reassured him that he had been right to resist the novelty of a dramatic change of face. He was still alone, however, and still puzzled by past relationships. His Moorish-style home was still being re-modelled ('I expect them to be putting the finishing touches just as I'm taking my last breath,'[69] he said). He was still juggling his multiple business concerns. He was still, in short, living his life on his own terms: 'I doubt if I have more than 70,000 hours left, and I'm not about to waste any of them.'[70]

CHAPTER XV

Old Cary Grant

Everyone grows older, except Cary Grant.
GRACE KELLY

Preserving what is left is more important than mourning what is lost.
CARY GRANT

'How old Cary Grant?' the telegram from the inquisitive magazine editor is supposed to have asked. 'Old Cary Grant fine – how you?' Cary Grant is supposed to have replied. 'I wish I could say it was true,' Grant said of the anecdote, 'but it's not.'[1] It really *ought* to have been true: it captured his distinctive *mélange* of edgy evasiveness and easy charm very neatly, and, as a statement, it was accurate – old Cary Grant *was* fine.

If the anecdote was typical of Grant, so then was the manner in which he disowned it. He seemed, at the end of the seventies, to be remarkably well adjusted to his life as a 'former movie star'. While some ageing actors have been known to encourage flattering anecdotes about themselves, even when they are apocryphal, Grant appeared, by comparison, refreshingly irreverent about his past career.[2] Recalling the montage of clips from his most memorable movies that had been shown when he was awarded his special Academy Award, he said: 'You know, in some of them I couldn't even remember being on a particular set or making a particular scene. Some I do. There were some that were very pleasant. I may have enjoyed working with a particular leading lady. But often I don't even remember being there. I would say, "My God, was that me?".'[3] He turned down a lucrative five-million-dollar advance for his memoirs, saying: 'I'm much keener on living now than writing about the past . . . nobody is ever truthful about his own life. There are always ambiguities. Deeply unsatisfactory. I'd rather not be guilty of that.'[4]

His determination to keep his gaze fixed firmly on the future, however, was shaken by the deaths of so many of his closest friends. Howard Hughes died in 1976, Howard Hawks in 1977, Barbara Hutton in 1979, Alfred Hitchcock in 1980, Ingrid Bergman and Eric Leach – his favourite cousin – in 1982 and David Niven in 1983. He was particularly distressed by the tragic deaths of Princess Grace (in 1982, from a car accident) and Lord Mountbatten (in 1979, murdered by the IRA). After attending the memorial service for Mountbatten at Westminster Abbey, Grant confided to a friend: 'I'm absolutely pooped, and I'm so goddamned old . . . I'm going to quit all next year. I'm going to lie in bed . . . I shall just close all doors, turn off the telephone, and enjoy my life.'[5] As the eighties began, he seemed calmer, less prone to the old bouts of indecision and moodiness: 'I've got to live to be 400 to do all the things I've got to do. But even if I don't live that long – even if I die soon – it's been a wonderful life.'[6] Bill Weaver observed how Grant's remarkable good health and stamina enabled him to persevere with all his numerous business activities; he continued to rise before six o'clock each morning in order to follow the New York Stock Market, constantly reviewing his portfolio of mostly blue-chip stocks, and attending several board meetings each month. He still found time for more pleasurable pursuits: 'I admit I used to worry that when you reached a certain age, things stopped happening. But I don't worry about that any more because – and it's a pleasure to tell you – they don't stop happening. I haven't stopped doing anything simply because of my age.'[7] He was, during all the years Weaver knew him, 'quite simply never ill [nor] did he seem to suffer from the palest traces of jet-lag, showing exceptional resilience after long flights across the Atlantic and eager, always, to make plans rather than go to bed to rest and adapt to the change in hour.'[8]

Although hopeful movie proposals were still responded to flatly with the phrase 'fat chance', Grant did begin to relent as far as tributes were concerned. In 1980, the Los Angeles County Museum of Art offered a two-month retrospective of more than forty Cary Grant movies. The following year, Grant was awarded a prestigious Kennedy Center Honor for Achievement in the Performing Arts.[9] In 1984, his presence was *de rigueur* at a ceremony marking the sixtieth anniversary of MGM, when the studio celebrated the occasion by re-naming its theatre on the MGM lot the Cary Grant Theater.[10] In 1982, he had been named 'Man of the Year' by the international show-business fraternity known as the Friars Club. At the dinner gala held in his honour in the Grand Ballroom of New York's Waldorf-Astoria Hotel, George Burns made a speech in which he claimed to have been introduced to Grant by Abraham Lincoln's widow,[11] Peggy Lee sang 'Mr Wonderful', and Tony Bennett, Sammy Cahn, Cy Coleman and Frank Sinatra offered musical tributes to Grant. After finishing his own short speech of thanks, Grant became overwhelmed by the moment: 'I find myself tearful with happiness quite often these days. I cry at great talent. I'm deeply affected by the works of certain writers, by certain singers, phrases of music, the perfection of Fred Astaire . . . Such things can trigger off a complexity of emotions, but you see, to indulge in one's emotions, publicly and unashamedly, is a privilege permitted the elderly.'[12]

Grant's sanguine disposition owed a good deal to the fact that he had his new partner by his side: Barbara Harris.[13] They had met for the first time in London in 1976, when Grant arrived at the Royal Lancaster Hotel for the annual Fabergé trade show and noticed Harris, the hotel's public relations officer. For two years their relationship was one of ardent friendship; he would telephone her often, and she would sometimes visit him in California. Both were wary of making a commitment; Grant was, after all, forty-six years her senior, and he had four failed marriages behind him. In time, however, they became inseparable, and, when they discovered that in California a couple who have been living together for three years do not need a marriage licence, they began to discuss their future together. Grant, before proposing marriage to Harris, was anxious to make sure that such a move would not cause his daughter to become estranged from him. 'Look,' he is reported as saying to her, 'how would you feel if I asked Barbara to marry me? I'm getting on. I need her.'[14] Jennifer Grant is said to have responded with tears of joy.

Cary Grant's fifth wedding took place in the living-room of his Beverly Hills home on 15 April 1981, with only his daughter, his lawyer Stanley Fox and wife, the judge and his wife, and two servants as witnesses. The news was made public ten days later, after the couple had attended a celebration in honour of the twenty-fifth wedding anniversary of Prince Rainier and Princess Grace. While

222

the media began to dwell on the age difference, Grant and Harris appeared concerned only to make the most of what time they had left to spend together. 'Cary had not been a happy man,' remarked Prince Rainier. 'It was only when he met Barbara that he found what he had been searching for: the everyday happiness that lasted all day, all night, day after day, month after month, year after year.'[15] Bea Shaw recalls: 'When I went to the house, he'd say, "Let me go get my old lady." He touched her all the time. You know, when a man is really in love, how he wants to touch a woman? He touched her hand; he put his arm around her; he stroked her. And that said more to me than anything he could say about her. And she was that way with him.'[16]

Later that year, Grant gave an unusual interview in which he described a typical day in his life at the age of seventy-seven:

> I suffer from insomnia. Always have. I usually wake around three and read for an hour or so . . . I probably drop off about four and wake again between 6.30 and seven . . . My houseman leaves a tray outside our bedroom door . . . If my daughter Jennifer, who is 14, is staying with us I have to get up and dress to drive her to school . . . My male secretary arrives at nine and we go through the mail, having to refuse a helluva lot of requests to open this or that . . . I do most of my business on the phone. I go to board meetings but I've no illusion about why I'm there – it's always for my P.R. ability . . . Most mornings I deal with my solicitors . . . In the afternoon – oh, Barbara, what do I *do* in the afternoon? Just more of the same, I guess. Certainly I don't crook a finger to keep fit. I take no exercise whatsoever. Barbara thinks I'm fit now because I started life as an acrobat . . .
>
> We like a very quiet life. We have a wonderful couple who look after us . . . Both marvellous cooks, so we have meals at home. We watch television sometimes. More often we play cards. Do you know Spite and Malice? Marvellous game . . . We go to bed sometimes at eight, sometimes as 12.[17]

If it was surprising that the very private Grant was prepared to discuss his home-life with a journalist, it was far more of a shock when, the following year, he decided that he would go out and about and reminisce about his movie career in front of an audience.

Nancy Nelson, senior vice-president of a New York lecture bureau, first approached Grant with the idea of a lecture tour in the summer of 1981. Several other eminent movie stars from Hollywood's 'golden era' had started 'An Audience With . . .'-style events, but Grant, who had always been so reticent about his movie past, and who had usually avoided any opportunities to appear in public, represented a considerable challenge. 'I can't commit myself to anything because I don't know when I'll be available,'[18] he protested. Nelson was persistent, and Grant began to take the idea more seriously. He said that, as his wife was British and had not seen much of the United States, he might consider those opportunities which would provide him with an excuse to take her on sight-seeing trips – particularly if the venues were in areas he had visited years before with the Pender troupe. 'I might be willing to break in my act if you get a cancellation,'[19] he told her, although he was very careful to make clear that he was not promising anything. On 21 October 1982, Steve Allen was to have been the guest speaker in front of an audience of twenty-six hundred people at the Flint Center of the DeAnza Community College in Cupertina, about forty miles from San Francisco. He cancelled. A last-minute replacement was needed. Nelson contacted Grant, and Grant, after negotiating a contract that ensured (as it always would do in the future) that no filming or tape-recording would be allowed, agreed to appear.

The format of the evening session was devised by Grant. The event would begin with the eight-minute montage of memorable moments from his movie career that had been shown at the 1970 Academy Awards show. 'I'll show some film clips in which I look moderately young,' he said, 'and then come out on stage looking incredibly aged.'[20] On the screen, Grant would be seen walking towards Frank Sinatra to collect his honorary Oscar; at that moment, Grant, in person, would appear on stage, timing his entrance to perfection. He coped very well with the new experience of working without a script. He sat centre-stage, alone in front of his admirers, and, for more than two hours, reminisced and answered questions from the audience about his life and career. The response was extraordinary. As soon as he appeared, the audience rose to give him a long standing ovation. 'If you won't sit,' he told them, '*I'll* sit.'[21] Asked why he was prepared finally to meet his admirers, he said, 'To regain my self-confidence.'[22] When it was all over, he seemed genuinely surprised by the enthusiastic reaction of all those who had come to see him. He had not anticipated such warmth after being largely away from the public eye for sixteen years.

Rich Little, the impressionist, recalls Grant saying to him at this time, 'You're not really doing *me* in your show?' When Little replied that he was, Grant said, 'Do they *remember* me?'[23] 'When he retired, he stepped away from all the adoration', recalled his friend, Bea Shaw. 'And I think it was important for him to know people still loved him and wanted to see him and hear him speak. It was invigorating.'[24] Although he was delighted to discover that his popularity remained so high, he did not commit himself immediately to any tour. He had other things to do, and the negotiations were as unpredictable and as protracted as before. It was, recalls Nelson, 'cat and mouse all over again'.[25] She did not, however, give up. In May 1983, the company she worked for moved to Connecticut; a month later, she received a telephone call from Grant, encouraging her to break away and establish her own agency: 'Do that, and you can have me as a client. I won't be the biggest one you'll ever have. After all, I'm not going to do very much. But it'll be good for you to have me.'[26]

He devised a ninety-minute one-man show called *A Conversation with Cary Grant*. He stipulated that he would not appear in any big cities where the press might crowd in on him, and he arranged for all proceeds, except for his travelling expenses, to go to the college or charitable organisations that were sponsoring his appearances. Aided by his wife Barbara, who helped with booking arrangements and public relations, he started making occasional, low-key, appearances. From 1982 until 1986, he made thirty-six public appearances in such places as Red Bank, New Jersey; Joliet, Illinois; Texarkana, Texas; Sarasota, Florida; and Schenectady, New York. His audiences ranged from elderly movie fans to college students who had discovered his movies on late-night television. He described these evenings as 'ego-fodder',[27] adding: 'I know who I am inside and outside, but it's nice to have the outside, at least, substantiated.'[28] The presenter of Grant's first *Conversation* believes that Grant 'had a need to show Jennifer and Barbara that he still had vitality and star attraction. He enjoyed interacting with people. He was truly interested in them. But if he hadn't had these two wonderful women in his life, I don't think he would have ventured out on that stage.'[29]

Before each engagement it was his custom to give two telephone interviews to local newspaper reporters. Although his appearances were not intended as grand occasions, they proved to be keenly anticipated and highly popular. When two dates were announced for appearances at La Mirada Civic Theater in California, all 1,264 seats sold out within twenty-four hours.[30] He approached each event with the same attention to detail as he had shown when making movies. His entrance and exit were planned and timed carefully, and he was always present as the technicians set up the lighting and sound equipment. A reporter from *Variety* described him as 'a real pro', noting that 'he even supervised the placement of microphones in each aisle of the former movie palace's orchestra and balcony'.[31] It had been more than half a century since his days in vaudeville, but the experience of how to deal with a live audience had not been forgotten: 'Wearing a tuxedo, he succeeded in achieving a warm intimacy in the large hall while maintaining a sophisticated celebrity aura.'[32]

He was surprisingly relaxed about the range of questions asked by members of the audience, even if he did not answer all of them with equal candour. On the subject of Mae West, he was very candid indeed: 'She did her own thing to the detriment of everyone around her. I don't admire superficiality.'[33] He said that he did nothing to preserve his health and good looks: 'I just breath in – and out . . . I don't smoke . . . Do everything in moderation. Except making love.'[34] He dismissed the suggestion that he might make another movie: 'Put that in your "fat-chance" department.'[35] He mocked his own image: 'I'm a fake. Watch me waddle off stage. And catch me going upstairs sometime.'[36] He talked about his daughter – 'We level with each other. I know when she's looking at me she's not thinking, "I wonder if I can get this old goat for a BMW"'[37] – and his wife – 'Barbara's the woman who has made me the happiest', adding, when she joined him on stage, 'Pretty good for an old geezer like me, isn't she?'[38]

He was never more familiar to the audience, however, than when he was being charmingly evasive:

Question: Would you do a pratfall?
Answer: It's all I can do to walk.

Question: You've [*nervously*] always been a fan of mine!
Answer: That's true. I have.

Question: What would you like for dinner if we were married?
Answer: The way you say that, I'd probably skip dinner.

Question: Why did Hitchcock make so many suspense films?
Answer: Money.

Question: What's good about being eighty?
Answer: The fact that one is living, I suppose.[39]

When the ninety minutes were up, he would glance at his watch, give one of his perfect comic double-takes and ask the audience, 'Don't any of you want to go *home*'[40] All the events were over-subscribed, all were organised with consummate professionalism and all were warmly received. 'Grant's sharp, fast, perceptive answers to questions belied his age,'[41] said *Variety*. He was, once again, a box-office and critical success.

From January to April 1983, the Grants took time off and relaxed on a world cruise aboard the *Viking Sky*. On 18 January 1984, Grant turned eighty. His old friend Roderick Mann produced an article to mark the occasion: 'Anyone who knows this man well will tell you that he does not spend time peering into the windows of his past. Ask him a question about his career and he'll answer courteously – though questions about his favorite film or actress are a sure-fire way to make his eyes glaze over.'[42] Mann went on: 'In the 25 years I've known this man, he has done hardly any exercise at all and always eaten like a timberwolf,' and yet his rude good health and rare good looks made him 'a walking, talking, breathing example for every man over 60 to cherish'.[43] 'I don't feel my age,' said Grant. 'Not often, anyway. I don't have a magic formula. I used to have a vodka before dinner but I've given that up. I still have a glass of wine with a meal. If I have a secret at all it's that I do just what I want. I think that stops the ageing process as much as anything.'[44] He still tried to depict himself as a man of surprisingly modest sartorial tastes, but he could never disguise entirely the old habits: 'Jaeger's – you know, that's a wonderful business – very kindly made me this cable-stitched sweater specially. They'd dropped them from stock and they know how much I like them.'[45] The general impression was of a man in fine health, remarkably similar in many ways to the debonair star the public remembered. Grant did not make any plans to celebrate his eightieth birthday (there was nothing to talk about, he said – he was still old, he was still fine), but he could not prevent the international media from drawing attention to the date's significance. A Chicago newspaper published a large, black-bordered photograph of him on its front page to commemorate his birthday; it seems that many people, glancing at the paper on their way to work, assumed that Grant had died, and one local radio station went so far as to announce the 'fact'. When contacted later in the day by reporters, Grant was greatly amused: 'I never felt better in my life.'[46] The celebrations continued. Tributes were recorded, seasons of his movies organised, books published[47] and various honours offered. He kept his distance.

He was content to lead a relatively quiet life at home with his wife. 'There was a serenity about him at eighty,'[48] said Peter Bogdanovich. He had finally found a relationship that worked. Barbara Grant shared his tastes, his values and his sense of humour. They were rarely apart from each other during the last few years of his life. 'Cary said he wanted to remarry Barbara every five years,' recalls Abigail Van Buren.[49] They would, on occasion, invite a few close friends around for elegant dinner parties (Grant was a caviar gourmand, and, as one guest recalls, he 'ate mountains of it . . . his and other people's'[50]), but for most of the time they seemed perfectly happy in each other's company. Jennifer Grant was attending Stanford University,[51] but she often spent weekends with her father and stepmother in Los Angeles. 'She has to do what she wants to do,' Grant said of his daughter. 'I can't, nor would I, impose my wishes on her. I love her and I pray for her. But she has her own life to live. I can merely spend the rest of my life loving her, enjoying her, hoping she enjoys me.'[52]

Grant's life had acquired – at last – a general semblance of normality. The *Bristol Evening Post* journalist Alston Thomas met him during one of his last visits to his birthplace, and was struck by the change in him:

A lady colleague of mine took him on a tour of Bristol. He spoke of the Saturday mornings his mother took him shopping, he pointed out the cinema where he'd seen his first Pearl White serials, and he even insisted on being taken to his favourite fish and chip shop. At the end of it all he told me, 'I wish she'd asked me more. I was enjoying it so much.' At that moment I felt at last Archie Leach had come happily home.[53]

It was later in 1984, however, that Grant began to have serious cause to be concerned about his health. In October, following a week of dizzy spells and headaches, he checked himself into Cedars-Sinai Medical Center in West Hollywood. After undergoing a number of routine tests, it was concluded that he had suffered a mild stroke. He was advised to ease up on his hectic schedule of personal appearances and business meetings, but, as soon as he began to feel well again, he continued with most of his obligations. 'I know I'm overdoing it, going out night after night and travelling the country,' he told his friend Henry Gris. 'It totally drains me at times, but I'm not going to stop. I have to show Barbara and Jennifer I'm still young at heart.'[54] The sudden sense of frailty was, for a man who had been so fit for so long, hard to come to terms with:[55]

Death? Of course I think of it. But I don't want to dwell on it. I must say, I don't want to attract it too soon. You know, when I was young, I thought they'd have the thing licked by the time I got to this age. I think the thing you think about when you're my age is how you're going to do it and whether you'll behave well.[56]

When it happened, it happened suddenly, unexpectedly, and not in Los Angeles or London or New York but in a quiet and remote Mississippi River town in the corn belt of the United States. Grant had agreed to take his *Conversation* show to Davenport, Iowa. It was another part of America that was unfamiliar to his wife, so he was pleased to have an opportunity to take her there. He found that he could fit the trip into their schedule for late November 1986, on his way to his annual appearance as a circus judge in Monaco. They arrived at Davenport's Blackhawk Hotel on 28 November, rested overnight, and the next day were taken on a tour of the city by a local businessman. At four o'clock in the afternoon, Grant arrived at the Adler Theater to supervise the technical rehearsal. He began to feel nauseous after an hour or so, and was helped from the stage by Barbara into his dressing-room. He refused to allow a doctor to be called, insisting that all he needed was some rest. At six o'clock, he was placed in a wheelchair and taken back to his hotel. In his room, his condition worsened, and Barbara – growing more concerned by the minute – called the theatre to cancel the evening's show. At 7.45 p.m., reportedly against Grant's wishes, a local doctor – Duane Manlove – was called; when he arrived, he took Grant's blood pressure, and advised him that he was very ill.[57] 'I realised he was having a stroke,' said the doctor. 'Grant's blood pressure was extremely high – my reading was 210 over 130.'[58] Grant still refused to be taken to hospital, in spite of the entreaties of those around him. 'By about eight-fifteen he was beginning to have a lot of pain, but he was still coherent,' recalled the doctor. 'He was talking about going back to Los Angeles and maybe seeing a doctor there. But I knew that was impossible . . . He didn't have that much time left to live. The stroke was getting worse. In only fifteen minutes he had deteriorated rapidly. It was terrible watching him die and not being able to help. But he wouldn't let us.'[59] At around 8.45 p.m., the cardiologist, James Gilson, arrived. Manlove and Gilson, taking matters into their own hands, requested an ambulance. A few minutes later, a paramedic team from the local St Luke's Hospital arrived. 'Grant kept calling his wife's name,' remembers one of the paramedics, 'and held his hand for her . . . As we took [him] out . . . he murmured to his wife, "I love you, Barbara . . . don't worry." And they squeezed hands.'[60] He was rushed to the intensive care unit, where a CAT scan revealed that he had suffered a massive stroke. At 11.22 p.m., on Saturday 29 November 1986, Cary Grant was pronounced dead. He was eighty-two years old.

Barbara Grant, although shaken, traced Jennifer by telephone to inform her of the news before it became public. At 2.45 a.m., she boarded a chartered Lear jet to accompany her husband's body back to Los Angeles. Reports of Grant's death began to flash around the world, and by the morning tributes were pouring in. President Ronald Reagan called Grant 'an old friend' and 'one of the brightest stars in Hollywood'.[61] James Stewart said that Grant 'was one of the great people in the movie business'.[62] Doris Day described him as 'a genius at what he did', adding that he 'had the looks, the charm . . . the classiest man I ever met'.[63] 'He was the one star', said Polly Bergen, 'that even other stars were in awe of.'[64] Frank Sinatra's brief response to the news was that he was 'saddened by the loss of one of the dearest friends I ever had. Nothing more to say, except that I shall miss him terribly.'[65] Tony Curtis declared that Grant 'represented the very best that all actors wish we could be. He was a great actor – more important, a great man – and a great human being.'[66] When the obituaries started to appear on the following Monday, they were unusually warm and affectionate. The *New York Times* called him 'a beloved figure',[67] the *Washington Post* said that 'he made things that other men had to work very hard at look very easy',[68] the London *Times* praised his 'magnificent technique',[69] while the *Los Angeles Times* described him as 'the sophisticated and urbane ideal of men and women throughout the world'.[70]

In accordance with Grant's wishes, his body was cremated, and no funeral service of any kind – even for the family – was held. 'That was very much in keeping with Cary,' Roderick Mann observed, 'the private man who didn't want the nonsense of a funeral.'[71] What happened to his ashes was never made public, but rumour has it that they were scattered to the wind in the hills surrounding his old house.[72] The probate of Grant's will[73] revealed that he bequeathed the bulk of his fortune to his wife and daughter. His widow received their Beverly Hills home and all its furnishings, his works of art and his cars. He also specified that half of what remained of the estate after taxes and miscellaneous bequests should be divided equally between his wife and daughter (Jennifer's half was to be administered through a special trust fund until she reached the age of thirty-five[74]). His clothing and other personal effects were to be divided by his attorney, Stanley Fox, among relatives and close friends (Frank Sinatra, Stanley Donen, Kirk Kerkorian and Roderick Mann were named specifically as recipients). Grant also left $150,000 to valued employees, $50,000 to the Motion Picture Relief Fund, $25,000 to Variety Clubs International, $20,000 to the John Tracy Clinic for the hearing-impaired and $10,000 to Dr Mortimer Hartman (the man who had introduced him to LSD). Typically, Grant concluded his will with the caveat that any beneficiary 'directly or indirectly' contesting or attacking the will would automatically lose his or her share. It has been estimated that Grant's fortune was somewhere in the region of $60 million at the time of his death.[75]

It had been twenty years since Cary Grant had made his last movie. During those final two decades, Grant refused, in the words of Richard Schickel, 'to succumb to age's great trap – tediousness –

refusing to pander to youth or to curiosity, he [became] what long years ago he set out to be – a gentleman. Of the old school.'[76] In one of his last major interviews, Grant had said: 'I know all too well that the day will come when I won't be around any longer. The prospect of that doesn't necessarily please me. That's another reason why I live for today.'[77] If the last few years of his life were – as they seem to have been – his happiest, it is perhaps not entirely coincidental that those years are among the ones we know least about. 'If I'm to be remembered by my family and friends,' Grant said, 'then let it be as someone who didn't rock the boat, who did moderately well at his craft, and was polite to his fellow man.'[78] As a summation of his life and career, it was, like most of his performances, memorably understated.

EPILOGUE

*Anyone who is on Cary's side is, of course,
on the side of the angels.*
RICHARD BROOKS

Don't investigate him. Learn from him.
PEOPLE WILL TALK

From Archie Leach to Cary Grant. What a giant step. And yet he became Cary Grant. He really became him.
DEBORAH KERR

I'd be a nut to go through all that again, but I wouldn't have missed it for anything.
CARY GRANT

'Cary Grant was not supposed to die,' said a *New York Times* editorial. 'Sure, we all knew he was getting on – he had the silver hair to prove it – and that his last movie was 20 years behind him. But die? Never. Cary Grant was supposed to stick around, our perpetual touchstone of charm and elegance and youth.'[1] In a way, of course, he still *is* that touchstone, preserved on film, no more distant or any less approachable than he was, for most of us, when he was alive, and yet, as the editorial added, 'we can never see him again without feeling a little pang, for now the substance behind that extraordinary shadow is gone'.[2]

Cary Grant is really missed. We miss his elegant animation on screen. His sense of fun. His *joie de vivre*. He kept the 'holiday in his eye'. He enjoyed himself and *looked* like he was enjoying himself. Accompanying the barking Mr Smith on the piano in *The Awful Truth*. Caught in Susan's silly frilly negligée in *Bringing Up Baby*. Teasing Hildy Johnson in *His Girl Friday*. Pushing Tracy Lord back through the front door in *The Philadelphia Story*. Dancing joyously in *Indiscreet*. Rolling the orange with his chin over the body of the stern-looking woman in *Charade*. Countless double-takes, sly winks and wry smiles. Taking great delight in sending himself up at every

235

opportunity. Thinking happy thoughts. He knew that he was in a movie, not in real life, and realised that this was a creative release rather than a cruel sentence. He *understood* movies.

His rare sense of decorum is also greatly missed. He was a star who always behaved impeccably, who treated his audience with respect and himself with an irreverent wit. The stars of today do not tend to behave like Cary Grant; their brash and boorish self-absorption stands in stark and sour contrast to his charming civility. Today we have stars eager to teach us about the finer points of terrorism, about the importance of physical fitness and about the threats to the environment. Today we have Don Johnson ranting at radio callers, 'I can do what I want! I'm famous and I'm bigger than you!'[3] Today we have Geena Davis complaining because Stephen Hawking has not yet replied to her helpful letter explaining to him how he might refute Heisenberg's Uncertainty Principle.[4] Today we have Whoopi Goldberg applauding her fellow celebrities during an orgy of self-congratulation at the Academy Awards show by telling them, 'Aren't we *wonderful?*'[5] Today we have stars inviting us into their homes, revealing to us their remodelled breasts, recounting their struggles to 'become' their roles, reading to us from their diaries and confiding to us all the intimate details of their 'private' drink and drug 'hell'.

Today we have stars whose crass deportment makes Cary Grant's discreet courteousness seem positively noble by comparison. He did not profess any special insight into the world of politics (although he had strong opinions of his own). Neither did he lecture us on the burdens of fame and the evils of money, nor bore us with the 'inside story' of his private torments (although he probably had his share). He just did his job as well as he could, made sure that he was rewarded handsomely for it, and never lost sight of how fortunate he was. While other stars might dream of being remembered as intellectuals, artists, novelists, philanthropists, freedom-fighters, peacemakers, 'gods' and 'goddesses', Cary Grant proposed as his simple epitaph: 'He was lucky, and he knew it.'[6]

He also knew when to stop. 'If one regrets the loss to the art of acting,' wrote Richard Schickel, 'one is really grateful to Cary Grant for stopping in his fit and prosperous (and heaven knows, extensive) middle age, fixing it in our minds permanently, [and] leaving us with such a pleasant image.'[7] Not all of his seventy-two movies[8] were uniformly good, and perhaps not many were truly great, but most were pleasantly unpretentious and well made, some were richly entertaining and an unusually high number were quite unforgettable. Grant's own performances – regardless of the material he had to work with – were invariably of the highest standard. He was a remarkable movie actor (making something that difficult look that easy was an extraordinary feat – compare Cary Grant with, say, Hugh Grant if one doubts it), perhaps, as David Thomson called him, 'the best and most important'[9] actor ever to have worked in Hollywood. 'It was genius,' said Alan J. Pakula. 'He never wasted a moment on the screen. Every movement meant something.'[10] Marcel Ophuls has expressed his admiration for the way that Grant, acting alongside James Stewart in *The Philadelphia Story*, 'stole an entire scene from him . . . with one movement of his head'.[11] If his solitary Academy Award was long overdue, it was, at least, awarded for the right thing: 'sheer brilliance'.

He had the other-worldly aura of a star but the down-to-earth nature of a character actor. Some stars inspire awe, or adoration, or respect, or lust, or even fear in their fans. Cary Grant inspired warmth. One *did* smile when one saw him. He was an unusually *likeable* star. He mixed Old World grace with New World glamour to win friends on both sides of the Atlantic, of both sexes, from all classes. 'Everyone thinks of him affectionately', said Pauline Kael, 'because he embodies what seems a happier time – a time when we had a simpler relationship to a performer . . . We were used to his keeping his distance – which, if we cared to, we could close in idle fantasy.'[12] Even though he remained such a private man, he was always a very public figure: 'He was everyone's favourite uncle, brother, best friend and ideal lover,' observed David Shipman; 'more than most stars he belonged to the public.'[13]

'Cary Grant – not his directors, not Paramount or RKO, not his fans – invented "Cary Grant",'[14] wrote one critic. Part of his peculiar appeal was that he reassured us that the price of social advancement did not have to amount to the betrayal of one's past. Fame never spoiled him. When Archie Leach was born, a gentleman was not meant to be anyone like him. When Cary Grant died, a gentleman was meant to be someone just like him. 'Cary Grant,' a critic claimed, 'has, probably more than any other actor, carried the burden of our dreams confidently, agreeably. If there was struggle involved in the creation of the comfortably elegant persona we know of as Cary Grant, he has kept it from us.'[15] There *was* a struggle, and he *did* keep it from us, but he overcame it because of who he was rather than who he became.

'He was very immature compared with me,' Cary Grant said of Archie Leach. 'But I quite liked him.'[16] Everyone really liked the idea of Cary Grant. 'Apart from being gorgeous, the adjective of many women's choice,' declared the *New York Times*, 'he is also a friend.'[17] That was the impression one was left with. A friend. 'If you like me,' said Grant, 'write you like me. If you don't like me, write you don't like me. I'm just a person.'[18] Everyone really liked the idea of Cary Grant, but many of us really liked the person, too.

Filmography

Cary Grant made seventy-two feature-length movies. His own personal list of his movies (which was sometimes given to journalists) omitted four titles: *The Devil and the Deep, Born to be Bad, When You're in Love* and *People Will Talk.* According to Nancy Nelson's *Evenings With Cary Grant* (p. 206), his own personal favourites were: *The Awful Truth, Bringing Up Baby, Gunga Din, His Girl Friday, The Philadelphia Story, None But the Lonely Heart, Notorious, To Catch a Thief, Indiscreet, North by Northwest, Charade* and *Father Goose.* (Further details concerning cast, plot and contemporary reviews can be found in Donald Deschner's *The Complete Films of Cary Grant,* Citadel Press, 1991.)

The director's name is in italics. A (c) *shows the film was in colour. Sp denotes Screenplay,* b/o *— based/on and Cin- Cinematography. An asterisk after Grant's name indicates that his performance was nominated for an Academy Award, while an asterisk after the title denotes an Academy Award nomination for Best Picture. V means that a movie exists on video, L/D on laser disk.*

1. THIS IS THE NIGHT. Paramount, 1932. *Frank Tuttle.*
Sp: Avery Hopwood.
b/o: play (*Pouche*) by Rene Peter and Henri Falk.
Cin: Victor Milner.
Cast: Lili Damita, Charles Ruggles, Roland Young, Thelma Todd, Cary Grant, Irving Bacon, Claire Dodd, Davison Clark.
Running Time: 80 minutes.

2. SINNERS IN THE SUN. Paramount, 1932. *Alexander Hall.*
Sp: Vincent Lawrence, Waldemar Young, and Samuel Hoffenstein.
b/o: story ('Beach-Comber') by Mildred Cram.
Cin: Ray June.
Cast: Carole Lombard, Chester Morris, Adrienne Ames, Alison Skipworth, Walter Byron, Reginald Barlow, Zita Moulton, Cary Grant, Luke Cogrove,

Ida Lewis, Russ Clark, Frances Moffett, Pierre De Ramey, Veda Buckland, Rita LaRoy.
Running Time: 70 minutes.

3.   MERRILY WE GO TO HELL. Paramount, 1932. *Dorothy Arzner.*
Sp: Edwin Justus Mayer.
b/o: play (*I, Jerry, Take Thee, Joan*) by Cleo Lucas.
Cin: David Abel.
Cast: Fredric March, Sylvia Sidney, Adrianne Allen, Richard 'Skeets' Gallagher, Florence Britton, Esther Howard, George Irving, Kent Taylor, Charles Coleman, Leonard Carey, Milla Davenport, Mildred Boyd, Cary Grant.
Running Time: 88 minutes.

4.   THE DEVIL AND THE DEEP. Paramount, 1932. *Marion Gering.*
Sp: Ben W. Levy.
b/o: story by Harry Hervey.
Cin: Charles Lang.
Cast: Tallulah Bankhead, Gary Cooper, Charles Laughton, Cary Grant, Gordon Wescott, Paul Porcasi, Juliette Compton, Arthur Hoyt, Dorothy Christy, Henry Kolker, Kent Taylor.
Running Time: 70 minutes.

5.   BLONDE VENUS. Paramount, 1932. *Josef von Sternberg.*
Sp: Jules Furthman and S. K. Lauren.
b/o: story by Josef von Sternberg.
Cin: Bert Glennon.
Cast: Marlene Dietrich, Herbert Marshall, Cary Grant, Dickie Moore, Gene Morgan, Rita La Roy, Robert Emmett O'Connor, Sidney Toler, Cecil Cunningham, Hattie McDaniel.
Running Time: 85 minutes. V.

6.   HOT SATURDAY. Paramount, 1932. *William A. Seiter.*
Sp: Seton I. Miller.
b/o: novel by Harvey Ferguson.
Cin: Arthur L. Todd.
Cast: Nancy Carroll, Cary Grant, Randolph Scott, Edward Woods, Lillian Bond, William Collier, Snr., Jane Darwell, Grady Sutton.
Running Time: 73 minutes.

7.   MADAME BUTTERFLY. Paramount, 1932. *Marion Gering.*
Sp: Josephine Lovett and Joseph Moncure March.
b/o: story by John Luther Long and play by David Belasco.
Cin: David Abel.

Cast: Sylvia Sidney, Cary Grant, Charles Ruggles, Irving Pichel, Helen Jerome Eddy, Sheila Terry.
Running Time: 86 minutes.

8. SHE DONE HIM WRONG.★ Paramount, 1933. *Lowell Sherman.*
Sp: Harvey Theu and John Bright.
b/o: play (*Diamond Lil*) by Mae West.
Cin: Charles Lang.
Cast: Mae West, Cary Grant, Gilbert Roland, Noah Berry, Snr., Rafaela Ottiano, David Landau, Rochelle Hudson, Owen Moore, Fuzzy Knight, Louise Beavers.
Running Time: 66 minutes. V. L/D.

9. THE WOMAN ACCUSED. Paramount, 1933. *Paul Sloane.*
Sp: Bayard Veiller.
b/o: magazine serial by Polan Banks, Rupert Hughes, Vicki Baum, Zane Grey, Vina Delmar, Irvin S. Cobb, Gertrude Atherton, J. P. McEvoy, Ursula Parrott, and Sophie Kerr.
Cin: Karl Strauss.
Cast: Nancy Carroll, Cary Grant, John Halliday, Irving Pichel, Louis Calhern, Jack La Rue, John Lodge.
Running Time: 73 minutes.

10. THE EAGLE AND THE HAWK. Paramount, 1933. *Stuart Walker.*
Sp: Bogart Rogers and Seton I. Miller.
b/o: story by John Monk Saunders.
Cin: Harry Fischbeck.
Cast: Fredric March, Cary Grant, Jack Oakie, Carole Lombard, Sir Guy Standing.
Running Time: 72 minutes.

11. GAMBLING SHIP. Paramount, 1933. *Louis Gasnier* and *Max Marcin.*
Sp: Max Marcin and Seton I. Miller.
b/o: story by Peter Ruric and adaptation by Claude Binyon.
Cin: Charles Lang.
Cast: Cary Grant, Benita Hume, Roscoe Karns, Glenda Farrell, Jack La Rue, Arthur Vinton.
Running Time: 72 minutes.

12. I'M NO ANGEL. Paramount, 1933. *Wesley Ruggles.*
Sp: Mae West and Lowell Brentano.
Cin: Lee Tover.
Cast: Mae West, Cary Grant, Edward Arnold, Ralf Harolde, Russell Hopton, Gertrude Michael, Kent Taylor, Dorothy Peterson, Gregory Ratoff.
Running Time: 87 minutes. V.

13.   ALICE IN WONDERLAND. Paramount, 1933. *Norman Z. McLeod.*
Sp: Joseph L. Mankiewicz and William Cameron Menzies.
b/o: story by Lewis Carroll.
Cin: Henry Sharp and Bert Glennon.
Cast: Charlotte Henry, Richard Arlen, Roscoe Ates, William Austin, Gary Cooper, Leon Errol, Louise Fazenda, W. C. Fields, Cary Grant, Sterling Holloway, Edward Everett Horton, Baby LeRoy, Mae Marsh, Jack Oakie, Edna May Oliver, May Robson, Charlie Ruggles, Alison Skipworth, Ned Sparks, Jacqueline Wells.
Running Time: 90 minutes.

14.   THIRTY DAY PRINCESS. Paramount, 1934. *Marion Gering.*
Sp: Preston Sturges and Frank Partos.
b/o: story by Clarence Budington Kelland.
Cin: Leon Shamroy.
Cast: Sylvia Sidney, Cary Grant, Edward Arnold, Vince Barnett, Edgar Norton, Henry Stephenson.
Running Time: 73 minutes.

15.   BORN TO BE BAD. United Artists, 1934. *Lowell Sherman.*
Sp: Ralph Graves.
Cin: Barney McGill.
Cast: Loretta Young, Jackie Kelk, Cary Grant, Henry Travers, Russell Hopton, Andrew Tombes, Harry Green, Marion Burns.
Running Time: 61 minutes.

16.   KISS AND MAKE UP. Paramount, 1934. *Harlan Thompson.*
Sp: Harlan Thompson and George Marion, Jnr.
b/o: play by Stephen Bekeffi and adaptation by Jane Hinton.
Cin: Leon Shamroy.
Cast: Cary Grant, Genevieve Tobin, Helen Mack, Edward Everett Horton, Lucien Littlefield, Mona Maris, Toby Wing, Clara Lou (Ann) Sheridan, Jacqueline Wells.
Running Time: 78 minutes.

17.   LADIES SHOULD LISTEN. Paramount, 1934. *Frank Tuttle.*
Sp: Claude Binyon and Frank Butler.
b/o: play by Guy Bolton and Alfred Savoir.
Cin: Harry Sharp.
Cast: Cary Grant, Frances Drake, Edward Everett Horton, Charles Arnt, Rosita Moreno, Nydia Westman, George Barbier, Charles Ray, Clare (Ann) Sheridan.
Running Time: 62 minutes.

18.   ENTER MADAME. Paramount, 1934. *Elliott Nugent.*

Sp: Charles Beckett and Gladys Lehman.
b/o: play by Gilda Varesi Archibald and Dorothea Donn-Byrne.
Cin: Theodor Sparkuhl and William Mellor.
Cast: Elissa Landi, Cary Grant, Lynne Overman, Sharon Lynn, Frank Albertson, Cecilia Parker, Diana Lewis.
Running Time: 83 minutes.

19.   WINGS IN THE DARK. Paramount, 1935. *James Flood.*
Sp: Jack Kirkland and Frank Partos.
b/o: story by Neil Shipman and Philip D. Hurn, adapted by Dale Van Every.
Cin: William C. Mellor.
Cast: Myrna Loy, Cary Grant, Roscoe Karns, Hobart Cavanaugh, Dean Jagger, Bert Hanlon, Russell Hopton.
Running Time: 75 minutes.

20.   THE LAST OUTPOST. Paramount, 1935. *Louis Gasnier* and *Charles Barton.*
Sp: Philip MacDonald.
b/o: story by F. Britten Austin and adaptation by Frank Partos and Charles Brackett.
Cin: Theodor Sparkuhl.
Cast: Cary Grant, Claude Rains, Gertrude Michael, Kathleen Burke, Colin Tapley.
Running Time: 75 minutes.

21.   SYLVIA SCARLETT. RKO, 1936. *George Cukor.*
Sp: Gladys Unger, John Collier, and Mortimer Offner.
b/o: novel by Compton Mackenzie.
Cin: Joseph August.
Cast: Katharine Hepburn, Cary Grant, Brian Aherne, Edmund Gwenn, Natalie Paley, Dennie Moore, Lennox Pawle, Daisy Belmore, Nolan Luxford.
Running Time: 94 minutes. V. L/D.

22.   BIG BROWN EYES. Paramount, 1936. *Raoul Walsh.*
Sp: Raoul Walsh and Bert Hanlon.
b/o: short stories by James Edward Grant.
Cin: George Clemens.
Cast: Cary Grant, Joan Bennett, Walter Pidgeon, Isabel Jewell, Lloyd Nolan, Douglas Fowley, Marjorie Gateson, Alan Baxter.
Running Time: 76 minutes.

23.   SUZY. MGM, 1936. *George Fitzmaurice.*
Sp: Dorothy Parker, Alan Campbell, Horace Jackson, and Lenore Coffee.

b/o: novel by Herbert Gorman.
Cin: Ray June.
Cast: Jean Harlow, Franchot Tone, Cary Grant, Lewis Stone, Benita Hume, Reginald Mason, Inez Courtney, Stanley Morner, Una O'Connor.
Running Time: 95 minutes. V.

24.   WEDDING PRESENT. Paramount, 1936. *Richard Wallace.*
Sp: Joseph Anthony.
b/o: story by Paul Gallico.
Cin: Leon Shamroy.
Cast: Joan Bennett, Cary Grant, George Bancroft, Conrad Nagel, Gene Lockhart, William Demarest, Inez Courtney, Edward Brophy.
Running Time: 81 minutes.

25.   THE AMAZING QUEST OF ERNEST BLISS [US: ROMANCE AND RICHES/AMAZING ADVENTURE]. Grand National, 1936 [US: 1937]. *Alfred Zeisler.*
Sp: John L. Balderston.
b/o: story by E. Phillips Oppenheim.
Cin: Otto Heller.
Cast: Cary Grant, Mary Brian, Peter Gawthorne, Henry Kendall, Leon M. Lion, John Turnbull, Arthur Hardy, Iris Ashley, Andrea Malandrinos, Alfred Wellesley, Marie Wright, Buena Bent, Charles Farrell, Hal Gordon, Quinton MacPherson.
Running Time: 70 minutes. V.

26.   WHEN YOU'RE IN LOVE [UK: FOR YOU ALONE]. Columbia, 1937. *Robert Riskin.*
Sp: Robert Riskin.
b/o: story by Ethel Hill and Cedric Worth.
Cin: Joseph Walker.
Cast: Grace Moore, Cary Grant, Aline MacMahon, Henry Stephenson, Thomas Mitchell, Catherine Doucet, Luis Alberni, Emma Dunn.
Running Time: 110 minutes. V.

27.   TOPPER. MGM, 1937. *Norman Z. McLeod.*
Sp: Jack Jerne, Eric Hatch, and Eddie Moran.
b/o: novel by Thorne Smith.
Cin: Norbert Brodine.
Cast: Constance Bennett, Cary Grant, Roland Young, Billie Burke, Alan Mowbray, Eugene Pallette, Arthur Lake, Hedda Hopper, Virginia Sale.
Running Time: 98 minutes. V (original and 'colorised' versions). L/D.

28.   THE TOAST OF NEW YORK. RKO, 1937. *Rowland V. Lee.*
Sp: Dudley Nichols, John Twist, and Joel Sayre.

b/o: book (*Book of Daniel Drew*) by Bouck White and story ('Robber Barons') by Matthew Josephson.

Cin: Peverell Marley.

Cast: Edward Arnold, Cary Grant, Frances Farmer, Jack Oakie, Donald Meek, Thelma Leeds, Clarence Kolb, Billy Gilbert.

Running Time: 109 minutes. V. L/D.

29.   THE AWFUL TRUTH.★ Columbia, 1937. *Leo McCarey.*

Sp: Vina Delmar.

b/o: play by Arthur Richmond.

Cin: Joseph Walker.

Cast: Irene Dunne, Cary Grant, Ralph Bellamy, Alexander D'Arcy, Cecil Cunningham, Marguerite Churchill, Esther Dale, Joyce Compton, Robert Allen, Robert Warwick, Claud Allister, Zita Moulton, Mary Forbes, and Asta the dog.

Running Time: 89 minutes. V. L/D.

30.   BRINGING UP BABY. RKO, 1938. *Howard Hawks.*

Sp: Dudley Nichols and Hagar Wilde.

b/o: story by Hagar Wilde.

Cin: Russell Metty.

Cast: Katharine Hepburn, Cary Grant, Charles Ruggles, May Robson, Walter Catlett, Barry Fitzgerald, Fritz Feld, Leona Roberts, George Irving, Tala Birell, Virginia Walker, John Kelly, and Asta the dog.

Running Time: 102 minutes. V (original and 'colorised' versions). L/D.

31.   HOLIDAY [UK: FREE TO LIVE]. Columbia, 1938. *George Cukor.*

Sp: Donald Ogden Stewart and Sidney Buchman.

b/o: play by Philip Barry.

Cin: Franz Planer.

Cast: Katharine Hepburn, Cary Grant, Doris Nolan, Lew Ayres, Edward Everett Horton, Henry Kolker, Jean Dixon, Binnie Barnes, Henry Daniell.

Running Time: 94 minutes. V. L/D.

32.   GUNGA DIN. RKO, 1939. *George Stevens.*

Sp: Joel Sayre and Fred Guiol.

b/o: story by Ben Hecht and Charles MacArthur, from a Rudyard Kipling poem.

Cin: John H. August.

Cast: Cary Grant, Victor McLaglen, Douglas Fairbanks, Jnr., Eduardo Ciannelli, Joan Fontaine, Montagu Love, Sam Jaffe.

Running Time: 117 minutes. V. L/D.

33. ONLY ANGELS HAVE WINGS. Columbia, 1939. *Howard Hawks.*

Sp: Jules Furthman.

b/o: story by Howard Hawks.
Cin: Joseph Walker.
Cast: Cary Grant, Jean Arthur, Richard Barthelmess, Rita Hayworth, Thomas Mitchell, Sig Ruman, Victor Kilian, John Carroll, Allyson Joslyn, Donald Barry, Noah Beery, Jnr.
Running Time: 121 minutes. V.

34.   IN NAME ONLY. RKO, 1939. *John Cromwell.*
Sp: Richard Sherman.
b/o: novel (*Memory of Love*) by Bessie Brewer.
Cin: J. Roy Hunt.
Cast: Carole Lombard, Cary Grant, Kay Francis, Charles Coburn, Helen Vinson, Katharine Alexander, Jonathan Hale, Peggy Ann Garner.
Running Time: 94 minutes. V. L/D.

35.   HIS GIRL FRIDAY. Columbia, 1940. *Howard Hawks.*
Sp: Charles Lederer.
b/o: play (*The Front Page*) by Ben Hecht and Charles MacArthur.
Cin: Joseph Walker.
Cast: Cary Grant, Rosalind Russell, Ralph Bellamy, Gene Lockhart, Porter Hall, Ernest Truex, Cliff Edwards, Clarence Kolb, Roscoe Karns, Frank Jenks, Regis Toomey, John Qualen, Helen Mack, Alma Kruger, Billy Gilbert, Marion Martin.
Running Time: 92 minutes. V (original and 'colorised' versions).

36.   MY FAVORITE WIFE. RKO, 1940. *Garson Kanin.*
Sp: Bella and Samuel Spewack.
b/o: story by the Spewacks and Leo McCarey.
Cin: Rudolph Mate.
Cast: Irene Dunne, Cary Grant, Randolph Scott, Gail Patrick, Ann Shoemaker, Scotty Beckett, Donald MacBride, Granville Bates.
Running Time: 88 minutes. V (original and 'colorised' versions). L/D.

37.   THE HOWARDS OF VIRGINIA [UK: THE TREE OF LIBERTY]. Columbia, 1940. *Frank Lloyd.*
Sp: Sidney Buchman.
b/o: novel (*The Tree of Liberty*) by Elizabeth Page.
Cin: Bert Glennon.
Cast: Cary Grant, Martha Scott, Sir Cedric Hardwicke, Alan Marshal, Richard Carlson, Paul Kelly, Irving Bacon, Elisabeth Risdon, Anne Revere, Richard Gaines, George Houston.
Running Time: 117 minutes. V.

38.   THE PHILADELPHIA STORY.★ MGM, 1941. *George Cukor.*
Sp: Donald Ogden Stewart.

b/o: play by Philip Barry.

Cin: Joseph Ruttenberg.

Cast: Cary Grant, Katharine Hepburn, James Stewart, Ruth Hussey, John Howard, Roland Young, John Halliday, Virginia Weidler, Mary Nash, Henry Daniell.

Running Time: 112 minutes. V. L/D.

39. PENNY SERENADE. Columbia, 1941. *George Stevens.*

Sp: Morrie Ryskind.

b/o: story by Martha Cheavens.

Cin: Joseph Walker.

Cast: Irene Dunne, Cary Grant,★ Beulah Bondi, Edgar Buchanan, Ann Doran, Eva Lee Kuney, Leonard Wiley, Wallis Clark, Walter Soderling, Baby Biffle.

Running Time: 120 minutes. V (original and 'colorised' versions). L/D.

40. SUSPICION.★ RKO, 1941. *Alfred Hitchcock.*

Sp: Samson Raphaelson, Joan Harrison, and Alma Reville.

b/o: novel (*Before the Fact*) by Francis Iles.

Cin: Harry Stradling.

Cast: Cary Grant, Joan Fontaine, Sir Cedric Hardwicke, Nigel Bruce, Dame May Whitty, Isabel Jeans, Heather Angel, Leo G. Carroll, Auriol Lee, Reginald Sheffield.

Running Time: 99 minutes. V (original and 'colorised' versions). L/D.

41. THE TALK OF THE TOWN.★ Columbia, 1942. *George Stevens.*

Sp: Irwin Shaw and Sidney Buchman.

b/o: story by Sidney Harmon.

Cin: Ted Tetzlaff.

Cast: Cary Grant, Jean Arthur, Ronald Colman, Edgar Buchanan, Glenda Farrell, Charles Dingle, Emma Dunn, Rex Ingram.

Running Time: 118 minutes. V. L/D.

42. ONCE UPON A HONEYMOON. RKO, 1942. *Leo McCarey.*

Sp: Sheridan Gibney.

b/o: story by Sheridan Gibney and Leo McCarey.

Cin: George Barnes.

Cast: Ginger Rogers, Cary Grant, Walter Slezak, Albert Dekker, Albert Bassermann, Ferike Boros, Harry Shannon, Natasha Lytess, John Banner.

Running Time: 116 minutes. V. L/D.

43. MR LUCKY. RKO, 1943. *H.C. Potter.*

Sp: Milton Holmes and Adrian Scott.

b/o: story ('Bundles for Freedom') by Milton Holmes.

Cin: George Barnes.

Cast: Cary Grant, Laraine Day, Charles Bickford, Gladys Cooper, Alan Carney, Henry Stephenson, Paul Stewart, Kay Johnson, Walter Kingsford, J. M. Kerrigan, Vladimir Sokoloff, Florence Bates.
Running Time: 100 minutes. V. L/D.

44.   DESTINATION TOKYO. Warners, 1944. *Delmer Daves.*
Sp: Delmer Daves and Albert Maltz.
b/o: story by Steve Fisher.
Cin: Bert Glennon.
Cast: Cary Grant, John Garfield, Alan Hale, John Ridgely, Dane Clark, Warner Anderson, William Prince, Robert Hutton, Tom Tully, Faye Emerson, John Forsythe.
Running Time: 135 minutes. V.

45.   ONCE UPON A TIME. Columbia, 1944. *Alexander Hall.*
Sp: Lewis Meltzer and Oscar Paul.
b/o: adaptation by Irving Fineman of radio play (*My Client Curly*) by Norman Corwin and Lucille Fletcher Herrmann.
Cin: Franz F. Planer.
Cast: Cary Grant, Janet Blair, James Gleason, Ted Donaldson, Howard Freeman, William Demarest.
Running Time: 89 minutes.

46.   NONE BUT THE LONELY HEART. RKO, 1944. *Clifford Odets.*
Sp: Clifford Odets.
b/o: novel by Richard Llewellyn.
Cin: George Barnes.
Cast: Cary Grant,★ Ethel Barrymore, Barry Fitzgerald, June Duprez, Jane Wyatt, George Coulouris, Dan Duryea, Roman Bohnen.
Running Time: 113 minutes. V.

47.   ARSENIC AND OLD LACE. Warners, 1944. *Frank Capra.*
Sp: Julius J. and Philip G. Epstein.
b/o: play by Joseph Kesselring.
Cin: Sol Polito.
Cast: Cary Grant, Priscilla Lane, Raymond Massey, Josephine Hull, Jean Adair, Jack Carson, Edward Everett Horton, Peter Lorre, James Gleason, John Alexander, Grant Mitchell.
Running Time: 118 minutes. V (original and 'colorised' versions). L/D.

48.   NIGHT AND DAY. Warners, 1946. (c) *Michael Curtiz.*
Sp: Charles Hoffman, Leo Townsend, and William Bowers.
b/o: life of Cole Porter.
Cin: Peverell Marley and William Skall.
Cast: Cary Grant, Alexis Smith, Monty Woolley, Ginny Simms, Jane

Wyman, Eve Arden, Victor Francen, Alan Hale, Dorothy Malone, Selena Royle, Mary Martin.
Running Time: 132 minutes. V.

49. NOTORIOUS. RKO, 1946. *Alfred Hitchcock.*
Sp: Ben Hecht.
b/o: idea by Alfred Hitchcock.
Cin: Ted Tetzlaff.
Cast: Cary Grant, Ingrid Bergman, Claude Rains, Louis Calhern, Mme Leopoldine Konstantin, Ivan Triesault, Reinhold Schunzel, Moroni Olsen.
Running Time: 103 minutes. V. L/D.

50. THE BACHELOR AND THE BOBBYSOXER [UK: BACH-ELOR KNIGHT]. RKO, 1947. *Irving Reis.*
Sp: Sidney Sheldon.
Cin: Robert de Grasse and Nicholas Musuraca.
Cast: Cary Grant, Myrna Loy, Shirley Temple, Rudy Vallee, Ray Collins, Harry Davenport, Johnny Sands, Don Beddoe, Veda Ann Borg.
Running Time: 95 minutes. V. L/D.

51. THE BISHOP'S WIFE.★ RKO, 1947. *Henry Koster.*
Sp: Robert E. Sherwood and Leonardo Bercovici. (Additional, uncredited, dialogue: Billy Wilder and Charles Brackett.)
b/o: novel by Robert Nathan.
Cin: Gregg Toland.
Cast: Cary Grant, Loretta Young, David Niven, Monty Woolley, James Gleason, Gladys Cooper, Elsa Lanchester, Sara Haden.
Running Time: 105 minutes. V. L/D.

52. MR BLANDINGS BUILDS HIS DREAM HOUSE. RKO, 1948. *H. C. Potter.*
Sp: Norman Panama and Melvin Frank.
b/o: novel by Eric Hodgins.
Cin: James Wong Howe.
Cast: Cary Grant, Myrna Loy, Melvyn Douglas, Sharyn Moffett, Connie Marshall, Louise Beavers, Lurene Tuttle, Reginald Denny.
Running Time: 94 minutes. V (original and 'colorised' versions). L/D.

53. EVERY GIRL SHOULD BE MARRIED. RKO, 1948. *Don Hartman.*
Sp: Don Hartman and Stephen Morehouse Avery.
b/o: story by Eleanor Harris.
Cin: George E. Diskant.
Cast: Cary Grant, Betsy Drake, Franchot Tone, Diana Lynn, Alan

Mowbray, Elisabeth Risdon, Richard Gaines, Harry Hayden, Leon Belasco, Fred Essler, Anna Q. Nilsson.
Running Time: 84 minutes. V. L/D.

54.   I WAS A MALE WAR BRIDE [UK: YOU CAN'T SLEEP HERE].
20th Century-Fox, 1949. *Howard Hawks*.
Sp: Charles Lederer, Leonard Spiegelgass, and Hagar Wilde.
b/o: novel by Henri Rochard.
Cin: Norbert Brodine and O. H. Borradaile.
Cast: Cary Grant, Ann Sheridan, William Neff, Eugene Gericke, Marion Marshall, Randy Stuart.
Running Time: 105 minutes. V.

55.   CRISIS. MGM, 1950. *Richard Brooks*.
Sp: Richard Brooks.
b/o: story ('The Doubters') by George Tabori.
Cin: Ray June.
Cast: Cary Grant, Jose Ferrer, Paula Raymond, Signe Hasso, Ramon Novarro, Gilbert Roland, Antonio Moreno, Leon Ames, Teresa Celli.
Running Time: 95 minutes.

56.   PEOPLE WILL TALK. 20th Century-Fox, 1951. *Joseph L. Mankiewicz*.
Sp: Joseph L. Mankiewicz.
b/o: play (*Dr Praetorius*) by Curt Goetz.
Cin: Milton Krasner.
Cast: Cary Grant, Jeanne Crain, Finlay Currie, Hume Cronyn, Walter Slezak, Sidney Blackmer, Katherine Locke, Will Wright, Margaret Hamilton.
Running Time: 109 minutes. V.

57.   ROOM FOR ONE MORE [UK: THE EASY WAY]. Warners, 1952. *Norman Taurog*.
Sp: Melville Shavelson and Jack Rose.
b/o: book by Anna Perrott Rose.
Cin: Robert Burks.
Cast: Cary Grant, Betsy Drake, Iris Mann, George Winslow, Clifford Tatum, Jnr., Gay Gordon, Malcolm Cassell, Larry Olsen, Lurene Tuttle.
Running Time: 97 minutes.

58.   MONKEY BUSINESS. 20th Century-Fox, 1952. *Howard Hawks*.
Sp: I. A. L. Diamond, Charles Lederer, and Ben Hecht.
b/o: story by Harry Segall.
Cin: Milton Krasner.
Cast: Cary Grant, Ginger Rogers, Charles Coburn, Marilyn Monroe, Hugh

Marlowe, Henri Letondal, Larry Keating, Esther Dale, George Winslow.
Running Time: 97 minutes. V. L/D.

59. DREAM WIFE. MGM, 1953. *Sidney Sheldon.*
Sp: Sidney Sheldon, Herbert Baker, and Alfred Lewis Levitt.
b/o: story by Alfred Lewis Levitt.
Cin: Milton Krasner.
Cast: Cary Grant, Deborah Kerr, Walter Pidgeon, Betta St John, Eduard
Franza, Buddy Baer, Les Remayne, Bruce Bennett.
Running Time: 98 minutes.

60. TO CATCH A THIEF. Paramount, 1955. (c) *Alfred Hitchcock.*
Sp: John Michael Hayes.
b/o: novel by David Dodge.
Cin: Robert Burks.
Cast: Cary Grant, Grace Kelly, Jessie Royce Landis, John Williams, Charles
Vanel, Brigitte Auber, Jean Martinelli, Georgette Anys.
Running Time: 103 minutes. V. L/D.

61. THE PRIDE AND THE PASSION. United Artists, 1957. (c) *Stanley
Kramer.*
Sp: Edna and Edward Anhalt.
b/o: novel (*The Gun*) by C. S. Forester.
Cin: Franz Planer.
Cast: Cary Grant, Frank Sinatra, Sophia Loren, Theodore Bikel, John
Wengraf, Jay Novello, Jose Nieto, Carlos Larranaga, Philip Van Zandt,
Paco El Laberinto, Julian Ugarte.
Running Time: 130 minutes. V.

62. AN AFFAIR TO REMEMBER. 20th Century-Fox, 1957. (c) *Leo
McCarey.*
Sp: Delmer Daves and Leo McCarey.
b/o: story by Leo McCarey and Mildred Cram.
Cin: Milton Krasner.
Cast: Cary Grant, Deborah Kerr, Richard Denning, Neva Patterson,
Cathleen Nesbitt, Robert Q. Lewis, Charles Watts, Fortuno Bonanova,
Matt Moore, Louis Mercier, Geraldine Wall, Sarah Selby.
Running Time: 114 minutes. V. L/D.

63. KISS THEM FOR ME. 20th Century-Fox, 1957. (c) *Stanley Donen.*
Sp: Julius J. Epstein.
b/o: play by Luther Davis and novel (*Shore Leave*) by Frederic Wakeman.
Cin: Milton Krasner.
Cast: Cary Grant, Jayne Mansfield, Leif Erickson, Suzy Parker, Ray Wal-
ston, Larry Blyden, Nathaniel Frey, Werner Klemperer, Jack Mullaney.

Running Time: 103 minutes.

64.   INDISCREET. Warners, 1958. (c) *Stanley Donen*.
Sp: Norman Krasna.
b/o: play (*Kind Sir*) by Norman Krasna.
Cin: Frederick A. Young.
Cast: Cary Grant, Ingrid Bergman, Cecil Parker, Phyllis Calvert, David Kossoff, Megs Jenkins, Oliver Johnston Middleton Woods.
Running Time: 100 minutes. V.

65.   HOUSEBOAT. Paramount, 1958. (c) *Melville Shavelson*.
Sp: Melville Shavelson and Jack Rose.
Cin: Ray June.
Cast: Cary Grant, Sophia Loren, Martha Hyer, Charles Herbert, Mimi Gibson, Paul Peterson, Eduardo Ciannelli, Harry Guardino, Murray Hamilton.
Running Time: 112 minutes. V. L/D.

66.   NORTH BY NORTHWEST. MGM, 1959. (c) *Alfred Hitchcock*.
Sp: Ernest Lehman.
Cin: Robert Burks.
Cast: Cary Grant, Eva Marie Saint, James Mason, Jessie Royce Landis, Leo G. Carroll, Philip Ober, Josephine Hutchinson, Martin Landau, Adam Williams, Edward Platt, Robert Ellenstein, Les Tremayne, Philip Coolidge, Patrick McVey, Edward Binns, Ken Lynch.
Running Time: 136 minutes. V. L/D.

67.   OPERATION PETTICOAT. Universal, 1959. (c) *Blake Edwards*.
Sp: Stanley Shapiro and Maurice Richlin.
b/o: story by Paul King and Joseph Stone.
Cin: Russell Harlan.
Cast: Cary Grant, Tony Curtis, Joan O'Brien, Dina Merrill, Arthur O'Connell, Gene Evans, Richard Sargent, Virginia Gregg, Robert F. Simon.
Running Time: 124 minutes. V. L/D.

68. THE GRASS IS GREENER. Universal, 1960. (c) *Stanley Donen*.
Sp: Hugh and Margaret Williams.
b/o: play by Hugh and Margaret Williams.
Cin: Christopher Challis.
Cast: Cary Grant, Deborah Kerr, Robert Mitchum, Jean Simmons, Moray Watson.
Running Time: 104 minutes. V. L/D.

69.   THAT TOUCH OF MINK. Universal, 1962. (c) *Delbert Mann*.
Sp: Stanley Shapiro and Nate Monaster.

The Awful Truth (1937): 'You're all confused, aren't you?'
Bringing Up Baby (1938): 'I'm not quite myself today!'

Grant – the nervous young actor – and Dietrich – the star – in *Blonde Venus* (1932).

'You can be had': Mae West as the strong woman and Grant as the seduced male in *She Done Him Wrong* (1933).

The kiss that opens and closes: Grant and Ingrid Bergman in *Notorious* (1946). 'Tell me, why are you so *good* to me?' Grant with Eva Marie Saint in *North by Northwest*.

Grant – reprising his unworldly academic from *Bringing Up Baby* – with Marilyn Monroe, and her acetates, in *Monkey Business* (1952).
Holiday (1938) with Hepburn: 'When you looked at that face of his, it was full of a wonderful kind of laughter at the back of the eyes.'
'Even in the dark, I know where your eyes are looking': Grant with Grace Kelly in *To Catch a Thief* (1955).

Grant as Ernie Mott in *None But the Lonely Heart* (1944): 'a lone wolf barking in a corner, plain disgusted with a world I never made and don't want none of.'

'Character teaches above our wills': Grant with Ronald Colman and Jean Arthur in *The Talk of the Town* (1942).

Grant accepts his belated Academy Award in 1970, for 'unique mastery of the art of screen acting'.

The democratic gentleman, with the deportment of the Old World and the disposition of the New.

Cary Grant, movie star, mid-career: an immaculate image.

'How do you shave in there?' The intimate stranger in *Charade* (1963), who may be a murderer, a thief or a bureaucrat, but who is still, unmistakably, Cary Grant.

Archie Leach as Cary Grant: an uneasy early pose, a furtive look, an unexamined past, an uncertain future.

Private lives or public postures? Grant and Randolph Scott, inviting idle speculation.

A rare picture of Bob Pender troupe appearing in *Jack and the Beanstalk* at the Theatre Royal Drury Lane, 1910. Archie Leach would join eight years later.

b/o: story by Stanley Shapiro and Nate Monaster.
Cin: Russell Metty.
Cast: Cary Grant, Doris Day, Gig Young, Audrey Meadows, Alan Hewitt, John Astin, Richard Sargent, Joey Faye.
Running Time: 99 minutes. V. L/D.

70. CHARADE. Universal, 1963. (c) *Stanley Donen.*
Sp: Peter Stone.
b/o: story ('The Unsuspecting Wife') by Peter Stone and Marc Behm.
Cin: Charles Lang.
Cast: Cary Grant, Audrey Hepburn, Walter Matthau, James Coburn, George Kennedy, Ned Glass, Jacques Marin, Paul Bonifas, Dominique Minot, Thomas Chelimsky.
Running Time: 113 minutes. V.

71. FATHER GOOSE. Universal, 1964. (c) *Ralph Nelson.*
Sp: Peter Stone and Frank Tarloff.
b/o: story ('A Place of Dragons') by S. H. Barnett.
Cin: Charles Lang, Jnr.
Cast: Cary Grant, Leslie Caron, Trevor Howard, Jack Good, Verina Greenlaw, Pip Sparke, Stephanie Berrington, Jennifer Berrington, Lourelle Felsette, Nicole Felsette, Sharyl Locke, Simon Scott, John Napier.
Running Time: 116 minutes. V.

72. WALK, DON'T RUN. Columbia, 1966. (c) *Charles Walters.*
Sp: Sol Saks.
b/o: story by Robert Russell and Frank Ross (and their screenplay for *The More the Merrier,* Columbia, 1943).
Cin: Harry Stradling.
Cast: Cary Grant, Samantha Eggar, Jim Hutton, John Standing, Miiko Taka, Ted Hartley, Ben Astar, George Takei, Teru Shimada, Lois Kiuchi.
Running Time: 114 minutes. V.

Bibliography

Cary Grant

Archer, Eugene, 'The Good Gray Grant', *New York Times*, Section II, 22 August 1965, p. 7.

Ashman, Chuck and Pamela Trescott, *Cary Grant* (London: W. H. Allen, 1987).

Bacon, James, 'The Secret of Ageless Cary Grant', *Made in Hollywood* (New York: Warner Books, 1977).

Barton, Jane, 'Cary Grant Wows Schenectady', *Variety*, 18 July 1984, pp. 2 and 149.

Battelle, Phyllis, 'Mrs Cary Grant Talks About Marrying (and Divorcing) Cary Grant', *Ladies' Home Journal*, April 1968, pp. 107, 168–9, 172.

Benson, Sheila, 'The Pleasure of His Company', *Los Angeles Times*, Calendar, 15 January 1984, p. 17.

Bergquist, Laura, 'Curious Story Behind the New Cary Grant', *Look*, 1 September 1959, p. 50.

Bogdanovich, Peter, 'Cary Grant', *Picture Shows* (London: George Allen & Unwin, 1975).

Britton, Andrew, *Cary Grant: Comedy and Male Desire* (Newcastle upon Tyne, Tyneside Cinema, 1983).

Buehrer, Beverley Bare, *Cary Grant: A Bio-Bibliography* (New York: Greenwood Press, 1990).

Canby, Vincent, 'A Lightness of Heart and Touch', *New York Times*, 1 December 1986, p. B10.

Cohn, Al, 'Cary Grant – Still the Cream of Bristol', *Los Angeles Times*, Calendar, 11 January 1976, pp. 27–9.

Corliss, Richard, 'Cary Grant: 1904–1986', *Film Comment*, February 1987, p. 78.

Davis, Debra Sharon, 'Cary Grant: A Candid Conversation with America's Epitome of Elegance', *Playboy Guide: Fashion for Men*, Spring–Summer 1981, pp. 31–5.

Decker, Cathleen, 'Cary Grant: A Self-Made Man of Wit and Charm', *Los Angeles Times*, 1 December 1986, pp. 1, 20–21.

Deschner, Donald, *The Complete Films of Cary Grant* (New York: Citadel, 1991).

Donaldson, Maureen with William Royce, *An Affair to Remember: My Life With Cary Grant* (London: Futura, 1989).

Eyles, Allen, *Cary Grant Film Album* (London: Ian Allen, 1971).

Flatley, Guy, 'About Cary Grant – From Mae to September', *New York Times*, Section II, 22 July 1973, p. 1.

Gamarekian, Barbara, 'Kennedy Center Honors Basie, Grant, Robbins, Serkin and Helen Hayes', *New York Times*, 7 December 1981, p. 17.

Gehman, Richard, 'The Ageless Cary Grant', *Good Housekeeping*, September 1960, pp. 64–6, 144–60.

Gehman, Richard, 'The Ageless Cary Grant', *Good Housekeeping*, September 1960, pp. 64–6, 144–60.

Godfrey, Lionel, *Cary Grant: The Light Touch* (London: Robert Hale, 1981).

Govoni, Albert, *Cary Grant: An Unauthorised Biography* (London: Robert Hale & Company, 1973).

Graham, Sheilah, 'Cary', *Scratch an Actor* (London, W. H. Allen, 1969).

Grant, Cary, 'What it Means to be a Star', *Films and Filming*, July 1961, pp. 12–13 and 42.
—'Archie Leach', *Ladies' Home Journal*, 3 parts, January/February, March and April 1963.

Guthrie, Lee, *The Lives and Loves of Cary Grant* (New York: Drake Publishers Inc., 1977).

Harris, Warren G., *Cary Grant: A Touch of Elegance* (London: Sphere, 1988).

Higham, Charles and Roy Moseley, *Cary Grant: The Lonely Heart* (London: New English Library, 1989).

Hoge, Warren,'The Other Cary Grant', *New York Times Magazine*, 3 July 1977, pp. 14–15, 28–9, 32–3.

Hubler, R. G., 'Cary Grant, Hollywood's Indestructible Pro', *Coronet*, August 1957, pp. 34–41.

Kael, Pauline, 'The Man from Dream City', *When the Lights Go Down* (New York: Holt Rinehart Winston, 1980).

Katz, Ephraim, 'Cary Grant', *The Macmillan International Film Encyclopedia* (London: Macmillan, 1994).

Kaye, Mary, 'Now Cary Stars in the Business World', *Bristol Evening Post*, 16 June 1972, p. 7.

Kehr, Dave, 'A Leading Man Among Leading Men: Cary Grant Dies at 82', *Chicago Tribune*, Section 1, 1 December 1986, p. 2.

Kobal, John, 'An Affair to Remember: Grant on Videotape', *American Film*, April 1987, pp. 59–61.

Krzys, Jane, 'The Girl That Cary Couldn't Resist', *Bristol Evening Post*, 4 April 1989, p. 7.

Lilly, Doris, 'A Day at the Office with Cary Grant', *Ladies' Home Journal*, November 1970, pp. 142–3.

McIntosh, William Currie and William D. Weaver, *The Private Cary Grant* (London: Sidgwick and Jackson, 1987).

Mann, Roderick, 'Cary Grant: Doing What Comes Naturally', *Los Angeles Times*, Calendar, 11 June 1978, p. 39.
—'Cary Grant at 80 – Still a Touch of Mink', *Los Angeles Times*, Calendar, 15 January 1984, pp. 16–17.

Michaelson, Judith, 'An Intimate Chat with Cary Grant', *Los Angeles Times*, Calendar, 18 March 1985, pp. 1–4.

Midforth, G. N., 'Film Star Visits His Old School', *Bristol Evening Post*, 28 November 1933, p. 13.
—'The Secret Behind Cary Grant's Visit', *Bristol Evening Post*, 2 December 1933, p. 5.

Nelson, Nancy, *Evenings With Cary Grant: Recollections in His Own Words, and by Those Who Knew Him Best* (New York: Warner Books, 1993).

Ostroff, Roberta, '"How Do You Like Being Cary Grant?" "I Like It Fine"', *Los Angeles Times*, 1 December 1972, pp. 26–9.

Pace, Eric, 'Cary Grant, Movies' Epitome of Elegance, Dies of Stroke', *New York Times*, 1 December 1986, pp. 1 and B10.

Peters, Pauline, 'A Life in the Day of Cary Grant', *Sunday Times Magazine*, 1 February 1981, p. 70.

Platman, Kerry, 'The Cary Grant Story', *Bristol Evening Post* (3 parts), 9–11 May 1983.

Reid, Helen, 'Why I'll always love Bristol, by Cary Grant', *Western Daily Press*, 30 November 1983, pp. 12–13.

Robinson, Jeffrey, 'Cary Grant: "I've lived my life"', *Redbook*, March 1987, pp. 28–34.

Schickel, Richard, *Cary Grant: A Celebration* (London: Pavilion, 1983).
—'The Acrobat of the Drawing Room: Cary Grant 1904–1986', *Time*, 15 December 1986, p. 95.

Schuelke, Kent, 'Cary Grant', *Interview*, January 1987, p. 44.

Shipman, David, 'Cary Grant', *The Great Movie Stars – The Golden Years* (London: Warner Books, 1993).

Siskel, Gene, 'Cary Grant: Hollywood's debonair and durable screen idol . . . without feet of clay', *Chicago Tribune*, Section 6, 15 February 1976, pp. 2–6.
—'Grant's private life adds luster to a public image', *Chicago Tribune*, Section 3, 16 February 1976, pp. 1–2.
—'The Real Cary Grant', *Chicago Tribune*, 7 December 1986, Section 13, pp. 6–8.

Taylor, John Russell, 'Cary Grant', *Films and Filming*, January 1987, pp. 14–15.

Thomas, Alston, 'Cary's Agreement', *Bristol Evening Post*, 30 January 1973, p. 4.
—'The enigma who was Cary Grant', *Bristol Evening Post*, 1 December 1986, p. 4.

Thomson, David, 'Tall, dark and terribly handsome: Cary Grant', in A. Lloyd (ed.), *Movies of the Fifties* (London: Orbis, 1982).
—'Cary Grant', in *A Biographical Dictionary of Film*, revised edition (London: André Deutsch, 1994).

Vermilye, Jerry, *Cary Grant: A Pyramid Illustrated History of the Movies* (New York: Pyramid Publications, 1973).

Walker, Alexander, 'Romantic but ruthless . . . they all loved Cary', *London Evening Standard*, 1 December 1986, p. 13.
—'Cary Grant and the Harry Lime Connection', *It's Only a Movie, Ingrid* (London: Headline, 1988).

Wansell, Geoffrey, *Cary Grant: Haunted Idol* (London: Collins, 1983).

Wolfe, Tom, 'Loverboy of the Bourgeoisie', in *The Kandy-Kolored Tangerine-Flake Streamline Baby* (London: Picador, 1981).

General

Abramson, Harold A. (ed.), *The Use of LSD in Psychotherapy and Alcoholism* (New York: Bobbs–Merrill, 1967).

Adler, Larry, *Me and My Big Mouth* (London: Blake, 1994).

Adorno, T. W. and Hanns Eisler, *Composing for the Films* (London: Athlone, 1994).

Agee, James, 'Comedy's Greatest Era', in Daniel Talbot (ed.), *Film: An Anthology* (Berkeley: University of California Press, 1966).

Allen, Irving Lewis, *The City in Slang: New York Life and Popular Speech* (New York: Oxford University Press, 1993).

Amies, Hardy, *The Englishman's Suit* (London: Quartet, 1994).

Anger, Kenneth, *Hollywood Babylon* (New York: Dell, 1981).
—*Hollywood Babylon II* (London: Arrow Books, 1986).

Atkins, T. R. (ed.), *Sexuality in the Movies* (New York: Da Capo Press, 1984).

Babington, Bruce and Peter William Evans, *Affairs to Remember: The Hollywood Comedy of the Sexes* (Manchester: Manchester University Press, 1989).

Bacon, James, *Made in Hollywood* (New York: Warner Books, 1977).

Bagehot, Walter, *The English Constitution* (London: Fontana, 1993).

Balio, Tino (ed.), *The American Film Industry* (Madison: University of Wisconsin Press, 1984).

Barker, Kathleen, *The Theatre Royal Bristol 1766–1966* (London: Society for Theatre Research, 1974).

Barsley, Michael, *Left-Handed People: An Introduction into the History of Left-Handedness* (North Hollywood: Wilshire Book Company, 1979).

Bart, Peter, 'Billing Without Cooing', *New York Times*, 15 November 1964, p. 12.

Barthes, Roland, *Roland Barthes*, trans. R. Howard (London: Macmillan, 1977).
—*A Lover's Discourse*, trans. R. Howard (London: Jonathan Cape, 1979).

Bartlett, Donald L. and James B. Steele, *Empire: The Life, Legend and Madness of Howard Hughes* (New York: W. W. Norton, 1979).

Baudelaire, Charles, *The Painter of Modern Life and Other Essays* (New York: Da Capo Press, 1986).

Baxter, John, *The Hollywood Exiles* (London: Macdonald and Jane's, 1976).

Bego, Mark, *The Best of Modern Screen* (London: Columbus Books, 1986).

Benjamin, Walter, *One Way Street* (London: New Left Books, 1979).
—*Illuminations* (London: Fontana, 1992).

Bennett, Alan, *Writing Home* (London: Faber, 1994).

Berg, Scott, *Goldwyn* (London: Hamish Hamilton, 1989).

Berger, John, 'My mother's secrets', *New Statesman & Society*, 10 June 1988, pp. 36–8.

Bergman, Andrew, *We're in the Money* (Chicago: Elephant Paperbacks, 1992).

Bergman, Ingrid with Alan Burgess, *Ingrid Bergman: My Story* (London: Michael Joseph, 1980).

Bogdanovich, Peter, *The Cinema of Alfred Hitchcock* (New York: Doubleday, 1963).

Braudy, Leo, *The Frenzy of Renown* (New York: Oxford University Press, 1986).

Brill, Lesley, *The Hitchcock Romance: Love and Irony in Hitchcock's Films* (Princeton: Princeton University Press, 1988).

Britton, Andrew, *Katharine Hepburn: Star as Feminist* (London: Studio Vista, 1995).

Brode, Douglas, *The Films of the Fifties* (Secaucus, NJ: Citadel Press, 1976).

Bryson, Bill, *Made In America* (London: Minerva, 1995).

Cady, Edwin Harrison, *The Gentleman in America* (Syracuse: Syracuse University, 1949).

Bibliography

Callow, Simon, *Charles Laughton: A Difficult Actor* (London: Methuen, 1987).

Canby, Vincent, 'Charting Stars Across the Decades', *New York Times*, Section II, 14 December 1986, pp. 23 and 31.

Carey, John, *The Intellectuals and the Masses* (London: Faber, 1992).

Cassidy, John, 'Kirk's Enterprise', *The New Yorker*, 11 December 1995, pp. 44–53.

Cavell, Stanley, *Pursuits of Happiness* (Cambridge, Mass.: Harvard University Press, 1981).

Challis, Christopher, *Are They Really So Awful? A Cameraman's Chronicle* (London: Janus, 1995).

Chandler, Charlotte, *The Ultimate Seduction* (London: Quartet, 1985).

Chaplin, Charles, *My Autobiography* (Harmondsworth: Penguin, 1966).

Cooke, Alistair, 'The Legend of Gary Cooper', *America Observed* (London: Reinhardt, 1988).

Curtis, Tony with Barry Parris, *Tony Curtis: The Autobiography* (London: Heinemann, 1994).

David, Hugh, *Heroes, Mavericks and Bounders: The English Gentleman from Lord Curzon to James Bond* (London: Michael Joseph, 1991).

Dawson, Jeff, 'It's Just Not Cricket', *Empire*, July 1995, pp. 72–6.

Durgnat, Raymond, *The Crazy Mirror: Hollywood Comedy and the American Image* (London: Faber, 1969).

Dyer, Richard, *Stars* (London: British Film Institute, 1982).

Eagleton, Terry, *The Crisis of Contemporary Culture* (Oxford: Clarendon Press, 1993).

Eames, John Douglas, *The Paramount Story* (New York: Crown, 1985).

Emerson, Ralph Waldo, *The Selected Writings of Ralph Waldo Emerson*, ed. Brodis Atkinson (New York: Random House, 1968).
—*Essays and Poems* (London: J. M. Dent, 1995).

Evans, Robert, *The Kid Stays in the Picture* (London: HarperCollins, 1994).

Fitzgerald, F. Scott, *The Great Gatsby* (Harmondsworth: Penguin, 1950).
—*The Crack-Up, with other Pieces and Stories* (Harmondsworth: Penguin, 1965).

Fleming, Charles, 'The Predator', *Vanity Fair*, February 1996, pp. 54–60, 112–15.

Forster, E. M., *Howards End* (Harmondsworth: Penguin, 1989).

Fraser, John, *America and the Patterns of Chivalry* (Cambridge: Cambridge University Press, 1984).

French, Philip, *The Movie Moguls* (London: Weidenfeld and Nicolson, 1969).

Freud, Sigmund, 'The "Uncanny"', in *Art and Literature* (Harmondsworth: Penguin, 1990).

Friedrich, Otto, *City of Nets: A Portrait of Hollywood in the 1940s* (London: Headline, 1987).

Gabler, Neal, *An Empire of Their Own* (New York: Crown, 1988).

Garber, Marjorie, *Vice Versa: Bisexuality and the Eroticism of Everyday Life* (London: Hamish Hamilton, 1996).

Gilbert, Douglas, *American Vaudeville: Its Life and Times* (New York: Dover, 1940).

Goffman, Erving, *The Presentation of Self in Everyday Life* (New York: Doubleday, 1959).
—*Frame Analysis* (New York: Harper, 1974).

Goldman, William, *Adventures in the Screen Trade* (London: Warner Books, 1993).

Gomery, Douglas, *Shared Pleasures: A History of Movie Presentation in the United States* (London: BFI, 1992).

Goolrick, Robert Cooke, 'To the Manner Born: The Genteel Art of the Gentleman', *On the Avenue*, 4 June 1988, pp. 18–19.

Gottlieb, Sidney, (ed.), *Hitchcock on Hitchcock* (London: Faber, 1995).

Gow, Gordon, *Hollywood in the Fifties* (New York: A. S. Barnes, 1971).

Graham, Sheilah, *Scratch an Actor* (London: W. H. Allen, 1969).

Granger, Stewart, *Sparks Fly Upward* (New York: G. P. Putnam's Sons, 1981).

Greene, Graham, *The Pleasure Dome*, ed. John Russell Taylor (Oxford: Oxford University Press, 1980).

Griffith, Richard (ed.), *The Talkies: Articles and Illustrations from a Great Fan Magazine 1928–1940* (New York: Dover, 1971).

Hadleigh, Boze, *Conversations With My Elders* (London: GMP, 1989).

Handell, Leo A., *Hollywood Looks at its Audience* (Urbana: University of Illinois Press, 1950).

Hart, Moss, *Act One: An Autobiography* (London: Secker & Warburg, 1960).

Haskell, Molly, *From Reverence to Rape*, second edition (Chicago: University of Chicago Press, 1987).

Hecht, Ben, *A Child of the Century* (New York: Simon & Schuster, 1954).

Heymann, C. David, *Poor Little Rich Girl* (Secaucus, NJ: Lyle Stuart, 1984).

Higham, Charles, *Howard Hughes: The Secret Life* (London: Pan, 1994).

Hillier, Jim (ed.), *Cahiers du Cinema: The 1950s* (London: RKP, 1985).

Honri, Peter, *Working the Halls* (London: Futura, 1974).

Hopper, Hedda and James Brough, *The Whole Truth and Nothing But* (Garden City, NY: Doubleday, 1963).

Hotchner, A. E., *Sophia: Living and Loving* (London: Michael Joseph, 1979).

Humphries, S., '"Hurrah for England"': Schooling and the Working Class in Bristol', in *Southern History*, vol. 1, 1979, pp. 171–207.

Hyams, Joe, *Mislaid in Hollywood* (London: W. H. Allen, 1973).

James, C. L. R., *American Civilization*, ed. A. Grimshaw and K. Hart (Oxford: Blackwell, 1993).

James, Henry, *The Beast in the Jungle and Other Stories* (New York: Dover, 1993).

Jennings, Dean, *Barbara Hutton* (London: W. H. Allen, 1963).

Jewell, Richard B. and Vernon Harbin, *The RKO Story* (New York: Arlington House, 1982).

Johnson, Terry, *Plays: One* (London: Methuen, 1993).

Kael, Pauline, *Kiss Kiss Bang Bang* (London: Arrow Books, 1987).

Kanin, Garson, *Hollywood* (New York: Viking, 1974).
—*Together Again!* (Garden City, NY: Doubleday, 1981).

Karnick, Kristine Brunovska and Henry Jenkins (eds.), *Classical Hollywood Comedy* (London: Routledge, 1995).

Keane, Marian, 'The Designs of Authorship: An Essay on *North by Northwest*', *Wide Angle*, no. 1, 1980, pp. 44–52.

Kerr, Walter, *The Silent Clowns* (New York: Knopf, 1975).

Kobal, John, *People Will Talk* (London: Aurum Press, 1986).

Korda, Michael, *Charmed Lives* (New York: Random House, 1979).

Koszarski, Richard, *The Astoria Studio and Its Fabulous Films* (New York: Dover, 1983).

Kracauer, Siegfried, *The Mass Ornament*, ed. Thomas Y. Levin (Cambridge, Mass.: Harvard University Press, 1995).

Lacey, Robert, *Grace* (London: Pan, 1994).

Lambert, Gavin, *On Cukor* (New York: Putnam, 1972).

Larkin, Philip, *Required Writing* (London: Faber, 1983).

Leary, Timothy, *Flashbacks* (Los Angeles: Tarcher, 1983).

Leitch, Thomas M., *Find the Director and Other Hitchcock Games* (Athens: University of Georgia Press, 1991).

Leonard, Maurice, *Mae West: Empress of Sex* (London: HarperCollins, 1991).

Levin, Martin (ed.), *Hollywood and the Great Fan Magazines* (London: Ian Allen, 1976).

Lewis, Kevin, 'A World Across From Broadway: The Shuberts and the Movies', *Film History*, vol. 1, no. 1, 1987, pp. 39–51.

Lloyd, Ann (ed.), *Movies of the Fifties* (London: Orbis, 1982).

Lowenthal, Leo, *Literature, Popular Culture and Society* (Palo Alto: Pacific Books, 1968).

Loy, Myrna with James Kotsilibas-Davis, *Myrna Loy: Being and Becoming* (London: Bloomsbury, 1987).

McBride, Joseph, *Frank Capra: The Catastrophe of Success* (London: Faber, 1992).

McCann, Graham, *Marilyn Monroe: The Body in the Library* (Oxford: Polity, 1988).
—*Woody Allen: New Yorker* (Oxford: Polity, 1990).
—*Rebel Males: Clift, Brando and Dean* (London: Hamish Hamilton, 1991).

McGilligan, Patrick, *George Cukor: A Double Life* (London: Faber, 1992).

McNamara, Brooks, *The Shuberts of Broadway* (New York: Oxford University Press, 1990).

Macintyre, Ben, 'A Veteran Hustler Who Hypnotises America', *The Times*, 14 April 1995, p. 14.

Macnee, Patrick with Marie Cameron, *Blind in One Ear* (London: Harrap, 1988).

Major-Ball, Terry, *Major Major: Memories of an Older Brother* (London: Duckworth, 1994).

Marshall, Michael, *Top Hat & Tails: The Story of Jack Buchanan* (London: Elm Tree Books, 1978).

Mason, James, *Before I Forget* (London: Sphere, 1982).

Mason, Philip, *The English Gentleman: The Rise and Fall of an Ideal* (London: André Deutsch, 1982).

Mast, Gerald (ed.), *Bringing Up Baby* (New Brunswick, NJ: Rutgers University Press, 1988).

May, Larry, *Screening Out the Past: The Birth of Mass Culture and the Motion Picture Industry* (New York: Oxford University Press, 1980).

Modleski, Tania, *The Women Who Knew Too Much: Hitchcock and Feminist Theory* (New York: Methuen, 1988).

Morley, Sheridan, *Tales from the Hollywood Raj: The British Film Colony On Screen and Off* (London: Weidenfeld and Nicolson, 1983).
—*The Other Side of the Moon* (London: Weidenfeld and Nicolson, 1985).

Morin, Edgar, *The Stars* (London: John Calder, 1960).

Naremore, James (ed.), *North by Northwest* (New Brunswick, NJ: Rutgers University Press, 1993).

Niven, David, *The Moon's a Balloon/Bring on the Empty Horses* (London: Coronet, 1985).

Olivier, Laurence, *Confessions of an Actor* (New York: Simon & Schuster, 1982).

Ophuls, Marcel, 'The Last of the Good Guys', in John Boorman and Walter Donohue (eds.), *Projections 4½ (London: Faber, 1995).*

Orwell, George, 'The Lion and the Unicorn', in The Penguin Essays of George Orwell (Harmondsworth: Penguin, 1984).

Osborne, John, *Damn You, England* (London: Faber, 1994).

Paglia, Camille, *Sexual Personae: Art and Decadence from Nefertiti to Emily Dickinson* (New Haven: Yale University Press, 1990).

Parish, James Robert, *Ghosts and Angels in Hollywood Films* (Jefferson, North Carolina: McFarland & Company, 1994).
—and Don E. Stanke, *The All-Americans* (New York: Arlington House, 1977).

Peary, Danny (ed.), *Close-Ups* (New York: Simon & Schuster, 1988).

Peary, Gerald, 'Odets of Hollywood', *Sight and Sound*, Winter 1986, pp. 59–63.

Plato, *Philebus*, trans. R. A. H. Whitehead (Harmondsworth: Penguin, 1982).

Priestley, J. B., *English Journey* (London: Mandarin, 1994).

Proust, Marcel, *Remembrance of Things Past*, 3 vols, trans. Terence Kilmartin (Harmondsworth: Penguin, 1983).

Rose, Jonathan, *The Edwardian Temperament 1895–1919* (Ohio: Ohio University Press, 1986).

Rosten, Leo C., *Hollywood: The Movie Colony, the Movie Makers* (New York: Harcourt, Brace & Co, 1941).

Russell, Rosalind with Chris Chase, *Life is a Banquet* (New York: Random House, 1977).

Russo, Vito, *The Celluloid Closet* (New York: Harper & Row, 1987).

Schickel, Richard, *The Men Who Made the Movies* (London: Elm Tree, 1977).
—*Intimate Strangers: The Culture of Celebrity* (Garden City, NY: Doubleday, 1985).

Schlesinger, Arthur M., *Learning How to Behave: A Study of American Etiquette Books* (New York: Macmillan, 1946).

Shaw, Bernard, *Pygmalion* (Harmondsworth: Penguin, 1957).

Sheldon, Sidney, *Bloodline* (London: HarperCollins, 1993).

Sinyard, Neil and Adrian Turner, *Journey Down Sunset Boulevard* (Ryde, Isle of Wight: BCW, 1979).

Sklar, Robert, *Movie-Made America* (New York: Random House, 1975).

Smith, R. Dixon, *Ronald Colman, Gentleman of the Cinema* (London: McFarland, 1991).

Soloman, David (ed.), *LSD: The Consciousness-Expanding Drug* (New York: Berkeley Medallion, 1966).

Bibliography

Spoto, Donald, *The Dark Side of Genius: The Life of Alfred Hitchcock* (London: Frederick Muller, 1988).

Steinberg, Cobbett, *Reel Facts* (Harmondsworth: Penguin, 1981).

Stevens, Jay, *Storming Heaven* (London: Flamingo, 1993).

Taylor, John Russell, *Strangers in Paradise: The Hollywood Émigrés 1933–1950* (London: Faber, 1983).

Thompson, Paul, *The Edwardians: The Remaking of British Society*, second edition (London: Routledge, 1992).

Thomson, David, *Movie Man* (New York: Stein and Day, 1967).
—*America in the Dark* (London: Hutchinson, 1978).
—*Warren Beatty: A Life and a Story* (London: Secker & Warburg, 1987).

Truffaut, François, *Hitchcock* (London: Paladin, 1986).

Tyler, Parker, *The Hollywood Hallucination* (New York: Simon & Schuster, 1970).

Tynan, Kenneth, 'Shouts and Murmurs', *Observer*, 7 April 1968, p. 26.
—*The Sound of Two Hands Clapping* (London: Jonathan Cape, 1975).
—*Profiles* (London: Nick Hern, 1989).

Updike, John, *Self-Consciousness* (New York: Knopf, 1989).

Viertel, Salka, *The Kindness of Strangers* (New York: Holt, Rinehart and Winston, 1969).

von Sternberg, Josef, *Fun in a Chinese Laundry* (London: Columbus, 1987).

Walker, Alexander, *Sex in the Movies* (Harmondsworth: Penguin, 1968).
—*Stardom* (New York: Stein and Day, 1970).
—*Superstars* (London: Phaidon Press, 1978).
—*Fatal Charm: The Life of Rex Harrison* (London: Weidenfeld and Nicolson, 1992).

Warshow, Robert, *The Immediate Experience* (Garden City, NY: Doubleday, 1962).

Wearing, J. P., *The London Stage 1910–1919* (Metuchen, NJ: Scarecrow Press, 1982).

Wells, J. C., *Accents of English 2: The British Isles* (Cambridge: Cambridge University Press, 1982).

West, Mae, *Goodness Had Nothing To Do With It* (London: World Distributors, 1962).

West, Nathanael, *The Day of the Locust* (Harmondsworth: Penguin, 1991).

Wharton, Edith, *The Custom of the Country* (New York: Charles Scribner's Sons, 1913).

Whittemore, Don and Philip Alan Cecchettini, *Passport to Hollywood* (New York: McGraw-Hill, 1976).

Wilde, Larry, *Great Comedians Talk About Comedy* (New York: Citadel, 1969).

Wiltshire, Bruce, *Role Playing and Identity: The Limits of Theater Metaphor* (Bloomington: Indiana University Press, 1982).

Wittgenstein, Ludwig, *Culture and Value*, trans. Peter Winch (Oxford: Blackwell, 1980).

Wray, Fay, *On The Other Hand* (New York: St Martin's, 1988).

Zinman, D., *Fifty Films from the Fifties* (New York: Arlington House, 1979).

Zolotow, Maurice, *Billy Wilder in Hollywood* (London: Pavilion, 1988).

Zukor, Adolph with Dale Kramer, *The Public is Never Wrong* (New York: G. P. Putnam's Sons, 1953).

Notes

'The Two Hour Old Baby' (1961), by Carl Reiner and Mel Brooks; transcribed from volume 2 of *The Complete 2000 Year Old Man* (1994) Brooksfilms Limited and Clear Productions, Inc., released by Rhino Records Inc.

PROLOGUE

Oscar Wilde: 'Pen, Pencil and Poison', *Complete Works of Oscar Wilde* (London: Collins, 1989), p. 995.

Noel Gallagher: 'Some Might Say', Creation Songs Ltd/Sony Music Publishing, 1995.

1. The phrase is Pauline Kael's. See 'The Man from Dream City', in Kael's *When the Lights Go Down* (New York: Holt Rinehart Winston, 1980) pp. 3–32. Kael's is by far the most impressive and original discussion of Grant. David Thomson's entry on Grant in his *A Biographical Dictionary of Film*, revised edition (London: André Deutsch, 1994) is much shorter but, again, brilliantly insightful. Richard Schickel's *Cary Grant: A Celebration* (London: Pavilion, 1983), written to mark Grant's eightieth birthday, is not as distinctive, but it contains some highly intelligent analyses of Grant's image and roles. Of the conventional biographies of Grant: Charles Higham and Roy Moseley's *Cary Grant: The Lonely Heart* (London: New English Library, 1989) is detailed but sometimes compromised by its over-imaginative and sensationalised treatment of certain themes; Geoffrey Wansell's *Cary Grant: Haunted Idol* (London: Collins, 1983) is a balanced account which draws on an interview with Grant himself; Lionel Godfrey's *Cary Grant: The Light Touch* (London: Robert Hale, 1981) is particularly good on Archie Leach's childhood in Bristol; and William McIntosh and William Weaver's *The Private Cary Grant* (London: Sidgwick and Jackson, 1987) is informative about Grant's later business activities. Andrew Britton's *Cary Grant: Comedy and Male Desire* (Newcastle upon Tyne: Tyneside Cinema, 1983) is an interesting but somewhat manipulative academic monograph

268

concerning Grant's screen image. Maureen Donaldson's *An Affair to Remember* (London: Futura, 1989) is a memoir of the relationship she had with Grant during the period 1973–7; it is not always convincing, but it does offer one a sense of Grant's later lifestyle. Nancy Nelson's invaluable *Evenings With Cary Grant* (New York: Warner Books, 1993) comes with the approval of Grant's widow and daughter, and contains fascinating material drawn from his private papers. Beverley Bare Buehrer's *Cary Grant: A Bio-Bibliography* (New York: Greenwood Press, 1990) includes a very helpful – but not comprehensive – bibliography of books and articles relating to Grant's life and career. Chuck Ashman and Pamela Trescott's slight *Cary Grant* (London: W. H. Allen, 1987), Albert Govoni's unbalanced *Cary Grant: An Unauthorised Biography* (London: Robert Hale, 1973) and Warren G. Harris's informative *Cary Grant: A Touch of Elegance* (London: Sphere, 1988) are biographies of more limited ambition.

2.   The woman was Audrey Hepburn, the movie was *Charade* (1963).

3.   Alfred Hitchcock quoted in Nelson, p. 211.

4.   James Mason, *Before I Forget* (London: Sphere, 1982), p. 408.

5.   Eva Marie Saint quoted in the *Los Angeles Times*, 1 December 1986, p. 20.

6.   James Stewart quoted in the *Los Angeles Times*, 1 December 1986, p. 20.

7.   Frank Sinatra, speaking at the Academy Awards ceremony, on 7 April 1970, as he announced the presentation to Cary Grant of a special Oscar for his achievements in movie acting.

8.   Stanley Donen quoted in Nelson, p. 106.

9.   Donen, in the television documentary *Cary Grant: The Leading Man* (1988), written and produced by Gene Feldman and Suzette Winter, a Wombat Production (first broadcast in the US on Cinemax, 4 April 1988).

10.   Radio City Music Hall opened on 27 December 1932. It is situated at Rockefeller Center; built in the art deco style, it has 5,874 seats, with an opulent foyer and a ceiling eighteen metres high. In 1979 the interior was declared a landmark and restored. It was Grant's favourite movie theatre. 'As far as we're concerned,' Tom Rogers, the director of Radio City at the time, is reported as saying, 'Cary is the Music Hall's uncontested star' (see Govoni, *Cary Grant*, London: Robert Hale, 1973, p. 209).

11.   Noted by Cary Grant, interviewed by Al Cohn, *Los Angeles Times*, 11 January 1976, p. 27.

12.   In a *People* magazine poll marking the centenary of Hollywood, Grant was rated the 'Greatest Male Movie Star of All Time (reported in the *Bristol Evening News*, 4 February 1987). He has figured at the top of similar polls in the US and Britain since his death. He has, for example, figured in the top five in *Time Out*'s readers' poll of the best movie actors (he was placed fourth, behind De Niro, Brando and James Stewart, in the most recent one: see *Time Out*, 25 October 1995, p. 17). In *Premiere* (UK) magazine's issue marking the centenary of cinema, Grant was named as the male 'idol of the thirties' (January 1996, p. 56).

13.   Kael, 'The Man from Dream City', p. 24.

14.   Schickel, *Cary Grant: A Celebration*, p. 154.

15.   *Premiere* (UK edition), August 1995, p. 90.

16.   Thomson, 'Cary Grant', pp. 300–301.

17.   Kennedy's choice of Grant is quoted in Nelson, p. 43. Luciano's is referred to in Kael, 'The Man from Dream City', p. 5.

18.   The remark has been quoted widely. Slightly different versions appear in Schickel, *Cary Grant: A Celebration*, p. 145, and Alexander Walker, 'Cary Grant and the Harry Lime Connection', *It's Only a Movie, Ingrid* (London: Headline, 1988), p. 70. Grant offers an explanation of it in Al Cohn, 'Cary Grant – Still the Cream of Bristol', *Los Angeles Times*, 11 January 1976, pp. 28–9.

19.   Thomson, 'Cary Grant', p. 302.

20.   Leslie Caron, in *Cary Grant: The Leading Man* (documentary).

21.   The phrase was, of course, coined first by Walter Bagehot in *The English Constitution* (London: Fontana, 1993), p. 102.

22.   Cary Grant quoted in Nelson, p. 311.

23.   *Ibid.*

24.   Guy Flatley, 'About Cary Grant', *New York Times*, 22 July 1973, p. 1.

25.   Editorial in the *Washington Post*, 2 December 1986, p. A18.

26.   Kenneth Tynan, 'Shouts and Murmurs', *Observer*, 7 April 1986, p. 26. He returned to the idea of the 'High Definition Performance' in his later collection, *The Sound of Two Hands Clapping* (London: Jonathan Cape, 1975, p. 8), describing it as 'the ability – shared by great athletes, sportsmen, bullfighters and conversationalists as well as stage performers – to communicate the essence of one's talent to an audience with economy, grace, no apparent effort, and absolute, hard-edged clarity of outline'.

BEGINNINGS

Walter Benjamin: quoted by Terry Eagleton in his *The Crisis of Contemporary Culture* (Oxford: Clarendon Press, 1993), p. 21. The usual English translation of Benjamin's remark is found in his *Illuminations* (London: Fontana, 1992), p. 252: 'Social Democracy thought fit to assign to the working class the role of redeemer of future generations, in this way cutting the sinews of its greatest strength. This training made the working class forget both are nourished by the image of enslaved ancestors rather than that of liberated grandchildren.'

None But the Lonely Heart (1944): screenplay by Clifford Odets.

Chapter I

Cary Grant: Walker, 'Cary Grant and the Harry Lime Connection', p. 73.

Jimmy Monkley: *Sylvia Scarlett* (1936): screenplay by Gladys Unger, John Collier and Mortimer Offner.

1. Pauline Kael, 'The Man from Dream City', p. 9.

2. *Ibid.*, p. 5.

3. *Ibid.*

4. F. Scott Fitzgerald, *The Great Gatsby* (Harmondsworth: Penguin, 1950), p. 95.

5. *Ibid.*

6. *Ibid.*

7. *Ibid.*, p. 8.

8. *Ibid.*

9. E. M. Forster, *Howards End* (Harmondsworth: Penguin, 1989), p. 58. See John Carey's *The Intellectuals and the Masses* (London: Faber, 1992).

10. Forster, *ibid.*, p. 127.

11. *Ibid.*, p. 66.

12. *Ibid.*, p. 224.

13. His baptismal certificate records his middle name in its contracted form of 'Alec', but his birth certificate identifies it as Alexander. There is little doubt that his parents named him 'Archibald Alexander'.

14.   Elsie Leach's maiden name is often wrongly referred to in print as 'Kingdom' (e.g. Kael, p. 9), and Grant himself, on one occasion, spelt it 'Kingdom' (in the first of his three-part article 'Archie Leach' for *Ladies' Home Journal*, January/February 1963, p. 133 – although this could merely have been a typographical error), and even the registrar, after altering his initial mistake, rendered the name as 'Kingsdon' on the birth certificate.

Cary Grant's 'Archie Leach' appeared in three parts in the *Ladies' Home Journal* in January/February, March and April 1963, subsequently referred to as 'Archie Leach' part 1, 2 and 3. (See also Chapter XI, note 60.)

15.   John William Elias Leach was born on 9 February 1899 and died on 7 February 1900. The official cause of death, listed on the birth certificate, was 'tubercular meningitis', although Donaldson (p. 176) claims that Grant once told her that he believed that the baby had died from gangrene after his mother had accidentally caught his hand in the door. Not only is this implausible, it is not supported by any documentary evidence.

16.   Grant, 'Archie Leach', part 1, p. 134.

17.   Higham and Moseley (p. 286) claim – rather enigmatically – that 'Stewart Granger and Ray Austin confirmed from first-hand knowledge that Cary Grant was circumcised'.

18.   See, for example, Kael, p. 9, Schickel, *Cary Grant: A Celebration*, p. 19, and McIntosh and Weaver, p. 22. Higham and Moseley (p. 286) admit that while some of their interviewees said they believed that Grant was Jewish, an 'almost equal number stated that he failed to mention any Jewish origin'.

19.   Kael, p. 9.

20.   The number of Jewish families in Bristol at that time was very low indeed. In 1901, the total number of Jews living in Britain as a whole was estimated to be 157,090, with a high proportion (one-third) of that number concentrated in the East End of London and, to a lesser extent, the north of England (*The Jewish Year Book*, London, 1901, pp. 177–8).

21.   Quoted by Nelson, p. 296.

22.   Apart from his financial donation, he also attended certain fund-raising events: on 20 October 1953, he participated in the 'City of the Ages, the Great Historical Drama and Tribute to Three Thousand Years of Jerusalem', along with José Ferrer, Gregor Piatigorsky, Jan Peerce and Edward G. Robinson. On 28 November 1953, he served as one of the narrators of the Israel Bond Event when Jerusalem had its 3000th Anniversary Bond Event in Chicago; President Harry S. Truman was guest speaker, and

Charlton Heston and Jeff Chandler also made appearances. One should note that Grant contributed to, and supported, several causes other than those with Jewish connections. Several other Hollywood stars, with no Jewish ancestry, are also known to have contributed to Jewish charities during this period, including Frank Sinatra (see *Sunday Times Magazine*, 29 October 1995, p. 38).

23. See Higham and Moseley, p. 51. Grant told Gene Siskel ('Cary Grant', *Chicago Tribune*, 15 February 1976, p. 2) that he inherited his dark, olive-tinted skin from his 'beautiful mother'.

24. Grant's papers contain a record he kept of the date (6 May 1983) of a telephone call he made to his correspondent (Debbie Rosen of Pompano Beach, Florida) to confirm this fact. The telephone call was not, for Grant, an unusual way of responding to such queries; he would note some basic details of his reply at the base of the correspondent's letter and place it in his files. (See Nelson, p. 297.) Another – perhaps even more significant – piece of evidence that seems to confirm that Elsie Leach was Grant's biological mother is a letter he wrote her in 1966, shortly after the birth of his daughter, in which he says the experience made him appreciate 'all you must have endured to have me' (Nelson, p. 271).

25. See Higham and Moseley, pp. x, xi, 2, 51, 78, 81, 162, 177, 217 and 222.

26. *Ibid.*, p. 2. The authors do not provide a source for this allegation.

27. *Ibid*, p. x.

28. *Ibid.*

29. *Ibid.*, pp. 83 and 162. The authors do not provide a source for this claim.

30. Fred Marks, Senior Managing Editor at Marquis *Who's Who*, explained that 'we have no archival material from the early 1960s and no material at all with Cary Grant's signature affixed to it', and so the reason why the change was made, and by whom, remains unclear (correspondence with the author, 21.9.95).

31. *Current Biography 1941* (New York: H. W. Watson, 1942), pp. 339–40; *Current Biography 1965*, pp. 170–73. He does not appear in equivalent editions of the UK *Who's Who*.

32. Such inaccuracies have been taken at face value by countless newspapers over the years. The London *Times*, for example, in its obituary of 1 December 1986 (p. 18), refers to an 'Alexander Archibald Leach'. The

Daily Telegraph (1 December 1986, p. 3) makes the same mistake, as well as describing his school as 'Fairfield Academy'.

33. He also – elsewhere – described *both* of his parents as 'churchgoing people . . . of Episcopalian Protestant faith' ('Archie Leach', part 1, p. 133).

34.   It was not particularly unusual for working-class families at that time to move so frequently. Before Archie was born, the couple lived at 30 Brighton Street. In 1904: 15 Hughendon Road; 1911: 5 Seymour Avenue; 1915: a shared house in Picton Street.

35.   Grant, 'Archie Leach,' part 1, p. 133.

36.   *Ibid.*

37.   *Ibid.*

38.   *Ibid.*

39.   Donaldson, p. 62.

40.   Charles Chaplin, *My Autobiography* (Harmondsworth: Penguin, 1966), p. 22.

41.   Grant, 'Archie Leach', part 1, p. 134.

42.   Grant recalled that he usually went to the cinema in Zetland Road on Saturday afternoons, when he could go upstairs for twopence (the Claire Street cinema cost around sixpence for admission). See Helen Reid, 'Why I'll always love Bristol, by Cary Grant', *Western Daily Press*, 30 November 1983, p. 12.

43.   Grant, 'Archie Leach', part 1, p. 136.

44.   *Ibid.*

45.   In an interview with Helen Reid – 'Cary's Cherished Childhood', *Western Daily Press*, 3 December 1980, p. 7 – Grant recalled seeing the Pearl White serial 'The Clutching Hand'. He may have misremembered the title, mistaking it for *The Iron Claw* (1916), which would have been shown at around this time.

46.   Grant, 'Archie Leach', part 1, p. 134.

47.   *Ibid.*, p. 52.

48.   Quoted by Kerry Platman, 'The Cary Grant Story', part 2, *Bristol Evening Post*, 10 May 1983, p. 31.

Chapter II

Marcel Proust, *Remembrance of Things Past*, vol. III (Harmondsworth: Penguin, 1983), p. 658.

Cary Grant: Warren Hoge, 'The Other Cary Grant', *New York Times Magazine*, 3 July 1977, p. 29.

1.   The precise date of Elsie Leach's disappearance is unknown, but one can place it cautiously within 1913. Grant said that he was nine when she left ('Archie Leach', part 1, p. 50). Some biographers suggest − without citing any evidence − that Elsie disappeared the following year, in 1914, when Archie was ten (see Higham and Moseley, p. 12, and Wansell, p. 39).

2.   Elsie Leach did still dance at local clubs, so the question was not as odd as it might seem; her cousin, Ernest Kingdon, has noted that she had her dancing shoes sent on to her when she was in Fishponds 'because they had dances at the institute [institution]' (Godfrey, p. 24).

3.   The relationship was not particularly unusual among working-class couples at that time. Divorce was rare. See, for example, Chapter 4 of Paul Thompson's *The Edwardians* (London: Routledge, 1992).

4.   Higham and Moseley, p. 12.

5.   This was the explanation that Grant himself gave to numerous interviewers throughout his career (e.g. Platman, part 1, p. 31) and it was the one which was included by him in his autobiographical article, 'Archie Leach', part 1, p. 136. See also the accounts in Ashman and Trescott (p. 32), Buehrer (p. 2), Donaldson (p. 41), Godfrey (p. 23), Govoni (p. 26), Harris (p. 13), Kael (p. 9), McIntosh and Weaver (p. 23), Nelson (p. 16), Schickel (p. 23) and Wansell (p. 40).

6.   Grant, 'Archie Leach', part 1, p. 136.

7.   *Ibid.*

8.   Platman, part 2, p. 31.

9.   See 'C.R.H.', 'Peep Into Old Fishponds', *Bristol Evening Post*, 10 November 1933, p. 9.

10.   Nelson, p. 248.

11.   Godfrey, p. 24.

12.   The couple had a son, Eric Leslie Leach, born on 5 September 1921, while Archie was away in the United States.

13.   Donaldson, p. 43.

14.   Grant said very little (at least for public consumption) about his father's behaviour, although Donaldson (p. 179) claims that Grant discussed it with her, saying: ' "Why hadn't he told me the truth? . . . Why hadn't he written me and told me? It's the least he could have done. My God, I had told the press she was *dead* because that's the only thing I could think after all these years." ' Nelson (pp. 24–5) reproduces a letter dated 5 May 1918 written by Elias to Elsie Leach in the sanatorium ('I remain your loving husband'), suggesting that Elias wrote occasionally to his wife after her incarceration, but possibly without his son's knowledge. What *is* clear, however, is that Elsie Leach's relatives had not kept in touch with Elias once he had sent her to Fishponds, which suggests – along with Ernest Kingdon's insistence that Elsie was stable and sane – that Elias's actions had not been approved of by his wife's family.

15.   All of Grant's biographers put the date of Elias Leach's death – incorrectly – as 2 December 1935 (Buehrer, pp. 7 and 32; Godfrey, p. 76; Harris, p. 81; Higham and Moseley, p. 64; Nelson, p. 66; and Wansell, p. 121). In Grant's own article, 'Archie Leach' (part 1, p. 134), he refers to it as '1933'. The 'births, marriages, deaths and in memoriam' section of the *Bristol Evening Post* of 2 December 1935 (p. 25), however, includes the following entry: 'LEACH – In loving memory of my dear brother Elias, passed peacefully away December 1. Ever remembered by his loving sister Hetty and children.'

16.   Grant, 'Archie Leach', part 1, p. 134. Quoted in numerous sources: see, for example, Harris, p. 81.

17.   This date refers to the moment when Grant was notified formally of his mother's situation; it is very likely, but not certain, that this was also the moment when he first learned for certain that she was still alive. If Grant *did* know before this point, we have no firm evidence that can prove it. Wansell (p. 108) claims that Grant had known early on about Elsie Leach's existence in Fishponds, but that he did not see her again until his father suggested it during Grant's visit to Bristol at the end of 1933 (Wansell does not, however, identify his source for this information). The contemporary article which may have caused – or contributed to – the confusion is G. N. Midforth's 'The Secret Behind Cary Grant's Visit' (*Bristol Evening Post*, 2 December 1933, p. 5): Midforth spoke enigmatically of how 'one day' the 'real story' behind Grant's visit might be told, 'but not yet, and not by me'. He added that this 'secret' was known 'to only a small number of people in the city, and is essentially a personal matter', but, if it was made public, it 'would make Bristolians proud of their splendid son'. Midforth had reported previously (28 November) that Grant's trip was 'to visit his parents'

and to 'make arrangements for his wedding to Virginia Cherrill', so the mere existence of both parents could not have been the 'secret' he refers to a few days later. Godfrey (p. 61) refers to an interview given by Grant to a newspaper upon his return from Bristol to London which says that he 'saw my father, my uncles, my cousins and my aunts and had a wonderful time' – no mention was made of any reunion with his mother. In the absence of any unambiguous evidence to the contrary, I suspect, like the majority of biographers (e.g. Godfrey, p. 78; Harris, p. 81; McIntosh and Weaver, p. 121; Nelson, p. 70), that Grant discovered the truth about his mother in the months following his father's death. Although the precise date remains open to question, one suggestion can be discounted: Higham and Moseley (p. 81) put the date at somewhere between 27 June and 19 October 1938, when Grant was shooting *Gunga Din*; they quote Phyllis Brooks as saying that a 'stunned' Grant received an 'astonishing telegram' telling him that 'his mother was alive and had been let out of the asylum'. The problem with this is that Grant had started receiving letters (sent from Grantchester, Westbury-on-Trym, Bristol) from his mother at least a year earlier.

18. Donaldson, p. 180.

19. Godfrey, p. 78.

20. Grant, 'Archie Leach', part 1, p. 136.

21. The movie was *Every Girl Should Be Married* (1948).

22. Higham and Moseley, p. 260; see also pp. 196–7. Of Grant's other biographers, accounts of his relationship with his mother range from those which stress the negative aspects (see, for example, Donaldson, pp. 41–2; Wansell, pp. 123–5, 199 and 276), through those – the majority – which favour a more ambivalent approach (e.g. Godfrey, p. 80; Harris, pp. 220–21; McIntosh and Weaver, pp. 120–24; Nelson, pp. 16–17, 70–72, 247–50) to the few which depict the relationship in generally positive tones (e.g. Ashman and Trescott, p. 72).

23. See, for example, Godfrey, p. 79.

24. Wansell, p. 282.

25. Hoge, p. 29.

26. Donaldson, p. 180.

27. Jeffrey Robinson, 'Cary Grant: "I've lived my life"', *Redbook*, March 1987, p. 28.

28. Nelson, p. 72.

29.   Grant, 'Archie Leach', part 1, p. 136.

30.   *Ibid.*

31.   Letters page, *Bristol Evening Post*, 21 April 1989, p. 8.

32.   Nelson, p. 249.

33.   *Ibid.*, p. 94.

34.   Quoted by Ashman and Trescott, p. 128.

35.   Alston Thomas, 'The enigma who was Cary Grant', *Bristol Evening Post*, 1 December 1986, p. 4.

36.   Nelson, p. 121.

37.   Godfrey, p. 80.

38.   Grant, 'Archie Leach', part 1, p. 136.

39.   Nelson, pp. 70−71.

40.   See, for example, other letters reproduced in Nelson, pp. 94 and 121.

41.   Doris Davis, who was married to the manager of the Commercial Cable Company in Bristol, told Godfrey (p. 79) that Grant 'used to cable regularly to his mother'.

42.   Nelson, pp. 271−2.

43.   *Ibid.*, p. 71.

44.   It is certainly the case that Grant, when asked by interviewers about his parents, spoke particularly warmly about his father (see, for example, Wansell, p. 122, who quotes him as saying that Elias was his 'first hero' and 'a wise and kindly man and I loved him very much'), and Nelson (pp. 39−40) reproduces examples of their correspondence which suggest that the relationship was relatively affectionate, although other sources, such as Donaldson (pp. 178−9), claim that Grant − in private − was more ambivalent in his feelings for his father.

45.   See Robinson, p. 28.

46.   Grant, 'Archie Leach', part 1, p. 134.

47.   *Ibid.*, p. 133.

48.   Harris, p. 181.

49.   Grant, 'Archie Leach', part 3, p. 152.

50.   Nelson, p. 16.

51.   Quoted in Wansell, p. 46.

Chapter III

Cary Grant, 'Archie Leach', part 3, p. 149.

Federico Fellini: Charlotte Chandler, *The Ultimate Seduction* (London: Quartet, 1984), p. 111.

1.   In his various *Who's Who* entries, Cary Grant (or whoever completed the forms on his behalf) referred to the school as 'Fairfield Academy, Somerset'. Bristol was, in those days, in Somerset, but the 'Academy' suggests an American hand.

2.   The 1902 Education Act established Local Education Authorities and encouraged them to extend educational provision at both elementary and secondary levels. Working-class children who were judged to be intellectually able were supposed to be given the opportunity to climb a rung or two up the social ladder by acquiring a secondary education. One result of the subsequent debates in Parliament concerning social inequality during the period of Liberal rule between 1906 and 1914 was the Free Place Regulations, introduced to ensure that all secondary schools aided by grants 'shall be made fully accessible to children of all classes'. Grammar schools offering at least one-quarter of their places free to pupils from elementary schools were rewarded with higher grants. The numbers of working-class children affected, however, remained disappointingly low. Only four or five working-class children out of 1,000 could hope to win scholarships to secondary schools. In 1912, although the proportion of children attending these schools had doubled during the previous ten years, four-fifths of children aged between fourteen and eighteen had never attended secondary school (see Jonathan Rose, *The Edwardian Temperament 1885–1919*, Ohio: Ohio University Press, 1986, p. 178).

3.   Grant, 'Archie Leach', part 1, p. 138.

4.   Godfrey, p. 27.

5.   Grant, 'Archie Leach', part 1, p. 136.

6.   G. N. Midforth, 'Film Star Visits His Old School', *Bristol Evening Post*, 28 November 1933, p. 13.

7.   In all of Grant's movies (with the single exception of *Indiscreet*), he played right-handed characters, and so someone else's hand was filmed in close-up whenever he had to be seen writing something down. According to Nelson (p. 15), one of Grant's favourite books was *A Social History of*

Left-Handers, written by 'a technician with the BBC': 'This technician was editing the recorded speeches of King George VI, erasing the King's stammer,' said Grant. 'He knew that many people stammer because they're frustrated, but wondered what could possibly frustrate a king. It seems George had been naturally left-handed but was forced as a child to use his right hand.'

Nelson does not name the author of this book, and I can find no record of such a title. I believe, therefore, that she, or Grant, misremembered the details, and that the book was, in fact, entitled *Left-Handed People: An Introduction into the History of Left-Handedness* (North Hollywood: Wilshire Book Company, 1979) by Michael Barsley (the first US edition, in 1967, was titled *The Other Hand*). Barsley did work for the BBC as a producer whose duties included royal broadcasts, as he notes at the start of Chapter XXV: 'The author's attention was brought to [the subject of stammering] in a vivid way by having to edit, for radio programmes, the speeches and other public pronouncements of King George VI,' a task that obliged Barsley to 'cut out, on tape, the pauses in his talk, in order to make a coherent message' (p. 168).

8.   Grant, 'Archie Leach', part 1, p. 136.

9.   *Ibid.*, p. 134.

10.   *Ibid.*, p. 138. 'The only person who ever remarked upon the tooth's absence was Mack Sennett . . . who came backstage to visit me in New York years later, and surprised me by saying that his camera-trained eye had noticed it from the audience.'

11.   *Ibid.*, p. 136.

12.   *Ibid.*, p. 138.

13.   Reid, p. 12.

14.   Grant, 'Archie Leach', part 1, p. 138.

15.   Cohn, p. 29.

16.   Cathleen Decker, 'Cary Grant: A Self-Made Man of Wit and Charm', *Los Angeles Times*, 1 December 1986, p. 20.

17.   Godfrey, p. 76.

18.   Grant, 'Archie Leach', part 1, p. 138.

19.   *Ibid.*

20.   *Ibid.*

21.   *Ibid.*, p. 140.

22. Nelson, pp. 22–3.

23. This is another contentious – and somewhat baffling – issue. Higham and Moseley (pp. 6–12) are alone among Grant's biographers in claiming that Archie Leach first made contact with Pender in 1910; the only evidence they adduce for this is a reference to a photograph of the Pender troupe in a copy of the *Pall Mall* magazine of January 1910 ('A small boy watching in the background at a rehearsal *may have been* Archie Leach', p. 286, italics are mine). According to Higham and Moseley, Elias Leach 'gave Archie to Pender as an extra member of the troupe', in spite of the fact that the boy was only six and that Elsie surely could not have approved. They go on to claim that Archie toured with the troupe in Bristol, Berlin, Paris and London during 1910; he is then supposed to have accompanied the troupe to New York, sailing on 15 March 1911 (p. 9), appearing at the Folies Bergère Theater at the invitation of Jesse L. Lasky. When the engagement ended, the decision was made, we are told, to return Archie to Bristol (p. 12). At some point late in 1911 he is meant to have 'reappeared, no doubt in a state of disappointment and irritation, at the drab and humdrum Bishop Road Infant School' (p. 12). As I have found no records which support this thesis, I have not referred to it in the main body of the text. Grant himself was never precise about the date of the first contact with Pender, but as he said he was 'not yet fourteen' when he wrote his letter to Pender ('Archie Leach', part 1, p. 140), one can assume that it was probably some time in the second half of 1917.

24. Higham and Moseley (pp. 6–7, 14) note that Pender's troupe was also sometimes known as 'Bob Pender's Little Dandies', the 'Pender Troupe of Giants' and 'Bob Pender's Nippy Nine Burlesque Rehearsal'. Grant, in 'What it Means to be a Star' (*Films and Filming*, July 1961, p. 12), refers to the troupe as 'the Bob Pender Acrobats', and, in 'Archie Leach', part 1 (p. 140), as 'knockabout comedians'.

25. In J. P. Wearing's *The London Stage 1910–1919* (Metuchen, New Jersey: Scarecrow Press, 1982), for example, there is a record of Pender playing the Clown in *Jack and the Beanstalk* at Drury Lane in 1911 (in a cast that included Harry Randall) and in *Hop O' My Thumb* at the same venue the following year (in a cast that included Jimmie James).

26. Reid, p. 12.

27. Grant, 'Archie Leach', part 1, p. 140. Faked notes seem to have been particularly in vogue among schoolchildren in Bristol at the time as a means of disguising truancy (see S. Humphries, ' "Hurrah for England": Schooling and the Working Class in Bristol', *Southern History*, vol. 1, 1979, p. 188).

28. See Grant, 'Archie Leach', part 1, p. 140.

29. For another version of Leach's flight from Bristol, see Higham and Moseley, p. 6.

30. For obvious reasons, it is difficult to be sure of the extent to which such Masonic links were common among music-hall performers, but Terry Major-Ball has told me that he knew that his father (who was a music-hall artiste based, eventually, in London) and many of his fellow performers were Masons (interview with the author, 19 September 1995).

31. Grant, 'Archie Leach', part 1, p. 140.

32. *Ibid.*

33. *Ibid.* Bob Bennett, one of his old schoolfriends, told Kerry Platman (part 2, pp. 30–31): 'I expect there's something to the story that he was expelled for going into the girls' department, but, when we talked about it years later, he told me that he honestly couldn't remember why he had been thrown out.' When Platman asked Grant about the incident, he laughed and said: 'I'm not going to tell you why.' He never denied his earlier explanation, however, and most of his biographers accepted it (see Ashman and Trescott, p. 39; Harris, pp. 21–2; Wansell, p. 53).

34. Higham and Moseley, p. 15.

35. *Ibid.*

36. Godfrey, p. 38.

37. *Ibid.*

38. Grant, 'Archie Leach', part 1, p. 140.

39. Nelson, p. 27.

40. It is, in fact, not entirely unlikely that at some point during this period Archie Leach may have come into contact with Tom Major-Ball (father of John Major). Both men were staying in Brixton at around the same time (Leach with the Penders at 247 Brixton Road, Major-Ball in rented accommodation at 144 Coldharbour Lane). Terry Major-Ball has told me that, although he does not recall hearing his father talk of any meeting with Leach, he did say that he met most of the acts from this period, and it is certainly the case that Leach and Major-Ball appeared on the same circuits and had several mutual friends who were fellow performers. 'Another common thread, of course, was the snobbery and intolerance I'm sure they both experienced as they tried to better themselves' (interview with the author, 19 September 1995).

41.   Grant, 'Archie Leach', part 1, p. 140.

42.   *Ibid.*, p. 142.

43.   *Ibid.*

CULTIVATION

To Catch a Thief (1955): screenplay by John Michael Hayes.

Bringing Up Baby (1938): screenplay by Dudley Nichols and Hagar Wilde.

Chapter IV

F. Scott Fitzgerald, 'Echoes of the Jazz Age', in *The Crack-Up* (Harmondsworth: Penguin, 1965), p. 10.

Cary Grant, 'Archie Leach', part 3, p. 149.

1.   Kael, 'The Man from Dream City', p. 15.

2.   *Ibid.*

3.   Grant, 'Archie Leach', part 3, p. 148.

4.   The Hippodrome had opened on 12 April 1905. In 1923, as B. F. Keith's Hippodrome, it had become a vaudeville house, and in 1928 it was re-opened as a cinema: the RKO Hippodrome. It closed again in 1932, re-opened in 1933 and was taken over by Billy Rose in 1935 before being demolished in 1939.

5.   It has been estimated that, by the mid-1920s, there were more than 1,000 movie theatres in New York City alone. Many of them were concentrated in Times Square and on the 'subway circuit' in various neighbourhoods. Among the most notable of the period was the Roxy Theater at 50th Street and 7th Avenue (seating 6,000), the Paramount Theater (seating 3,700) and the Loew's State (seating 3,300) on Times Square. See Douglas Gomery's excellent *Shared Pleasures* (London: BFI, 1992) for information on the movie theatres of this era.

6.   Some vaudeville promotors – including B. F. Keith and E. F. Albee – opened their own movie theatres.

7.   Grant, 'Archie Leach', part 2, p. 35.

8.   *Ibid.*, pp. 24 and 35.

9.   Quoted by Donaldson, p. 153.

10.   Grant, 'Archie Leach', part 2, p. 35.

11.   Quoted by Donaldson, p. 152.

12. Grant, 'Archie Leach', part 2, p. 35.

13. Nelson, pp. 34–5.

14. Grant, 'Archie Leach', part 2, p. 38.

15. Grant, 'Archie Leach', part 1, p. 142.

16. *Ibid.*

17. Quoted by Midforth, 'Film star visits his old school', p. 13.

18. Grant, 'Archie Leach', part 2, p. 38.

19. *Ibid.*

20. *Ibid.*

21. Kael, 'The Man from Dream City', p. 11.

22. Lucrezia Bori (1887–1960), the Spanish soprano, was associated with the New York Metropolitan Opera from 1912 to 1936. She would at this time have been easing her way back into her repertoire after five years of serious throat problems.

23. Grant spells the name incorrectly as 'Tilyew' in his 'Archie Leach', part 2, p. 38.

24. Grant, 'Archie Leach', part 3, p. 87.

25. Nelson, p. 39.

26. *Ibid.*, p. 40.

27. *Ibid.*, p. 39.

28. For details of some of his engagements at this time, see Buehrer, pp. 160–1.

29. This is yet a6nother confusing moment in Grant's biography. According to his brief article for *Films and Filming* magazine ('What it Means to be a Star', p. 12), he survived in New York for 'two years' after the departure of the Pender troupe, and then, he claims, he 'returned to England, where without very much trouble I landed small parts in musical comedies'. He does not give precise details of where or when he played, nor of when he arrived back in the US. As the article contains several inaccuracies concerning his past, one must treat this information cautiously. Buehrer (p. 161) suggests that Archie Leach joined a minor repertory company – the Nightingale Players – in 1925, touring England in its productions of *No, No, Nanette* and *The Arcadians* and returning to New York in 1927. Several biographers refer – always briefly and rather vaguely – to a brief tour of

England during this period (see, for example, Harris, pp. 38–9). Evidence of such a tour – as far as Archie Leach's presence is concerned – is, as far as I have been able to ascertain, scant and highly questionable. Nancy Nelson's *Evenings With Cary Grant* does not refer to such a tour, even though she had access to Grant's private papers and is usually an extremely reliable source. A possible explanation has been put forward by Higham and Moseley (p. 34), who claim (they provide no source) that Archie Leach published a brief biographical essay in the *Post-Dispatch* while he was on tour in St Louis in 1930, full of invented details (such as that he had started his career as a pugilist, and that he had returned briefly to England in the mid-twenties). This, they allege, was the original source for the subsequent references to Leach's 'English tour'. I am inclined to agree with them, and, for that reason, I have not referred to this 'tour' in the text.

30. Grant, 'Archie Leach', part 3, p. 149.

31. The sobering fate of Mr Ritter, and his lasting impact on Grant, is recounted by James Bacon in *Made in Hollywood* (New York: Warner Books, 1977), pp. 213–14.

32. Grant, 'Archie Leach', part 3, p. 149.

33. Nelson, p. 38.

34. Grant, 'Archie Leach', part 3, p. 149.

35. *Ibid.*

36. Nelson, pp. 40–41.

37. Hammerstein's theatre, on Broadway and 53rd Street in Manhattan, opened in 1927. It struggled to make enough money to stay open, and, in 1934, was converted into Billy Rose's Music Hall, a casino and nightclub. In 1949 CBS converted the theatre into a television studio for the *Ed Sullivan Show*, and it was renamed the Ed Sullivan Theater in 1967. In the 1990s it became the venue for the David Letterman show.

38. Quoted by Grant, 'Archie Leach', part 3, pp. 149–50.

39. *Ibid.*, p. 150.

40. By the late 1920s, the Shuberts owned over one hundred theatres around the country. Among those in New York City were the Shubert Theater (1913) and the Broadhurst Theater (1917) – both on 44th Street – the Booth Theater (1913) on 45th Street and the Barrymore Theater (1928) on 47th Street. See Brooks McNamara, *The Shuberts of Broadway* (New York: Oxford University Press, 1990).

41. Quoted by Kael, 'The Man from Dream City', p. 12.

42.   The Astoria Studio was situated at 35th Avenue between 34th and 37th streets in Astoria, just across the East River. Between 1921 and 1927 around one-quarter of the movies produced by Paramount were made there. In 1988, it became the site of the Museum of the Moving Image. See Richard Koszarski, *The Astoria Studio and Its Fabulous Films* (New York: Dover, 1983).

43.   Quoted in Nelson, p. 45.

44.   The report has been quoted in numerous accounts; I take it from Ephraim Katz's entry on Astaire in his *The Macmillan International Film Encyclopedia* (London: Macmillan, 1994), p. 56.

45.   Robinson's 'Cary Grant: "I've lived my life"', p. 28, suggests that Grant's collar-size was a slightly more modest 17 inches.

46.   Grant, 'Archie Leach', part 3, p. 150.

47.   *Ibid.*

48.   Harris, p. 47, quoting critics Percy Hammond and Arthur Pollack.

49.   Buehrer, p. 164.

50.   Grant, 'Archie Leach', part 3, p. 150. It seems that he really liked the city: Nelson (pp. 46–7) claims that these engagements in St Louis 'began a love affair with the city that was to last until the end of his life'.

51.   Grant, 'Archie Leach', part 3, p. 151.

52.   Wansell (p. 80) suggests that Leach accepted the movie offer after *Nikki* closed at the end of October 1931. Buehrer (p. 5), Godfrey (pp. 46–7), Harris (p. 49) and Higham and Moseley (p. 36) all make similar claims. Nelson, however, who, unlike the others, had access to Grant's own records, puts the date as 8 May 1931 – *before* he opened in *Nikki* (see pp. 48–9).

53.   The 1970 Oscars ceremony did, in fact, use a brief clip from the movie.

54.   Nelson, pp. 48–9.

55.   It *seems*, as far as one can tell, that nothing came *directly* from the appearance, although some writers, such as Higham and Moseley (p. 36), have suggested that an invitation from Paramount for Leach to visit Hollywood may have resulted from this work. It is not an entirely implausible conjecture, but it remains no more than that.

56.   Fay Wray confirmed this to Nelson, pp. 49–50.

Chapter V

Nathanael West, *The Day of the Locust* (Harmondsworth: Penguin, 1991), p. 6.

Cary Grant, quoted in Nelson, p. 55.

1.   Mae West repeated the claim – much to Grant's irritation – in countless interviews. See, for example, Chandler, p. 60.

2.   See Donaldson, pp. 256–7.

3.   Recounted in Ashman and Trescott, p. 58, and Harris, pp. 51–2.

4.   Grant, 'Archie Leach', part 3, p. 152.

5.   Roderick Mann, 'Cary Grant: Doing What Comes Naturally', *Los Angeles Times*, 11 June 1978, p. 39.

6.   Grant, 'Archie Leach', part 3, p. 152.

7.   This was not, strictly speaking, correct. Harold Lockwood (1887–1918) had been a fairly popular romantic leading man during the silent era (his movies included *The Fighting Lieutenant*, 1913, and *Broadway Bill*, 1918), but he had died of influenza complicated by pneumonia at the age of thirty-one – nearly fourteen years before Archie Leach arrived in Hollywood.

8.   Grant, 'Archie Leach', part 3, p. 152.

9.   Quoted by Nelson, p. 54.

10.   He changed his name legally in 1942.

11.   See, for example, the account in Wansell, pp. 89–90.

12.   See Alistair Cooke, 'The Legend of Gary Cooper', *America Observed* (London: Reinhardt, 1988).

13.   Quoted by Wansell, p. 89.

14.   Grant, 'Archie Leach', part 1, p. 50.

15.   *Ibid.*

16.   Moss Hart, *Act One: An Autobiography* (London: Secker & Warburg, 1960), p. 252.

17.   Sidney Sheldon, *Bloodline* (London: HarperCollins, 1993), p. 18.

18.   Nelson, p. 19.

19.   Sheldon, p. 19.

20. Nelson, p. 13.

21. *Ibid.*

22. *Ibid.*

23. Grant, 'Archie Leach', part 1, p. 142.

24. Fairbanks married Mary Pickford in 1920. The previous year they had joined Chaplin and D. W. Griffith in forming United Artists.

25. Schickel, *Cary Grant*, p. 30.

26. Grant, 'Archie Leach', part 1, p. 142. Fairbanks invited the Pender troupe to watch him work on the set as he made *The Thief of Bagdad* (1924) when the troupe passed through Los Angeles on its first tour of the US.

27. See Grant, 'Archie Leach', part 1, p. 142.

28. Sam Goldwyn, for example, would never carry anything in his pockets because he was so determined to show off the cut of his suit – even a single coin, he felt, might ruin the immaculate look (see Philip French, *The Movie Moguls*, London: Weidenfeld and Nicolson, 1969, p. 30).

29. Nelson, p. 29.

30. Such a claim has been made by Walker, 'Cary Grant and the Harry Lime Connection', p. 70. One can certainly hear Grant's English accent quite clearly in *The Amazing Quest of Ernest Bliss* (1936), in which he plays an upper-class Englishman and modulates his diction accordingly.

31. Peter Honri, *Working the Halls* (London: Futura, 1974), p. 136.

32. Godfrey, p. 41.

33. Honri, p. 175.

34. See Nelson, p. 41.

35. *Ibid.*, p. 33.

36. Schickel, *Cary Grant*, pp. 29–30.

37. Although Terry Major-Ball recalls that his father, returning to England after a number of years in the US (performing on the same circuits as Archie Leach and the Pender troupe), did not seem to have acquired any noticeable trace of an American accent (interview with the author: 19 September 1995). For an interesting account of the significance of slang and dialect in New York at the time, see Irving Lewis Allen, *The City in Slang* (New York: Oxford University Press, 1993).

38. See, for example, Schickel, *Cary Grant*, pp. 29–30, and Higham and Moseley, p. 30.

39. Richard Corliss, 'Cary Grant: 1904–1986', *Film Comment*, February 1987, p. 78.

40. Nelson, p. 267.

41. Walker, 'Cary Grant and the Harry Lime Connection', pp. 70–71.

42. David Thomson, 'Tall, Dark and Terribly Handsome', in A. Lloyd, ed., *Movies of the Fifties* (London: Orbis, 1982), pp. 186–7.

43. James Agee, 'Comedy's Greatest Era', in Daniel Talbot, ed., *Film: An Anthology* (Berkeley: University of California Press, 1966), p. 131.

44. Walter Kerr, *The Silent Clowns* (New York: Knopf, 1975), p. 11.

45. Kael, 'The Man from Dream City', p. 8.

46. *Ibid.*

47. Thomson, 'Tall, Dark and Terribly Handsome', pp. 186–7.

48. Grant, 'Archie Leach', part 2, p. 40. Sir Gerald DuMaurier (1873–1934) was an actor-manager, renowned for his throwaway technique and his relaxation of manner, who made his stage reputation in elegant criminal roles, such as *Raffles* (1906). A. E. Matthews (1869–1960) had a long career playing numerous comedy roles. Jack Buchanan (1890–1957) was sometimes referred to as 'Britain's Fred Astaire'; he was a star of musicals in London and on Broadway, and his movies included *Break the News* (1938) and *The Band Wagon* (1953). Ronald Squire (1886–1958), another actor-manager, noted for his work in light comedy, can be seen briefly in the Reform Club scenes in *Around the World in Eighty Days* (1956).

49. Walker, 'Cary Grant and the Harry Lime Connection', p. 73.

50. Nelson, p. 55. Grant became a good friend of Lonsdale's.

51. Nelson, p. 55. See *The Amazing Quest of Ernest Bliss* (1936) for a particularly good example of this awkwardness – one can see his clenched fist fixed firmly in his coat pocket throughout several early scenes.

52. Philip Larkin, *Required Writing* (London: Faber, 1983), p. 224.

53. The journalist was Jim Tully, writing in *Picturegoer* in 1936; quoted in David Shipman, *The Great Movie Stars*, vol. 1 (London: Warner Books, 1993), p. 41. Grant later said that it was Baxter whom he felt he had replaced when he became a star (see Nelson, p. 52).

54. Edgar Morin, *The Stars* (London: John Calder, 1960).

55. Martin Levin, ed., *Hollywood and the Great Fan Magazines* (London: Ian Allen, 1976), p. 7.

56. Quoted by Wansell, p. 90.

57. *Ibid.*

58. *Ibid.*, p. 102, quoting Julie Lang Hunt.

59. *Ibid.*, p. 90.

60. *Ibid.*, pp. 90–91, quoting Elisabeth Goldbeck.

61. Quoted by Eric Pace, 'Cary Grant', *New York Times*, 1 December 1986, p. B10.

62. Nelson, p. 85.

63. *Ibid.*

64. Apart from the *His Girl Friday* reference, he calls himself 'Archie' in *Gunga Din* (1939) and inserts a number of biographical references into several other movies, such as *None But the Lonely Heart* (1944) and *To Catch a Thief* (1955). Pace (p. B10) has also claimed that 'Archie Leach' can be glimpsed on one of the headstones in *Arsenic and Old Lace* (1944), although, after several viewings, I have not been able to confirm this.

65. Grant was honoured by the New York Friars Club when it named him 'Man of the Year' and held a dinner for him at the Waldorf-Astoria Hotel on 16 May 1982.

Chapter VI

Cary Grant: Debra Sharon Davis, 'Cary Grant: A Candid Conversation with America's Epitome of Elegance', *Playboy Guide: Fashion for Men*, Spring –Summer 1981, p. 32.

Fedora (1978): screenplay by Billy Wilder and I. A. L. Diamond.

1. Quoted by Nelson, p. 50.

2. The advertisement was featured in *Motion Picture Herald*, 14 November 1932, and reprinted in Andrew Bergman, *We're in the Money* (Chicago: Elephant Paperbacks, 1992) p. xxi.

3. See French, pp. 16, 34 and 43–4; John Douglas Eames, *The Paramount Story* (New York: Crown, 1985); and Adolph Zukor, *The Public is Never Wrong* (New York: G. P. Putnam's Sons, 1953).

4. Nelson, pp. 54–5.

5. Quoted by Harris, p. 54.

6. The actor Tony Randall said of *The Devil and the Deep*: 'Cary Grant was all right in it . . . [He] didn't try to do anything; he kept it as simple as possible. But the others, Tallulah included, went ape' (quoted in James Parish and Don E. Stanke, *The All-Americans*, New York: Arlington House, 1977, p. 22).

7. Walker, 'Cary Grant and the Harry Lime Connection', p. 81.

8. *Ibid.*

9. *Ibid.*, p. 80.

10. Schickel, *Cary Grant*, p. 39.

11. See Sheridan Morley, *Tales from the Hollywood Raj* (London: Weidenfeld and Nicolson, 1983).

12. *Ibid.*, pp. 139–40.

13. John Russell Taylor, *Strangers in Paradise* (London: Faber, 1983), p. 92.

14. Morley, *Tales from the Hollywood Raj*, p. 131.

15. *Ibid.*, p. 1.

16. Donald Spoto, in his *The Dark Side of Genius: The Life of Alfred Hitchcock* (London: Frederick Muller, 1988, p. 210), notes that Alma and Alfred Hitchcock were not keen to re-involve themselves with the 'stuffy English gentlefolk' in Los Angeles, and Simon Callow, in his *Charles Laughton: A Difficult Actor* (London: Methuen, 1987, p. 44), says that Laughton preferred to concentrate on his work rather than seek out the British community in Hollywood.

17. Grant told Sheridan Morley (*The Other Side of the Moon*, London: Weidenfeld and Nicolson, 1985, p. 154) that he felt Niven was 'more educated, I think a more intelligent man, than I was'. Morley notes (p. 52), however, that Niven also preferred to 'go native' rather than settle into the British colony.

18. The observation is recorded in George Sanders's autobiography, and quoted by Morley, *Tales from the Hollywood Raj*, p. 131.

19. The relationship, however, as well as the house-sharing, attracted the gossip columnists, who began to imply that Scott and Grant were bisexuals (see Chapter IX).

20. Grant, 'Archie Leach', part 2, p. 40.

21. Nelson, pp. 57–8.

22. John Springer in *Cary Grant: The Leading Man* (1988 documentary).

23.   Josef von Sternberg, *Fun in a Chinese Laundry* (London: Columbus, 1987), p. 264.

24.   Mae West, *Goodness Had Nothing To Do With It* (London: World Distributors, 1962), pp. 134–5.

25.   *Ibid*.

26.   Chandler, p. 60.

27.   See Higham and Moseley, p. 49.

28.   See Wansell, p. 100.

29.   Kael, 'The Man from Dream City', p. 6.

30.   *Ibid*.

31.   Grant appeared in one more movie in 1933 – *Alice in Wonderland* – although 'appear' is not quite the right word, as he was completely obscured by the man-sized turtle shell and rubber mask he was obliged to wear as the Mock Turtle.

32.   Quoted by Nelson, p. 58.

33.   Quoted by Harris, p. 60.

34.   According to the *Bristol Evening Post* (2 December 1933, p. 5), two of his movies were showing when he returned to his hometown: *The Eagle and the Hawk* and *She Done Him Wrong*.

35.   See Chapter IX for a discussion of Grant's marriages and other close relationships.

36.   One of which was *The Last Outpost* (1935), in which he played, in the words of Graham Greene's review, an 'incurably light-minded and rather stupid British officer' (quoted in Deschner, *The Complete Films of Cary Grant*, New York: Citadel, 1991, p. 86).

37.   Quoted by Godfrey, p. 64.

38.   The movie was released in the UK in 1936. It was released in the US, with the alternative title *Romance and Riches*, in 1937. A video version, missing certain scenes, was released in the US by Vintage Video (1985) and in the UK by Creation Entertainments (1996) under the title *The Amazing Adventure*. The alternative titles have confused some writers: Ashman and Trescott, for example (pp. 82–3), claim that Grant came to London to make *The Amazing Quest of Ernest Bliss*, and then, just before returning to California, made 'another quickie movie which had two alternative titles, *Romance and Riches* and *Amazing Adventure*'; there was, in fact, no 'quickie

movie', just several different titles for the same one. Grant played Bliss, a wealthy young man bored with life, who bets his doctor £50,000 that he can earn his own living for a year. He works as an oven salesman, a porter and a chauffeur, falls in love with a secretary (Mary Brian), fights some con men and returns, successful but more compassionate, at the end. Grant and Brian are considerably better than the rest of the cast, and the movie is moderately entertaining in spite of its poor production values. The quite extraordinary fight scene, in which Grant's wild leaps and rolls suggest a not entirely serious approach to the whole affair, and another sequence set in Covent Garden are probably the two most memorable moments in the movie. The central theme of the movie would be returned to on several occasions in the future: consider, for example, *Sullivan's Travels*, 1941; *Arthur*, 1981; and *Life Stinks*, 1991.

39.   Quoted by Nelson, p. 68.

40.   It is this 'gender-subversion' theme which so excites academic writers; Andrew Britton's *Katharine Hepburn: Star as Feminist* (London: Studio Vista, 1995) devotes an entire chapter ('Gender and Bisexuality') to the movie, and is probably the best discussion of this kind. As a movie, however, I would still argue that it is considerably less painful to write about than to watch.

41.   Boze Hadleigh, *Conversations With My Elders* (London: GMP, 1989), p. 84.

42.   Hepburn's diary entry was quoted in an interview she gave to David Robinson in *The Times*, 24 November 1973, quoted in Patrick McGilligan, *George Cukor: A Double Life* (London: Faber, 1992), p. 127.

43.   See McGilligan, p. 127, and Hadleigh, p. 84. For a contemporary discussion of the 'crisis' in Hepburn's career, see Kirtley Baskette, 'Is Hepburn Killing Her Own Career?', *Photoplay*, September 1935, reproduced in Richard Griffith, ed., *The Talkies* (New York: Dover, 1971).

44.   Quoted by Nelson, pp. 68–9.

45.   Schickel, *Cary Grant*, pp. 51–2.

46.   Interviewed by Schickel, *The Men Who Made the Movies* (London: Elm Tree, 1977), p. 182.

47.   Quoted by Nelson, p. 69.

48.   Excerpts from contemporary reviews reproduced in Deschner, p. 90.

49.   Quoted by Nelson, p. 34.

50.   Quoted by Nelson, p. 69.

51. Quoted in Parish and Stanke, p. 22.

52. Quoted by Wansell, p. 95.

53. See Chapter X.

STARDOM

Sullivan's Travels (1941): screenplay by Preston Sturges.

Cary Grant: Wansell, p. 242.

Chapter VII

Ralph Waldo Emerson, 'Manners' (1844), *Essays and Poems* (London: J. M. Dent, 1995), p. 252.

Cary Grant: one of his favourite expressions, quoted in Donaldson, p. 319 (and ad-libbed by Grant in the movie of the same name, and again near the start of *North by Northwest*).

1. Emerson, 'Manners', p. 252. The association has been made before, by Stanley Cavell, in his *Pursuits of Happiness* (Cambridge, Mass.: Harvard University Press, 1981), p. 235.

2. Schickel, *Cary Grant*, p. 74.

3. Quoted by Nelson, p. 82.

4. *Ibid.*

5. Ralph Bellamy in *Cary Grant: The Leading Man* (1988 documentary).

6. See Harris, p. 89.

7. Quoted by Nelson, pp. 71–2.

8. Judging from the final draft of Vina Delmar's screenplay, the most memorable scenes and dialogue in the movie owe a great deal to the improvisations on set by the actors and director. The restaurant scene, for example, is much more subtle and finely paced on the screen than it is in the text (Ralph Bellamy's nice playing of Daniel Leeson's shyness in the presence of Toots is missing in the more *louche* written version, which ends up with Toots having her stage act brought to an abrupt end by detectives charging her with indecency), and the later scene set in the home of Jerry's prospective in-laws is remarkably sluggish and clumsy in the text compared to the screen version.

9. Bellamy, in *Cary Grant: The Leading Man* (1988 documentary).

10. Andrew Britton, in *Cary Grant: Comedy and Male Desire*, p. 3, is too

eager to present Grant's character as devious in contrast to Irene Dunne's; in fact, both are rightly suspicious of the other's explanations. Watch her eyes as she waits to see if Jerry is convinced by her story of the improbable events that led to her and Armand having to stay overnight in 'the nastiest little inn you ever saw'. In a scene late on, Lucy, hoping to win Jerry back, asks Armand if he will tell Jerry that her story of their innocent night together was true; they look nervously at each other, and then Armand, with a wry smile, says, 'Oh, I'll be glad to . . . but, er, does he carry a gun?' Lucy is certainly *better* at deceit than Jerry – who fails to remove the California stickers on his 'Florida' oranges and acquires a fake tan when any of the newspaper reports could have told him that it was cold and wet on his 'vacation' – but neither Lucy nor Jerry is meant to seem above suspicion.

11.   Quoted by Nelson, p. 81.

12.   *Ibid.*

13.   Interviewed by Schickel, *The Men Who Made the Movies*, p. 182.

14.   *Ibid.*, p. 183.

15.   Leo Lowenthal, 'The Triumph of Mass Idols' (1943), *Literature, Popular Culture and Society* (Palo Alto: Pacific Books, 1968), p. 135.
    Horatio Alger (1832–99) was a former Unitarian minister turned schoolmaster who became one of America's most popular novelists with his boys' adventure stories (such as the *Ragged Dick* series). His positive themes drew on the optimism generated in a period of exceptional economic growth in the north-east of the country. His unlikely heroes (industrious yet penniless newsboys, destitute but honest boot-blacks, oppressed yet virtuous servants and orphaned but optimistic factory hands), who came from poor small-town origins to find power and prosperity in the big city, embodied the American ideal of equality of opportunity. Up until around the middle of the twentieth century it was common for children to be presented with his books for use as models for achieving success.

16.   Emerson, 'Manners', p. 244.

17.   *Ibid.*, pp. 254–5.

18.   *Ibid.*, p. 239.

19.   Henry James, 'The Jolly Corner' (1908), *The Beast in the Jungle and Other Stories* (New York: Dover, 1993), pp. 96–7.

20.   See, for example, Edith Wharton's *The Custom of the Country* (New York: Charles Scribner's Sons, 1913).

21.   See, for example, the treatment of Nick Carraway in F. Scott Fitzgerald's *The Great Gatsby*.

22.   Emerson, 'Manners', p. 250.

23.   *Ibid.*, p. 240.

24.   C. L. R. James, *American Civilization* (Oxford: Blackwell, 1993), p. 145. James produced a manuscript, entitled *Notes on American Civilization*, during the period 1938–53 when he lived in the US. After his enforced departure from America he never had the opportunity to complete the project, but this draft of the text was published posthumously in 1993.

25.   For an interesting discussion of this theme, see Bruce Babington and Peter Evans, *Affairs to Remember* (Manchester: Manchester University Press, 1989), Chapter 1.

26.   Harris (p. 278), notes that a book called *Christianity, Social Tolerance and Homosexuality* claimed that the first publicly recorded use of the word 'gay' in 'a homosexual context' was Grant's improvised 'I just went *gay* all of a sudden!' in *Bringing Up Baby*. There are, however, numerous examples of Grant using the word in its old-fashioned sense years after he had appeared in this movie.

27.   Strictly speaking, the 'real' name of this remarkably talented celebrity dog was 'Skippy', but he was known to movie-goers as 'Asta' because of his appearances as Asta in *The Thin Man* series.

28.   Frank S. Nugent, writing in the *New York Times* (4 March 1938), said that he was content when he watched the movie 'to play the game called "the cliché expert goes to the movies"'. Otis Ferguson, in the *New Republic* (2 March 1938), disagreed, judging it to be 'funny from the word go' (see Gerald Mast, ed., *Bringing Up Baby*, New Brunswick, NJ: Rutgers University Press, 1988, pp. 265–8). The movie cost $1,096,796 to make. In its initial run, domestic revenues totalled $715,000 and foreign revenues amounted to $394,000, giving a combined total of $1,109,000 – a modest profit. In a 1940–41 re-issue, domestic revenues were $95,000 and foreign revenues $55,000 – an additional $150,000. The total revenues of $1,259,000 meant, when RKO closed its books on the movie, that it had made a final profit of $163,000 (see Mast, pp. 13–16).

29.   Pauline Kael, *Kiss Kiss Bang Bang* (London: Arrow Books, 1987), p. 241.

30.   *Life* magazine (28 February 1938) described Hepburn's performance as 'the surprise of the picture' (see Mast, p. 15).

31. Quoted in Mast, p. 260.

32. Kael, 'The Man from Dream City', pp. 6–7.

33. Quoted in Mast, p. 260.

34. Quoted in Harris, p. 96.

35. Garson Kanin, *Together Again!* (Garden City, NY: Doubleday, 1981), p. 145.

36. Quoted by Nelson, p. 86. Bogdanovich's remark is referred to in the context of *Bringing Up Baby*, but when Schickel (*The Men Who Made the Movies*, pp. 108–9) quotes Hawks recalling the same piece of advice he suggests that it was for *His Girl Friday*, made the following year and released in 1940.

37. See Mast, p. 13.

38. Katharine Hepburn quoted by Higham and Moseley, p. 77.

39. Quoted by Nelson, p. 84. He did the same at the end of *North by Northwest* (1959), rescuing Eva Marie Saint.

40. McGilligan, p. 141.

41. *Holiday* was the first of two movie adaptations directed by Cukor of plays by Philip Barry; the second, *The Philadelphia Story*, also co-starred Grant and Hepburn.

42. Hepburn quoted by Nelson, p. 83.

43. *Ibid.*, p. 85.

44. When, in 1970, *Sylvia Scarlett* was selected as the opening movie of a Museum of Modern Art retrospective of George Cukor's *œuvre*, Cukor objected and requested that *Holiday* replace it (see McGilligan, p. 128).

45. See Chapter X.

46. Kael, *Kiss Kiss Bang Bang*, p. 278.

47. Kael, 'The Man from Dream City', p. 18.

48. *Gunga Din* earned the studio more than $3.1 million, even though a foreign release was hampered by the impending war in Europe (and the movie only reached English cinemas after the end of the Second World War).

49. Although Grant has several lines such as 'Hello, Judy. Come on, Judy. Now, Judy', he never says, 'Judy, Judy, Judy'. Like *Casablanca*'s 'Play it again, Sam', the line has been invented and immortalised by a succession

of impersonators (beginning, Grant believed, with Larry Storch). James Cagney joked about this kind of popular misquotation when he received his Life Achievement Award from the American Film Institute in 1974: 'Actually,' he said, 'I never said, "You dirty rat!" What I actually said was, "Judy! Judy! Judy!" '

50.   The movie remains, I am aware, an ambiguous one in its treatment of this relationship. See, for example, the brief but pertinent discussion in Molly Haskell's *From Reverence to Rape* (Chicago: University of Chicago Press, 1987), pp. 209–10.

51.   F. Scott Fitzgerald, *The Great Gatsby*, p. 49.

Chapter VIII

Cary Grant, 'Archie Leach', part 3, p. 38.

Roland Barthes, *A Lover's Discourse* (London: Jonathan Cape, 1979), p. 135.

1.   See Tino Balio, ed., *The American Film Industry* (Madison: University of Wisconsin Press, 1984), and Philip French, *The Movie Moguls*.

2.   See Chapter 4 in Gomery.

3.   Kael, 'The Man from Dream City', p. 3. The same point is made by Corliss (p. 78): 'most men wanted to be Cary Grant, and most women wanted to have him'.

4.   Quoted by Nelson, p. 375.

5.   *Ibid.*, quoting Peter Stone, screenwriter.

6.   *Ibid.*, p. 376, quoting the singer Steve Lawrence.

7.   Kael, 'The Man from Dream City', p. 4.

8.   *Ibid.*, p. 5.

9.   *Ibid.*, p. 4.

10.   *Ibid.*, p. 5.

11.   It was also an image which was ambiguous enough to seem either English or American (or sometimes simply stateless). He played an Englishman in at least nine movies: *The Last Outpost* (1935); *The Amazing Quest of Ernest Bliss* (1936); *Sylvia Scarlett* (1936); *Gunga Din* (1939); *Suspicion* (1941); *None But the Lonely Heart* (1944); *The Pride and the Passion* (1957); *The Grass is Greener* (1961); and *Walk, Don't Run* (1966). He also played (without attempting the accent) a Frenchman in two movies: *Suzy* (1936)

and *I Was a Male War Bride* (1949), and an Italian in one: *An Affair to Remember* (1957).

12.   Quoted by Nelson, p. 376.

13.   I take the phrase 'intimate stranger' from Richard Schickel's *Intimate Strangers: The Culture of Celebrity* (Garden City, New York: Doubleday, 1985), although I use it here to refer to Grant's particular ambiguity as a public personality.

14.   Schickel, *Cary Grant*, p. 147.

15.   The allusion is to Freud's 1919 essay on 'The "Uncanny"'. Freud defines the uncanny as something that seems unfamiliar yet intimate, frightening one because the homely (*das Heimliche*) has returned as its opposite (*das Unheimliche*), 'for this uncanny is in reality nothing new or alien, but something which is familiar and old-established in the mind and which has become alienated from it only through the process of repression'; according to Freud, one can speak of a living person as uncanny 'when we ascribe evil intentions to him' (Freud, 'The "Uncanny"', *Art and Literature*, Harmondsworth: Penguin, 1990, pp. 363–4). Grant's screen persona, I would argue, is strangely familiar without (usually) seeming frightening (although, in his more dramatic movies, such as *Suspicion* and *Notorious*, this odd intimacy is played on for its more unsettling qualities).

16.   Roberta Ostroff, ' "How Do You Like Being Cary Grant?" "I Like It Fine" ', *Los Angeles Times*, 1 December 1972, p. 28.

17.   Schickel, *Cary Grant*, p. 147.

18.   Roderick Mann, 'Cary Grant at 80 – Still a Touch of Mink', *Los Angeles Times*, 15 January 1984, p. 17.

19.   Grant, 'Archie Leach', part 3, p. 38.

20.   Quoted by Nelson, p. 127.

21.   *Ibid.*, pp. 106–7.

22.   Mann, 'Cary Grant at 80', p. 17.

23.   Quoted by Truman Capote, 'The Duke in his Domain', *A Capote Reader* (London: Hamish Hamilton, 1987), p. 536.

24.   Schickel, *Cary Grant*, p. 77.

25.   *Ibid.*

26.   *Ibid.*

27.   Kael, 'The Man from Dream City', p. 6.

28. The phrase is Babington and Evans's (see p. 101).

29. Such as in *Gunga Din* (1939), when Grant's character receives an invitation to a regimental ball, and he winces as the name 'Archibald Cutter' is read out, with every syllable enunciated with disbelief at the absurdity of it.

30. Sometimes the in–jokes would be intended solely for his own amusement. For example, in *The Bachelor and the Bobbysoxer* (1947), he has his character say that he was taught art at school by a 'Miss Hallett'; one of Archie Leach's schoolmates, Ellen Kathleen Hallett, had gone on to be an assistant to their former art teacher (see Higham and Moseley, p. 13).

31. It is likely that Howard Hawks, when he was planning, or shooting, *Bringing Up Baby*, saw a rough cut of *The Awful Truth*. Another shared reference was 'Vance' – Susan's surname in the former, Jerry's fiancée's surname in the latter. Hawks was a good friend of Leo McCarey, and Grant was already known for his ad-libbing, so the cross-references were probably quite deliberate (see Mast, p. 7).

32. The relevant dialogue in *The Awful Truth* is reproduced in Chapter VII.

33. Kael, 'The Man from Dream City', p. 24.

34. Corliss, p. 78.

35. Kael, 'The Man from Dream City', p. 3.

36. Walker, 'Cary Grant and the Harry Lime Connection', pp. 72–3.

37. Andrew Britton has discussed this kind of inversion of the conventional Hollywood roles in the context of what he terms 'positive bisexuality', movies which feature 'the elimination of the differential of social/sexual power within the heterosexual couple', and which 'use Grant to formulate a type of masculinity which is valuable and attractive by virtue of the sharing of gender characteristics with women' (*Cary Grant*, p. 10).

38. Kael, 'The Man from Dream City', p. 3.

39. Walker, 'Cary Grant and the Harry Lime Connection', p. 73.

40. Thomson, 'Cary Grant', p. 301.

41. Charles Baudelaire, 'The Painter of Modern Life', *The Painter of Modern Life and Other Essays* (New York: Da Capo, 1986), p. 29.

42. Kael, 'The Man from Dream City', p. 4.

43. Schickel, in *Cary Grant*, p. 44, argues that Kael herself made this mistake.

44. Kael, 'The Man from Dream City', p. 4.

45. *Ibid*.

46. Grant advising John Forsythe, quoted by Nelson, p. 161.

47. When Grant wanted a vehicle for Betsy Drake (his wife-to-be), he chose a story which was probably the most basic and overt example of the woman in pursuit of the man – *Every Girl Should Be Married* (1948) – and he worked very hard to help her to dominate most scenes.

48. Kael, 'The Man from Dream City', p. 29. Andrew Britton reaches a similar conclusion – by a different route – when he says that, 'uniquely in the popular cinema, Grant's acting *creates* the attractiveness of male femininity and of the relationships enabled by it' (*Cary Grant*, p. 17).

49. Billy Wilder's failure to procure the services of Grant, in spite of Grant's willingness to work with him, became something of a running joke. Certain characters – Leon in *Ninotchka*, Linus in *Sabrina* and Frank Flannagan in *Love in the Afternoon* – in movies that Wilder *did* make had been written specially for Grant, only for other obligations to force Grant to pass. Wilder, perhaps sensing defeat, has someone *impersonate* Grant in *Stalag 17* and *Some Like It Hot*. See Chapter XIII.

50. Maurice Zolotow, *Billy Wilder in Hollywood* (London: Pavilion, 1988), p. 191.

Chapter IX

Cary Grant: Nelson, p. 312.

Mandy Rice-Davies: at the trial of Stephen Ward, on being informed that Lord Astor had claimed that her allegations about himself and his house parties were untrue; reported in the *Guardian*, 1 July 1963.

1. Joan Fontaine spoke the lines in the trailer shown to promote the movie.

2. Quoted by Nelson, p. 109.

3. Camille Paglia, in *Sexual Personae: Art and Decadence from Nefertiti to Emily Dickinson* (New Haven: Yale University Press, 1990, p. 533), has commented on what she sees as the unusual, androgynous image of the Hollywood gentleman: 'The idiomatic qualities are *smoothness* and *elongation*: smooth both in manner and appearance, long in ectomorphic height and Nordic cranial contour.' She goes on, somewhat speculatively, to link Grant

with this 'androgyne of manners': 'I think, for instance, of the astounding narrowness of Cary Grant's shiny black evening pumps in *Indiscreet* (1958). The smoothness and elongation of figure are best shown off by a gleaming tuxedo, signifying a renunciation of masculine hirsutism.' A more general discussion – although equally speculative – can be found in Marjorie Garber's *Vice Versa* (London: Hamish Hamilton, 1996), which contends that stars are 'bisexual' when performing, in the sense that they tap into the suppressed fantasies of both men and women in the audience.

4.   John Kobal, 'An Affair to Remember', *American Film*, April 1987, pp. 59–60. Kobal was homosexual, and it might be tempting to conclude that his interpretation of Grant's ambiguous image said more about him than it did about Grant; this would, however, be too simplistic a response, as similar interpretations have been made by heterosexual critics.

5.   Quoted by Nelson, p. 333.

6.   Peter Bogdanovich, 'Cary Grant', *Picture Shows* (London: George Allen & Unwin, 1975), p. 100.

7.   Quoted by Nelson, p. 79.

8.   *Public Enemy*, starring James Cagney and directed by William A. Wellman, was released by Warner Brothers in 1931.

9.   In 1951 Grant played a character in *People Will Talk* – Noah Praetorius – whose reticence about his past causes his colleagues to grow increasingly suspicious of him. The principled ending, one suspects, was particularly attractive to Grant.

10.   See Alston Thomas, 'Cary's Agreement', *Bristol Evening Post*, 30 January 1973, p. 4, and 'The enigma who was Cary Grant', p. 4.

11.   Quoted by Nelson, p. 314.

12.   *Ibid.*, p. 317.

13.   Rick Ingersoll, in *ibid.* See also Grant, 'Archie Leach', part 2, p. 35.

14.   David Niven, *The Moon is a Balloon/Bring on the Empty Horses* (London: Coronet, 1985), p. 273.

15.   *Ibid.*, pp. 273–4.

16.   Grant, 'Archie Leach', part 1, pp. 53 and 133.

17.   The beach house was later renumbered 1093 Ocean Front. Nelson (p. 65), who had access to Grant's private papers, puts the date when they moved in as 'late summer 1935'; Higham and Moseley (p. 69) put it a year later, as August 1936.

18. Quoted by Harris, p. 63.

19. *Ibid.*, p. 64.

20. Niven, p. 159. Niven says he moved into the house with 'Robert Coote, an excellent English actor, and a mysterious Australian named Walter Kerry Davis'.

21. Quoted by Nelson, p. 65.

22. Robinson, p. 32.

23. Quoted by Higham and Moseley, p. 59. *One Way Passage* was, however, the romantic play that Grant later said 'has always been my favorite' (Siskel, 'Cary Grant', p. 3), so, *perhaps*, the reference was not *quite* as devious as it seemed.

24. Betty Furness (1916–1994) appeared in more than thirty movies during the thirties, and became well known from the fifties onwards as a consumer advocate on US television.

25. Edith Gwynn quoted in Higham and Moseley, p. 59.

26. Dean Jennings, *Barbara Hutton* (London: W. H. Allen, 1963), p. 162. It was particularly ironic, bearing in mind the history of tense exchanges between the two, when Grant was voted the winner of the annual Louella Parsons Award in 1982 by the Hollywood Women's Press Club for 'presenting the best image of Hollywood to the world'.

27. Kenneth Anger's *Hollywood Babylon* (New York: Dell, 1981, p. 250), for example, reprinted an old cartoon from the thirties which referred to Grant as the star of a movie called 'Who's a Fairy?', as well as the notorious movie magazine pictures of Scott and Grant at home. Larry Adler, more pertinently, claimed to have witnessed the two men 'stroking each other' at a Hollywood party (*Me and My Big Mouth*, London: Blake, 1994, p. 74).

28. Randolph Scott, in contrast, did not attract the same kind of attention. He was married twice – first, briefly, to the heiress Mariana du Pont, then, from 1944, to Patricia Stillman, who survived him when he died in 1987. Higham and Moseley do, however, seem, from the very beginning, to be extraordinarily ill-disposed towards him, describing him as having a 'horsey face', 'an air of calculating laziness' and the 'soul of a cash register'. Since, they claim, Scott 'could not act, film making was just an easy path to acquiring a personal fortune' (p. 42).

29. Nelson, p. 315. Grant also told Judith Michaelson ('An Intimate Chat with Cary Grant', *Los Angeles Times*, 18 March 1985, p. 1) that he had developed 'a skin like a rhino' when it came to the scandal sheets. Inter-

viewed by Kent Schuelke ('Cary Grant', *Interview*, January 1987, p. 44), he remarked on the posthumous sensationalistic studies of Alfred Hitchcock: 'I deplore these idiotic books written about him when the man can't defend himself. Even if you do defend yourself against that kind of literature, it gets you nowhere.'

30.   Higham and Moseley, p. xi.

31.   *Ibid.*

32.   *Ibid.*, p. x. I have already noted in Chapter II the problems with this depiction of Grant's mother.

33.   Grant, 'Archie Leach', part 1, p. 133.

34.   Higham and Moseley, p. 4.

35.   *Ibid.*, p. 33.

36.   *Ibid.*, p. 20.

37.   *Ibid.*, p. 30.

38.   *Ibid.*, pp. x–xi.

39.   *Ibid.*, p. 227. A similar piece of heavy-handed manipulation occurs in an early chapter on Grant's time in New York, where the authors announce solemnly that 'There is no record of his having any love-affairs with women at the time' (p. 32), but they choose not to add that there is also no record of Grant having any love-affairs with men at that time – there may be gossip about either, or both, but the absence of 'records' is, of course, not remotely surprising.

40.   *Ibid.*, p. 186.

41.   *Ibid.*, p. 196. The assistant's name was Ray Austin.

42.   A point seldom appreciated when lazily tangential remarks are made about certain stars. A particularly regrettable example, for obvious reasons, is my own passing reference to Grant in *Rebel Males* (London: Hamish Hamilton, 1991), p. 8.

43.   Robert Evans, *The Kid Stays in the Picture* (London: HarperCollins, 1994), p. 76. Evans has recalled being informed early on in his career by a movie executive that he was a homosexual and that he had been on intimate terms with Montgomery Clift and Rock Hudson. 'There's one problem,' Evans said. 'I never met any of 'em' (pp. 75–6).

44.   McGilligan, p. 346.

45.   Quoted by Higham and Moseley, p. 63. Kenneth Anger, not

surprisingly, notes many of the other stars of that period who were the subjects of rumours concerning their 'real' sexuality: see, for example, *Hollywood Babylon I* on Garbo, Dietrich and Claudette Colbert (p. 246), and *Hollywood Babylon II* on Clark Gable (p. 63).

46. *Ibid.*, p. 174.

47. Alexander Walker, in his *Fatal Charm: The Life of Rex Harrison* (London: Weidenfeld and Nicolson, 1992, p. 299), has noted that rumours circulated 'about almost every celebrated English actor of the time'. It was, in fact, not uncommon at that time in Hollywood for homosexuality to be referred to as 'the English disease' (see Harris, p. 93). Rumours sometimes surrounded English *women* as well: see, for example, Julie Andrews's rebuttal of the long-running allegations concerning her 'lesbianism' in Jonathan Van Meter's 'Victor/Victorious', *Vanity Fair*, October 1995, pp. 56–61. Grant noted in his article, 'Archie Leach' (part 3, p. 151), that he was once told, when he complained of being 'romantically-linked' by gossip columnists with women he had never met, 'Never mind . . . It would be much worse if they printed you were out with a different young *boy* every night.' The fact that a similar response was offered by Hollywood publicists and executives in 1995, when Hugh Grant was caught *in flagrante delicto* with the prostitute Divine Brown, suggests that homophobia, in spite of the ubiquitous red ribbons sported at all Hollywood social occasions in the early 1990s, is still very real in the movie industry.

48. Niven, p. 274.

49. *Ibid.*, p. 275.

50. *Ibid.*

51. Sal Mineo quoted in Hadleigh, p. 9.

52. *Ibid.*, p. 22.

53. Garson Kanin quoted by Nelson, p. 315.

54. *Ibid.*

55. *Ibid.*, quoting David Tebet.

56. *Ibid.*, p. 60.

57. Quoted by Higham and Moseley, p. 212.

58. Quoted by Nelson, p. 49.

59. *Ibid.*, p. 50.

60. John Baxter, *The Hollywood Exiles* (London: Macdonald and Jane's, 1976), p. 121.

61. Nelson, p. 308.

62. *Ibid.*, p. 61.

63. *Ibid.*, p. 66.

64. *Ibid.*, p. 68. Higham and Moseley (p. 68) acknowledge that Brian, when asked, 'rejects decisively' the suggestion that Grant was bisexual.

65. Quoted by Harris, p. 105.

66. Quoted by Higham and Moseley, p. 80.

67. Quoted by Nelson, p. 98.

68. *Ibid.*, p. 73.

69. Quoted by Higham and Moseley, p. 89.

70. Quoted by Godfrey, p. 150. The television movie, *Sophia: Her Own Story* (1980), went ahead eventually, with John Gavin playing Cary Grant.

71. Quoted by Nelson, pp. 308–9.

72. McIntosh and Weaver, p. 124. Of those women to whom Grant was linked romantically during the fifties and sixties, Luba Otsevic, Alma Cogan and, especially, Clotilde Feldman were among the most widely reported (see Wansell, pp. 260–64, and Nelson, p. 284).

73. Niven, p. 492.

74. Grant, 'Archie Leach', part 3, p. 151.

75. *Ibid.*

76. Quoted by Harris, p. 133.

77. Jennings, p. 153, quoting Igor Cassini.

78. *Ibid.*, p. 171.

79. McIntosh and Weaver, p. 118.

80. Although when they appear on screen together, particularly in *Room for One More* (1952), there seems to be a genuine warmth about the way they act with each other.

81. See Chapters XIII and XV.

82. Robinson, p. 34. A similar explanation was included in Hoge, p. 28.

83. McIntosh and Weaver, p. 77.

84.   Sheilah Graham, 'Cary', *Scratch an Actor* (London: W. H. Allen, 1969), p. 26.

85.   Niven, p. 492.

86.   Quoted by Nelson, p. 323.

87.   Grant, 'Archie Leach', part 3, p. 151.

88.   *Ibid.*

89.   Quoted by Nelson, p. 362.

90.   *Ibid.*, p. 315, interviewed by Phillip Wuntch. See also Donaldson, Chapter 8.

91.   Hoge, p. 33. A similar account is given by Ray Austin, one of Grant's former assistants, in Higham and Moseley, p. 197.

92.   Robinson, p. 34. On one occasion, however, Grant did take exception to the gossip. In November 1980, on Tom Snyder's NBC television show *Tomorrow*, Chevy Chase said of Grant, 'He really was a great physical comic, and I understand he was a homo . . . What a gal!' Grant filed a ten-million-dollar lawsuit against Chase. The suit stated that Chase's remarks held Grant up to 'shame, ridicule and humiliation', and added that his allegations 'are completely, totally, and absolutely false, and have no basis whatsoever in truth and fact' (see *Variety*, 19 November 1980, p. 5). The suit was settled out of court. (Shipman's entry on Grant – in *The Great Movie Stars*, p. 277 – claims mistakenly that Robin Williams, rather than Chase, was sued.)

93.   Quoted by Morley, *Tales from the Hollywood Raj*, p. 176.

94.   Even when the younger stars, such as Niven, did return, they were hardly greeted with enthusiasm. Niven was passed from the RAF to the Navy until he was finally accepted by the Rifle Brigade. See Morley, *The Other Side of the Moon*, pp. 108–11.

95.   Quoted by Godfrey, p. 100, interviewed by Quentin Reynolds.

96.   See Higham and Moseley, p. 116.

97.   Godfrey, p. 101.

98.   Morley, *Tales from the Hollywood Raj*, p. 176. Grant was quoted later on as saying of Niven that 'I admired him very much for going back and fighting in the war: that was a wonderful thing to have done'. However, Gladys Cooper remembers that when the two men appeared together shortly after the war in *The Bishop's Wife* (1947), she sensed 'a very faint feeling of tension between David and Cary on the set whenever the subject

of the war came up, which was not often'. The irony was that Niven, when he did return home to join up, was patronised by the same press that had attacked his colleagues who had stayed put. One journalist wrote at the time: 'We like him for being at such pains to come home and fight with us, but we have a feeling that his conscience may have done him wrong' (see Morley, *The Other Side of the Moon*, pp. 111 and 153–4).

99.   See Higham and Moseley, pp. 72, 92, 95, 112 and 121. They claim that Grant was first used to report on anti-Semitism in Hollywood, and that, in 1940, he travelled to New York via the Panama Canal on Special Orders, and that he liaised with Alexander Korda and Noël Coward when they were in Los Angeles on Intelligence business. In support of this claim, the authors refer to 'a telegram to Roy Moseley by Sir William Stephenson, head of British Security Coordination', which, it is implied, confirms Grant's involvement in the Intelligence Services (p. 85).

100.   The relevant files on Grant remain classified in London. See Higham and Moseley, p. 148.

101.   Higham and Moseley (p. 149) claim that the award, 'according to the historian at MI6, Nigel West, was customarily given to individuals who had performed special Intelligence services for the Allied Governments'. Another – or additional – reason, however, might have been the fact that Grant donated all of his salaries from *His Girl Friday* and *The Philadelphia Story*, and part of his salary from *Arsenic and Old Lace*, to the War Relief Fund.

102.   He changed his name legally to Cary Grant at the same time.

103.   Binnie Barnes quoted in Nelson, p. 117.

104.   Grant himself was not apolitical, but his views were not easy to fit neatly into party political categories. In 1950, in one of his very rare statements about political matters, he expressed the wish that he 'would like to see a woman as President' (see Nelson, p. 170). He became a good friend of John and Robert Kennedy in the late fifties (and when they were in the White House they would often telephone him), but he was also supportive of his old friend Ronald Reagan in the seventies and early eighties, and was probably a left-of-centre Republican in US terms.

105.   Nelson, pp. 132–3.

106.   Another intriguing association that almost happened during this period was Carol Reed's plan to cast Grant as Harry Lime in *The Third Man* (1949). The role was given eventually to Orson Welles. (See Walker, 'Cary Grant and the Harry Lime Connection'.)

107. Higham and Moseley, p. 145.

108. Grant quoted in Wansell, p. 317.

109. Ingrid Bergman with Alan Burgess, *Ingrid Bergman: My Story* (London: Michael Joseph, 1980), p. 263.

110. Grant, 'Archie Leach', part 2, pp. 40–42. Grant was, again, one of the first to come to the defence of Charlie Chaplin when he was ostracised in the US during the McCarthy era.

111. Quoted by Godfrey, p. 190.

112. *Ibid.*

INDEPENDENCE

North by Northwest (1959): screenplay by Ernest Lehman.

Chapter X

Cary Grant, 'What it Means to be a Star', p. 12.

Ernie Mott, *None But the Lonely Heart* (1944): screenplay by Clifford Odets.

1. Grant quoted in Hoge, p. 33.

2. *Cary Grant: The Leading Man* (1988 documentary).

3. Niven, pp. 492–3.

4. Grant quoted by Nelson, p. 87.

5. *Ibid.*, p. 75.

6. By 1943, for example, Grant's income had reached nearly $330,000, putting him in the 93 per cent income-tax bracket.

7. Scott Berg, in his account of the negotiations that led up to the making of *The Bishop's Wife*, says that Grant's agent was Jules Stein. There is no other source – to my knowledge – that refers to Stein as Grant's agent (nor, indeed, as an important business associate of Grant's). At best, it seems, Stein may have been acting, in this case, as his informal representative. See Scott Berg, *Goldwyn* (London: Hamish Hamilton, 1989), p. 424.

8. See Higham and Moseley, p. 96.

9. *Ibid.*, p. 135.

10. They began doing so in the 1950s.

11. Nelson, pp. 145–6. The movies included: *Indiscreet* (1958: a Grandon

production); *Operation Petticoat* (1959: a Granart Company production); *The Grass is Greener* (1960: Grandon Productions, Ltd.); *That Touch of Mink* (1962: a Granley Company–Arwin Productions, Inc.–Nob Hill Productions, Inc.); *Father Goose* (1964: a Granox Company production); and *Walk, Don't Run* (1966: a Granley Company production). Grant also owned the negative of *Penny Serenade*. When Grant realised that his movies would, eventually, be sold for television, he made it clear that he would no longer appear as the star of any movie unless he acquired ownership of the negative seven years after the movie was released; he sold his equity in seven of his movies for over two million dollars in the early 1970s to National Telefilm Associates.

12.   Chaplin, *My Autobiography*, p. 291.

13.   Grant, 'Archie Leach', part 3, p. 148.

14.   Graham, p. 26.

15.   Walker, 'Cary Grant and the Harry Lime Connection', p. 76.

16.   Examples also include *Once Upon a Honeymoon* (1942), a comedy marred by some peculiar lapses into bad taste, and *Once Upon a Time* (1944), a whimsical tale about a theatrical producer and a performing caterpillar.

17.   Quoted by Nelson, p. 104.

18.   Quoted by Harris, p. 149. The demeanour of the director, Michael Curtiz, was an acquired taste, as, indeed, was his notoriously unpredictable Hungarian-orientated English. David Niven (p. 341) recalls one flare-up on a Curtiz set when the director, exasperated, cried out: 'You lousy bums . . . you think I know fuck nothing . . . well, let me tell you – I know FUCK *ALL!*'

19.   See Garson Kanin's account of how Grant was approached to appear in this movie in *Hollywood* (New York: Viking Press, 1974), pp. 76–7.

20.   For later examples, see Chapter XIII.

21.   James Mason, p. 333.

22.   See Higham and Moseley, p. 177.

23.   One way in which Grant ensured that his popularity remained high was his exploitation of radio as a mass medium. From the late thirties until the early fifties, Grant took part, on average, three or four times per year in truncated radio versions of some of his movies. He starred in an adaptation of *The Awful Truth*, for example, on 15 October 1936 on Cecil B. De Mille's famous CBS 'Lux Radio Theater' (his co-stars were Claudette Colbert and Phyllis Brooks). Other shows featured versions of such movies as *Only*

Angels Have Wings, The Philadelphia Story, Mr Lucky, The Talk of the Town, The Bachelor and the Bobbysoxer, Mr Blandings Builds His Dream House, Every Girl Should Be Married and *People Will Talk*. Apart from being very lucrative, these radio slots allowed Grant to prepare and promote his movies simply and effectively (see Buehrer, pp. 167–71, and Deschner, p. 274).

24.   As Kael observes (*Kiss Kiss Bang Bang*, p. 232), for years after its release 'any film society or school movie series could count on *Arsenic and Old Lace* to make money'.

25.   See Joseph McBride, *Frank Capra: The Catastrophe of Success* (London: Faber, 1992), p. 445.

26.   The movie was shot between 20 October and 16 December 1941. As the play ran for 1,444 performances on Broadway, the movie was not seen by any audience until 1943 – when Capra screened it for military audiences only – and did not receive its theatrical release until 1 September 1944.

27.   Quoted by McBride, p. 445.

28.   Quoted by Nelson, p. 112.

29.   *Ibid.*, p. 111.

30.   *Ibid.*, p. 112. Grant did, however, contribute indirectly to one of Capra's most impressive artistic achievements. The movie rights to Philip Van Doren Stern's short story, 'The Greatest Gift', were purchased by RKO for $10,000 in 1943 at the urging of Grant. Frank Capra bought the rights from RKO in 1945 and made the story the basis of *It's a Wonderful Life* (1946). See McBride, Chapter 17.

31.   Harris, p. 231.

32.   Quoted by Nelson, p. 102.

33.   Grant, 'Archie Leach', part 2, p. 42.

34.   Quoted by Nelson, pp. 151–2.

35.   *Ibid.*, p. 152, quoting Stanley Fox.

36.   See Kanin, *Together Again!*, p. 148.

37.   McIntosh and Weaver, p. 89. For an interview with Grant on his sartorial tastes, see Davis, pp. 31–5.

38.   Higham and Moseley, p. 205.

39.   Quoted by Harris, p. 180.

40. James Bacon, *Made in Hollywood*, p. 36.

41. *Ibid.*, p. 35.

42. Eric Stacey quoted in Higham and Moseley, p. 142.

43. Christopher Challis, *Are They Really So Awful?* (London: Janus, 1995), p. 174.

44. Quoted by Nelson, p. 102.

45. Bogdanovich, 'Cary Grant', p. 103.

46. See Higham and Moseley, pp. 206–7.

47. Mason, p. 409.

48. Quoted by Nelson, pp. 88–9.

49. *Ibid.*, p. 104.

50. *Ibid.*, p. 184.

51. Schickel, *Cary Grant*, p. 104.

52. Bacon, p. 34. Grant did, however, win a David Donatello award (an Italian 'oscar') – see Siskel, 'Cary Grant', p. 3.

53. Nelson, p. 255.

54. *Ibid.*, p. 151.

55. *Ibid.*, p. 105. Grant, in turn, spoke warmly of Stewart's talents: 'Jimmy had the ability to talk naturally . . . He knew that . . . it's not always so *easy* to get a thought out. It took a little while for the sound men to get used to him, but he had an *enormous* impact. And then, some years later, Marlon [Brando] came out and did the same thing all over again – but what people forgot is that Jimmy did it first. And he affected *all* of us' (Bogdanovich, 'Cary Grant', p. 134).

56. *Ibid.*, p. 106.

57. Kael, 'The Man from Dream City', p. 20.

58. Maurice Richlin quoted by Nelson, p. 227.

59. *Ibid.*, p. 161, quoting Jerry D. Lewis.

60. *Ibid.*, p. 227, quoting Cleveland Amory.

61. Sidney Buchman's other screenwriting credits included *Mr Smith Goes to Washington*, *Here Comes Mr Jordan* and *Holiday*. His career reached a peak in the mid-forties, when he became vice-president and assistant production

chief at Columbia. In 1951, he admitted former membership of the Communist Party of the USA to the House Un-American Activities Committee; when he refused to name names, he was found guilty of contempt of Congress, fined $150 and blacklisted.

62. See Jennings, pp. 165–6.

63. *Ibid.*, p. 178.

64. Quoted by Nelson, p. 131.

65. Higham and Moseley, pp. xi–xii.

66. Quoted by Harris, p. 138.

67. See my introduction to T. W. Adorno and Hanns Eisler, *Composing for the Films* (London: Athlone, 1994).

68. Nelson, pp. 129–30. Odets, in turn, was grateful to Grant, describing him as a 'hero out of a Joseph Conrad novel . . . You share with the heroes of those novels a strange quality of decency, which is not a poor word when used this way. It is a quality of goodness that comes from the heart, whether one wills it or not; and it is everywhere evident in the film.'

69. Kael, 'The Man from Dream City', p. 24.

70. Quoted by Nelson, p. 131.

71. Cohn, p. 29.

72. *The Road to Victory* (Warner Brothers, 1944), directed by LeRoy Prinz and featuring appearances by Grant, Bing Crosby, Frank Sinatra, Charles Ruggles, Dennis Morgan, Irene Manning, Jack Carson, Jimmy Lydon and Olive Blakeney.

73. Vincent Canby, 'A Lightness of Heart and Touch', *New York Times*, 1 December 1986, p. B10.

74. Grant, 'What it Means to be a Star', p. 42.

75. An example of one of Wilder and Brackett's new lines is the remark by the elderly scholar: 'You know, for quite a while now, every time I passed the cemetery, I felt as if I were apartment hunting.' There is some disagreement about how happy Grant was with his role in this movie. According to Higham and Moseley (pp. 153–4), Grant was asked originally by Sam Goldwyn to play the part of the bishop, alongside Niven as the angel, and then, after a re-write of the screenplay, Goldwyn switched their roles. Berg (p. 424), however, claims that 'Goldwyn had considered but one actor to play Dudley – Cary Grant'. Grant was signed by Goldwyn for a fee of almost half a million dollars – the biggest sum he had ever paid

an actor, but, in a move which contradicted the view of Grant as being obsessed with money, Grant took himself off the payroll for six weeks while Goldwyn searched for a director (see Berg, pp. 425–6).

76.   See Deschner, p. 209.

77.   The review appeared in the *New York Times*, and is quoted in Wansell, p. 182.

78.   Schickel, *Cary Grant*, p. 143.

79.   The others were Bing Crosby, Betty Grable, Abbott and Costello, Gary Cooper, Bob Hope, Humphrey Bogart, Clark Gable, Spencer Tracy and Ingrid Bergman.

Chapter XI

Ludwig Wittgenstein, *Culture and Value* (Oxford: Blackwell, 1980), p. 76.

Cary Grant: Robinson, 'Cary Grant', *Redbook*, p. 32.

1.   Quoted by Nelson, p. 55 (my italics).

2.   Bacon, p. 34.

3.   Laura Bergquist, 'Curious Story Behind the New Cary Grant', *Look*, 1 September 1959, p. 50.

4.   John Updike, *Self-Consciousness* (New York: Alfred A. Knopf, 1989), p. 241.

5.   Quoted by Godfrey, p. 143.

6.   She was nearly twenty years his junior. Her grandfather had built the Drake Hotel in Chicago, but the family suffered huge losses in the stock-market crash of 1929.

7.   Drake – a promising player of light comedy – was returning after appearing at London's Wyndham's Theatre in the imported Broadway play, *Deep Are the Roots*. Grant was returning after a visit to his mother in Bristol and a business meeting with Sir Alexander Korda.

8.   Judges of the Venice Film Festival awarded it a special prize for 'positive treatment of social problems regarding childhood and adolescence'. Reviews, however, were mixed: the *Hollywood Reporter* said that Grant was 'witty, debonair but always real', and Drake was 'superb', while the *Manchester Guardian Weekly* judged the movie to be the kind of comedy which brought 'to the European mind a deep, deep depression' (see Deschner, pp. 211–12).

9.   Frederick Brisson quoted by Harris, p. 168.

10.   *Ibid.*, p. 76.

11.   Quoted by Wansell, p. 114.

12.   Niven, p. 491.

13.   Niven quoted in Wansell, p. 329.

14.   Robinson, p. 34.

15.   Grant, 'What it Means to be a Star', p. 12.

16.   Updike, p. 241.

17.   Quoted by Harris, p. 227.

18.   Quoted by Nelson, pp. 166–7.

19.   William Goldman, *Adventures in the Screen Trade* (London: Warner Books, 1993), p. 9.

20.   Quoted by Nelson, p. 166.

21.   *Ibid.*, p. 230, quoting Judy Quine.

22.   Niven, p. 491.

23.   *Ibid.*, p. 493.

24.   *Ibid.*

25.   Grant, 'What it Means to be a Star', p. 12.

26.   Quoted by Nelson, p. 228.

27.   Grant makes a passing reference to him on p. 86 of his 'Archie Leach', part 3.

28.   Nelson, p. 228.

29.   *Ibid.*, p. 169.

30.   *Ibid.*, p. 228.

31.   George Orwell, 'The Lion and the Unicorn', *The Penguin Essays of George Orwell* (Harmondsworth: Penguin, 1984), p. 147.

32.   Donaldson, p. 104.

33.   Quoted by Nelson, p. 229.

34.   F. Scott Fitzgerald, *The Crack-Up*, p. 55.

35.   See Higham and Moseley, p. 167.

36.   The couple announced their separation on 19 October 1958; Drake was granted her divorce on 14 August 1962. They remained close friends, and Drake was one of the beneficiaries of Grant's will.

37.   Grant, 'Archie Leach', part 3, p. 151.

38.   Drake studied in the early sixties with Alfred Cannon at UCLA's Neuro-Psychiatric Institute. She went on to do volunteer work at the Institute and became a director of the psychodrama programme.

39.   For an interesting account of the use of LSD in California at the time, see Jay Stevens, *Storming Heaven* (London: Flamingo, 1993), Chapter 7.

40.   Nelson, p. 231.

41.   *Ibid.*

42.   Grant, 'Archie Leach', part 3, p. 152.

43.   Bacon, p. 34.

44.   Robinson, p. 32.

45.   Who or where, exactly, these doctors were was not made clear; see Hoge, p. 15. He did, however, tell Geoffrey Wansell (p. 14) of 'a country house where you can spend a week taking LSD and discovering about yourself'. The movies he made during this period included *An Affair to Remember* (1957), *Kiss Them for Me* (1957), *Indiscreet* (1958), *Houseboat* (1958), *North by Northwest* (1959) and *Operation Petticoat* (1959).

46.   Robinson, p. 32.

47.   Grant, 'Archie Leach', part 3, p. 152.

48.   Hoge, p. 29.

49.   See Higham and Moseley, pp. 192–3.

50.   *Ibid.*, p. 193.

51.   *Ibid.*, p. 194, quoting Timothy Leary.

52.   Quoted by Stevens, p. 194. Stevens suggests that Huxley might well have been referring to Hartman and Chandler.

53.   Bergquist, p. 50.

54.   Grant, 'Archie Leach', part 3, p. 152.

55.   Joe Hyams's account of the meeting with Grant – and its consequences – is included in his memoir, *Mislaid in Hollywood* (London: W. H. Allen, 1973), Chapter 8.

56. Hyams, p. 87.

57. *Ibid.*

58. *Ibid.*, p. 88.

59. *Ibid.*

60. See *ibid.*, pp. 90–98; Higham and Moseley, pp. 210–14; Wansell, pp. 259–61. After lengthy – and often acrimonious – negotiations between Hyams and Stanley Fox, Grant agreed, in 1960, to be interviewed by Hyams about his life and career for the *Ladies' Home Journal* (under the by-line 'By Cary Grant as told to Joe Hyams'). Grant then decided that he would prefer to re-write the articles himself, and told the editors of the magazine that they could only publish the text in the form in which it was submitted: 'There are mis-spellings and some of the grammar is awkward . . . If a reader notices these things, he'll say "Cary doesn't know how to spell" and he will be right . . . Let the readers judge me as I really am and not by an image they may have of me as polished up by someone else' (Hyams, p. 97). The editors agreed – although they did, surreptitiously and much to Grant's anger, correct a few spelling and grammatical errors.

61. Flatley, p 1.

62. See, for example, Robinson.

63. Quoted by Nelson, p. 233.

64. *Ibid.*

65. Niven, p. 496.

66. Grant, 'What it Means to be a Star', p. 12.

67. *Ibid.*

68. Quoted by Nelson, pp. 232–3.

69. Bacon, p. 34.

Chapter XII

Cary Grant: Robinson, p. 28.

Alfred Hitchcock: Chandler, p. 99.

1. Tom Wolfe, 'Loverboy of the Bourgeoisie', *The Kandy-Kolored Tangerine-Flake Streamline Baby* (London: Picador, 1981), p. 137.

2. Quoted by Godfrey, p. 143.

3. Wolfe, p. 137.

4. *Ibid.*

5. Kael, 'The Man from Dream City', p. 30.

6. Walker, 'Cary Grant and the Harry Lime Connection', p. 69.

7. See Wolfe, p. 139.

8. Kael, 'The Man from Dream City', p. 30.

9. *Ibid.* The effect is probably most remarkable in *Indiscreet* (1958).

10. Wolfe, p. 136.

11. Quoted by Nelson, p. 172.

12. Quoted by Harris, p. 180.

13. Quoted by Wansell, p. 231.

14. See Nelson, p. 175, and Siskel, 'Cary Grant', p. 3.

15. Nelson, p. 175.

16. *Ibid.*, pp. 208–9. The respect was mutual: Patrick Macnee has claimed that Hitchcock was 'slightly in awe of Cary Grant' (see Macnee, *Blind in One Ear*, London: Harrap, 1988, p. 198).

17. Hitchcock, 'Elegance Above Sex', in Sidney Gottlieb, ed., *Hitchcock on Hitchcock* (London: Faber, 1995), p. 96.

18. Quoted by Nelson, p. 175. Grant told Debra Sharon Davis (pp. 32–4): 'I'm attracted to women who are secure. One gets secure as one accomplishes. A person tries to meet another on the same plateau, the same intellectual level . . . I like women without artifice. The social belles of my day, the long cigarette-holder types with little bonnets and jangling bracelets and all that stuff, were artificial, I don't go for that.'

19. Gottlieb, p. 95.

20. Quoted by Nelson, p. 176.

21. Grant was, apparently, genuinely uneasy about Kelly's driving skills, and, ironically, she died when she crashed her car on the same route in 1982.

22. Kael, 'The Man from Dream City', p. 5.

23. Eugene Archer, 'The Good Gray Grant', *New York Times*, Section II, 22 August 1965, p. 7.

24. See A. E. Hotchner, *Sophia: Living and Loving* (London: Michael Joseph, 1979), in which Loren recalls that she 'never doubted for a second

that Cary loved me as much as I could hope to be loved by a man' (p. 95). They had met just before the beginning of the production. The affair marked, effectively, the end of Grant's marriage to Betsy Drake. George Barrie has said that 'Cary never talked much about romances with famous women, but he did tell me he loved Sophia Loren' (Nelson, p. 185). Grant proposed to her, but, after some indecision, she returned to Carlo Ponti, whom she subsequently married. Grant acted alongside her again in *Houseboat* (1958), a rather lifeless romantic comedy made all the more uncomfortable for the painfully ironic scene in which Grant and Loren are married. 'She broke my heart,' he told Donaldson (p. 264).

25. Thomson, 'Tall, dark and terribly handsome', p. 186.

26. Nelson, p. 251.

27. Leslie Caron, in *Cary Grant: The Leading Man* (1988 documentary).

28. *Ibid.*

29. *Motion Picture Herald* review of *Kiss Them for Me*; reproduced in Deschner, pp. 231–2.

30. Schickel, *Cary Grant*, p. 154.

31. Kael, 'The Man from Dream City', pp. 30–31.

32. *Ibid.*, p. 31 (my italics).

33. *Ibid.*

34. *Ibid.*

35. Goldman, p. 133.

36. Grant, 'What it Means to be a Star', p. 13.

37. Kael, 'The Man from Dream City', p. 6.

38. *Ibid.*, p. 32.

39. The woman was Audrey Hepburn, the movie was *Charade* (1963). Grant's original response, which he decided subsequently to omit, was: 'Like porcupines make love – very carefully' (see Siskel, 'Cary Grant', p. 3).

40. *An Affair to Remember* was director Leo McCarey's re-make of his own 1939 movie *Love Affair*, starring Irene Dunne and Charles Boyer. McCarey said that the chief difference between the original and the re-make was 'very simply the difference between Charles Boyer and Cary Grant. Grant could never really mask his sense of humour – which is extraordinary – and that's why the second version is funnier' (Wansell, p. 243). Nora Ephron's *Sleepless in Seattle* (1993) is more of a meditation on the Grant–

Kerr version than another re-make, while Warren Beatty's *Love Affair* (1995) was the least inspired – and least successful – of all the movie versions.

41.   Wolfe, p. 137.

42.   *Ibid.*, p. 139.

43.   Brendan Gill's review for *The New Yorker,* quoted in Deschner, p. 256.

44.   Grant invested a considerable sum of his own money in *North by Northwest,* and he also negotiated an exceptional contract that gave him approval of most aspects of the movie. He certainly did well financially: he was paid an outright salary of $450,000 plus ten per cent of the gross profit on all earnings over $8 million, plus an additional $5,000 per day beginning seven weeks after the contract was signed and continuing until the production was complete (and, since those seven weeks came and went before shooting had even begun, Grant's income was, in the end, massive). (See Nelson, pp. 211–12.)

45.   See Grant, 'Archie Leach', part 2, p. 42.

46.   Filming started on 18 October 1962. Grant was sixty by the time the movie was released.

47.   Quoted by Nelson, p. 241.

48.   *Ibid.*

49.   The dialogue also shows that Grant's love of in-jokes and ad-libs had not faded. Early on in the movie, as he escorts Hepburn to her hotel room, he announces: 'We're here.' 'Where?' asks Hepburn. 'On the street where you live.' It was an ad-lib that referred to the Lerner and Loewe song in *My Fair Lady,* the movie version of which Grant had declined to appear in but which he knew Audrey Hepburn was to start shooting immediately after *Charade.*

50.   Robinson, p. 32.

51.   Wolfe, p. 137.

RETIREMENT

Insignificance (1982) by Terry Johnson in *Plays: One* (London: Methuen, 1993), p. 22.

Sleepless in Seattle (1993) by Jeffrey Arch, Larry Atlas, David S. Ward and Nora Ephron.

Chapter XIII

Roger O. Thornhill, *North by Northwest* (1959): screenplay by Ernest Lehman.

Cary Grant: Godfrey, p. 165.

1.   Quoted in Nelson, p. 266.

2.   *Ibid.*, p. 265.

3.   Interview with Murray Schumach in the *New York Times*, quoted in Godfrey, p. 163.

4.   Reviews by Arthur Knight and Philip Hartung, cited in Deschner, p. 264.

5.   *Hollywood Reporter*, cited in Deschner, p. 265.

6.   Quoted in Wansell, p. 273.

7.   The portly Charles Coburn – one of the stars of *The More the Merrier* – won the Oscar for Best Supporting Actor for playing the character on whom Grant's would be based. Contrary to appearances, both men were similar ages when they played the role (Coburn had been sixty-six, Grant was sixty-two). Both of them are inveterate scene-stealers, although Coburn stole his scenes from the excellent Jean Arthur and Joel McCrea. Grant's performance is, as usual, slyly self-referential: at one point a young woman exclaims, 'You're *married*?' to which Grant, dead-pan, replies, 'Yes. I'm old enough!'; he also cannot resist slipping in a couple of playful references to two of his earlier movies – in the amusing scene set in the cramped kitchen, he can be heard whistling Henry Mancini's love theme from *Charade*, and humming the theme song from *An Affair to Remember*. (One oddity is the fact that Grant's character is seen smoking a cigar in several scenes; as his hatred of smoking was great enough to cause him to refuse to be in the same room as someone with a lighted cigarette, one assumes that he devised a way to fake the action.)

8.   Deschner, p. 267.

9.   *Ibid.*

10.   Quoted in Wansell, p. 292.

11.   It was Grant's twelfth-biggest box-office success. Above it, in order of priority, were: 1. *Operation Petticoat*; 2. *That Touch of Mink*; 3. *North by Northwest*; 4. *Charade*; 5. *Father Goose*; 6. *Notorious*; 7. *The Bachelor and the Bobbysoxer*; 8. *To Catch a Thief*; 9. *The Pride and the Passion*; 10. *I Was a*

Male War Bride; 11. *Night and Day*. (Listed in the 65th Anniversary issue of *Weekly Variety*, and reproduced in Deschner, p. 274.)

12.   Wansell, p. 293.

13.   See, for example, Mann, 'Cary Grant', p. 39.

14.   Graham, pp. 32–3.

15.   Quoted in Nelson, p. 271.

16.   Dyan Cannon was born Samille Diane Friesen in Tacoma, Washington, on 4 January 1939. Grant first made contact with her in 1961, after he saw her in an otherwise forgettable television soap opera entitled *Malibu Run* (formerly entitled *The Aquanauts*). They started going out together soon after. He proposed to her sometime in early 1964. (See Phyllis Battelle, 'Mrs Cary Grant Talks About Marrying (and Divorcing) Cary Grant', *Ladies' Home Journal*, April 1968, pp. 107, 168–9, 172.)

17.   Quoted in Nelson, p. 107.

18.   See Jennings, p. 167.

19.   *Ibid.*, p. 168.

20.   *Ibid.*, pp. 174–7.

21.   The source is Jill St John, who first encountered Grant when Lance Reventlow took her to meet his former step-father (see Nelson, p. 136). When Reventlow died in a plane crash (on 24 July 1972, at the age of thirty-six), Grant was grief-stricken. St John recalls that, on the way to the funeral, Grant looked through a large manila envelope containing 'everything Lance ever sent him – cards, letters from camp, letters from school, postcards, gift enclosures, Christmas cards, Easter cards – from about the age of six years to maybe twelve' (Nelson, p. 137).

22.   See Donaldson, p. 232.

23.   Grant, 'Archie Leach', part 1, p. 133 (italics are mine).

24.   Hoge, p. 28.

25.   Battelle, p. 107.

26.   Quoted in Nelson, p. 274.

27.   *Ibid.*, p. 273 (italics are mine).

28.   Quoted by Decker, p. 21.

29.   Grant had, in fact, become an increasingly difficult star to persuade to take on new projects since he first took a break from Hollywood in the

early fifties. Mike Todd had seen him as one of the few stars who could hold together the story of his epic *Around the World in Eighty Days* (1956); David Niven took the role when Grant turned it down (Wansell, pp. 234–5). Grant almost agreed to do – and later regretted not doing – David Lean's *The Bridge on the River Kwai* (1957) – William Holden took his role (Nelson, p. 269); he also rejected Stanley Donen's offer of the role of the devil (played in the end by Ray Walston) in *Damn Yankees* (1958) (Buehrer, p. 18) and George Cukor's request for him to play opposite Marilyn Monroe in 1960's *Let's Make Love* (Buehrer, p. 18). He wanted to attempt a big-budget musical, but he turned down what became Robert Preston's role in *The Music Man* (1962) and what became Rex Harrison's role in *My Fair Lady* (1964) (Nelson, pp. 267–8). Rock Hudson took the role intended for Grant in the 1964 Howard Hawks movie *Man's Favorite Sport?* (Buehrer, p. 19).

30.   The Alan Bennett project – and Grant's involvement in it – is referred to in Walker's biography of Rex Harrison, p. 298. Alan Bennett himself, however, has told me that the screenplay – which was written during the period 1966–7 – 'never looked like actually going into production, Cary Grant or no Cary Grant', and he is not even certain that Grant ever read it (correspondence with the author, 15 January 1996).

31.   See Gottlieb, p. 160. Hitchcock first mentioned the project at the end of the 1940s.

32.   See Wansell, p. 314.

33.   Grant said he was tempted, 'but in the end I decided it would be too much work. I mean, I've *done* all that – almost 70 times [72 in fact] – and it's a tiresome and very strenuous business' (Flatley, p. 1). Sir Laurence Olivier took the role.

34.   See Buehrer, p. 19, and Flatley, p. 1. George Segal took the role.

35.   Buehrer, p. 19.

36.   Graham, p. 23.

37.   Higham and Moseley, pp. 243–4. The project was to be directed by Mervyn LeRoy.

38.   Nelson, p. 269. According to Harris (pp. 245–6), Hawks and Grant also considered a movie version of *Don Quixote*, with Grant in the title role and Cantinflas as Sancho Panza.

39.   Nelson, p. 268. Dyan Cannon had already been considered for the

role in the movie when Beatty first approached Grant. See also Donaldson, pp. 253–5.

40. See Donaldson, p. 254, and Siskel, 'Cary Grant', p. 3.

41. See Maurice Leonard, *Mae West: Empress of Sex* (London: Harper-Collins, 1991), pp. 343–4. Their combined ages would have been 160 when the proposed movie was made.

42. Harris, p. 184. The offer was made in 1955, after Grant attended the opening of West's new nightclub act at Ciro's.

43. Quoted by Nelson, pp. 266–7.

44. Evans, p. 146.

45. *Ibid.*

46. Cohn, p. 27. Grant's reply was: 'I hardly know how to go about playing myself.'

47. See Nelson, p. 268.

48. *Ibid.*

49. Robinson, p. 34.

50. See Battelle, pp. 107, 168–9 and 172.

51. Grant even recorded a single for her – 'Christmas Lullaby' (Columbia 4–44377) in 1967 (the other side features Peggy Lee singing 'Here's To You').

52. Robinson, p. 34.

53. Quoted by Godfrey, p. 165.

54. Cohn, p. 27.

55. Mann, 'Cary Grant at 80', p. 17.

56. The couple had taken Jennifer to Bristol in the summer of 1966 to see Elsie Leach. See reports in the *Bristol Evening Post*: 15 July 1966, p. 1; 16 July, p. 1; and 23 July, p. 1. In another move which adds to the doubts about Grant's 'Jewishness' (Chapter 1), Grant, while in Bristol, attempted to have his daughter baptised in the same parish church where he had been christened; the baptism did not, in the end, occur, because the minister would not waive the condition that obliged the parents to bring up the child as an Episcopalian (Cannon did have a Jewish mother, and neither Grant nor Cannon wished to impose any religious point of view on their daughter, see Nelson, pp. 274–5).

57. Nelson, pp. 275–6.

58. Battelle, p. 172.

59. *Ibid*.

60. New York *Daily News*, 21 March 1968, p. 1. Cannon's suit was reported widely in newspapers of the time.

61. St John's Hospital in Elmhurst, Queens.

62. In later testimony, two psychiatrists – Dr Judd Marmor and Dr Sidney L. Pomer – who had been instructed by the court to examine Grant, gave fairly favourable reports concerning his emotional state. Dr Marmor told the court that he had found no evidence of any deleterious effects resulting from Grant's LSD therapy; he said that Grant had told him that the drug had helped 'deepen his understanding of himself, and helped cure his shyness and anxiety in dealing with other people', and Marmor had formed the opinion that Grant was 'an emotional individual', but no more so than he had seen in other actors he had examined. Dr Pomer also testified that he had found no evidence of 'irrationality, erratic behavior or incoherence' in Grant (see Govoni, pp. 203–4). Virginia Cherrill, Grant's first wife, was one of those friends who offered to appear as character witnesses to contradict some of the allegations being made against him (Wansell, p. 332).

63. See Higham and Moseley, p. 246.

64. Graham, p. 23.

65. Quoted in Nelson, p. 279.

66. *Ibid*.

67. See Graham, p. 25.

68. Quoted in Nelson, p. 277.

69. For example, Grant arranged for Cannon to be included in the cast of *Bob and Carol and Ted and Alice* (1969), asking Columbia's head of production, Mike Frankovich, to intervene and persuade the director, Paul Mazursky, to try her for the role (see Wansell, pp. 304–5). Grant remained close to all four of his former wives; he symbolised this fact by always wearing a gold chain around his neck with three charms attached, representing the religions of each of his wives – a St Christopher for Virginia Cherrill (a Catholic), a small cross for Barbara Hutton and Betsy Drake (Protestants) and a Star of David for Dyan Cannon (he also had one of Jennifer's first baby teeth encased in Lucite). (See Donaldson, p. 109.)

70. Grant quoted in Hoge, p. 33.

71.   McIntosh and Weaver, pp. 72–3. Grant arranged for permanent bodyguards, day and night, for Jennifer after the murder of Sharon Tate.

72.   Hoge, p. 33.

73.   Battelle, p. 172.

74.   Wansell, p. 237. He did, however, make a single exception: he appeared, briefly, as a tramp in an unbilled cameo role on a local television show in Los Angeles in 1950 called *Dave and Charlie* (see Deschner, p. 273).

75.   The exception was Grant's occasional war-time appearances at US Army camps in serviceman shows.

76.   Nelson, p. 289.

77.   He also received a large block of Fabergé stock.

78.   Mary Kaye, 'Now Cary Stars in the Business World', *Bristol Evening Post*, 16 June 1972, p. 7.

79.   Grant also had at his disposal a company helicopter kept by the East River in New York. For contemporary accounts of his work for Fabergé, see 'How a Star Fits a Director's Chair' (no author given), *Business Week*, 21 December 1968, pp. 92–4, and Doris Lilly, 'A Day at the Office with Cary Grant', *Ladies' Home Journal*, November 1970, pp. 142–3.

80.   'How a Star Fits a Director's Chair', p. 93.

81.   *Ibid.*

82.   *Ibid.*, p. 92.

83.   *Ibid.*, p. 93.

84.   Kaye, p. 7.

85.   Thomson, 'Cary Grant', p. 301.

86.   See McIntosh and Weaver, Chapter 1.

87.   See Higham and Moseley, pp. 251–2.

88.   The montage was compiled by Jack Haley, Jnr., and Richard Dunlap.

89.   Academy Awards show, 7 April 1970, broadcast by NBC.

90.   Grant had spent the previous evening rehearsing the speech, which he had written himself, with his ex-wife, Dyan Cannon.

91.   The case was dropped as soon as it came to court. The baby, when unwrapped from its layers of clothing, was revealed to be half black. Bouron refused to take a blood test. Three years later, on 30 October 1973, she

was found in the boot of a car parked in a supermarket parking lot, beaten to death with a claw hammer.

92. Quoted by Nelson, p. 303.

93. *Ibid.*, p. 302.

Chapter XIV

Leo Braudy, *The Frenzy of Renown* (New York: Oxford University Press, 1986), pp. 587–8.

Cary Grant: Mann, 'Cary Grant', p. 39.

1. This has, in fact, been a fairly common argument among Grant's biographers (see, for example, Schickel, *Cary Grant*, p. 12).

2. Walker, 'Cary Grant and the Harry Lime Connection', pp. 69–70.

3. Donaldson, p. 197.

4. Chandler, p. 202.

5. Fitzgerald, *The Great Gatsby*, p. 97.

6. See, for example, Davis, p. 32. Siskel, however, in his 1976 interview ('Cary Grant', p. 2), notes: 'He doesn't disappoint you. He really *is* like he is in the movies', still elegant and 'outrageously handsome'.

7. See McIntosh and Weaver, p. 89.

8. *Ibid.*, p. 90.

9. *Ibid.*, p. 125.

10. *Ibid.*

11. Cohn, p. 29.

12. Donaldson, p. 129.

13. Mann, 'Cary Grant at 80', p. 39 (italics are mine).

14. *Ibid.*

15. *Ibid.*

16. McIntosh and Weaver, p. 96.

17. The other occasions in the seventies when Grant agreed to make public appearances included: Walt Disney World's Candlelight Ceremony (December 1972), Disneyland Candlelight Ceremony (December 1973 and December 1974) – Grant was, on all three occasions, the narrator; the Straw

Hat Awards in New York City (May 1975) – Grant was given a special plaque acknowledging the city's appreciation of his long career 'as a star and superstar in entertainment'; the Republican National Convention in Kansas City (19 August 1976) – he introduced Betty Ford; a special Bicentenary dinner at the White House honouring the visit of Queen Elizabeth (1976); the American Film Institute's salute to Alfred Hitchcock (7 March 1979); and the Academy Awards ceremony (9 April 1979) – Grant presented an honorary Oscar to Sir Laurence Olivier.

18. McIntosh and Weaver, p. 94.

19. *Ibid.*, p. 150.

20. *Ibid.*, p. 87.

21. Grant's involvement in the Shannonside project began in 1970, when William McIntosh encouraged him to lend his name and his financial support ($10,000) to the enterprise. The aim was to build an 'Irish–American' community village (situated inbetween Ballynacally and Kildysart) on the banks of the Shannon–Fergus rivers. Grant became a director of the company on 9 September 1971. Problems dogged the project. To raise capital the consortium entered into an agreement with Associated Mortgage Investors in the US, but the necessary $6 million was not found and bills went unpaid. The receivers came in during 1974, and the venture collapsed. (For an informative account of this episode, see McIntosh and Weaver, Chapter 9.)

22. See Buehrer, p. 22.

23. See Nelson, p. 288.

24. See McIntosh and Weaver, p. 149.

25. See Nelson, p. 341.

26. *Ibid.*, p. 287.

27. *Ibid.*, p. 318.

28. Decker, p. 21. See also Cohn, p. 27.

29. See Flatley, p. 1.

30. It won one: Best Actress for Glenda Jackson.

31. Cohn, p. 27.

32. See Higham and Moseley, pp. 118–19.

33. See McIntosh and Weaver, pp. 111–12.

34. For background information on Kerkorian's business dealings, and his controversial involvement in the movie industry, see John Cassidy, 'Kirk's Enterprise', *The New Yorker*, 11 December 1995, pp. 44–53; Ben Macintyre, 'A veteran hustler who hypnotises America', *The Times*, 14 April 1995, p. 14, and Charles Fleming, 'The Predator', *Vanity Fair*, February 1996, pp. 54–60, 112–15.

35. Kerkorian's father, an illiterate Armenian immigrant, had become a land baron in California's San Joaquin Valley before his son was born. See Fleming, p. 56.

36. *Ibid.*, p. 115.

37. MGM had opened the $106 million MGM Grand Hotel in Las Vegas in 1973; Grant presided over several of the festivities arranged for the month-long gala opening. (Kerkorian sold it to Bally Manufacturers in the mid-eighties; he opened the new MGM Grand Hotel in 1994.)

38. See McIntosh and Weaver, Chapter 7.

39. See Nelson, pp. 303–4.

40. *Ibid.*, p. 176.

41. Grant was an enthusiastic follower of baseball, and a supporter of the Los Angeles Dodgers.

42. For an amusing first-hand account of the chaos caused by Grant's fastidious design plans, see McIntosh and Weaver, Chapter 6.

43. *Ibid.*, p. 126.

44. Donaldson, p. 76. Morgan later became the victim of a grisly murder: in 1983, she was found, bludgeoned to death, in a Colfax Avenue apartment in Los Angeles (see Higham and Moseley, pp. 264–6, for a brief – and very speculative – account of her life).

45. McIntosh and Weaver, p. 125.

46. *Ibid.*, p. 126.

47. Donaldson's *An Affair to Remember* is her memoir of the relationship.

48. Grant singled Herne out as an accomplished pantomimist (see Grant, 'Archie Leach', part 1, p. 142).

49. Donaldson, p. 134.

50. Quoted in Donaldson, p. 198.

51. *Ibid.*, p. 201.

52. *Ibid.*, p. 313. The Browning poem was 'Apparent Failure'.

53. The Chesterfield Nursing Home in Clifton, Bristol, a private acute-care establishment. Elsie had lived previously in Coldharbour Road, Redland.

54. Godfrey (p. 192) quotes Elsie Leach's cousin, Ernest Kingdon, saying that 'we used to be very concerned about the electric fire. She had a habit of putting one on the table by her bed . . . She had a dizzy spell . . .'

55. Quoted by Nelson, p. 249.

56. See Thomas, 'The enigma who was Cary Grant', p. 4, and 'Cary's Agreement', pp. 4–5.

57. Quoted by Nelson, p. 307.

58. After his cousin died, Grant supported Eric's widow, Maggie, in the years that followed, and provided for her in his will. Grant's half-brother, Eric Leslie Leach, died of cancer on 23 November 1976, aged fifty-five. Grant had never acknowledged the existence of his half-brother in interviews, and saw him only very rarely. He did, on certain occasions, assist the family financially (Eric Leslie was married with six children, and he worked at the electric meter company in Bristol), and had helped set him up in business (see Nelson, p. 31), but it seems that the fact that Eric Leslie had been born after Elias had abandoned Elsie caused Grant to feel very bitter about the relationship (see Donaldson, pp. 294–7).

59. When he did visit, he usually stayed at the Royal Hotel (in the Churchill Suite) or sometimes in the Grand Spa or the Avon Gorge.

60. See Thomas, 'The enigma who was Cary Grant', p. 4.

61. He had a point. Grant visited the city considerably more often than, say, Edmund Burke, Bristol's most eminent Member of Parliament (1774–80), deigned to visit the 'swinish multitude', even though a statue of Burke (waving regally to his old constituents) now stands in the centre. Grant, in contrast, is not even mentioned in some of the tourist literature on the area.

62. Thomas, 'The enigma who was Cary Grant', p. 4.

63. Tom Shales, 'Woody: The First Fifty Years', *Esquire*, April 1987, p. 91.

64. Nelson, pp. 298–9.

65. *Ibid.*, p. 219.

66. *Ibid.*, p. 260.

67.   Mann, 'Cary Grant', pp. 259–60, quoting Sheila Benson (italics are mine).

68.   Cohn, p. 27.

69.   Mann, 'Cary Grant', p. 39.

70.   *Ibid.*

Chapter XV

Grace Kelly: McIntosh and Weaver, p. 153.

Cary Grant: Mann, 'Cary Grant', p. 39.

1.   *Ibid.*

2.   He might, of course, have decided that he had been beaten to it by his friend David Niven, whose two hugely successful volumes of auto-biography – *The Moon's a Balloon* (first published in 1971) and *Bring on the Empty Horses* (1975) – had covered many of the same incidents, and the same era, as any likely Grant memoir would do. Roderick Mann was a friend of both men, and he worked with Niven on his books. According to Mann, when *The Moon's a Balloon* was published, 'Cary was a bit teed off . . . He said, "That happened to me, not him." But everybody knew David took stories that happened to other people and melded them as though they had happened to him' (Nelson, p. 152).

3.   Quoted by Cohn, p. 27.

4.   Pauline Peters, 'A Life in the Day of Cary Grant', *Sunday Times Magazine*, 1 February 1981, p. 70.

5.   Quoted by McIntosh and Weaver, p. 151.

6.   Quoted in the *Los Angeles Times*, 1 December 1986, p. 21.

7.   Grant quoted by Robinson, p. 34.

8.   McIntosh and Weaver, p. 148.

9.   The Fourth Annual Kennedy Center Honors ceremony was held in Washington on 6 December 1981. Apart from Grant, the other recipients were Count Basie, Helen Hayes, Jerome Robbins and Rudolf Serkin. Rex Harrison presented Grant with his award. It was noted by Harrison that audiences around the world had 'loved the civilised grace and brilliance of Cary Grant', but not everyone had appreciated that he was also 'one of the most accomplished actors in the history of motion pictures, because civilised grace and comic brilliance are two of the most unique and rare qualities within an actor's range'. Since Grant's retirement, Harrison added, 'there

have been descriptions of many newcomers as "young Cary Grants". The fact is there is only one original, the supremely gifted man, whom we honor tonight for a magnificent career on the screen.' It was filmed by CBS-TV and broadcast on 26 December. (See Barbara Gamarekian, 'Kennedy Center Honors Basie, Grant, Robbins, Serkin and Helen Hayes', *New York Times*, 7 December 1981, p. 17.)

10.   The ceremony took place on 3 October 1984. Grant said, 'I've never had anything named after me . . . Oh, my mother once named her dog Archie' (Nelson, p. 349).

11.   See Harris, p. 287. The event, attended by 1,500 people, took place on 16 May 1982.

12.   Quoted by Nelson, p. 348.

13.   Barbara Harris was born on 30 September 1950 in Dar es Salaam, the youngest daughter of Lesley and James Harris. Her father was a British provincial commissioner in East Africa.

14.   Interview given to the *Star* publication in December 1981; quoted in McIntosh and Weaver, p. 157.

15.   Quoted by Nelson, p. 327.

16.   *Ibid.*, pp. 327–8. The marriage itself, and its apparent success, is another reason to be sceptical of the stylisation of Grant by some writers as a 'closet bisexual or homosexual'. George Cukor, for example, was enjoying a very open gay lifestyle in Los Angeles at this time, and Rock Hudson, although he did not acknowledge his homosexuality publicly until forced to, was very open about his sexuality around Hollywood. Grant, long retired and financially secure, had no obvious reason to continue to have such relationships with women if he regarded them as mere diversions for publicity purposes.

17.   Peters, p. 70.

18.   Quoted by Nelson, p. 3.

19.   *Ibid.*

20.   *Ibid.*, p. 6.

21.   *Ibid.*, p. 355 (italics are mine).

22.   *Ibid.*, p. 6.

23.   *Ibid.*, p. 353 (italics are mine).

24.   *Ibid.*, p. 355.

25. *Ibid.*, p. 7.

26. *Ibid.*, p. 8.

27. Michaelson, p. 1.

28. Quoted by Ostroff, p. 29.

29. Richard Henning quoted by Nelson, pp. 354–5.

30. *Ibid.*, p. 352.

31. Jane Barton, 'Cary Grant Wows Schenectady: Faces a Crowd of 1,000', *Variety*, 18 July 1984, p. 2.

32. *Ibid.*, pp. 2 and 149.

33. *Ibid.*, p. 149.

34. Quoted by Michaelson, p. 1.

35. *Ibid.*

36. Quoted by McIntosh and Weaver, p. 160.

37. Michaelson, p. 1.

38. Nelson, p. 365.

39. Questions taken from Nelson, pp. 362–3, and Michaelson, p. 1.

40. Nelson, p. 365.

41. Barton, p. 2.

42. Mann, 'Cary Grant at 80', p. 16.

43. *Ibid.*

44. Peters, p. 75.

45. *Ibid.*, p. 70.

46. Quoted by Ashman and Trescott, p. 18.

47. The very best of which was Schickel's splendid *Cary Grant: A Celebration*, one of the few biographies of himself that Grant admitted – in a typically roundabout way – to having read, and the only one that he was, discreetly, impressed by (see Nelson, p. 313).

48. Quoted by Nelson, p. 351.

49. *Ibid.*, p. 335. Their marriage was, in fact, blessed in a church wedding on 1 July 1986.

50. *Ibid.*, p. 330.

51.   Jennifer Grant graduated in 1987. She went on to work on projects for the homeless with a public-interest law firm in San Francisco, and it was also reported that she was studying acting. After her father's death, in response to the allegations about him in certain biographies, she organised (as associate producer) a documentary: *Cary Grant: A Celebration* (ABC, 3 November 1988). (See Jane Krzys, 'The Girl that Cary couldn't resist', *Bristol Evening Post*, 4 April 1989, p. 7.)

52.   Robinson, p. 34.

53.   Alston Thomas, in *Cary Grant: The Leading Man* (1988 documentary). The reporter he refers to may have been Helen Reid, who wrote an article about accompanying Grant on a drive around Bristol in 1983 ('Why I'll Always Love Bristol, by Cary Grant', pp. 12–13).

54.   Quoted by Harris, p. 294.

55.   Apart from the injury he experienced after his car accident in the late sixties, Grant's last serious bout of ill-health had occurred in 1948, during the filming of *I Was a Male War Bride*, when he became ill with hepatitis and jaundice (see John Kobal, *People Will Talk*, London: Aurum Press, 1986, pp. 238–9).

56.   Hoge, p. 28.

57.   See McIntosh and Weaver, p. 162, and Nelson, p. 369.

58.   Quoted by Harris, p. 2.

59.   *Ibid.*, pp. 2–3.

60.   *Ibid.*, pp. 3–4.

61.   *Los Angeles Times*, 1 December 1986, p. 20.

62.   *Ibid.*

63.   *Ibid.*

64.   Quoted by Harris, p. 295.

65.   *Los Angeles Times*, 1 December 1986, p. 20.

66.   *Ibid.*

67.   Pace, p. 1.

68.   Leader in the *Washington Post*, 2 December 1986, p. 18.

69.   *The Times*, 1 December 1986, p. 18.

70.   Decker, p. 1.

71.   Quoted by Nelson, p. 372. There was, however, a special tribute to Grant on 19 October 1988 at the Beverly Hilton Hotel, Beverly Hills, California, organised by the Princess Grace Foundation and attended by 940 admirers and friends.

72.   See Harris, p. 296.

73.   The will was dated 26 November 1984. Typically, Grant had ensured that it was a prudent document that covered most eventualities. He also authorised his executors 'to invest and reinvest any surplus money in their hands in every kind of property, real, personal or mixed, and every kind of investment, that *men of prudence, discretion and intelligence acquire for their own account*'.

74.   Until Jennifer Grant reached the age of twenty-one (in 1987), the Trustees were empowered by her father to support her; after she reached that age, they were instructed to 'pay to or apply for her benefit all of the net income from the trust estate, until my daughter attains the age of thirty-five'.

75.   McIntosh and Weaver, p. 164.

76.   Schickel, *Cary Grant*, p. 170.

77.   Robinson, p. 34.

78.   Quoted by Nelson, p. 375.

EPILOGUE

Richard Brooks: Higham and Moseley, p. viii.

People Will Talk (1951): screenplay by Joseph L. Mankiewicz.

Deborah Kerr: *Cary Grant: The Leading Man* (1988 documentary).

Cary Grant, 'Archie Leach', part 3, p. 154.

1.   'Cary Grant's Promise', editorial in the *New York Times*, 2 December 1986, p. 26.

2.   *Ibid.*

3.   Quoted in *The Times*, 21 April 1994, p. 14.

4.   *Empire*, July 1994, p. 103.

5.   Quoted in *The Times*, 21 April 1994, p. 14.

6.   Quoted in Harris, p. 297.

7.   Schickel, *Cary Grant*, pp. 167 and 170.

8.   Apart from his seventy-two 'official' appearances in movies, Grant made the following guest appearances: *Singapore Sue* (Paramount, 1932) – a short one-reeler in which he plays a sailor; *Hollywood on Parade* (Paramount, 1932–4) – another one-reeler featuring 'glimpses' of the studio's stable of actors; *Pirate Party on Catalina Isle* (MGM, 1936) – another short featuring countless stars as themselves; *Topper Takes a Trip* (MGM, 1939) – Grant was not available for this sequel to *Topper*, so footage from the original movie was used in several 'flashback' sequences; *Polio and Communicable Disease* (1940) – a hospital trailer short; *The Road to Victory* (Warner Brothers, 1944) – a ten-minute short promoting war loans; *The Shining Future* (1944) – another short; *Without Reservations* (RKO, 1946) – starring Claudette Colbert and John Wayne, Grant makes a brief unbilled appearance dancing with Colbert as a joke; *Christmas Seals* (c. 1947) – a short soliciting funds on behalf of Christmas Seals; *MGM's Big Parade of Comedy* (MGM, 1963) – a compilation movie with clips included from *Suzy* and *The Philadelphia Story*; *Ken Murray's Hollywood* (1965) – a compilation of candid camera footage; *Elvis: That's the Way It Is* (MGM, 1970) – Grant is glimpsed attending a festival in Las Vegas; *That's Entertainment, Part II* (MGM, 1976) – an excerpt is included from *The Philadelphia Story*; *Once Upon a Time . . . Is Now* (1977) – a movie made for television in which Grant's voice is heard.

9.   Thomson, *A Biographical Dictionary of Film*, p. 300.

10.   Quoted by Hoge, p. 33.

11.   Marcel Ophuls, 'The Last of the Good Guys', in John Boorman and Walter Donohue, eds., *Projections 4½* (London: Faber, 1995), p. 137.

12.   Kael, 'The Man from Dream City', p. 32.

13.   Shipman, p. 274.

14.   Corliss, p. 78.

15.   Benson, p. 17.

16.   Quoted by Schickel, *Cary Grant*, p. 172.

17.   'Cary Grant's Promise', *New York Times*, 2 December 1986, p. 26.

18.   Ostroff, p. 28.

Index

Index

Index

Index

B
GRANT   McCann, Graham
M
           Cary Grant

DUE DATE **BRODART**   02/97   24.95

OVERDUE FINES $.10 PER DAY

Bellmore Memorial Library

2288 Bedford Avenue

Bellmore, New York

(516) 785-2990

BE

3/99